THE WORKSHOP GUIDE TO
CERAMICS

THE WORKSHOP GUIDE TO

CERAMICS

Duncan Hooson and Anthony Quinn

BARRON'S

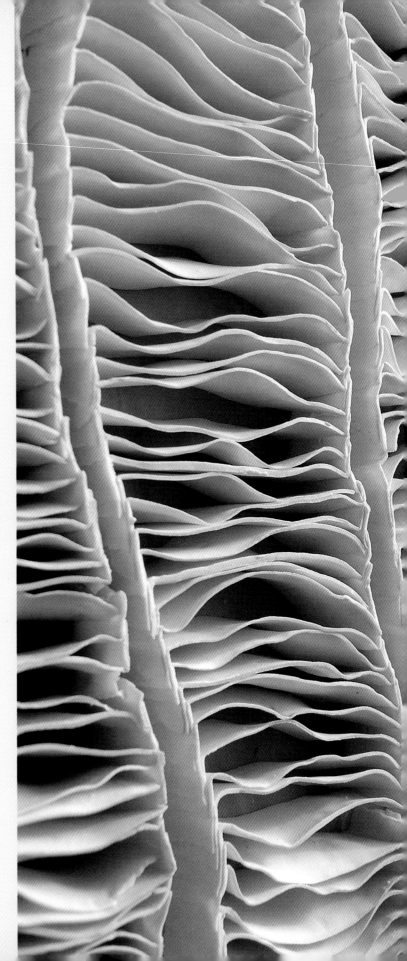

A QUARTO BOOK

BARRON'S

First edition for North America published in
2012 by Barron's Educational Series, Inc.

All inquiries should be addressed to:
Barron's Educational Series, Inc.
250 Wireless Boulevard
Hauppauge, New York 11788
www.barronseduc.com

Library of Congress Control No.: 2011939031

ISBN: 978-0-7641-6461-3

QUAR.SGCE

Conceived, designed, and produced by
Quarto Publishing plc
The Old Brewery
6 Blundell Street
London N7 9BH

Project Editor: Chelsea Edwards
Designer: John Grain
Art Director: Caroline Guest
Assistant Art Editor: Kate Bramley
Photographer: Phil Wilkins
Illustrator: John Woodcock
Picture Researcher: Sarah Bell
Copyeditor: Sarah Hoggett
Proofreader: Claire Waite Brown
Indexer: Helen Snaith

Creative Director: Moira Clinch
Publisher: Paul Carslake

Color separation by Pica Digital Pte Ltd,
Singapore

Printed by 1010 Printing International Limited,
China

10 9 8 7 6 5 4 3 2 1

Picture credits
Pages 1 and 10–11: Derek Wilson
Pages 2–3: Wouter Dam
Page 4: Fenella Elms (detail)
Page 5: Natasha Daintry (detail)
Page 6: Ken Eastman (detail)

Contents

Continued on the next page $\longrightarrow$

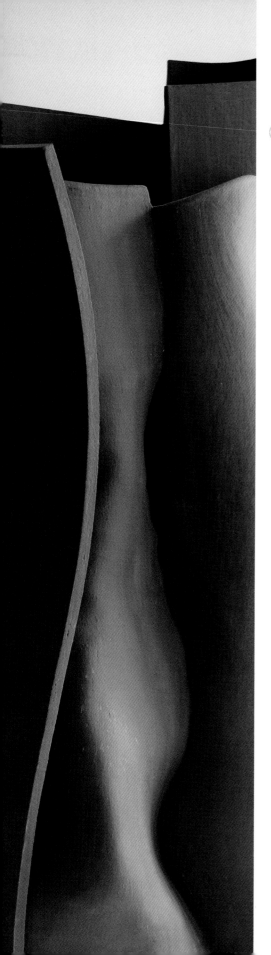

Contents continued

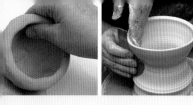

TECHNIQUE FILE

PUBLISHER'S NOTE

Ceramics can be dangerous. Always follow the instructions carefully, and exercise caution. Follow the safety procedures mentioned. As far as the techniques and methods described in this book are concerned, all statements, information, and advice given are believed to be accurate. However, neither the authors, the copyright holder, nor the publisher can accept any legal liability.

Materials, Tools, and Process (pages 20–51)

This comprehensive section looks at the extraordinary raw material of clay itself; examining the varieties available and their particular uses. An exhaustive directory of tools and equipment covers everything from simple hand tools to advanced machinery, and includes a guide on what to buy for your "beginner's kit." Details on setting up your own workshop, as well as an overview of the ceramic process, are also featured in this section.

Forming Techniques (pages 52–169)

From coiling vast forms to throwing delicate vases and modeling slip-cast pieces, this section details a wide range of forming techniques to suit every maker's need. In addition to hand-building and wheel-throwing methods, this chapter also covers lathe and whirler turning and computer-aided design.

Prefiring Surface Decoration (pages 170–217)

Here you will find a variety of methods for introducing color and texture to your work. This may come from decorating with slip, direct screen printing, burnishing, or any of the other extensive techniques included.

This book is organized into eight parts covering all you need to know about creating ceramic work.

ABOUT THIS BOOK

Navigator

This device provides an at-a-glance listing of all the sections included in the book as well as the subsections for that particular chapter.

Panel points

Faults and their remedies, hints and useful explanations of technical vocabulary are highlighted in these colored boxes.

Technique number

Each step-by-step technique is numbered and can be found by using the technique file listings on page 7.

Contextual examples

Stunning finished works by professional makers have been selected to contextualize the wide range of techniques covered.

Order of work

Shorthand instructions are provided for several of the techniques in order to help you memorize the key steps.

Step-by-steps

Clear step-by-step photographs are accompanied by concise instructions to help you complete the process. Each technique is numbered and a full listing of all the techniques can be found on page 7.

Inspirational pieces

Each part opens with an array of beautiful works that embody the techniques in the upcoming section.

Beginner's kit

Equipment that every beginner should have is indicated by this icon.

Diagrams

Clear diagrams are included to aid the understanding of various ceramic processes and features.

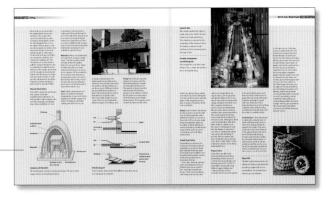

Recipes

Each recipe details the uses, firing ranges, and ingredients needed to achieve the glaze described and pictured.

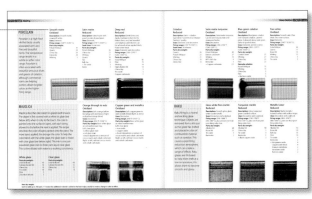

Firing (pages 218–243)

Learn about the myriad firing options open to today's maker: from reliable and controlled electric kilns to experimental processes such as sawdust firing. As well as explaining the results of different methods, this chapter also includes useful kiln diagrams.

Glazing (pages 244–261)

This chapter explores the process of protecting the fired ceramic surface by making it nonporous. Aside from the functional aspect of glazing, this section provides a range of glaze recipes and methods for their application.

Post-glaze Surface Decoration (pages 262–283)

Glazing does not have to be the end of the decorative process; there are a multitude of techniques that can be applied to extend the beauty of any form's surface.

Design (pages 284–295)

This chapter looks at the design process from finding that initial inspiration and recording it through to creating a technical drawing for others to work from.

Professional Practice (pages 296–307)

Discover how to set up professionally including how to price, sell, and exhibit your work. Also find out how to photograph and promote your pieces, as well as how to deal with commissions.

FOREWORD

The community of ceramics is generally one of overwhelming support and generosity of spirit. Throughout my involvement with this fascinating material called clay, I have been surprised and delighted by the sharing of information, the constant encouragement and care that exists in this industry. So, after getting your hands dirty and finding both your thoughts and hands stuck in clay, rest assured, they won't be stuck for long; support is out there and in this new book. Don't just sit and confront the material on a daily basis, go out and research and develop your ideas, take your sketchbook and camera to galleries and museums and take a fresh look at what is around you. Get inspired, then get stuck in!

We understand the subject matter is vast and have endeavored to include the relevant areas of practice to this book. This was all in response to my co-author's question "What do you think about writing a book together about stuff we know and do?" People from Stoke (the historic center of the UK ceramics industry), like myself, are said to have slip rather than blood running through our veins. Here's to the next generation to take this material forward and invent new work and uses. Come on you potters and clay makers!

Duncan Hooson

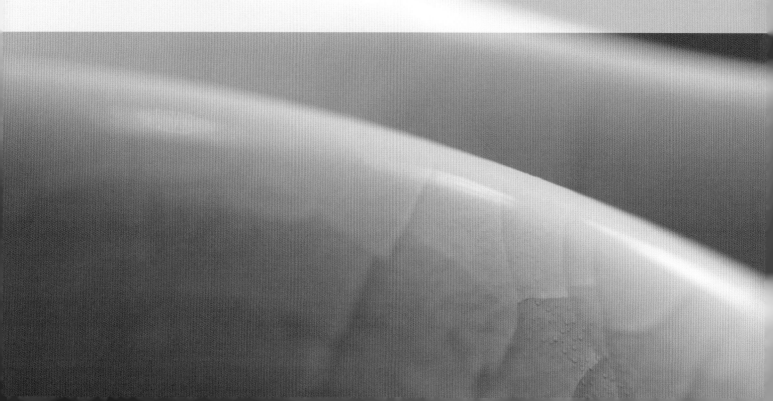

Ceramics is an activity that I fell into by accident over twenty years ago but have continued to be drawn deeper and deeper into the subject every day of my practice. The ability to transform and manipulate the clay material continues to fuel my enjoyment of the subject. Similarly this transformative material beguiles and challenges my practice as an educator and designer constantly.

The opportunity to collaborate on a book that endeavors to be so informative, so wide ranging in its ambition and so detailed in its exploration is exciting. To my mind there are very few books that deal with the subject in this way, that explore the relationship between techniques and qualities and guide the reader through this relationship with such clarity of purpose.

One of the key interests for me as an educator and writer is to expose readers to the tacit knowledge of the subject. This is the sort of knowledge that takes some time and a lot of practice to acquire. It is my intention that this book helps the reader overcome this barrier and allows them to dig deeper with confidence and purpose.

Anthony Quinn

One of the most alluring aspects for anyone intending to work in clay is the sheer breadth of potential applications for the material and the improvisational nature of the techniques. This has given rise to what is possibly the defining characteristic of contemporary practice —the breaking-down of the traditional barriers of art, craft, and design. Practitioners are ignoring traditional classifications and skills and following a very personal trajectory.

CONTEMPORARY PRACTICE

Artists are using volume manufacturing to address issues such as scale, repetition, and context. Neil Brownsword's work is a direct response to industry, often taking the cuttings, swarf (metal filings and shavings), and trimmings of industrial manufacture to make sculptural forms. Clare Twomey's work challenges our understanding of the concept of mass production and our consumption of it: her installation *Forever* reproduces the same object in an edition of 1345, installs them in a huge gallery space, and invites the public to take an object on the condition that the recipient allows people to view the work in their homes, effectively becoming a museum themselves. Ai Weiwei's sunflower seeds installation in the vast turbine hall at London's Tate Modern uses hand painting and slip casting to reproduce the simple sunflower seed in its millions. It challenges us to discard the beautiful singular object

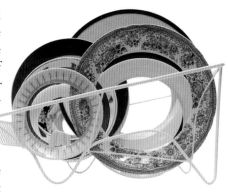

RESISTANCE
BY KJELL RYLANDER
His work offers the viewer a problematic image of a random collection of plates standing in a drying rack, devoid of their function by being reduced to their decorative rims, the viewer is left with more questions than answers.

SY SERIES
BY NEIL BROWNSWORD
This work challenges the viewer to engage with loss of tradition and skill while presenting ambiguous objects as archaeological remnants of the industrial process. These objects are often shown with films that juxtapose the craftsmanship of production with images of factories being demolished.

UNFIRED INSTALLATION
BY PHOEBE CUMMINGS
*The use of clay as a unfired material is central
to these site-specific installations. Knowing that
a bucket of water could instantly reclaim these
intricate works, adds to both the fragility and
allure of the viewing experience.*

EVERYDAY BEAUTY
BY ANDERS RUHWALD
*These coiled and hand-
built earthenware forms
are inspired by our personal
everyday journeys. These
pieces disturb preconceptions
about beauty in objects we
frequently overlook.*

MONUMENT
BY CLARE TWOMEY
*This eloquent and
intimidating installation
of broken ceramic objects
measures 30 ft (9 m) in height.
The artist recontexualizes
the industrial pitcher pile
by placing it in a gallery.*

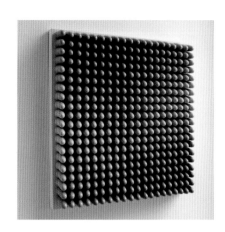

SWAB SKIN

BY JESSICA DRENK

This extraordinary piece has been made using Q tips soaked in porcelain. From building walls using wattle and daub to the creation of the silicon chip, the combination of clay with other materials has long been, and continues to be, explored.

REFLECTIVE PROPERTIES

BY DAWN YOULL

Through placement and association these intriguing slip-cast forms (center) pose questions for us to engage with. The objects act as signs and symbols creating a narrative for the viewer.

in amongst the mass and therefore overlook the workmanship that has produced each object.

Craft makers are using CAD (computer-aided design) technologies to produce unique objects that challenge the notion of the hand made, yet still reflect the quality and bespoke nature usually associated with their field. Michael Eden's *Wedgwoodn't* tureen is an example of a technology driving the craft to a new arena. His work very much speaks of material and the archetype, taking a traditional object such as a tureen that has now become redundant and building it in an ultra modern form and methodology. It breaks rules long associated with ceramics; perforated structures that were previously impossible take on forms that appear both traditional and futuristic at the same time. Tavs Jorgensen uses CAD programs and an electronic glove to form objects in a "virtual workshop" before employing rapid prototyping technologies to create those objects in clay. His previous training as a potter and designer bring a sympathy and fluidity to the otherwise systematic nature of the program. The technological development of clay from one of the most basic materials to one of the most advanced has also drawn industrial designers to working with it. Ami Drach and Dov Ganchrow's *+/- Hotplate* transplants technology from printing circuit boards to act as a heat reactive surface design that can keep food warm. The surface motif is playful and useful all at once.

YELLOW LINGHAM

BY KULDEEP MALHI

These slip-cast forms were influenced by the maker's interest in Indian Shaivism. These powerful multiple forms protrude from the wall with subtle, colorful glaze creating movement through the form.

UNIDENTIFIED VIEW

BY CAROLINE SLOTTE

This painstakingly beautiful work is achieved through a time-consuming process and a poetic attention to detail. An essential detail in the pattern has been isolated and highlighted through a reduction of all other visual details.

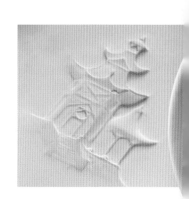

TANK SERIES
BY NAO MATSUNAGA
These forms are able to evade interpretation by incorporating both coiling and press-molding forming techniques. Matsunaga dismisses glaze and completes the forms with ink and wax.

ROLL CARBON CHAIR
BY SATYENDRA PAKHALÉ
This chair (center) marries the traditional skills of throwing and turning with the futuristic material of carbon fiber. The form is clad in high-shine carbon to give an otherworldly finish.

REINFORCED CLAY FURNITURE
BY MAARTEN BAAS
This collection of clay furniture seems to challenge gravity with its fragile appearance. The look is achieved by gestural hand-modeled clay over a metal skeleton.

Designers are reinventing craftsmanship and the idea of the unique within a mass-manufacture context. Studio Glithero is an Anglo-Dutch design group whose work celebrates craftsmanship and attention to detail in the making. Its *Running Mould* is a pair of plaster benches formed in the gallery space using the process of sledging; the work is a reminder of the loss of skills that were once widely used. Hella Jongerius uses the potential faults of the printing and firing processes to make unique objects within a factory and mass manufacture context. Her work with major companies such as Ikea and Nymphenburg has resulted in the idea of the bespoke being translated into many peoples' homes. Satyendra Pakhalé is an Indian industrial designer whose work is concerned with the translation of craftsmanship into an industrial context. His collection of limited-edition furniture re-contextualizes the craft of throwing or coiling and demonstrates a quality far removed from the potter's wheel. His *Roll Carbon* chair clads a hand-made ceramic form in a high-tech carbon fiber surface. Maarten Baas' furniture also uses clay, but with a surface quality entirely removed from that of Pakhalé. His hand-formed chairs seem to defy gravity and weight and challenge the user to sit if he or she dares. His collection seems to defy the logic of the material as it evolves into ceramic tables and floor fans.

One of the most prevalent trends within the contemporary field is the challenging of the ceramic archetype. Artists, makers,

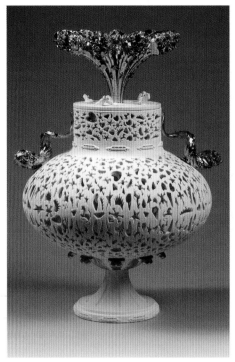

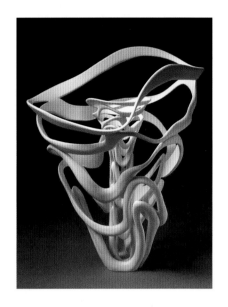

PSORIASIS I

BY TAMSIN VAN ESSEN

This piece makes use of a fault in the glazing process to create a beguiling, decaying surface on a reproduction apothecary jar. The juxtaposition of disease and medicine makes the final piece a more powerful vehicle.

À REBOURS

BY MICHAEL EDEN

By using 3D printing the artist challenges the ceramic convention and looks forward to the future and the beginning of new craft possibilities (center).

and designers have all been drawn to the breadth of ceramic tradition as a creative opportunity. One of the most poetic interpretations of tradition is Caroline Slotte's *Unidentified View*—hand-weathered plates that create a poignant tableau of nostalgia and silence. Her work is painstakingly transformed from thrift store to gallery by using a hand-held rotary tool to draw out interesting details from a pattern to create an alternative narrative. Barnaby Barford's work is no less poetic, if a little more direct in its inception. Barford collects unwanted ceramic figurines and brings them together in unlikely combinations to make work that acts as a mirror to our society. His work has a political and satirical bent; he has recently produced a stop-frame animation called *Damaged Goods*, which is a love story in a bric-a-brac store. Dutch designer Jo Meesters' *Ornamental Inheritance* uses mass-produced Chinese decorative objects and a sand-blasting machine to transform the decorative design into a skyline that shows McDonald's signs and wind turbines to speak of our desire for and consumption of objects and things.

The opportunity for ceramic sculpture has not waned in the light of this hybrid practice. Some makers work directly with clay to make large-scale sculptural works. Ah Leon produces breathtaking *trompe l'oeil* ceramic sculptures that take the potential for mimicry to a new level. His

PIERCED PORCELAIN SCULPTURE

BY JENNIFER MCCURDY

This fluid skeletal form pushes both the porcelain clay body and the technique of piercing to an extreme to create a dynamic expression of the material.

Moon Jar
by Grayson Perry
This coil-built vase provides a three-dimensional clay canvas for a variety of slip and surface decoration techniques. The layering of transfers and painted imagery brings a real depth and richness to the form.

work challenges our perception and understanding of the material as it transforms into a weathered wooden bridge or school desk. Edmund de Waal is both a potter and a sculptor; his pots are made in editions, often specific to a particular place or environment, and collected together in a thoughtful order that inspires a contemplation or meditative engagement. His most ambitious work to date, *Signs and Wonders*, is a massive circular shelf that has been installed in the dome of the Victoria and Albert Museum in London: placed on it is a huge collection of hand-made porcelain pots and dishes, reminding us of the museum's role in collecting what we possess in our homes.

The traditional crafts of ceramics are still thriving, and makers are finding increased opportunities with galleries, trade fairs, and collectors. The breadth of work is arresting, from Rupert Spira's delicate and elegant forms to Julian Stair's monumental funerary ware to Bodil Manz's decorative geometric simplicity.

The sheer breadth of contemporary practice means that this is one of the most vibrant and exciting periods for ceramic practice. We hope that, by including such work in this book, readers may be inspired to use the same techniques and add to the wealth of the medium.

Flower Jar Yellow
by Felicity Aylieff
The throwing used to make this work is on a monumental scale. The hand-painted motifs reference a domestic context but the scale of the piece (57 in, 146 cm) sits outside of the same notion of domesticity, making for an interesting juxtaposition.

HEALTH AND SAFETY

Due to the sheer breadth of techniques and materials used in ceramics, there are many health and safety issues to consider. Many of the precautions you need to take regarding the use of hazardous materials and heavy machinery are no more than common sense. Others involve planning out your workspace and organizing working practices sensibly.

When setting up your workshop, give some thought to the passage of materials and techniques through the workspace. Large workshops tend to have separate areas for each activity, which simplifies the health and safety issues related to each technique. If your working area is limited and therefore multifunctional, you will need a well thought-out working process in which dust, toxic materials, water, glaze, and clay are managed safely. This is entirely possible if you plan your working day and clean up properly between each activity. Make sure all individual containers and equipment can be moved to clean spaces on a regular basis.

Risk assessment

When you are working with any substances that may be hazardous to your health, it's important to make a proper risk assessment of your work environment. Consult official guidelines for advice on how to do this.

A risk assessment is an analysis of all the factors involved in undertaking a particular activity and formally logging the level of risk. It is good practice to carry this out in your own workshop. Look at the space you are using and at who is using it. Think about things like the risk of tripping, receiving an electric shock, fire and burns, handling hazardous materials, flying particles, and shelving collapse.

Look at how you are going to use equipment in particular spaces. Does your work space have appropriate storage? Can materials and containers be placed on wheeled boards (dollies) to aid easy moving for daily cleaning? Are there any trip hazards in passageways? Are materials correctly labeled and are you aware of the risks involved in using them? In each case, record whether you think the risk of an accident is low, medium, or high; if it's high, work out what you can do to lessen the risk.

Protective clothing

Many potential problems can be prevented by adopting good working practice at all times. Always wear protective clothing, such as overalls or aprons; these should be made from a polyester-type material that does not hold dust in the same way as natural fabrics, which should be avoided.

- Wear appropriate footwear when in workshops, especially when loading kilns and climbing ladders.
- When using any equipment and machinery, especially throwing wheels, all hair must be tied back with a headband.
- Cleaning and chipping bits off glaze shelves should be carried out in a secluded area and appropriate safety eye-glasses should be worn.
- Never look into kiln spy holes without wearing appropriate eye-wear.
- Wear foundry gloves to unpack kilns, and surgical gloves to protect skin and prevent cuts when using ceramic materials.
- Never remove protection guards from equipment or override any safety cutoff devices.

Glazing

When mixing glazes a dust mask is the minimum requirement, with a respirator being the best form of protection against inhaling dusts and toxins. If the workshop has extraction, then glazes must be mixed under extraction. You should also wear surgical gloves to prevent any skin irritation.

Cleaning

- Clean workbenches and equipment, including spray booths, after each activity by wet sponging. Make sure you clean any spillages immediately.

- Wash all tools after each session. Wet wipe all canvas after use and wash it periodically.
- Wet mop dusty floors daily rather than sweeping them, which simply creates clouds of dust that will stay airborne for hours. Small bits of clay that fall on the floor should be swept up immediately with a dust pan and brush.
- Rinse out water spray misters weekly.

Manual handling

Make sure that you observe safe lifting procedures when handling heavy bags of materials such as clay, plaster, or glaze.

When loading a kiln, assess how you are going to pack the shelves to prevent overstretching.

Adequate shelving is a key part of any studio and you must ensure that the height does not exceed what you can comfortably reach. Again, health and safety guidelines should be consulted to find out what the maximum shelving height recommended is.

Dealing with hazardous and toxic materials

Many glaze materials are either hazardous or toxic. Data sheets are available from suppliers for all materials and must be displayed if working in a group environment. Labels also need to be displayed for the range of materials stocked in cupboards. The data sheets will tell you everything you need to know in order to safely use and store such materials.

To avoid ingesting hazardous materials you should never eat or drink in the workshop.

Dust

Probably the biggest health and safety issue in the ceramics workshop is the dust, which can range from an irritant to toxic. Clay has tiny silica particles, which are particularly dangerous if inhaled because they build up in the lungs and can cause silicosis, traditionally considered a potter's disease. Silicosis and such problems are easily preventable by wearing respirators or masks and switching on an extractor fan. Always wet wash benches and floors.

Machinery

Wheels, lathes, pug mills, kilns, and many more machines associated with ceramics are all potentially dangerous; consult the Safe Systems of Work sheet for any machine before you use it, because this will give you the safe working specification of the machine and details of any features such as emergency stop switches. It is important to familiarize yourself with all machines before you use them; ideally, get someone to demonstrate its use. Always wear safety goggles and overalls or an apron, and secure any loose clothing or long hair so that it cannot be drawn into moving parts of the machine. Make sure that machines are turned off before fixing or adjusting them.

Kilns and firing

Kilns are very important pieces of workshop equipment and must be loaded and operated correctly each time. Follow kiln packing procedures at all times and only use the supplied kiln furniture for firing. Do not touch the kiln exterior while firing is in progress, since it can get very hot.

- Give careful consideration to where the kiln is placed. Kilns should never be in contact with surrounding walls. Suppliers will tell you how far from the wall they can be and provide other useful safety information.
- Ideally, kilns should be placed in a separate room; where this proves difficult, access should be restricted—especially in schools, where they are often placed in a cage. The metal surface areas will be very hot during and after firing and could cause burns.
- If the kiln is indoors, excellent ventilation is required to remove gases, fumes, and smoke directly from the kiln. This is normally achieved by installing extractor hoods above the kiln; if this cannot be done, open grilled windows or extractor fans will help. If you are using a kiln in a small studio, fire at night so that you can avoid working in the atmosphere.
- Exiting fumes can be harmful if inhaled, since firings give off different gases and fumes. Enamels, lusters, and transfer covercoat are particularly noxious and are to be avoided.
- Small to medium front-loading kilns need to be placed on rollers, because you need access to the back to repair and change the elements and contacts.
- Ideally, kilns should be placed on concrete slabs, floors, or ceramic tiles—and never on a wooden floor.

- When firing is in progress, there should be no combustible materials—for example, wooden boards on which work is drying—in the vicinity.
- Use only heavy-duty foundry gloves to unpack work from a warm kiln or to open vent bung bricks and covered spy holes.

Electric kilns All kilns should be fitted by a qualified electrician and should have relevant isolating safety control cutoff switches.

- Do not have water near any part of the kiln. When cleaning surfaces, use only a damp sponge and always switch the kiln off.
- Purchase the appropriate fire extinguisher for electric fires.
- All electric kilns should be fitted with padlocks or safety cutoff electric key locks. New kilns will be fitted with relevant safety cutoff devices.
- If the kiln is not reaching temperature, it is likely that at least one of the element banks has failed and needs to be changed. Once the kiln has been switched off and isolated, this is a straightforward procedure. If more than one bank has failed, replace the whole set.

Gas kilns Always check the terms of any local planning regulations, restrictions, and laws in relation to installing and using a gas kiln, as well your personal insurance.

- Full access is required all around gas kilns so that checking and maintenance can be carried out. You must have regular checks made on all pipework and burners to ensure there are no leaks that may cause an explosion.
- Gas is heavier than air and will sit at the lowest level, especially in corners where it can get trapped. Excellent ventilation is essential to allow any gas to disperse.
- Burners should have safety cutout devices to prevent gas going into the kiln if not alight.
- Explosions will occur if unlit gas enters the chamber at a low temperature and is then lit.

Ceramic fiber This is extensively used in kiln building due to its excellent thermal insulation properties. Keep up to date with current health and safety regulations regarding its use, since it is rated as carcinogenic and is also a skin irritant. New fibers are being developed which

are safer but they are not heat rated beyond 2280° F (1250° C).

Ceramic fiber is a mixture of alumina, silica flux, and china clay. It is easy to use but should always be handled with care wearing a dust mask and protective gloves. Always keep the material dry, because it will break down when wet. There is a liquid available that is painted on the surface to provide a bonding coat to help prevent the fiber from breaking down so easily.

Wood, salt, and soda firings Consult local planning regulations to see if you are allowed to do these firings. More makers are exploring soda firing, as it is believed to be considerably less toxic than salt and is tolerated in built-up communities.

Raku firing This involves working in direct contact with ceramics at very high temperatures. All precautions should be taken regarding the siting of the kiln. Loose pipework should be covered to prevent trip hazards and burners being pulled out of position. Wearing appropriate footwear and protective clothing—gloves, goggles, masks—is essential. Have buckets of water and a fire extinguisher close at hand and undertake any other fire precautions. If you are working with other people, carry out a full induction to cover safe working procedures and ensure everyone knows their individual role and responsibilities.

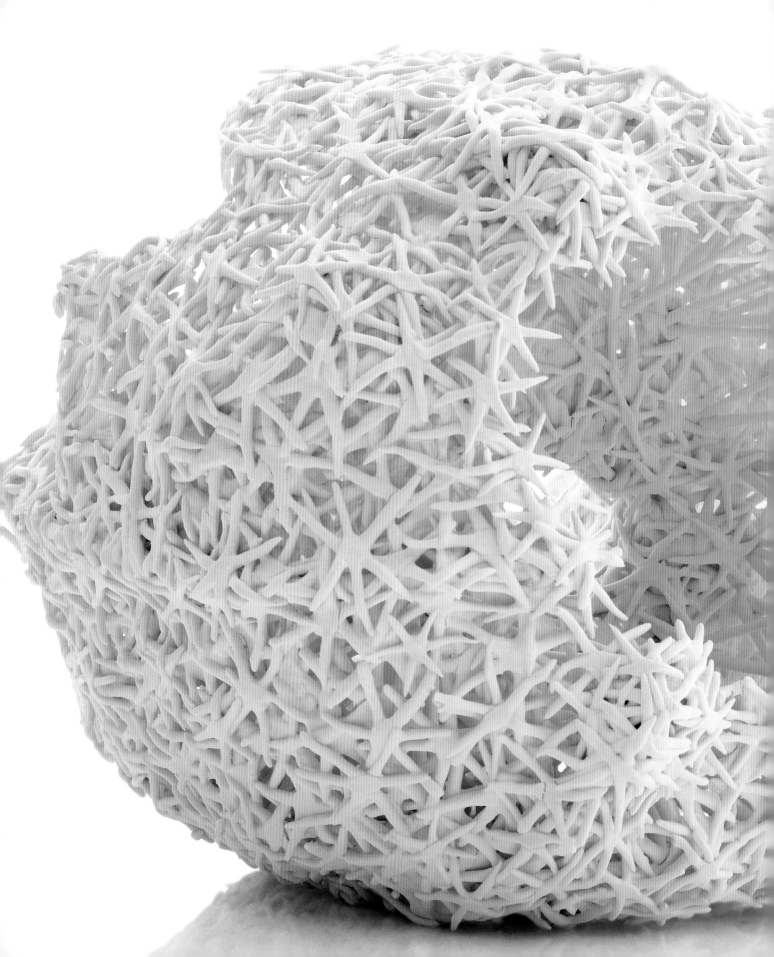

PART ONE

MATERIALS, TOOLS, AND PROCESS

Delicate porcelain sculpture
by Nuala O'Donovan
Clay can be made into a heavy solid block
or manipulated into a fine intricate web
as this porcelain form demonstrates.
Makers from left to right: Jochen
Rueth, Phoebe Cummings, and
Fernando Casasempere.

Clay is one of the planet's most abundant natural materials—probably the most abundant. It's there, in the ground, almost all over the world. Where it's found and the composition of individual clays is the end result of millions of years of ever-changing geological flux.

WHAT ON EARTH IS CLAY?

Often, clay is found on or very near the surface. Where roads are being built or foundations dug, where gardens are being carved out of the ground, seams and chunks of clay will be uncovered and discovered. Beyond town and city, you'll find clay where roads and highways have been cut through hillsides; in the banks of rivers and streams; in outcrops on beaches and cliffs. In each case, it will be in seams that are smooth and compact compared to the layers of sand, gravel, soil, and rocks that often surround them.

Types of clay

Most clays began life as felspathic and granitic rocks, which, millions of years ago, began to be decomposed by hydrothermal action (heated water in the earth's crust) and weathering agents (water, sun, ice, wind, heat, plants, animals).

MINED CLAYS

These materials can be used to create a range of different clay bodies or used as found.

Surface or red clay These are the most common and are found across the world, taking their color from iron oxide. Within this broad range of clays there are many different types, each with its own individual texture, color, and working quality. The color varies from white-gray through yellow ocher to dark iron red to almost black, depending on the clay's organic and iron content. Fusible, high in plasticity, with many having a low melting point, these clays are most commonly used and will be highly visible wherever you travel in the world as building bricks. Because of the extent of geological movement these clays have picked up other materials making them coarse when found; but once refined are highly plastic and smooth because the movement has broken down their particle size. These have a wide firing range with some melting as low as 1900° F (1050° C). Vitrification for many is around 2100° F (1150° C) through to 2200° F (1200° C).

Ball clay Ball clays are gray to blue to black in their natural state—the result of decomposed vegetable matter. When fired, however, they become white to buff colored. (The name "ball clay" dates from the early days of the British pottery industry. When clay was transported by packhorse it was shaped into balls to make it easier to load, carry, and unload.) Ball clay has a high level of plasticity, which is why it is often used in blended

Surface clays	Australia	China	Ghana	UK	USA
Fired to 2190° F 1200° C					
Fired to 1830° F 1000° C					
Wet					
Dry					

Geologically, clay divides into primary and secondary clays—also known as residual and sedimentary. Primary clay is less abundant than secondary clay and remains pretty much where it was formed. It is known as "kaolin" or, more commonly, "china clay"—the name a result of the belief that the kaolin found in China was the only one of its kind with a high level of plasticity. The word "kaolin" itself derives from a Chinese original—*gaoling* or *kao-ling*, meaning high hill—and came to the English language via French in the early 18th century.

Primary clay is often mined by using high-pressure water to wash the fine clay into suspension, thus separating it out from the surrounding gravelly rock and fine sand. It is then settled in vast tanks, where it is dried out and thus prepared for its many uses. One of its many uses is as filler in this paper. Because

of its purity, primary clay is rarely suitable for working in its natural state and usually mixed with other clay bodies. It is used in a blended body for its strength and whiteness and is an essential ingredient of porcelain and also used as an ingredient in glazes. It is extremely rare to find kaolin like that found in Jingdezhen in China that is usable as a clay body.

Secondary clays are those whose structure or location has significantly changed in some way since they were formed. They are found in sedimentary layers, shaped and formed by weathering and other geophysical processes. The weathering creates an extremely fine, laminated particle structure. These secondary clays are classified as stoneware, surface, fire, and ball clays. These clays can be used in their found state but are often used as ingredients to create clay bodies both commercially and by clay makers.

clay bodies. Their plasticity makes them very smooth because of their fine particle size and have a top firing range around 2400° F (1310° C).

Fire clay So called because it is often found near or next to coal seams or because of its highly refractory properties. It is very common worldwide and is found in a range of colors due to levels of metal oxides. It is usually coarse in texture and used widely in blended stoneware clay bodies because of its high firing (refractory) qualities.

Its firing range is 2200° F (1200° C) through to 2370° F (1300° C). It is also used as a common form of grog in clay bodies to give added greenware strength, lessen shrinkage, and to add texture. Grog is a material, usually made from clay, that has been fired and crushed—the action of production is referred to as calcining.

Stoneware clay This is a general term for natural clays that fit in between those of ball and fire and are quite rare to find; these are manufactured and commercially

blended from the other individual clay mineral ingredients.

Clay starts changing color the moment it is dug and continues to change through all the different stages of the ceramic process, as the water in the clay evaporates or is driven out by heat. The firing process burns the impurities away almost completely, leaving a considerably diminished color range, from white to gray to various tones of terracotta (Italian for "fired earth").

Although clay bodies do contain small amounts of other minerals, they

consist mostly of alumina and silica. It is the proportion of these two minerals, together with the other minerals that act as fluxes, that assists the fusing and melting of the clay body during the firing process. It takes millions of years for nature to make clay, transforming rock into a soft, malleable material, yet the hands of the maker can, within hours and with the heat of the kiln, effectively reverse that process, turning soft clay back into a permanent, rocklike substance. This is the transubstantiation of ceramics.

Materials for making clay	Ball clay	China clay	Fire clay	Potash feldspar	Quartz
Fired to 2280° F (1250° C)					
Wet					
Dry					

Unless you are going to dig your own clay, you will be using clay bodies that have been blended commercially. Each manufacturer will have a catalog of at least 50 types of clay body, with new variations appearing regularly. Each different body will have been designed for a different task or tasks and will, therefore, have different properties.

WHAT TO BUY OR DIG—AND OTHER CONSIDERATIONS

You will use different clays for different purposes. For example, for throwing you want clay that's highly plastic and bends easily, but for large slabs you will need grogged clay that does not warp.

Characteristics

There are a variety of characteristics that you need to consider when selecting a clay body: plasticity, greenware (unfired) strength, overall shrinkage rate, the textures you wish to create, and, of course, its response to your selected glazes, firing, temperature range, and resistance to warping at the higher temperatures.

Blending clays

Even after buying clay bodies, makers often continue the blending process. It's not uncommon to mix together varying quantities of up to three different bodies. Colleges often provide a mixed

body made up from scraps and unwanted work of different clays—a good way both to recycle a variety of clays and to make available a different clay body.

The basis of most prepared commercial clays is the highly plastic ball clay, with the addition of ceramic minerals such as feldspar, alumina, and silica or nonplastic materials such as kaolin, Cornish stone, or whiting.

The proportions of different clay ingredients in the mixture will determine what the clay body is to be used for. Purchased clays should give you a certain level of consistency and quality, but always bear in mind that they are made from a blend of natural materials. These materials are mined from different sites, and within any given area the pits and seams of materials will change. To eliminate color unpredictability, specific colors of clay will be added separately by the

Clay plasticity tests
You can easily assess the characteristic of plasticity by first rolling and bending clay into tight arches or loops. The grogged clay needed to be bent in stages and smoothed with a damp sponge to prevent cracking, while highly plastic ones will remain smooth.

Porcelain stoneware   White grogged stoneware   Iron-flecked stoneware   Smooth red earthenware

THE CHARACTERISTICS OF CLAY

These are the characteristics that you will be testing for when assessing the quality of clay for a particular purpose.

Plasticity For a maker, the most important property is the degree of plasticity—the movement of small particles that hold together and stay in place. Primary china clay is very pure, but its particles are large, so it is not very plastic. Secondary clays are more plastic—a result of the geophysical movement and erosion that break the material down, grinding it down to a smaller particle size. These tiny particles are 1,000 times smaller than a pinhead. Plasticity is often improved in a body by the addition of bentonite, a mineral similar in composition to primary clay.

The higher the plasticity, the more the clay will withstand stretching, pulling, and bending without the surface opening up or cracking. The more you handle clay, the drier it will become, because your skin absorbs water from the clay; this inevitably reduces the clay's plasticity. With experience, you will be able to make informed decisions on the different degrees of plasticity required for different tasks, techniques, and projects.

Greenware This stage will need to be considered depending on what work you are making. The larger and more complex the work gets the more you will have to consider the greenware strength. Larger works will benefit from a more coarse body made with the addition of grog or molochite. This clay is less plastic but able to withstand more additional weight and scale of making than finer clays; it will shrink a lot less so does not put as much strain on the form during drying and firing.

Shrinkage/warping The majority of clay you use will shrink during the making and firing process. Experienced makers enable such an allowance in the making process—particularly if making multiples of production ware. How much the clay shrinks will depend on the clay type and what temperature you fire it to. There is always the probability that work will warp and crack if it has a high shrinkage rate (above 15 percent). It may also make a difference to the glazes you use because of the compatibility fit.

Porosity The percentage of absorption after firing is how a clay is classified; earthenware, stoneware, and porcelain. It's useful to know the temperatures where the clay is porous, semiporous, and vitrified because you can then make informed decisions about the correct glaze to apply. Knowing something about this should prevent crazing with glaze fit and is essential if you are making work for exterior locations and functional work.

Texture Clay can be bought in fine, smooth, or grogged varieties. Manufacturers will often supply small sample bags to test. They realize that it's difficult to assess how a tactile material behaves simply by reading a label or catalog entry. Adding other ingredients to help with the plasticity or to create different textures in the clay is fairly straightforward. If you want to change the actual character of the clay by adjusting the formula it will require a certain amount of research, trial, and error.

Glaze response The color of the clay will determine the response of the glazes you apply. This can also relate to the number of coats of glaze that need to be applied depending on the effect required. However, you always have the option to change the clay's color by using clay slips.

You will make compromises along the way as you handle and use a wide variety of clays for particular projects and techniques, but, rather than being based on purely practical reasons, your choice of clay may stem from a personal and intuitive response to the color, texture, tactile and visual qualities of a particular type.

---

manufacturer. The only difference in certain clay bodies will be the added color.

A coarse body can be obtained by adding some form of sand or grog to a fairly plastic clay. The choice of ingredients for any clay body is dependent on what type of work you are going to make with it.

Mixing your own clay body from powder

Some makers buy clays in powder form, blending and mixing them in their workshops using a dough or cement mixer. This can be much less expensive; it also enables you to mix the clay to your own formula and have it at your own preferred consistency. If you go down this route, remember to factor the cost of your own time into this process.

You can mix and make your own clay body very easily; for large quantities, however, you need to have access to a dough mixer.

To make small amounts or test batches without using a dough mixer, put some water in a container to prevent a lot of dust from flying around. Then weigh out the dry powders and add them to the container. Add water until covered and leave the materials to soak for ten minutes. Depending on how well the ingredients have mixed and the consistency achieved, that

The ingredients of clay

Clay is not one thing; it's a material that is composed of many elements in different amounts. The basic chemistry of clay is alumina and silica. Chemically it's classed as hydrous aluminum silicate. The different properties of found clay and variations from one batch to another in different locations around the world is the reason why clays are often blended to perform more predictably. Natural clays are categorized by their geological formation: ball clays, kaolin/china clay, fire clay, stoneware clay, and surface clay. Manufacturers create clay bodies, which will give you a tried-and-tested firing range and color.

Alumina This white powder is generally unaffected by standard kiln temperatures. It has a melting point of above 3630° F (2000° C). It's added to the body in different ways: in its pure form or as additional ingredients in clays, frits, and feldspars. Feldspars are a group of rock-forming minerals that make up as much as 60 percent of the Earth's crust.

Silica This property is found in many forms but commonly as beach sand and quartz. It has a melting point of approximately 3000° F (1650° C). It is added to the body in different ways: in its pure form, in clays, feldspars, frits, talc, and wollastonite.

Water Clay naturally contains water, but it is also added as part of the blending process to combine the particles together.

Firing ranges

Whatever stage of firing you are at, it should come near to the point of vitrification (when the clay no longer absorbs water). This will vary according to the type of ware or composition of the body, but the following is a general guide to vitrification temperatures. Suppliers will put the firing range information on the bag for each particular clay.

Terracotta ware, bricks, and red tiles	1650–1900° F (900–1040° C)
General earthenware	1900–2080° F (1040–1140° C)
Fine earthenware	2010–2190° F (1100–1200° C)
Stoneware	2190–2370° F (1200–1300° C)
Porcelain	2260–2460° F (1240–1350° C)
Bone china	2240–2250° F or 2340–2410° F (1230–1240° C or 1280–1320° C)

should be the end of the process. If you have had to add a large amount of water to enable a thorough mix, then this will need to be laid out onto a plaster bat to partially dry (see page 143). If making 22 lb (10 kg) or more it will need to be mixed with either an electric drill with a plaster mixing blade attachment or a glaze mixer.

When making large amounts with a dough mixer you can achieve the correct consistency immediately, as you add the water while mixing. Without a dough mixer, however, you usually have to add a lot more water to get the ingredients to mix. So, if the mixture is too wet, you may need to put it through a 30–60-mesh sieve (depending on the consistency) and then lay it on a plaster bat to dry, as with recycling clay (see page 29).

The clay needs to be stored ideally in a brick or concrete bay covered in plastic for at least six months; the longer you leave it the better. Fresh clay improves with age, because the bacteria aids its plasticity. Ideally you would then put the clay through a pug mill to further blend and expel air before use.

Dig it: sourcing and refining clay

Digging, identifying, and refining your own clay will give you a real sense of what the material you are dealing with actually is. Found clay may not supply you with your specific needs, but the process provides an invaluable basic understanding of your chosen material. You can

DIGGING IN BEDLAM'S BACKYARD BY DUNCAN HOOSON AND GILES CORBY
A site-specific sculpture was created to prospect for clay and ceramic shards. This shows the entrance tunnel. The exterior was clad in metal, and the interior with terracotta to create the sense of going to mine for materials.

Digging for clay
In some places clay can be found on the surface, but in other areas you will need to dig for it.

	Earthenware			Stoneware		Porcelain	
Recipe	1	2	3	1	2	1	2
Ingredients	%	%	%	%	%	%	%
Fire clay	-	-	-	-	60	-	-
Ball clay	65	30	48	25	20	-	17
Kaolin	14	25	25	25	-	-	-
Flint	11	35	4	-	10	-	8
Whiting	10	-	-	-	-	-	25
Cornish stone	-	15	23	25	-	-	25
Sand (silver)	-	-	-	25	-	-	-
Feldspar	-	-	-	-	10	25	-
Bentonite	-	-	-	-	-	5	-
Quartz	-	-	-	-	-	15	-
Firing temprature	1980–2050° F (1080–1120° C)			2300–2340° F (1260–1280° C)		2340–2410° F (2800–1320° C)	

test and then combine your local clay with a commercial one to give it a different character. Some found clays, for example, do not have great plasticity by themselves, but can be used effectively when blended with others.

Once you think you have found some local clay, a quick test to see if it might be useful is to wet the material and rub it together. If it appears and feels sticky, then it contains clay. Roll it into a ball and see if it stays together; if it does, then dig out more. One final test is to check its plasticity: try rolling a small coil and forming it around your finger. If it does form a ring, then it is definitely worth investigating.

When you have found your clay, allow it to dry out along with all the other materials—soil, organic matter, stones, and so on—that you found with it. This will allow it to break down quickly when introduced to water—a process known as slaking.

The following test is a good demonstration of how wet and dry clays break down. Put two samples of the same clay—one dry, one wet—into separate glasses and add water. Watch how quickly the dry clay disintegrates, while the wet one will stay the same for days, or even weeks.

Breaking down clay
These images demonstrate how quickly clay breaks down when bone dry. The wet clay at the top was placed in water and left for a day. It will remain like this for some time. The dry clay in the centre was put into water and then photographed five minutes later and is shown at the bottom. Now it is ready for reclaiming and wedging.

REFINING PROCESS

Hopefully these steps will inspire you to go out wherever you are and start digging the stuff out below your feet. Once you start you will be amazed at the range of colors and places you can find clay. Get digging!

TECHNIQUE FILE **01**

1 Discard as much waste material as possible from your found clay—twigs, stones, and so on. Let the remaining materials dry out completely before crushing them into small pieces with a rolling pin or hammer. Place the material in a container and pour water in until covered. Stir and leave to stand for a day to allow the heavier materials, including the clay, to settle to the bottom.

2 Pour away the top half of the mixture. Stir the remaining mixture until it has a yogurtlike consistency that will easily pass through a sieve, then push it through a 30-mesh sieve. The liquid-fine clay will pass straight through. This can then be pushed through a 60–80-mesh sieve to refine the mixture further.

3 Pour the liquid-fine clay mixture onto a plaster bat or any other absorbent material and spread the mixture across the full surface area to speed up the drying process. The time the clay takes to dry will depend on the quantity and thickness of the clay slop: because this was a thin layer it had dried enough to collect into clay body in 30 minutes, whereas large amounts will take at least one day.

4 Once the clay has dried, it should easily come away from the bat with a rubber kidney or by pressing a gathered lump of clay on top of it to compress it together.

World clays
The color of clay will vary depending on where in the world it has been extracted.
1 UK   3 Pakistan
2 China   4 Japan

Testing clay

The tests that you need to carry out for any clay are for plasticity, shrinkage rate, porosity, firing range, and vitrification (melt) point.

To test your clays, make sample bars measuring 6 x ¾ in (15 x 2 cm). Within this, mark a central line 4 in (10 cm) long. By taking measurements and recording them at stages throughout the ceramic process, you will be able to compare them and assess accurately their suitability for use. You can always add other clay materials to found clays to make them usable.

Testing plasticity Plasticity depends on what ingredients the clay body is made up from. It is the particle size of clay that determines its plasticity and a mixture of particle sizes is preferable in a clay to hold it together. You can test plasticity by squeezing, rolling, bending, and twisting the clay; plastic clay should have an almost elastic feel when any pressure is applied.

Testing shrinkage Clay shrinks at the three different stages of the ceramic process: first, when it is drying out through water evaporation; second, when it is bisque—first fired to 1830° F (1000° C); third, when glaze fired, especially at top stoneware temperatures of 2340° F (1280° C). The more heavily grogged the clay body is, the less it will shrink. Most commercial clays shrink by between 10–12 percent, unless sold as low-shrink bodies. Porcelain shrinks by around 15–18 percent. By measuring the center line at each stage through the process you will see the shrinkage rate overall: when wet, when dry, when bisque fired, and at final earthenware temperatures. If the shrinkage rate is beyond 15 percent then the clay may prove problematic to use for many forming techniques because of cracking and warping problems when drying and firing.

Testing porosity You need to know the porosity of the bisque-fired clay to enable you to apply glaze. Many found surface clays have low melting points, so the density of the clay is far greater after the bisque firing as the body starts to vitrify and close up. This is in contrast to the majority of commercial clays, which are designed to be fairly porous at 1830° F (1000° C). This may mean that you have to mix less water into the glaze than normal before you apply it; alternatively, you can bisque fire to a lower temperature to make the body more porous. To test these clays for porosity, firing range, and vitrification point you can fire three bars of clay to temperatures in between 1830–2200° F (1000–1200° C). When testing the range of any found clay, always make a walled clay tray for it to sit in during firing. When reaching stoneware temperatures, the clay can become liquid and drip onto your kiln shelves and elements; a costly experiment. This should give you an idea of the firing range; from this you can then select the point where it's still porous but not absorbing water so quickly. This will give you some indication of the potential usefulness and the functionality of the clay. The less porous the clay is the stronger it is.

Testing the vitrification point The word "sintering" is used to explain the firing stages up to the point of vitrification when the clay particles are beginning to fuse together. If kaolin is present or added it will increase the firing range. When the clay no longer absorbs water you have reached the vitrification point. Some clays will have a shiny appearance at this point and some can be used as interesting slips or glazes. All clays will melt at different temperatures; the standard table of classification is to provide a general guide for the firing range for earthenware, stoneware, and porcelain. The majority of commercially available kilns are not recommended to go beyond 2370° F (1300° C).

Reclaiming and recycling clay

Clay should always be worked with at its optimum consistency; if it goes past this point, it will need to be recycled.

No matter what method of forming techniques you are using, there will always be times when you are left with dry bits of clay: remnants from cutting slabs to fit, shavings from leveling edges and bases, handles that didn't look quite right, and turning waste from wheel-thrown forms. The wonderful thing about clay is that, until it goes in the kiln to fire, it can be recycled with relatively little effort; it does not matter how long it has been sitting around.

As previously discussed, it is far easier to break down dry clay than wet clay: this process is called slaking. Collecting semidry lumps at the end of making sessions, breaking them into small pieces, and adding small amounts of water can be enough to refresh clay without having to completely recycle it. As you put the bits back into a bag or clay bin, sprinkle water in between each layer before finally wrapping the clay in plastic.

If, however, the bits of clay can no longer be pressed together, put the semidried bits of each clay in a separate bucket to allow them to completely dry (or put them all in one bucket or trash can if you are creating a mixed body). Pour in water until the pieces are completely covered, allow to soak for a day, and the clay will quickly disintegrate. If you keep adding to this mixture with dry pieces of clay, make sure there is plenty of water in the bucket. Avoid putting in semidry lumps, since these will not break down as quickly.

Give the mixture a good stir and slop it out onto a plaster bat or concrete slab to dry out over a few days. Make sure that the bat or slab is sitting on wooden slats so that air can circulate underneath it to dry it out after use. Check the clay throughout the day to assess the drying and turn it over when necessary so that it dries out evenly on both sides and through the middle. Then wedge (see page 30) the mixture or put it through a pug mill and store it in plastic, ready for reuse. If the clay is not as plastic as you would like, then next time add small amounts of fire clay, ball clay, or bentonite to the initial mix.

SLAKING OR RECYCLING CLAY

This process should become part of your making routine and adds to the understanding of the material and best consistency for particular techniques.

TECHNIQUE FILE 02

1 Collect scraps of the same clay together in an appropriately sized container; you need one with a lid to prevent dust particles from flying around. Before adding water the clay should be bone dry, like the clay on the left of the image, and broken into small lumps.

2 Cover the clay with water and allow the mixture to break down over a few days; this process is known as slaking. You can keep adding more over months by adding both clay and water to this mixture before slopping out; the downside will be the rotten smell!

3 Slop the clay out onto a plaster bat. Form ridges in the slurry to increase the surface area, so that the clay dries more quickly. Keep checking to see how the slurry is drying; if it dries out too much you will need to repeat the process from the beginning. You can pull the soft clay to one side, pull away the stiffer clay on the bottom, and spread out the slurry again. Alternatively, cover it with plastic and leave it to dry overnight, so that you can check the condition the following day.

4 As the base dries it should easily come away from the bat. The larger and heavier the mass, the easier it will compress and collect together. At this stage, if the clay is going to be stored for any length of time, it should be softer than if needed for immediate use.

5 Pick up any remaining residue and scrape the bat clean with a rubber kidney. Do not use anything that will scratch the bat, since you do not want the clay to be contaminated with any other material—especially plaster. The bat should always be cleaned with a wet sponge to eliminate any leftover clay, because dry lumps will break down into dust particles.

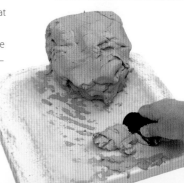

It is important to know how to prepare clay ready for use. New bags of clay will have had the air knocked out of them at the manufacturer; any other bits and pieces, especially reclaimed clay, need to be mixed together to achieve an even consistency and expel any air pockets since, if left, air pockets can cause the work to blister, split, or even explode during the firing process.

CLAY PREPARATION AND ADDITIONS

Some clay workers see the task of getting rid of air pockets as good preparation for the day's work ahead, while others avoid it whenever possible. Purchasing a de-airing pug mill is one solution, but it needs to be cleaned out before each different clay is used.

If you do not have a de-airing pug mill, choose a stable and suitably absorbent surface at a height that allows you to apply downward pressure. The clay must be soft; if it is too hard, it will layer and not compress together. If the clay is stiff, then push your fingers into the clay, fill the holes with water, squash the clay together until blended,

and then continue with wedging. Alternatively, cut slices of clay about ¾ in (2 cm) thick and put slurry in between to create a sandwich, and then wedge. (This is also how you would mix in grog and blend different clay bodies together.)

Always prepare the clay on a porous surface. If the clay is very wet, then knead it on a plaster bat (see page 143) to absorb some of the water. The different core-forming techniques demand slightly different consistencies of clay, depending on what you want to achieve. Wedging is the opposite of bread making, where you are trying to add air. It can be difficult to prepare small lumps of clay and easier to handle a larger lump and then cut off smaller pieces as required. There are three main methods: overhead wedging, ox-head kneading, and spiral kneading. It will take practice to achieve the desired results.

Your body position is very important when preparing the clay. You need to apply downward pressure so, depending on the height of your workbench, you may need to stand on a sturdy platform. Always take one step back from the surface and place one leg in front of the other. This will allow your body to move forward and back in a rocking action. It will also allow you to extend your arms to full length both in front of you and above. In addition you will have better balance when lifting the clay above your head and throwing it back down again.

Adding other materials to clay

Some additives melt or burn away in the clay to create cavities and decorative effects; some combine with the clay to create properties that can have an industrial, technological, scientific, or environmental impact; others lower the melting point; while paper and other cellulose fibers add

OVERHEAD WEDGING

This method is a useful way of mixing big lumps of clay. The name is derived from cutting the block at an angle into a wedge shape.

1 Form the clay into a wedge shape and cut the block up from the base to the top at an angle of 45 degrees.

2 Lift the clay above your head and slam it down onto the block so that the cut, flat side comes down and hits the top of the ridge. As the flat surfaces connect, the air should be knocked out. Pick up the block and rotate it through 90 degrees. Repeat this process at least five times, until the mix is even in consistency.

THE IDEAL OX-HEAD SHAPE

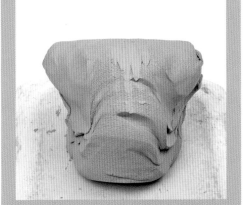

This is the ideal shape to finish ox-head kneading with. From this you can either form the clay into one ball or cut off smaller pieces as required. Try not to trap any air pockets while forming your other pieces. Keeping the clay compact is the most difficult aspect to overcome. If it proves too difficult, then reduce the size of the lump. If the clay is too hard and not compressing together, then soften it with water. When cutting, look to see that the surface is smooth and compact. If it is not, then continue kneading until this is achieved.

strength at the greenware and bisque stages. The main additive that you will encounter is grog.

Grog is clay that has been fired and ground down into different sizes and is identified as a number. The lower the number, the coarser it is. It ranges from coarse grit, which adds texture, through to a fine powder, which will improve the strength of certain clay bodies and lessen the warping at high temperatures. Molochite is a white grog that is a calcined form of china clay. It is mainly added to white firing clays such as T material, which is an expensive, but excellent general-purpose hand-building clay, suitable for large work. Molochite can also be used with dark clays to create a speckled surface, especially in work where the surface is scraped back. These substances can be kneaded or wedged into the clay.

TECHNIQUE FILE 04

OX-HEAD KNEADING

With ox-head kneading you push the clay away from you and pull it back in a rocking motion while at the same time applying pressure at the sides to keep the shape compact. This is useful for small to medium amounts of clay.

1 Make sure the clay is "putty" soft. It will be easier to knead by selecting a lump of clay that forces your hands apart. Knock the lump into a rough ball shape. Position yourself so that you can rock backward and forward. Place one hand on each side of the clay ball at the top and push forward.

2 As you push the clay forward, apply inward pressure from the sides: this will help to keep the clay compact. From your shoulders it should feel as if you are pushing forward to a point in a "V" shape. Rock the clay back and push forward again. If you are not applying enough pressure from the sides, the clay will quickly turn into a long roll.

TECHNIQUE FILE 05

SPIRAL KNEADING

This is similar to ox-head kneading, but it's almost as if one arm takes over while the other relaxes. This method is good for larger clay lumps.

1 Make sure the clay is "putty" soft and knock it into a rough ball shape. This method allows you to control large lumps of clay; you only need to hold a small amount of it as you push down, turn, and repeat. You should see a layering, which forms the lump into a spiral shape.

2 If you are preparing the clay for wheel throwing, then as you knock it into a ball, make sure the spiral is visible at the top before you place it on the wheel head, to avoid trapping air underneath. Some wheel throwers say that this spiral makes it easier to center the clay on the wheel.

Definitions within ceramics can seem confusing because there are so many exceptions to general rules. As makers find other successful ways to make, glaze, and fire, the standard processes change and the rule book is challenged.

CATEGORIES OF CLAY DEFINITIONS

At first, the definitions in ceramics can seem confusing because they refer to clay, materials, different types of work, kiln firings, and also temperatures. Once you understand that temperatures govern how things are described, everything will start to fall into place.

The transformation of clay into a permanent material happens in set stages during the ceramic change from 840–1200° F (450–700° C). At 1070° F (570° C), something called "quartz inversion" takes place. This is when the molecular structure goes through a physical change. The higher the temperature, the harder and denser clays become until they reach their individual vitrification point.

The main classifications are earthenware and stoneware, and sometimes left out of this generalization is porcelain.

The term "earthenware" is used to describe a clay whose firing temperatures range from 1760–2080° F (960–1180° C). "Stoneware" describes a clay fired between 2190–2370° F (1200–1300° C). Porcelain is fired between 2260–2460° F (1240–1350° C). Within these categories there are low, medium, and high firing temperatures. Materials are fired to many different temperatures within these ranges, until they are either just about to or have fused. By selecting different temperatures, the maker can create different tactile and visual qualities.

Earthenware
We are surrounded by earthenware in the form of bricks even though, in cities the world over, steel and glass are fast taking over. Other contemporary common uses for earthenware include garden pots, roofing tiles, chimney pots, and domestic functional ware.

Earthenware clay can be found in large deposits all over the world. It forms the majority of the clay that we dig up, providing different colors depending on the organic matter and impurities within it. These impurities often burn away

Layered glaze vessels
by Morten Lobner Espersen
These hand-built heavily grogged stoneware forms are covered in layers of glaze. The work is fired several times after another layer of glaze is added. Each firing adds to the crawling and dripping as the glaze eats away at the surface.

during firing to give a range of colors from ocher to orange-brown. Earthenware clay is often referred to as red clay (the red actually being more brown); we also call it terra-cotta, even though that translates from the Italian as "fired earth," which could be the definition for all ceramics. The higher the temperature at which you fire this clay, the darker it will become, up to its various vitrification points (dependent on the minerals it contains). Different percentages of iron oxide determine the color and provide a flux. The iron oxide also gives it a lower melting point than stoneware clays. The color and strength of earthernware is determined by where in the world the clay is fired, in what type of kiln, and at what temperature. Keeping the light orange color will make the work softer and more porous. Many makers use slip decoration in conjunction with earthenware, because the earthenware provides an attractive dark background against which decorations stand out well.

You can buy commercially blended white earthenware clay, which is a mixture of ball clays and other powdered minerals. This will fire to a white/buff color and is generally used by makers who do not want to apply decoration over a white slip coating on the red clay. It can be difficult to handle with certain forming techniques and is not as tolerant due to its fineness as other clays that have more texture. Careful, slow drying is required when pieces or sections have been added to the main body.

The common glaze-firing temperatures for earthenware are in between 1940–2150° F (1020 –1180° C). You need to decide how functional you want the work to be: glazing makes the work more hygienic and less porous. You also need to use the correct fit of glaze, meaning that the clay and glaze are compatible, so that crazing, which is caused by the different shrinkage rates of the glaze and the clay body, does not occur. You will have to test the glaze colors you want to work with on the clay. (Stoneware clays also can be fired to these temperatures, but will suffer from glaze fit faults for this reason.)

Industrial earthenware is often fired to a high bisque range of 2080–2150° F (1140–1180° C), almost to vitrification. This is then glazed and fired at a lower temperature of 1940–1980° F (1060–1080° C). This can be difficult to achieve

Earthenware body samples
The clay loops show the plasticity of the clay body. The stamped part of the fired tile demonstrates how different glazes break over the raised surface.

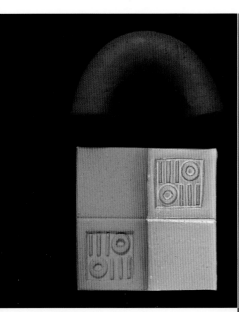

Standard red earthenware, half tin-glazed

Grogged red earthenware, half-covered in clear glaze

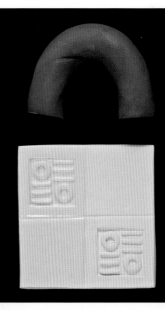

Low temperature white body, half transparent-glazed

in a studio setup, because the clay has started to lose its porosity. Getting the glaze onto the bisque ware can be difficult and will require repetitive testing, unless it is mixed with an adhesive. Red earthenware has such a strong background color that it will affect the color response of many transparent glazes, which is why it is often used with slips. Red clay is still one of the cheapest clays to purchase. The firing of earthenware can take place with any fuel and in any kiln.

Stoneware

Not surprisingly, the name derives from its stonelike quality and appearance. Stoneware is much stronger than most earthenware, because it has been fired to a higher temperature. This clay is usually fired between 2190–2370° F (1200–1300° C), with some clays, especially ones for industrial use, fired even higher.

Stoneware is similar in mineral composition to stones, since both have been exposed to heat treatment in different ways (stones being formed naturally and the ceramic artificially blended from minerals and clay). There are many more commercially available stoneware clay bodies than earthenware. They come blended with

different sizes of grogs, which create a wide range of very fine to coarse clays for different purposes. Fine stoneware bodies are ideal for smooth surfaces where fine detail is key, and for domestic functional ware. Coarse ones are responsive to textural treatment and ideal for large-scale sculptural work. All are hard-wearing and some are suitable for external locations.

Stoneware is fired in many different types of kilns with different heat-generating materials, creating different kiln atmospheres. The two most common types of kiln atmospheres are referred to as "oxidized" and "reduced."

In oxidation, depending on which type of kiln you are firing, the flow of air into the chamber of the kiln is unrestricted, and complete combustion of the fuel takes place as the temperature steadily rises. In a reduction firing, however, the air intake is restricted and, instead of fully combusted fuel giving off carbon dioxide, carbon monoxide is produced. As this is an unstable gas, it quickly combines with oxygen atoms in the clay body and glazes of the work, changing their chemical composition and color.

Reduction is not appropriate in electric kilns, so electric kilns produce oxidized, or more

STONEWARE SCULPTED VASE BY JOCHEN RUETH
Stoneware's appearance can reflect the heating and cooling of the material. This piece looks like it could have been formed by the force of nature.

Stoneware and porcelain body samples

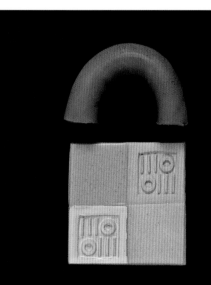

Buff stoneware, one quarter transparent-glazed, one quarter tin-glazed

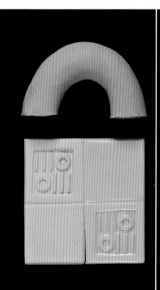

Smooth white stoneware, half transparent-glazed

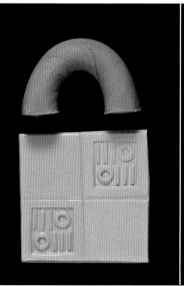

T material, half transparent-glazed

Standard porcelain, half transparent-glazed

correctly, neutral firings. Localized reduction can take place in electric kilns by placing wood into the kiln, but this will cause smoke and lessen the life of the kiln's element wire—something that is not advisable. If you want to experiment with reduction, you can place the work in sealed containers called saggars with combustible materials (see page 240). These will reduce the internal atmosphere inside the saggar.

If fired to vitrification point, stoneware is generally (depending on the clay body) nonporous. The coarser the clay, the more "open" the body, which can result in porosity. Certain clays will hold water without being glazed but over several weeks may allow a small amount of water through to form a damp patch underneath. For functional ware, it is usually better to glaze—especially if the piece is likely to come into contact with food, for hygiene purposes.

Porcelain

There appears to be an insatiable appetite for porcelain's clear celadon blues and greens, which shows no sense of abating in the next few years, as many makers push this white material into new places and spaces. Found in China and other areas of the world as a primary clay, porcelain has not been on much of a journey since first formed. In the hands of clay makers its aesthetic journey has gained pace. There is a range of commercially blended bodies made from the whitest clays available. Its white fired color provides a pure blank canvas; this especially allows transparent glazes to clearly shine. It highlights any incized lines where the glaze will create rich pools of color.

PORCELAIN BLOCK SCULPTURE
BY FERNANDO CASASEMPERE
These solid blocks of porcelain clay show the deep fissures of tension created during the firing process. The structure's balance seems to be flexing at the moment of collapse.

Porcelain recipe

China clay	25%
Ball clay	25%
Feldspar	25%
Silica	25%

Porcelain paper clay, half transparent-glazed

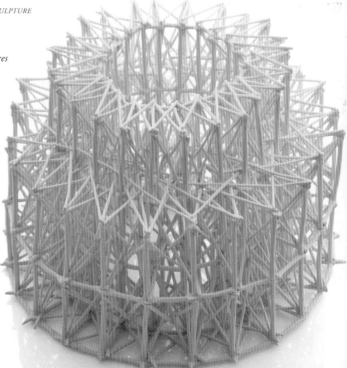

INTRICATE PORCELAIN SCULPTURE
BY NUALA O'DONOVAN
This fascinating three-dimensional form explores the irregularities in constructing repeated pattern. The work is built slowly and pushes the boundaries of what is technically achievable with porcelain.

DELICATE BONE CHINA
BY ALAN WHITAKER
This fine bone china work is inspired by the sand formations on beaches. It plays with the qualities associated with the material by demonstrating its translucent nature.

Porcelain is usually fired above 2280° F (1250° C), with or without glaze, to leave a surface with a slight sheen that does not mark easily. It can be fired to its recommended vitrification point to make it nonporous and, depending on the shape of the form, will quickly start to distort and crack. When fired it is a very dense, strong, and durable material that is resistant to acid and bacteria, which is why it is used for many industrial purposes.

Porcelain is not highly plastic and will require regular handling to gain experience of its capabilities. Certain rules and mystique have built up around the material, but generally those who use it regularly find their own way with it. Slow drying, especially where attachments have been added, helps reduce the risk of cracks. The thinner the clay and the higher above 2280° F (1250° C) it is fired, the more translucent it becomes, to the point where shadows can be seen through it. Porcelain's shrinkage is the greatest of all clays, ranging between 15–18 percent.

A range of porcelain bodies is available from commercial suppliers and you can also make up your own to suit your particular needs. Generally it is not suited for large-scale working without the addition of 7 percent fine molochite and/or 1 percent cellulose fibers; this amount should not change the nature of the porcelain.

Other types of clay

Many clays are being explored within the field of contemporary ceramics as makers are continually expressing different ways to use them. The following are a small sample of those that would have been thought of as more specialist in the studio context only two generations ago.

Bone china This type of clay contains calcined animal bone, which acts as a flux to create an almost glasslike substance when fired above 2260° F (1240° C). Contemporary makers use it for its whiteness and translucency. It has long been used industrially for these characteristics, along with its fineness and extreme strength. It is used mainly as a slip-casting clay, but can be purchased as a plastic clay body. Bone china does not have a wide maturing range— the time between the sintering (fusing) stage and vitrification. This can present problems depending on the forming technique you are using, since the structural relationship is more critical than some other clays and will quickly distort and lose its shape. As with some other industrial-type clay bodies, it can be bisque-fired to near its maturing range between 2250 and 2300° F (1230 and 1260° C). It is then usually glaze fired below 1980° F (1080° C).

Bone china does not have very good plasticity, which can make using it with the core-forming techniques difficult. Its beautiful properties

Bone china made from casting slip, half transparent-glazed

Black stoneware, one quarter transparent-glazed, one quarter tin-glazed

Recipes

These two recipes offer the starkest of contrasts within the ceramic color vocabulary.
They can be used together.

Black wash recipe		Bone china recipe	
(given in parts)		(given in percentages)	
China clay	10	Calcined bone	50 %
Manganese dioxide	3	China clay	25 %
Cobalt oxide	3	Feldspar	25 %
Red iron oxide	3		

add to its allure, but it does not have much mechanical strength before firing, which can therefore lead to a high failure rate through cracking and distortion.

Black clay This clay was made fashionable by Wedgwood's jasperware, which was left with an unglazed, matte surface. Today the main reason to use black clay is to highlight the surface qualities that the making and handling leave on the work: to show how you have manipulated the surface, leaving either subtle evidence of mark making, joining, or any other qualities that you want visible on the final surface. Otherwise, you could simply use a black slip on any clay and glaze over this. The unglazed black clay can be combined with partially glazed and contrasting slipped areas to make full use of the richness of the clay surface.

Black clays are supplied commercially as both earthenware and stoneware bodies in a variety of textures from smooth to very coarse, depending on the grog content. They are very plastic and are suitable for all the main core-forming techniques. They come in a color range from chocolate to black and the color will darken the higher you fire them toward vitrification. You should strictly follow the supplier's recommended firing range because errors of overfiring the top temperature will result in pools of clay as they melt due to the high oxide content. Don't confuse the earthenware black clay with the stoneware clay in the same firings. The temperature will always be on the bags and will vary depending on the supplier.

You can make your own earthenware black clay body by starting with a red clay and adding 5–10 percent black body stain or manganese oxide. Other oxides such as cobalt, black iron, and copper can be tried, and all of these will add subtle variations to the final color.

An alternative to using a black clay body is to use a black wash at the glazing stage. Unlike a glaze—which will cover some of the subtleties of the surface—the wash is so thin, but saturated in oxide to produce a dense color, that it will leave the underlying marks visible.

Sculpting/architectural clay bodies A variety of clays—sometimes referred to as marl—are sold for sculpting or architectural purposes, commercially blended to enable large-scale working. Working at a large scale magnifies and increases the number of problems associated with the greenware strength, shrinkage, and crack resistance during making and drying, and with the tensions that clay goes through during the firing and cooling stages.

Marl is made from a combination of stoneware clays and grog or molochite to open the structure of the body, enabling quicker drying and adding to its greenware strength. This reduces its plasticity, so you may have to adapt your usual

CUT BLACK CLAY VESSEL BY SARAH-JANE SELWOOD *This piece was wheel thrown and finished to a high degree, before being subtracted and reconstructed.*

Architectural grogged stoneware clay with transparent glaze on the left side

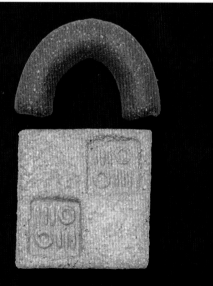

Raku grogged stoneware clay with transparent glaze on the left side

ARCHITECTURAL CLAY SCULPTURE
BY RAFAEL PEREZ
This sculpture demonstrates both the energy and drama of the material: how clay can be manipulated to create extraordinary forms.

RAKU SCULPTURE
BY ROWENA BROWN
This raku-fired tower form made with a heavily grogged clay demonstrates that finely constructed work can survive the rigorous raku firing process.

working methods. Once you use it, however, it may become your preferred clay due to its greater tolerance levels.

These clays will have high stoneware vitrification points because of the added materials that almost get in the way of the finer clay particles when melting and knitting together. This will be important if making work for exterior locations, because you do not want any water penetration or absorption in the clay; this will freeze in cold weather and cause damage to the work.

Raku clay This clay is made specifically to survive the raku firing process and is similar to many sculpture bodies. The raku process relies on the rapid firing and cooling (usually within one hour) of clay work that has been previously bisque fired. The work is taken out of the red-hot kiln at around 1830° F (1000° C), which puts the clay through severe thermal shock.

Raku clays are generally prepared to be coarse and with an open texture, created by the large percentage of grog or molochite in the clay. You can create your own raku clay simply by wedging (see page 30) grog or molochite into a prepared body or adding them at the recycling stage (see page 29). The addition of the grog helps prevent cracks and splits. Other clays than these can be used successfully for raku, but it is worth testing them to see which survive this ordeal by heat.

Paper clay A paper clay body is a blended mixture of clay and paper; it is also referred to as "fiber body" due to the cellulose present in paper. The term can describe any clay body that contains between 5–50 percent paper content.

The percentages of clay and paper you mix together will be important depending on what you want to make and on what core-forming techniques you are using, as all of the main ones are possible. The amount of paper content affects the texture, final strength, and durability. Paper clay is now commercially available in a variety of forms.

Paper clay has changed many of the basic forming rules in recent years, particularly in joining procedures. Complex structures can be built because fresh new clay can be stuck onto bone-dry or even bisque-fired clay by using paper-clay slurry as the glue and bond. It can also be enough to simply wet areas to be joined. In the dry state, the hollow fibers of cellulose provide the capillaries for the wet clay to bond and knit together. Armatures for sculpture made from wire mesh can be used, but are generally not needed. Paper clay can be fired to all temperatures, when the paper will burn away; this will also reduce its weight. Make sure you have excellent ventilation (as you already should have) since smoke and fumes can be created during the early stages of the firing, depending how much paper you have used in the mix.

To make your own paper clay, it is best to start with a clay slurry; this either entails breaking down an existing clay (see page 29) or starting with your own mix of dry ingredients. Use either a plasterer's mixing blade in an electric drill or a ceramic glaze mixer, and create a clay slurry, which should be the texture of thick cream. Select your paper: newspaper, tissue paper, and egg cartons are all suitable; alternatively you can buy cellulose fiber from builders' merchants and

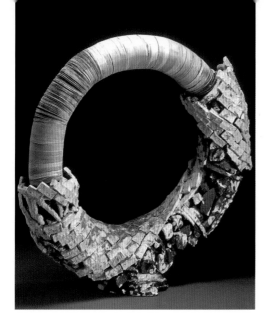

some ceramic suppliers. Soak your chosen fiber in water to break it down and then mix further in the bucket with your blender. Depending on which paper you have used, squeeze out the excess water. The paper can then be blended with the slurry. Cellulose insulation can be added without first soaking because of the fine nature of this particular paper. Mix until the mixture is lump free and slop out onto a plaster bat to dry. When sufficiently dry, it can be used as sheets, or wedged and stored in a cool dark space in airtight bags or containers to prevent mold growth.

There are health issues and hazards around the storage of paper clay, and many makers who use it regularly make up a quantity to use within one to two weeks. It can quickly start to rot and smell. If mold does appear on the surface, scrape it off and spray with a mixture of water and a very small amount of bleach. If the clay has turned black inside, it should be thrown away. A very small amount of bleach can be added to the water in the initial mixture to help prevent this. Certain fibers, such as cellulose insulation, have added boron and borax to aid in fire prevention, which seems to prevent this rotting. Research on the Internet will provide up-to-date information, as clay makers share their knowledge.

Casting clays These are liquid clays that are poured into plaster molds to create forms and are referred to as "slip." The majority of industrial manufacturing processes use this type of clay to enable repeated forms, a process that is referred to as "slip casting." Casting slip can be purchased in small 11-lb (5-kg) containers or much larger quantities from commercial suppliers. Makers who use large quantities usually make their own using a machine called a blunger. Most clays can be made into a casting slip with the aid of a liquid called a deflocculent. This helps to keep the clay particles in suspension and decreases the need for a large amount of water to be added to the slip. It also assists with reducing the overall shrinkage rate.

Casting slips enable you to repeat forms and make small or large additions. They also make it possible to make very thin forms of a single clay or create walls made up of multilayered, different-colored clays by pouring one on top of the other.

Egyptian paste This specially prepared body is not commercially available. It is a self-glazing clay body in which the glaze is supplied by soluble salts of soda that are drawn to the surface of the work as it dries. Care must be taken in handling the clay in order not to disturb the soda or rub it off. The outer layer of soda crystals reacts with the clay body during firing to form a glaze coating with the added color from the pigment or stain present in the body. A historical example of Egyptian paste is the clay beads from ancient Egypt, which acquire a brilliant turquoise from the soda and copper reaction. Most of the basic oxides, such as iron, manganese, cobalt, and chrome, can be used in this way with colored body stains that will provide a wide range of bright colors.

Egyptian paste is used not as a functional clay body, but for its colorful decorative effects. The addition of minerals to give greater strength and durability to the body would counteract the particular qualities of color. Because the paste has a poor mechanical strength while being formed, it is only used for small objects such as beads and decorative bowls. Care must be taken in the firing to ensure that the glaze does not adhere to the kiln shelf, by firing on alumina. Beads should be supported on straight lengths of element wire to prevent contact with the kiln shelves and each other. The work is best fired once, to approximately 1830° F (1000° C) or below.

PAPER CLAY RING
BY GRAHAM HAY
Paper clay enables greater flexibility to construct forms that can better support themselves during the making, drying, and firing stages.

MOLDED VASES
BY KATHRYN HEARN
Creating form with plaster molds and casting clay of different colors enables you to repeat form and investigate different surface treatments. These repeated forms are made unique by the surface treatment, which creates very different square patterns.

TOOLS FOR GENERAL USE

Each making process uses specific tools and equipment, but there are some tools that are used across all making methods and that form the basic tool kit. These can be purchased from most ceramic suppliers, who will stock a good selection of these items.

Clay cutters

Technique: Cutting clay, cutting items off the wheel.
Uses: Clay cutters (cutting wire) are used to cut slices from a large block of clay, and for wedging, slabbing, and cutting items off the wheel head after throwing.
Range available: Available in 12–18-in (30–45-cm) lengths and in different gauges in nylon with hardwood toggles, stainless steel, and twisted wire form to produce shell ridging on the underside of thrown forms.
🧰 **Skill level:** Basic.

Rubber kidneys

Technique: Smoothing.
Uses: Rubber kidneys are generally used for smoothing plastic clay surfaces and in press molding. Very soft rubber kidneys can be used to smooth decals when fixing them.
Range available: Now available in many sizes and gauges, but generally 3 x 2 x ¼ in (100 x 55 x 6 mm), 4¾ x 2 x ¼ in (122 x 57 x 6 mm), and 5½ x 2½ x ⁵⁄₁₆ in (138 x 64 x 8 mm). Smaller and larger, heavier and more flexible varieties are available through different suppliers.
🧰 **Skill level:** Basic.

Metal kidneys and palettes

Technique: Scraping and refining the clay surface.
Uses: Smoothing and trimming leather-hard clay and plaster; burnishing. Serrated kidneys are used for rapid shaping and texturing of the clay surface and rectangular palettes for angled surfaces.
Range available: Two thicknesses—flexible and very flexible. Kidneys are available in sizes ⅜ x ³⁄₁₆ in (90 x 45 mm) and ⁷⁄₁₆ x ³⁄₁₆ in (102 x 45 mm). Rectangular palettes are ½ x ¼ in (125 x 51 mm) and serrated kidneys ⅜ x ³⁄₁₆ in (95 x 45 mm).
🧰 **Skill level:** Basic.

Needles

Technique: Trimming pot rims, piercing, and sgraffito work.
Uses: Can be used to measure the thickness of clay to ensure evenness. They are generally used as a sgraffito and piercing tool, but fine needles are also useful for accurately trimming the rims of pots.
Range available: Generally available in two sizes—fine and thick. Needles can also be made from bodkins fixed into bottle corks.
🧰 **Skill level:** Basic.

Potter's and other knives

Technique: Cutting and fettling.
Uses: Potter's knives are used for cutting clay at all stages of making. They are also used when fettling the surfaces of mold-made wares, in slip casting, and so on. Craft knives are useful for many applications, including clay and paper work.
Range available: A general-purpose potter's knife has a very sturdy 2-in (54-mm) blade shaped to a point. Craft knives are available from most stationers in multipacks.
🧰 **Skill level:** Basic.

Palette knife

Technique: Cutting, stirring, mixing, and scraping.
Uses: A multipurpose knife, but generally used for mixing or grinding colors for various methods

of surface decoration. Also used for cutting and scraping clay and other surfaces and stirring liquids.
Range available: In many sizes, with blades ranging from 2½ to 10 in (63 to 250 mm).
🧰 **Skill level:** Basic.

Sponges

Technique: Finishing, cleaning, and decorating.
Uses: Natural sponges are used for fettling and finishing clay surfaces, soft soaping in mold making, applying coats of slip and glaze for overall or decorative coverage effects, and mopping up when throwing on the wheel. Synthetic sponges are generally used for cleaning surfaces and mopping up but can be cut into shapes for slip or glaze stamp decoration.
Range available: Small to large, fine to coarse texture. Always have a selection, including a large bench sponge, on hand.
🧰 **Skill level:** Basic.

Rolling pin and roller guides

Technique: Slabbing.
Uses: Rolling pins are used for rolling clay for slab building; roller guides ensure an even thickness of clay.
Range available: Generally available in 14- and 20-in (355- and 510-mm) lengths. A child's-size rolling pin is useful for jewelry and small slabs. Rolling guides should be chosen to match the thickness of slab required; most builders' merchants will have a range of battening that can be cut to the required size.
🧰 **Skill level:** Basic.

Double-ended strip tool

Technique: Turning, trimming, and carving.
Uses: With sharp ground-steel cutting edges, these tools are designed for fine and medium cutting, turning foot rings, trimming excess clay, carving, and decorating leather-hard surfaces.
Range available: A large selection of both single- and double-ended

Selection of ribs

strip tools is available for specific tasks, but a simple tool that is squared at one end and rounded at the other is a good basic for all-round use.
🧰 **Skill level:** Basic.

Hole cutters

Technique: Cutting holes or squares.
Uses: Producing holes in lamp bases, teapots, and so on; also used to cut out decorative patterns in leather-hard surfaces. The blades are half round to prevent clogging as the clay is cut.
Range available: Round hole cutters are usually available in several sizes to make holes from ⅛ to ½ in (3 to 13 mm); square cutters from ¹⁄₁₆ to ¼ in (2.4 to 6 mm).
🧰 **Skill level:** Basic.

Double-ended cleanup brush

Technique: Cleaning delicate surfaces.
Uses: These spiral brushes are invaluable for cleaning out small holes and delicate surfaces on

Fettling knife, mold-maker's knife, and mold trimming knife

handles and so on. The long end can be used for larger and deeper openings and the small end for fine sculpture and cutout work.
Range available: One size.
Skill level: Basic.

Surform

Technique: Shaving excess clay and plaster.
Uses: Surforms (the blades are also known as rasp blades) are used for reducing the thickness of clay walls, leveling rims, and shaping sculptural forms, and can be used to texture clay surfaces. In mold making they are used to reduce the bulk of the mold immediately after casting in plaster and for rounding off sharp edges.
Range available: Blades are available as curved, flat, round, and half round to fit relevant-sized planes.
Skill level: Basic.

Wooden bats/boards

Technique: Supporting work in many studio processes.
Uses: Boards allow maneuverability of items at all stages of making, drying, and storing. Round bats are also used on the pottery wheel to avoid distortion of thrown items when lifting off.
Range available: Most pottery suppliers have a range of boards; building suppliers also have boards that can be cut to requirement.
Skill level: Basic.

THROWING AND TURNING TOOLS

The tool kit for throwing needs only a few additional items to the basics. However, there are many tools listed here for specific use at the throwing, turning, or decorating stages that the maker will find useful to have as they become more proficient.

Dottle—sponge on a stick

Technique: Throwing, slip casting, and fettling.
Uses: A dottle is used in throwing to sponge up excess water from the insides of forms that cannot be reached by hand. In slip casting, it has a similar function but is also used to smooth over seam lines and irregularities in the cast surface and to soften rims.
Range available: Several shapes and sizes are available, with rounded, squared-off, and angled ends for specific uses.
Skill level: Basic to intermediate.

Wooden ribs

Technique: Generally used in throwing, but can also be used in other making techniques.
Uses: Ribs are generally used for smoothing and shaping pots on the wheel but can also be used in hand-building processes and as decorating tools.
Range available: Several sizes and shapes, large and small: angle curve, convex oval, flat concave, flat rectangular, flat curve.
Skill level: Basic to intermediate.

Large throwing rib with handle

Technique: Throwing and hand building.

Uses: A long-handled rib is used for smoothing and shaping the insides of pots that are difficult to reach with the hand when throwing or hand building. They can also be used for cutting and slicing.
Range available: Generally one size.
Skill level: Basic to intermediate.

Throwing sticks and stick with hook

Technique: Throwing.
Uses: This tool aids in the shaping and compressing of clay when throwing items that have a deep, narrow-neck where the hand cannot reach.
Range available: Different sizes and lengths, up to 12-in (300-mm) long.
Skill level: Basic to intermediate.

Bamboo comb tool and fluter

Technique: Throwing and hand building.
Uses: Generally used to texture and flute the surface of wheel-thrown wares when the clay is still relatively soft, but can also be used to similar purpose for hand-built items.
Range available: Comb tools are generally double ended, with three prongs at one end and four at the other. Fluters have the fluting device at one end and a two-pronged comb at the other.
Skill level: Basic to intermediate.

Calipers

Technique: Throwing and measuring.
Uses: Calipers are most often used for measuring the width of lids and galleries when throwing, but can also be used on hand-built objects

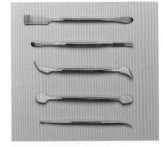

Steel turning tools

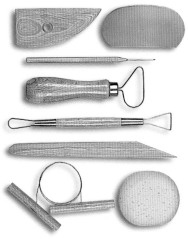

Beginner's throwing kit

where good fit is important. The calipers are set to a specific width and put aside until needed later.
Range available: Wooden, metal, and plastic, in several sizes from small to large.
Skill level: Basic to intermediate.

Stem turning tools

Technique: Turning foot rings, and decorating surfaces.
Uses: Stem tools are a type of turning tool with flat steel blades set on wooden handles. Each tool is multisided to allow great flexibility when turning pots of different shapes.
Range available: Pear-shaped, quadrilateral, triangular, and approximately 6½ in (165 mm) long.
Skill level: Basic to intermediate.

Steel turning tools

Technique: Turning bases on wheel-thrown items.
Uses: An alternative choice of turning tool in a good range of shapes for specific turning needs. These tools can also be used to score lines and other decoration on the surface of wares.
Range available: In both narrow and wide versions, these tools come with pointed, triangular, and pear-shaped ends, squared and rounded, and are approximately 6½ in (158 mm) long.
Skill level: Basic to intermediate.

HAND-BUILDING/ MODELING TOOLS

Some specific tools are required for hand building but modeling requires a number of very specific tools that are available in a huge selection of shapes and sizes. Ceramic suppliers generally sell modeling tools in useful packs as well as individually.

Cut-out tools

Technique: Precision cutting in hand building, slip casting, and so on.
Uses: These tools are used to cut openings and for pierced design work in leather-hard clay wares. The different blades available are suited to either heavier or delicate/fine-walled work and are double edged for reverse cuts and sharp turns.
Range available: Generally in two sizes: 5¾ in (148 mm) for heavier work and 4½ in (114 mm) for more delicate work.
Skill level: Basic to intermediate.

Salt and pepper drill

Technique: Hand building, slip casting, and throwing.
Uses: This double-ended tool has fine drills for making small holes in greenware. It is called a salt and pepper drill because the holes are fine enough to suit that purpose, but it can also be used for any purpose where holes are required.
Range available: One size generally but they can be homemade by fixing a fine drill bit into a cork or piece of wooden dowelling.
Skill level: Basic.

Strip tools

Technique: Surface decoration on greenware, turning, hollowing, and carving.
Uses: These tools are very useful for delicate work where precision carving or turning is required. Because of their shapes, they can be used to create carved decorative surfaces.
Range available: Round, circular, and semicircular, approximately 7¼-in (185-mm) long with wooden handles.
Skill level: Basic to intermediate.

Loop or ribbon tools

Technique: Turning, sculpting, modeling, and carving.
Uses: These tools have many uses: turning clay from wheel-formed pots, hollowing and carving out fine modeled work, and creating fluted and other decorative surface

details. Heavy-duty loop tools are used to carve or hollow out large amounts of clay from models and sculptures.
Range available: A good selection of double-ended tools in varying shapes and sizes is available for every need, including heavy-duty tools for large-scale work.
🧰 **Skill level:** Basic to intermediate.

Metal sculpture/modeling tools

Technique: Hand building, modeling, shaping, and carving clay or plaster.
Uses: Invaluable in the tool kit for precision smoothing, scraping, texturing, burnishing. With long handles and available in many shapes, these tools give flexibility to work both outside and inside a form.
Range available: Pointed, curved, serrated, palette-ended, hooked, spear-shaped, and many more.
🧰 **Skill level:** Basic to intermediate.

Boxwood modeling tools

Technique: Modeling, hand building, and decorating.
Uses: A selection of wooden tools is essential for the tool kit. They have many uses, including blending clay when coiling, cleaning up angles when slabbing, compressing, burnishing, texturing, and fine detailing in modeling.
Range available: Vast selection of shapes and sizes with flat, curved, and serrated edges.
🧰 **Skill level:** Basic.

Coilers

Technique: Hand building, and coiling.
Uses: Coilers are used to make coils in different sizes quickly and easily from a block of clay. They are useful for short- to medium-length coils for making small forms, and for decorative purposes.
Range available: Generally ½ in (13 mm), ¾ in (19 mm), and 1 in (25 mm) in diameter.
Skill level: Basic.

Rubber-ended shapers

Technique: Modeling.
Uses: Silicone- or rubber-tipped

shapers are used to manipulate clay in modeling. They are made so that most materials won't stick to them, making them ideal for working with clay.
Range available: Several sizes, shapes, and degrees of firmness. The shaper is held and used like a brush.
Skill level: Basic to intermediate.

DECORATING TOOLS

The maker will generally need some of the following tools for the many methods of surface decoration—brushes, in their various forms being the most essential, but many of the tools listed have a multifunctional use so will be helpful in other processes also.

Sgraffito tools

Technique: Surface decoration.
Uses: A simple, double-ended tool for drawing into clay is an essential basic for this decorating technique. The needle-type point at one end and spear-shaped point at the other produce lines of different thickness and depth.
Range available: Double- and single-ended versions.
Skill level: Basic.

Sgraffito tool with brush end

Technique: Surface decoration.
Uses: Having a brush at one end of the tool helps when cleaning away excess clay as the sgraffito decoration is applied to leather-hard clay. A paintbrush will do the same job, but having both tools in one is invaluable.
Range available: Specialist ceramic suppliers only.
Skill level: Basic.

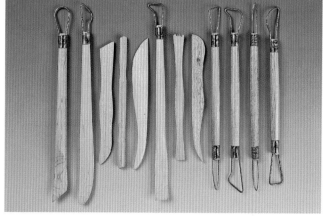

Boxwood and loop tools

 Beginner's Kit
When this symbol appears next to a tool it indicates that it is an essential tool for a beginner.

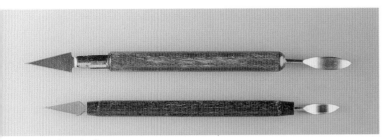

Lace tools

Lace tool

Technique: Surface decoration.
Uses: Looking much like other sgraffito tools, lace tools are specifically designed to help in the application of slip-soaked lace to greenware figurines. They can also be used as standard sgraffito tools.
Range available: Double-ended tool with one pin end and one spear end.
Skill level: Basic to intermediate.

Twisted wire, double-ended loop tool

Technique: Turning and texturing surfaces.
Uses: Good for turning textured foot rings and creating surface detail on wheel-thrown wares, but can also be used to create textured detail on other greenware surfaces and works well when used over colored slip to reveal the clay body beneath.
Range available: Generally with one rounded and one triangular end.
Skill level: Basic to intermediate.

Slip trailers

Technique: Slip trailing, marbling, feathering, tube lining, and glaze trailing.
Uses: Slip trailers are traditionally used to draw or trail decorative patterns and designs onto leather-hard and dry clay surfaces. They are also useful for other slip techniques such as marbling and feathering, and can similarly be used for glaze.
Range available: Available in several sizes but generally bulb-shaped with interchangeable nozzles ranging from super-fine to thick for varied effects.
Skill level: Basic to intermediate.

Double-tip texture rollers

Technique: Surface texture.
Uses: A handy tool for creating fine and medium pinpricked textured surfaces. Use for relief detail on models for mold making or any hand-built item requiring a roughened texture detail.
Range available: One type: double ended with roller action, generally blue.
Skill level: Basic to intermediate.

Hake brushes

Technique: Applying slip, glaze, or color.
Uses: Broad Japanese hake brushes are generally used for laying on larger areas of color, be it oxide, stain, slip, or glaze. The brush is loaded with the decorative material and then evenly applied to a surface as it is rotated on a whirler or banding wheel. These brushes can also be used to make broad, sweeping painterly strokes on the clay surface.

Slip trailer

Range available: In several sizes from narrow to very wide.
Skill level: Basic to intermediate.

Mop brushes

Technique: Applying slip, glaze, or color.
Uses: Traditionally used for the application of glaze, but also good for slip, underglaze colors, or any surface treatment that requires a thick application.
Range available: A good range of long- and short-handled brushes is available from most pottery suppliers.
Skill level: Basic.

Miscellaneous brushes

Technique: Brushes are used in the making process and for many types of surface decoration.
Uses: Generally thin, fine brushes are used for delicate work such as china painting, luster, and enamel work and thicker brushes are used where a more robust design is to be applied. Liners, as the name suggests, are used for applying lines of color to surfaces; they can also be used in a painterly way. Cut liners are used to paint Japanese-style designs on surfaces.
Range available: There is a huge range of brushes available, but they can be very expensive. Choose carefully and buy brushes for specific purposes.
Skill level: Basic.

Hake brushes

MOLD-MAKING TOOLS

This section lists all the tools required for mold making from basic- to advanced- and semi-industrial-level techniques. Some of the tools cross over to other disciplines and can be used at various stages—from the design process through to the end product.

Riffler file

Technique: Mold and model making.
Uses: Generally, riffler files have a curved face for filing concave surfaces. They are designed to be used in hard-to-reach or unusually shaped areas when making and finishing plaster models and molds and are extremely useful for detailed carving work.
Range available: Small- to medium-sized files are available in an assortment of cross-sectional shapes and profiles.
Skill level: Intermediate to advanced.

Fettling knife

Technique: Fettling mold-made surfaces.
Uses: A fettling knife is designed and shaped with a small blade specifically for cutting and finishing the surfaces of mold-made ceramics—for example, to cut away the spare at the top of slip-cast items and to neaten seams at the leather-hard/dry stage.
Range available: The design may vary between suppliers.
Skill level: Basic to intermediate.

Greenware seam-line cleaner

Technique: Fettling and cleaning.
Uses: An alternative to a fettling knife for cleaning back the seams and rims on slip-cast forms at the greenware stage; also useful for removing raised blemishes on other surfaces, including excess glaze.
Range available: Only from certain pottery suppliers. The tool has a sprung steel cutting head and a plastic handle.
Skill level: Basic to intermediate.

Carborundum/abrasive block

Technique: Multiple studio uses.
Uses: Abrasive blocks are used for grinding, smoothing, and refining ceramic surfaces such as the undersides of fired pots, where glaze may have dripped or the surface is rough. They are also used to clean used kiln shelves and to sharpen tools and can be used as a sanding device when mold making.
Range available: Generally available as a white sintered alumina block from most pottery suppliers.
🧰 **Skill level:** Basic.

Carborundum paper/wet and dry

Technique: Mold and model making and fettling.
Uses: Wet, the paper is used in plaster model making to finish and polish the surface to a perfect level before mold making. It is also used to tidy up sharp edges on molds. Occasionally, wet and dry paper can be used to fettle the edges and bases on casts.
Range available: Widely available as wet-and-dry sandpaper.
Skill level: Basic to intermediate.

Vernier gauge/dial caliper

Technique: Measuring.
Uses: This tool is a measuring instrument consisting of an L-shaped frame with a linear scale along its longer arm and an L-shaped sliding attachment to read directly the dimension of an object. A Vernier gauge allows for very accurate measurement.
Range available: From specialist suppliers; try engineering suppliers.
Skill level: Intermediate to advanced.

Spring caliper

Technique: Measuring.
Uses: Spring calipers are used for measuring and marking out diameters, both internally and externally. They have many applications and are an essential tool at design level and when making maquettes, models, and molds.
Range available: In several shapes and sizes.
Skill level: Basic to advanced.

Engineer's square

Technique: Measuring.
Uses: An engineer's square is used to test a right angle and determine a perpendicular surface when model making for plaster molding and for making the molds themselves. It can be used for other applications where the accuracy of an angle is crucial.
Range available: Several sizes, with blades from 2 to 36 in (5 to 91.5 cm).
Skill level: Basic to advanced.

Surface gauge

Technique: Measuring and marking.
Uses: A surface gauge is used to scribe accurate lines into plaster models to mark the center point for

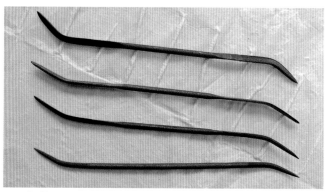

Needle files

two-part molds or other points for multipart molds. The gauge can be used for other applications in the studio where accurate lines need to be marked—in greenware or when decorating—and is useful for finding the center of round-section objects.
Range available: A gauge of this type is available from most ceramic suppliers.
Skill level: Basic to advanced.

Pair of compasses

Technique: Designing, measuring, and model making.
Uses: Essential at all levels of design and making. When used in conjunction with indelible pencils, they can be used for dividing a plaster model up to find a center line.
Range available: Widely available in different sizes and styles from stationers and art supply stores.
Skill level: Basic.

Plastic card/sheet

Technique: Making templates.
Uses: Plastic sheet can be cut out quite easily to make template shapes for throwing profile details and for checking that plaster model profiles are consistent with technical drawings. Other tools can also be made from it, including kidneys and ribs, and texturing and burnishing tools.
Range available: In several thicknesses, from thin and very flexible to rigid and Perspex from specialist suppliers.
Skill level: Basic to advanced.

Chisel

Technique: Turning plaster.
Uses: Chisels are used to turn plaster that has been attached to a cup head on a lathe in the model-making process.
Range available: A large range available from most builders' suppliers.
Skill level: Intermediate to advanced.

Needle files

Technique: Profile and tool making.
Uses: Needle files are used to finish and smooth the outline surfaces of templates and profiles used in the sledging technique of model making. They can also be used for refining tools made for other applications in the workshop.
Range available: In a selection of shapes, they are often sold in kit form from specialist suppliers.
Skill level: Basic to advanced.

Circular tapering file

Technique: Tool and profile making.
Uses: Another tool for refining the inner and outer surfaces of templates, profiles, and other tools specifically made for model- and mold-making processes.
Range available: From builders' suppliers and specialist stores.
Skill level: Basic to advanced.

Spring calipers

🧰 **Beginner's Kit**
When this symbol appears next to a tool it indicates that it is an essential tool for a beginner.

Piercing saw

Technique: Tool and profile making.

Uses: This saw is commonly referred to as a jeweler's saw and consists of an adjustable frame with jaws for clamping the ends of a fine, wirelike blade that can be fitted in different lengths. In the ceramic studio, it is used to cut sheet metal and Perspex for profiles and templates in plaster model making.

Range available: From specialist jewelry suppliers.

Skill level: Intermediate to advanced.

Fret saw

Technique: Cutting profiles and templates.

Uses: Used to cut out larger profile and template shapes for use when model and mold making, hand building, or throwing to keep the shape of the item as it is built.

Range available: Small and large versions, available from most builders' suppliers.

Skill level: Intermediate to advanced.

Mold frames

Technique: Making plaster molds.

Uses: Not an essential item, but useful when making multiple molds because they can be sized according to the model and save the time of having to build a holding wall using other methods.

Range available: One size allows small to large molds to be made, but the frame can easily be made at home with wooden boards and angle brackets to any size required.

Skill level: Basic to intermediate.

Soft soap/mold-maker's size

Technique: Multiple-part mold making.

Uses: Used in the production of plaster molds to prevent surfaces from sticking together. The soap forms a barrier through which subsequent plaster layers cannot be absorbed, allowing the parts to separate easily.

Range available: Buy as mold-maker's size or soft soap.

Skill level: Basic to intermediate.

MISCELLANEOUS TOOLS

For the most part the tools in this section represent essential items required for a working studio, with the exception of a few items that have specific uses.

Lucy tool

Technique: Hand building and cleaning molds.

Uses: This double-ended, spear-shaped plastic tool is designed for cleaning clay from plaster molds to avoid scraping and damaging the surface, but it is also useful for hand building—to smooth surfaces and burnish—and as a modeling tool and scraper for internal and external greenware surfaces.

Range available: Generally blue plastic, with one large and one thin spear-shaped end. Available from most ceramic suppliers.

Skill level: Basic.

Bow harp

Technique: Slabbing.

Uses: The bow harp enables a stack of slabs to be cut from a single block of clay by repeatedly repositioning the wire up or down in the grooves on the frame before drawing through the clay.

Range available: In two sizes: medium (12 in/300 mm) and large (18 in/457 mm); replacement wires are also available.

Skill level: Basic.

Bow trimmer

Technique: Hand building, molding, and throwing.

Uses: This small, one-handed bow is generally used for trimming away excess clay, especially in press-molded or slab work, but it can also be used to level and trim the rims

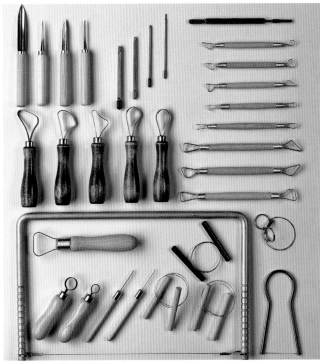

Assorted tools

of wheel-thrown work and other hand-built wares.

Range available: In different styles from different suppliers.

Skill level: Basic.

Sieves and lawns

Technique: Preparation of slips, glazes, and colors.

Uses: Essential items for the pottery studio, these tools are used for processing hand-dug clay to remove stones, and for mixing slip and glazes so that the constituents are blended together properly and colors are properly distributed through a mix. Small cup lawns are ideal for sieving colors that are usually used in small amounts, as are flat slip sieves, which sit over a container.

Range available: In mesh sizes 20, 30, 40, 60, 80, 100, 120, and 200 in beechwood frames 8 in (203 mm) or 10 in (245 mm) in diameter.

Skill level: Basic.

Sieves

Rotary glaze sieve

Technique: Rapid sieving of raw materials.

Uses: Designed for mixing slips and glazes, this device fits onto any round container and holds 2 gallons (9 liters) of material. It can be used to sieve dry materials and is operated by a turning handle that rotates brushes over a screen.

Range available: Supplied with 60, 80, and 100 size sieves. The bowl is 16 x 5½ in (405 x 140 mm); frame length 24½ in (620 mm); screen diameter ½ in (12 mm).

Skill level: Basic.

Digital scales

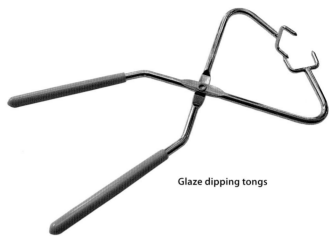

Glaze dipping tongs

Steel hacksaw

Technique: General cutting of materials and plaster work.
Uses: Cutting plaster blocks, cutting markers for cracked molds and general cutting requirements in the studio. Old and broken blades can be used for texturing and scoring.
Range available: From builders' suppliers with a metal, U-shaped frame and assorted fine-toothed blades.
Skill level: Basic to advanced.

Plastic measuring jugs

Technique: Measuring ingredients.
Uses: For measuring water content when mixing slips, glazes, plaster, and other liquid mixtures. It is useful to have several jugs in different sizes.
Range available: From pottery suppliers or general hardware stores.
Skill level: Basic.

Bowls, buckets, funnels, and scoops

Technique: All areas of studio practice.
Uses: Apart from the obvious uses, large bowls are good for dipping plates or flatware in slip or glaze. Buckets, especially with fitted lids, are used to contain dry materials and liquid mixtures like slip, glaze, and even plaster when mold making. Funnels are used to decant wet or dry materials into containers, and scoops are used for dry materials, usually when weighing.
Range available: Available in different sizes from pottery suppliers or general hardware stores.
Skill level: Basic.

Tile cutters

Technique: Slabbing and tile making.
Uses: Tile cutters are a quick and reliable tool for cutting multiple, uniformly sized tiles from clay slabs.
Range available: Square in several sizes 1, 4½, and 6 in (28, 108, and 152 mm); hexagonal—3¼ in (82 mm); rectangular—4 x 2 in (100 x 50 mm); round—4 in (100 mm). Mini cutters in various shapes are available from some suppliers for application as surface decoration.
Skill level: Basic.

Glaze dipping tongs

Technique: Glazing.
Uses: Dipping tongs are used to dip ceramic pieces directly into glaze. Generally made from heavy steel, they usually have sharp gripping points for minimal contact with

the pieces being dipped for even coverage of glaze. They can be used to dip objects in other liquids where minimal contact is required.
Range available: Pottery suppliers all have different versions of the same thing.
Skill level: Basic.

Pestle and mortar

Technique: Preparing raw materials.
Uses: A pestle and mortar is useful for hand grinding raw materials that may be lumpy by nature or have solidified in storage, and colors such as stains and oxides before mixing into clay, slips, or glazes.
Range available: In several sizes from small to very large, from pottery suppliers and kitchenware stores.
Skill level: Basic.

Glaze hydrometer

Technique: Mixing glaze.
Uses: Floats like a fishing float in

glaze. Invaluable to enable easy repetition of optimum glaze consistency from one batch to another; important in repeat and mass-production wares.
Range available: From pottery suppliers.
Skill level: Basic.

Beam and gram scales

Technique: Weighing raw materials.
Uses: No studio can work without scales to weigh raw materials, because most recipes for glaze and slip preparation, plaster work and addition of colors and oxides to clay bodies require very precise measurement to be successful.
Range available: Triple beam balance scales accurate to 0.1 g are supplied with a weight set of 2 x 1,000 g and 1 x 500 g to increase the weighing capacity. Gram scales are useful for weighing minute quantities of stains and oxides, weighing up to 50 g in 1-g divisions.
Skill level: Basic.

Flexible rubber buckets

Technique: Mold and model making.
Uses: For mixing plaster. Flexible rubber buckets are easier to handle when pouring plaster; they allow for larger mounts to be mixed and are easier to clean out than buckets with rigid walls.
Range available: Available from most hardware stores.
Skill level: Basic.

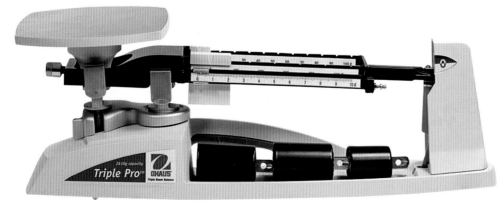

Beam scales

 Beginner's Kit
When this symbol appears next to a tool it indicates that it is an essential tool for a beginner.

HEALTH AND SAFETY EQUIPMENT

Health and safety in the ceramic workplace is of paramount importance because of all the potentially hazardous materials that are being used. Every studio requires the following basic equipment.

Dust mask

For mixing dry materials as in glaze making, plaster work, and cleaning.

Respirator

For handling and preparing more dangerous materials and some forms of firing such as raku.

Heat-resistant gloves

For handling hot wares from the kiln and kiln furniture or raku firing.

Safety goggles

For grinding, mixing certain materials, raku, and smoke firing.

Apron

To protect clothes from dust and other dangerous materials; for this reason, aprons should be nylon and easily wipeable.

Dust mask

Respirator

WHEELS

Wheels are available in many shapes and sizes, but the main consideration for purchasing one should first and foremost be comfort, because they can be a strain on the back. The electric wheel is the most versatile where great production is required, but many potters still choose a momentum wheel for aesthetic reasons.

Electric wheel

Technique: Throwing.
Uses: For production throwing and turning of tableware, kitchenware, and decorative items, and for turning clay models for plaster mold making. Set at very slow, the wheel can be used for banding slip or glaze onto greenware or bisque-fired forms.
Range available: Many electric wheels are available, from tabletop types to large wooden-framed versions with seats or for standing. See pottery equipment suppliers for advice for specific needs.
Skill level: Intermediate to advanced.

Momentum/kick wheel

Technique: Traditional form of throwing.
Uses: The same uses as for electric wheels, but driven by kicking a treadle that operates a heavy fly wheel to build up momentum and torque to center and throw the clay.
Range available: Modern momentum wheels are constructed on a fabricated steel frame in either sitting or standing

versions. Available from pottery equipment suppliers.
Skill level: Intermediate to advanced.

Lining/banding wheel

Technique: Decorating or hand building.
Uses: Lining wheels are floor standing and adjustable to enable work to be set at exactly the right position. Use in the same way as a bench whirler for hand building, modeling, sculpting, and surface decorating.
Range available: Generally made from steel and aluminum, and available from most pottery equipment suppliers.
Skill level: Basic.

Banding wheel

Electric wheel

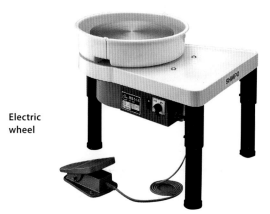

Momentum wheel

GENERAL STUDIO EQUIPMENT

The items listed in this section would generally be required to establish a ceramic studio for good and efficient working practice. Not all the items need to be purchased from dedicated suppliers because they are readily available from craft stores or can be adapted from other equipment.

Wedging bench

Technique: The preparation of clay.
Uses: Every studio needs a sturdy bench with a semiabsorbent surface, for wedging and kneading clay in preparation for hand building and throwing.
Range available: Different-sized benches are available from most pottery equipment suppliers, but they can be homemade by securing a paving slab to the top of a sturdy wooden table.
🧰 **Skill level:** Basic.

Hair dryer

Technique: Hand building.
Uses: Handy for the hand builder, especially when coiling, because it allows the maker to dry the clay to a firmer state before adding subsequent coils. Also useful for firming up pinched sections before joining and any other processes where the clay needs to be firmer before it can be worked on further.
Range available: Use an old one preferably—but readily available from electrical suppliers in all shapes and sizes.
🧰 **Skill level:** Basic.

Large plastic bins

Technique: Clay recycling and storage.
Uses: Apart from the obvious use of storage, plastic bins are used for clay recycling. Use one to collect dry clay and another to slake clay down for pugging later. Keep different clays in individual bins and mark each appropriately.
Range available: Widely available from hardware stores; choose heavy-duty plastic for better durability, with well-fitting lids.
🧰 **Skill level:** Basic.

Gallon mixer

Technique: Preparation of glaze and slip.
Uses: An invaluable aid for the rapid mixing of glazes and slips. Best results are achieved by adding the required amount of water to the bucket before adding the dry ingredients progressively as the machine is operating. The machine is designed to prevent a vortex or splashing.
Range available: Pottery suppliers have their own design of machine but all perform the same task.
Skill level: Basic.

Sedimentation tank

Technique: Safe water drainage.
Uses: Helps protect the environment from the potentially dangerous materials used in the pottery studio and prevents the blocking of drains with clay, plaster, or other residues. The tank fits under the studio sink and collects sediment but allows water to flow to drains.
Range available: Several types are available, but a portable system on wheels is best for emptying collected sediment.
Skill level: Basic.

SEMI-INDUSTRIAL EQUIPMENT

The items of equipment listed in this section have specific uses and can be quite large. Therefore, they are generally used in mass-production studios, but some can be useful in the smaller studio as well.

Slab roller

Technique: Slab building.
Uses: Efficient and reliable method of rolling large sheets of clay into slabs for hand building and tile making. The design of the machine allows for infinitely variable thicknesses of clay to be rolled by adjusting the height of the roller.
Range available: Widely available from pottery equipment suppliers in large and small versions.
Skill level: Basic.

Clay blunger

Technique: Making slip.
Uses: Blunging is the process by which raw lump, powdered, or plastic clay is mixed with water and reduced to slip for casting or decoration. This machine produces large quantities of slip suitable for production making.
Range available: Available in several sizes from pottery equipment suppliers.
Skill level: Basic to advanced.

Whirler

Technique: Model and mold making.
Uses: For turning plaster models and the manufacture of professional-quality working molds. Due to rotational motion the whirler produces primarily symmetrical objects.
Range available: The whirler is a specialist piece of equipment, it will usually have a plaster head (wheel) and can be either a manual whirler, with no power source, used for mold making only, or a motorized whirler used for making models and molds. Some models have a reverse setting, which means the whirler can spin both ways.
Skill level: Intermediate to advanced.

Ball mill

Technique: Grinding raw materials.
Uses: A ball mill is a specific type of grinder—a cylindrical device used to grind raw ceramic materials to a finer particle size. It is especially useful for grinding oxides and colored stains to a finer state before adding to slips, glazes, and clay bodies.
Range available: Available in several sizes from pottery equipment suppliers.
Skill level: Advanced.

Pug mill

Technique: Processing clay.
Uses: Pug mills are used to process reconstituted clay, mix different clays together to form another clay body, de-air, and extrude clay ready for use.
Range available: Available in several sizes and in flat/bench-mounted and upright forms from pottery equipment suppliers.
Skill level: Basic to intermediate.

Extruder

Technique: Extruding for hand building.
Uses: For the production of coils and shaped strips of clay for making items such as handles. Many potters now construct forms entirely from larger extruded shapes. Most extruders are available with a selection of dies for different purposes.
Range available: Generally wall mounted, but some suppliers now sell extruders fitted to a stand for maneuverability and for use where a solid wall is not available for fixture.
Skill level: Basic to intermediate.

🧰 **Beginner's Kit**
When this symbol appears next to a tool it indicates that it is an essential tool for a beginner.

Jigger and jolley machine

Technique: Mechanical system for forming wares over and inside plaster molds.

Uses: The jigger refers to the metal part that forms the back of an item where the face is formed by a plaster mold—usually plates, saucers, and shallow bowls. The jolley works in the opposite way so that the outside is formed by the mold and the metal tool forms the inside to make hollowware such as cups and deep bowls. A useful machine for repeat production.

Range available: From some pottery equipment suppliers.

Skill level: Intermediate to advanced.

Vibratory sifter

Technique: Making slip and glaze.

Uses: This electronically operated vibrator is ideal for rapidly sieving slip and glaze in both small and large quantities.

Range available: Most pottery suppliers have their own version of this machine, but some machines sieve larger amounts than others, so check that the machine meets your requirements.

Skill level: Basic.

Slip pump and casting table unit

Technique: Slip casting.

Uses: Allows for multiple casting of molds from a tank that holds large quantities of casting slip, through a hose and hand-controlled nozzle. A casting table has a dowelling top, which allows molds to drain excess slip into a holding tank beneath; the tank, in turn, has a drainage pipe for emptying and cleaning—useful for production work.

Range available: Most suppliers have their own version of pump and table/unit.

Skill level: Basic to intermediate.

Drying cabinet

Technique: Hand building, throwing, and mold making.

Uses: These cupboards are designed to aid the even drying of clayware and plaster molds by a thermostatically controlled heating element. Open mesh shelves allow for the free movement of air around the items drying within.

Range available: From some pottery equipment suppliers in narrow and wide sizes.

Skill level: Basic.

Lathe

Technique: Model and mold making.

Uses: For turning plaster models, primarily for the manufacture of symmetrical pieces from which molds are made.

Range available: Dedicated plaster lathes are difficult to come by, but wood-turning lathes can sometimes be converted for use with plaster. Look for secondhand lathes on shopping and ceramic websites.

Skill level: Intermediate to advanced.

Band saw

Technique: Tool making.

Uses: Band saws are used to cut templates and profile shapes for model- and mold-making techniques, hand building, and wheel-thrown wares. They can also be used to cut materials into tools for specific use or a specific shape.

Range available: Small to very large industrial sizes; available from builders' suppliers.

Skill level: Intermediate to advanced.

Circular sander

Technique: Surface preparation or finish.

Uses: Circular sanders are very useful to refine any bisque- or low-fired surfaces where the clay is either left unglazed or evident through a transparent glaze.

Range available: Many—from building, wood working, and electrical suppliers.

Skill level: Intermediate

SPRAYING EQUIPMENT

There are a number of techniques that require a surface covering to be sprayed on for best effect, but spraying equipment is also helpful in the production studio where items may need to be processed quickly and uniformly.

Spray booth, fixed

Technique: Surface decoration.

Uses: This piece of equipment is designed to contain and extract dust and particles created in the process of spraying liquids such as glaze when decorating, which may be harmful if inhaled.

Range available: Varying according to manufacturer, but fixed spray booths are generally sited against a wall to allow ducting to the atmosphere; must conform to local government requirements.

Skill level: Basic to intermediate.

Spray booth, wet back

Technique: Surface decoration.

Uses: As for the fixed spray booth, working on the principle of a curtain of recycling water running down the rear face of the booth along with an extractor system to catch excess particles of glaze as it is sprayed.

Range available: In smaller sizes suitable for studio potters, schools, and colleges, and large sizes for production/industrial output.

Skill level: Basic to intermediate.

Compressor

Technique: Glazing and decorating.

Uses: Required to power a spray gun for application of decorative colors, slips, and glazes to the surface of green or bisque ware.

Range available: Several types are available from pottery equipment suppliers.

Skill level: Basic to intermediate.

Spray gun, cup, and hose

Technique: Glazing and surface decoration.

Uses: To glaze and surface decorate where an even application is important. Spraying gives the advantage of total control over the thickness of the covering for different and varied effects.

Range available: Most pottery equipment suppliers have a range of spray guns suitable for use with a compressor and spray booth.

Skill level: Basic to intermediate.

Compressor

When you first start out, you don't need to have every single machine, a kiln, or lots of space; machines and kilns can be hired, while professional networks grow and thrive on sharing and hiring of space and facilities. If you set up your workspace thoughtfully, it will grow in line with your career.

SETTING UP A WORKSHOP

This section helps you consider how your workspace might develop over time from a basic space through to fully functioning workshop.

Workshop requirements

The basic requirements are space to work and access to water. This may mean working at the kitchen table, although dust will become an important health and safety issue very quickly. It is more likely that a basement or shed will provide a convenient and free space to work. If the room has a sink then you should consider installing a sump trap below the sink to prevent clay, plaster, and glaze materials blocking the pipes. This allows these materials to settle in a tank that is easier to remove and clean. If you do not have access to running water then you can have a good strong bucket that you can bring to the space, or alternatively if your workshop is a shed at the end of the garden a waterbutt to collect rainwater is a good option (except during the frozen winter months).

Space If space is big enough, benches, shelving, and small kilns can be installed as necessary without too much trouble. This is a great opportunity for maximizing your potential without incurring large costs. If you do not have space at home, then a good start-up option is a shared studio. The benefits of such an arrangement are evident: if the shared studio is already established, you will be effectively renting a whole selection of machinery; if it is a new arrangement then, at least you will be entering into a community with shared responsibility for rent and other expenses.

Planning your workspace regardless of whether it is shared or not, it makes good sense to plan the path of a piece of work through the space. Understanding your practice

OVERVIEW OF THE STAGES IN THE CERAMIC PROCESS

PROCESS	DETAILS
GREENWARE	All work before bisque firing.
PREPARE CLAY Wedge/knead/mix.	New bags of clay will not require any preparation.
MAKE WORK. Store unfinished work wrapped in plastic. Can be kept indefinitely if sprayed with water and kept airtight and wrapped in plastic.	Add clay of the same consistency together, by blend or score and slurry method.
DRYING STAGES	
Leather hard	As soon as the clay starts to dry it is deemed leather hard until dry. Join clay using score and slurry method.
Dry. Standard drying time for work up to ¾ in (2 cm) thick can range from two days to two weeks.	Up to indefinite period depending on clay thickness, complexity of the form, room atmosphere and wrapping, don't try and join work.
Bone dry	If cold to the touch at room temperature the work is still damp, leave to dry further.
PACK KILN	Be careful not to touch the thermocouple sticking into the kiln which reads the temperature. Greenware work can touch.
BISQUE (FIRST FIRING) Standard firing for work to ¾ in (2 cm) thick 8–10 hours including up to 1 hour soak.	This may be higher than 1830° F (1000° C) depending on the clay and for vitrification purposes. Close bungs between 1110–1290° F (600–700 °C).
UNPACK KILN Firing and cooling depend on retention of the kiln: 1½–2½ days.	Bisque work can be glazed immediately and fired again or stored indefinitely. Don't open kiln door until heat temperature is below 390–300° F (200–150° C).
SELECT TEMPERATURE	Earthenware (E/W): 1650–2190° F (900–1200° C). Stoneware (S/W): 2190–2460° F (1200–1350° C).
GLAZE WORK	Make sure bisque is dust-free before applying glaze. Always check temperature range of materials.
PACK KILN	Glaze work should not touch in kiln.
GLAZE FIRING Depending on type of firing and fuel. Standard electric kiln neutral (oxidation)—earthenware 7–8 hours, stoneware 8–9 hours.	Select temperature.
UNPACK KILN Firing and cooling depending on heat retention of kiln: 1½–2½ days.	Don't open kiln door until temperature is below 300° F/150° C. Only partially open to cool down further. The kiln and the work is still very hot.
POST-GLAZE DECORATING TECHNIQUES	Enamels, transfers (decals), lusters. 1360–1830° F (740–1000° C)
PACK KILN/FIRE/UNPACK	Admire results.

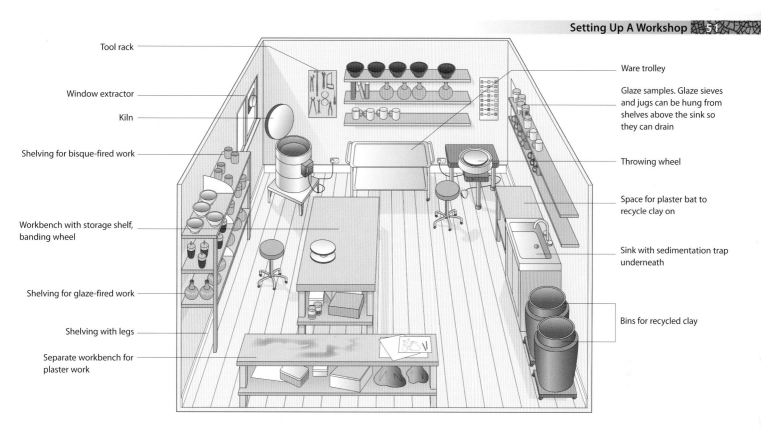

Tool rack

Window extractor

Kiln

Shelving for bisque-fired work

Workbench with storage shelf, banding wheel

Shelving for glaze-fired work

Shelving with legs

Separate workbench for plaster work

Ware trolley

Glaze samples. Glaze sieves and jugs can be hung from shelves above the sink so they can drain

Throwing wheel

Space for plaster bat to recycle clay on

Sink with sedimentation trap underneath

Bins for recycled clay

and the flow of your work will really help you utilize your space to its fullest potential.

If your space is limited, then the ability to store work, clean up, and switch from one activity to another is essential. This is not as difficult as it sounds: it simply requires planning and preparation.

If your workshop is spacious, then you might like to create zones for the different stages of your process—a damp area to allow you to work on a number of pieces, a space for drying, and a space for fired work to be decorated or glazed. Even so, it is a good idea to consider how one activity impacts on another. For example, as a general rule, glazing or on-glaze decoration should be separate from a plaster or clay workshop to minimize the contamination of the process by dust.

Lighting A well-lit space is ideal, but in some instances, especially when starting out, you might make the decision to choose a big space instead. If this is the case then you can get a good anglepoise lamp for your desk. Daylight bulbs are helpful and they are easy to obtain from electrical suppliers.

Equipment and storage The next step is to build the basic environment. Aside from kilns and other machinery, the most immediate requirements for a new studio are a good workbench and storage space. The workbench can either be bought or made; whichever solution you choose, the most important thing is that it should be large and stable and does not move while you try to work. To make a strong workbench with a large surface area, you can buy a standard fire door, which are usually quite strong, and add legs made out of strong wood. It is important to support the legs with cross braces. It is also a good idea to fix the workbench to the floor if you are able to.

An important consideration is the height of your workbench. If you move around quite a lot or change position and find that most of the time you are standing, then a tall bench (maybe 1 yd/1 m) with a stool to sit on is a good option. If, on the other hand, your activity is fairly fixed, and you spend long periods sitting down at normal desk height (27½ in/70 cm), then a standard desk with a good chair and a movable spotlight is a good

idea. A sheet of toughened glass or Plexiglass provides a perfectly flat surface for fine modeling jobs. Good shelving is essential. Racked, open shelving helps air circulate to aid drying, while horizontal shelving that starts at the same height as your workbench allows you to access things easily, and you can store raw materials in airtight plastic boxes directly below. If you are trying to keep work damp and workable, you can create a simple damp cupboard by stapling heavy plastic sheets to the front and sides of the shelves.

Your collection of tools will grow over time so, as you build your workshop, you should consider what you actually need. Some tools are essential and others a luxury.

A tool rack on the wall is a good space-saving device that also keeps tools visible and ready to hand. It's a good idea to relate your ideal "shopping list" of tools to sales or commissions: if you receive a commission, then buy the tool you need to complete the work, knowing that the job will pay for that particular piece of equipment. Keeping the tools clean is essential to ensure a long working lifetime, a whet stone, wet and dry paper,

and WD40 (spray oil) are important materials to keep tools in peak working condition.

There are five or six big machines used in ceramic studios. Kilns are the most obvious, followed by wheels, lathes, whirlers, extruders, pug mills, and slab rollers. In each case it is important to consider their output in relation to your activity. For example, a slab roller is desirable, but it takes up a lot of floor space, so unless you make a lot of slab-built work, it is less important than a kiln or wheel.

The storage of clay, plaster, glaze, and other raw materials is an essential piece of the studio puzzle. Ideally, these materials should be kept in a separate area in airtight containers. If this is impossible, then systematic storage in an otherwise unused space such as under a workbench is a clever solution, provided you leave ample leg room.

As your practice evolves a well-planned and fully-functioning appropriate workshop will help you to flourish.

PART TWO

FORMING TECHNIQUES

MIXED CLAY FORM
BY RAFAEL PEREZ
This powerful piece is a mixture
of clays and includes porcelain
fired to a high earthenware
temperature. The layering
echoes how the clay material
is naturally found.
Makers from left to right:
Natasha Daintry, Rebecca
Catterall, and Nicole Mueller.

Pinching is often the first technique encountered in ceramics. It's a simple way to start handling clay and understanding ceramic form; you are in constant contact with the clay, controlling it only by hand and getting used to working with a hollow form. It can seem like a very simple skill, but it still requires practice to perfect and has the potential to create a wide range of forms of varying scales.

HAND BUILDING: PINCHING

Starting with the pinching technique affords an ideal opportunity to try a variety of different clay bodies. It's beneficial to begin understanding how different clays behave and feel as early as possible. This will be the start of your journey with clay, enabling you to have personal preferences for future choices and uses. Once you have had the chance to appreciate different clays and their characteristics you could try selecting samples of different colors and textures and blending them together. This will create marbled effects, if not overdone, and also shows the compatibility of different clays. You will also start to see how manufacturers can blend their clay bodies for specific textures, colors, and uses.

Working properties
You will gain an understanding of clay's working properties—how different applications of pressure directly affect the clay and how quickly forms can grow, for example. If a form has not been considered you will see how quickly it goes out of shape. Consider this a design lesson or a type of play, with no intended outcome other than allowing the activity to direct the final result—let your hands do the talking.

As you handle the clay you will start to realize how quickly your hands absorb water from the material. The longer you handle clay, the more it will dry out. Adding a small amount of water with a damp sponge will quickly rehydrate the clay back to its original state. Introduce a lot of water, though, and you will see how quickly it turns into an uncontrollable mess.

Preparing clay for pinching can be done very simply by ripping the clay in half and pushing it back together again; this will expel many air pockets and the action of pinching while making will burst any that are left as you progress with your form.

Appreciating the technique
There are examples of pinched forms from many cultures in museum collections around the world. When given the opportunity, there is

PINCHED FORM

BY GABRIELE KOCH

Once you have control of any technique you can then fully explore its creative potential. This pinched and coiled form demonstrates a clear vision of simplicity, which allows the eye to settle on the subtle burnished and smoked surface qualities.

FORMING BY PINCHING

You will soon want to develop your forms further and realize their potential for use with other core ceramic techniques. Like the majority of making techniques, the gradual movement of clay in stages toward the final thickness will give you the greatest control over form.

1 Select a small amount of clay that just pushes your hands apart. To condition and prepare the clay you will need to use a simple form of wedging. This is achieved by tearing the lump in half and using some force to push the two pieces back together. Repeat this action several times.

2 Make the clay into a ball by cupping your hands around it. Slap and pat it, using some force, while turning the clay with both hands as they move around the form to create a sphere.

3 Cup the ball of clay in one hand and, with the other push your thumb down into the middle of the ball to a depth that leaves approximately ⅝ in (1.5 cm) at the base.

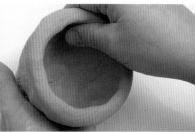

4 Starting at the base, press and pinch your thumb and fingers together. Use small, close-together movements on the clay surface. Don't apply too much pressure as you rotate the ball around in the palm of your hand. Try to make the wall of the form as even as possible by pinching where it feels uneven.

5 Gradually work your way around the form toward the top. The aim is to thin out the clay wall in stages from the base as your fingers travel upward. Avoid pinching the rim too hard—keep it thicker, otherwise it will start to flare out and you will lose control of the form.

6 Once you have achieved an even wall, start working with the rim of the form to decide on the final shape. To practice your control, the form described is a simple bowl. Obviously you can achieve a wide variety of more organic shapes by freely pinching in any direction.

7 You can develop the form further by turning it upside down and working on the sides and base with wooden paddles and plastic or metal ribs. You can either refine and define at this stage or wait until the form has dried out a little.

8 The rim will need further attention to complete the form and deciding on its appearance will help to convey the form's intention: the rim is the frame to any open form.

ADDING SLABS AND COILS

To increase the size of any pinched form you can extend the walls by adding slabs or using coils.

something very pleasing about handling pinched forms from the past (or even the present) where you can feel the maker's pressed finger marks on the interior and exterior surfaces.

Development of form

The size of a pinched form is generated by the initial size of the ball you have in your hand. When adding any clay make sure it's of a similar consistency to what you are working with to enable joining by pinching and blending. If either piece is harder then you will need to score and slurry the surface edges to enable joining. You would also do this if you were adding textured sections where you did not want to disturb the surface quality.

Distorting the form

Once a form is enclosed, the air trapped inside will form a useful support structure, enabling you to distort the shape in different ways:

Once you have completed your form it must have a small pierced hole somewhere, preferably discreetly hidden. This is to allow the air (which expands due to heat during the firing process) to escape. If there is no way out for air, the form will explode.

As you explore this technique you will realize how direct the contact with the clay is and why it's a useful starting point in handling the material. Once you have covered the principles of making pinched forms you will see how many different ways this basic technique can be applied to develop interesting forms, and its potential for use along with other core-forming techniques.

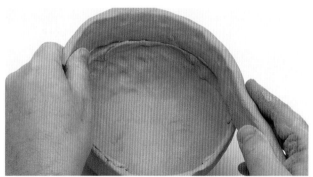

Flatten small amounts of clay onto canvas or into the palm of your hand. Apply these new sections onto the existing form by overlapping them. Press to blend and then carry on pinching to extend the form. You could develop the surface interest of forms by pressing these extra sections onto different textures and then applying them in the same way.

Roll out the coil of clay and apply it by blending to the interior and exterior (see page 61). Pinch the clay as before to achieve the desired thickness and form. You can apply as many coils as you wish in this way to increase the height and development of the form.

FAULTS & REMEDIES

A problem you may face when pinching is that the top or rim flares out too quickly.
Cut two or four "V" shapes into the walls opposite each other. Draw these together and overlap the sides, press, and remodel.

The rim or walls start cracking.
Add a very small amount of water using a damp sponge, then smooth over by blending and compressing. Don't overwet.

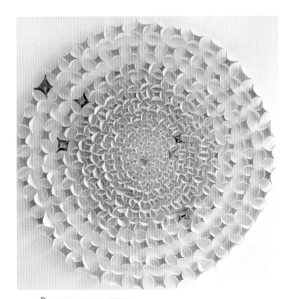

PINCHED INSTALLATION

BY VALÉRIA NASCIMENTO

This artwork consists of small slabs of clay that are pinched into shape. By producing multiples it extends the possibilities of scale.

ALTERING FORM AND SURFACE TEXTURE TECHNIQUES

Try some of the following ideas to provide quickly constructed maquettes (see page 292) for further development. Pinching is a simple technique but can offer a great insight into both the development of form and surface.

- Make and join other pinched forms to create complex multiple shapes.
- Use tools to cut away sections or pins to pierce intricate designs.
- Make pinched lids by cutting into the form and reshaping and defining the new edges.
- Make individual pinched/modeled feet to add to bases.
- Make individual pinched/modeled sculptural details.
- If a base is required, gently tap the proposed area on a flat surface to create a flat side to sit on.

- Roll around on a wooden surface to soften the surface and form.
- Roll on texture to create surface interest.
- Push with your fingers to manipulate soft organic forms.
- Use a variety of modeling tools to create surface designs and textures.
- Use strip tools to subtract negative surface designs.
- Use a variety of hard edges to create lines and indentations in the surface.
- Use small coils of clay to create areas to build on and from the form.

Faceted, pinched forms

ADDITIONS AND REFINEMENT TO SIMPLE PINCHED FORMS

Once the clay has stiffened after the initial pinching, you can alter forms using simple manipulation and modeled additions.

Small modeled additions can be either fully modeled then added or developed further once attached. If the clay is leather-hard these additions must be joined with the score and slurry technique (see page 72).

Marking areas to join more clay (in this case feet) will help aid decision making. Sketching on the surface can inspire potential ideas. All additions can be well attached by blending with an appropriate modeling tool.

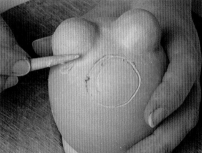

The base of any form is as important as anywhere else. It provides stability and should never be neglected. This base is being paddled to soften its appearance so that it stays in keeping with the form.

Use a flexible metal kidney at a steep angle to subtract clay. This will help to achieve a flowing even profile to the form.

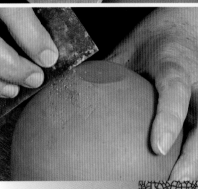

PINCHED SECTIONS

By joining two pinched sections together you can explore a range of basic hollow enclosed forms for either function or sculpture. These simple shapes can then be developed through surface texturing and clay additions.

1 Pinch two bowl forms as described, making sure the rims are going to meet. Score and slurry both rim edges to ensure good adhesion.

2 Gently push both forms together, twisting the rim backward and forward to ensure a good keyed fit and join.

3 Wipe away excess slurry, and smooth and blend the join.

4 To manipulate the form into different shapes you can reinforce this join with a small coil of clay placed onto the surface seam. Push and blend the added coil of clay to finish (see detail).

ALTERING FORM AND SURFACE TEXTURE

There are many ways you can explore altering the form and surface texture. Combining pinched forms together can create complex shapes and increase the surface area on which you can experiment with a variety of tools.

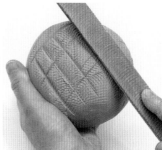

Metal kidneys are useful for flexing around forms to push and scrape the surface into shape.

Using a wooden spatula as a paddle, you can gently tap the sections into defined shapes.

Using a metal file can create a geometric pattern on the previously smooth surface.

By manipulating the clay with your hands you can transform the form into a more organic shape.

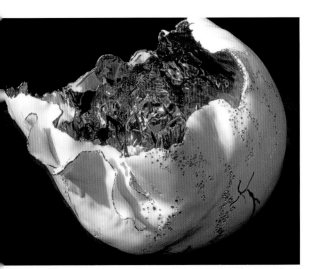

PINCHED PORCELAIN FORM
BY JASMIN ROWLANDSON
Clay can be pinched to a paper-thin thickness. It can be a simple vehicle to experiment with an extensive range of surface techniques.

OPEN FLOW WALL PIECE
BY FENELLA ELMS
Each component is individually made and placed together to create a flickering, swarming feeling of movement.

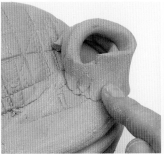

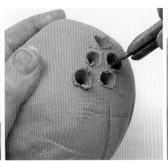

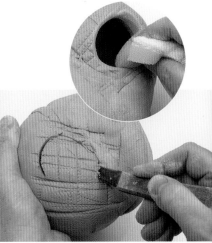

Loop or strip tools can be used to carve into the clay surface and make negative patterns.

Additions can be made to the form by using small coils, which can then be blended in.

A potter's knife is a useful tool for piercing through the form wall.

Cut out shapes to form lids and then smooth down the cut rim and lid to achieve a perfect fit (see detail).

Coiling can be an exciting and intuitive way to make ceramic forms. Once you understand a few basic principles of clay joining, drying, and shrinkage, the form can flow from your imagination with great immediacy, or follow a very specific design challenge. Choosing the appropriate clay will enable you to achieve the scale and design you envisage.

HAND BUILDING: COILING

For functional pieces you are limited only by the size of your kiln. There is no limit for decorative work or sculpture if you make composites and assemble them once fired, using balance, armatures, or adhesives. Think of buildings and bricks!

Coiled clay is seen clearly in Japanese ceramic forms that date approximately from 14,000 BCE. Functional ware has been extensively coil-built for storage and cooking since 12,000 BCE.

Jomon, meaning "twisted cord," was made by coiling forms that were beaten with sticks wrapped in cord to create some extraordinary objects. In early examples you can see how the coils have been used to create "wandering" woven patterns. Coil building has been used in many cultures, and you will find a wide range of examples in museums worldwide.

The method
The coiling technique involves using hand-rolled or machine-made coils or "ropes" of clay to build form. By placing one piece on top of another and joining them by blending and pinching together, forms can grow quite quickly. It will be useful for all future making to learn how to make a coil by hand, since you can use them with every other core technique, enabling you to "add on," fix, or strengthen certain areas. If you have an extruder or pug mill, then you can make a

COILED SCULPTURE
BY TINA VLASSOPULOS
This coil-built form demonstrates the skill and control that can be achieved with this technique. The beautiful, flowing line is finely balanced as though caught in between its decision to roll forward or backward.

die plate with several same-sized holes fixed to the end. This will produce whatever diameter coils you prefer working with and will save you time. The coils should always be thicker than the clay wall that you intend on making, since you will be thinning it as you pinch and blend the coils into place.

Whichever method you use, the coils are best kept wrapped in plastic while you are working, otherwise their small surface area will quickly start to dry out. For ease of making, always work on a turntable and a board. As the form grows, you will need to change position to remain above the top edge. Ceramic work is often governed by the height at which it is made. Sitting working at a table will produce tabletop ceramics!

The line between coils can be left unblended on the exterior for decorative effect, depending on the softness of the clay. If you are using stiffer clay, then running a small tool between this line on the outside will connect the clay and still leave the pattern visible. This prevents any horizontal splitting as it dries. Always make sure you have joined, blended, and sealed the inside very well. As clay dries, any gaps that are visible will shrink apart rather than merge together. Where you place each coil will depend on the direction you wish the form to take. If you want to push outward, you would place it on the outside edge. If you are tapering the form inward, then you would place it on the inside edge.

Stability

Always be aware of the stability of the form as it grows. By giving a gentle shake of the board you are working on you will see whether there is any movement of the wall. If so, then it's time to stop for a while and let it partially dry. When drying the wall to continue building, be careful not to dry your working edge. You could do as many coil builders do, and work on several forms at the same time. This means you will always have a form that's at the right stage to proceed with. The temperature of your working environment, the composition of the clay body, the different thicknesses in the wall, and the shape and changes in direction that you make will all affect

FORMING ROUND COILS BY HAND

Forming round coils by hand is a useful skill to acquire, which can be used in combination with other forming methods. The thickness of your coils will depend entirely on the scale of the form you are making. When you attach them together they will become slightly thinner as you blend and pinch.

1 Form the clay into an even roll by squashing it between the palms and fingers of both hands and working the coil around at the same time until it is about 1 in (2.5 cm) thick. The coil will start to drop and lengthen with gravity.

2 Working on a clean, flat surface, continue thinning and extending the length of the coil by rolling it. Use either the palms or fingers of both hands and apply gentle pressure from the middle as you roll backward and forward. The clay roll needs to revolve at least once each time, otherwise the coil will soon become flat and impossible to roll.

3 As you roll from the middle to the edges, fan out your fingers—this will help the clay to stretch and remain even and round. Any fluctuations in pressure will distort the coil; too much will result in the coil getting stuck to the table. As your fingers reach the ends of the coil, restart in the middle and repeat.

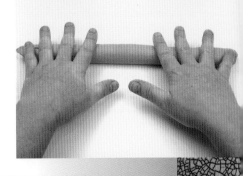

the stability of the clay wall. Remember, you cannot defy gravity in one making session!

Appropriate clays

You can use a wide variety of clays but they need to have a good degree of plasticity to enable you to bend them into place. If the clay is dry, or "short," in texture it will be problematic to join and will upset the rhythm of making. If you are a beginner, smooth, fine clay bodies will initially be more difficult to control and blend together. Medium-textured clay is ideal because it will allow for certain mistakes but will hold together well while making. Heavily grogged clay will be short and difficult to roll and extrude until you are more experienced. Try experimenting with blending your own clay bodies—you can add fire clay for greater plasticity, and for larger work

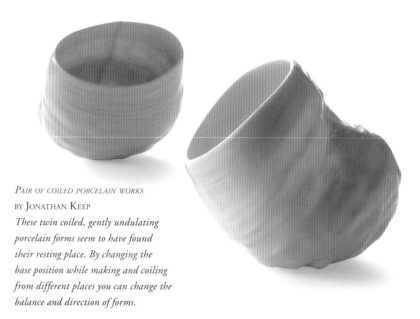

PAIR OF COILED PORCELAIN WORKS
BY JONATHAN KEEP
These twin coiled, gently undulating porcelain forms seem to have found their resting place. By changing the base position while making and coiling from different places you can change the balance and direction of forms.

BUILDING WITH ROUNDED COILS

This technique will respond very quickly to your hand movement and mood. Designs will help you visualize the three-dimensional form and will keep you from wandering into the organic, unless that's what you have planned.

1 If you have a clear idea of the form you wish to build, design a template and cut it out to start the process.

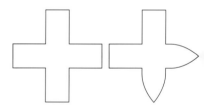

2 Use the template to cut out the shape of the base on a prepared slab (see page 70). You can also start a coil form from a pinched form, or coils placed in a plaster mold. If you form the base from coils and don't blend them very well, they may start to unwind and crack while they dry.

3 If the clay you are using to coil is the same as the base, you can put your first coil straight on. If you have chosen a different clay, score and slurry the joining edge only for the first coil (see page 72). There is no need after that as long as the clay is the same consistency.

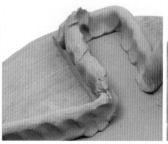

4 Apply one coil only and blend this thoroughly into the base so there are no gaps. Smooth all areas, since anything unblended and not smooth will be razor-sharp once fired.

5 Lay the next whole coil on, or blend as you go, holding the coil with the other hand. Usually the thumb is blending the inside down while your forefinger is on the outside coming up. But, as with other techniques, you will find your own preferred method.

you can add 20–30 percent grog, for example. For lighter final work try adding 30 percent sawdust. The grog and sawdust will also give the work greater mechanical (greenware) strength before firing. Clay manufacturers make a wide range of clay bodies developed specifically for different techniques.

Design control

Design and planning will become an important part of coil building as you develop the shape and scale of your forms. Creating certain forms will require very clear visualization—as you move the clay in different directions the supporting drying wall cannot then be altered. If you wish to make symmetrical forms, the easiest method is to make a template of your intended profile out of card, thin plywood, or MDF. You can

TECHNIQUE FILE 12

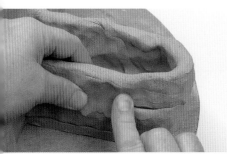

6 You may prefer to blend the inside first and then concentrate on the outside surface. You may also prefer to use a tool to do the blending, rather than your finger, depending on the type of clay you use.

CONSIDERING THE BASE

TECHNIQUE FILE 13

It is important to think about the base of any form before it either gets too dry or big to deal with. These steps highlight how they might be dealt with to finish them off before continuing to build the form.

1 Once the form has gained 5 in (12.5 cm), turn it over and check that the base is fully blended. You should now be thinking about how the form will sit on the surface, and how and where you will be glazing it.

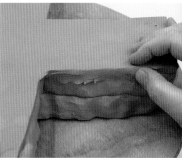

2 For example, will it have a defined glaze cut-off line, or an angle that creates a shadow underneath? Do you want to be able to see the bare clay?

3 Compress any raised grog and smooth any potential rough edges that could scratch the surface once fired. Any fired burrs will become razor-sharp, so it's vital they are removed before that stage.

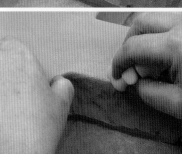

4 You could put a coil on the base to create a foot ring, but you would need to let this dry off a little before adding more weight, or leave it until the end of the day's work to add.

DEVELOPING THE FORM AS YOU BUILD

TECHNIQUE FILE **14**

Each coil can be joined and well blended with the previous one, or begun on the main body and developed independently.

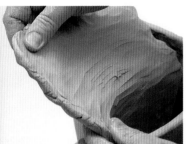

1 You can take the coil in any direction as long as the clay underneath will support the weight of clay being added. Once you have reached this point, dry off the clay below, either with heat or by leaving it to dry.

2 Add a wooden support with clay at both ends and paper between the clay wall and the clay support to prevent sticking. This can be left in place and will shrink away as the clay dries at both ends of the wooden support.

3 Once the clay is firm enough you can continue to add further coils to extend the form.

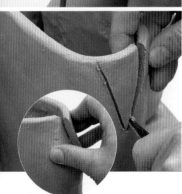

4 While building, if you find that the form is spreading out from your intended shape you can cut "V"s on opposite sides to pull the form in. Overlap the edges, blend them together, and continue adding coils (see detail). You can do this in as many places as you like, and right down to the base of the form if necessary. You can also cut out other shapes, depending on what's required.

COILED STRUCTURE
BY MERETE RASMUSSEN
The control of this coil-built form is finely balanced with a rhythmic movement. It shows the potential of this technique where the form does not always need to be built from the base up.

then place this repeatedly against the side of your work as you progress. Making templates of the whole profile means that you don't have to let the form wander into the unintentional organic. Because you will always be creating hollow forms, this means that, as they become larger, the supporting clay will need to be dry to support the clay on top. Once an area has dried you cannot go back and alter it. It's also not possible to add fresh wet clay to clay that has dried beyond leather-hard consistency, due to shrinkage. As you progress with this technique and your ideas develop, the form you are making does not have to be made from base to top. It can be made in any order your design requires, but you'll need to think about how to support it internally as it progresses.

Time frame and drying

Work can be made over as long a time frame as you require. The areas to be added to must be kept damp enough to take fresh clay, and the rest firm but not completely dry. Keep the working edge and at least the top 2 in (5 cm) wet by spraying with water and wrapping with fine polythene so that it clings to the surface. You can then wrap it in more polythene if you are continuing to build. If partial drying is required, leave some air in the bag to start the drying process. When a piece is completed, wrap it loosely to let air in slowly. If areas have become a little dry, soak several sheets of newspaper and place them on an area to rehydrate it. This method is also useful if you are leaving the piece for several days; you can use dishcloths in the same way. Keep checking to assess the wetness/dryness and remove the newspaper if the piece is adequately hydrated. When you are building with coils, there may be thicker and thinner areas. Due to these variations structural stresses can cause a piece to crack if it is dried too quickly. Large forms will generally require slow drying over several weeks to be on the safe side, until you start to know the clay you are using and the drying conditions of where you are working. You can help large, wide bases to dry by placing them on batons to let air circulate underneath.

Extruded coils

Extruded coils can be formed by making or purchasing a die plate, which is fixed to the end of a pug mill, hand-operated wall box, or smaller handheld extruder. If you are using different types of clays you'll need to clean the die plate and machine between each use. These machines can save you time if you are extruding a lot.

Support structures

When using soft clay coils there will be times when you will need temporary support or supporting sections all through the making and firing of work; this will depend on the clay and temperature you are firing the work to. Even with careful partial drying of the supporting clay you may build areas that are going to create an imbalance in the form, so need some temporary help for stability. Simple support from using clay and wood together may be all you need. The wood will form the main support, while clay

REFINING THE FORM

There are different ways to define and refine your coil building as you develop the form. Using a range of different tools will help you to achieve this.

Define the coil lines for decorative purposes by drawing a tool along them. This will also ensure they are well joined and will not part or crack during the drying.

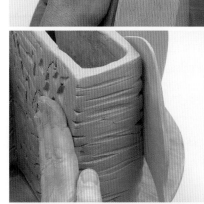

Define and refine the edges of a sharp-angled form by running a line down the center to which you can refer.

Use a paddle to beat and tap the form into shape. Support the clay wall while you do this.

Using the paddle to straighten the sides periodically will help to maintain control of a vertical form and sharpen the edge to enable further building.

To enhance the curve of any form, you can flex a metal kidney into shape and repeatedly draw it over the surface. This also has the benefit of compressing the joined coils.

USING COILS WITH SUPPORT FORMS

Using this forming method allows you to see the individual coil lines in the design. You can either blend the coils together on one side, or show them intact on both sides.

TECHNIQUE FILE 16

1 Place coils side by side on top of plaster molds ("hump molds"). The work made on any hump mold must be taken off before the day's end, otherwise the form will crack and split as the clay dries and shrinks.

2 When trimming the clay on plaster molds, be careful not to scratch the surface, since small amounts of plaster in the clay will cause damage during the firing process. Clay and plaster are not compatible, although they are used together.

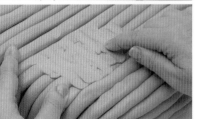

3 Blend the clay together on the outside surface. Depending on how firmly or lightly you press, you will leave lines visible on the inside.

4 Place coils inside the plaster mold to either create the shape of the mold or use part of the shape for a more sculptural form. These can then be blended together or left to display the method of making.

5 You can place coils into previously bisque-fired forms and, once again, either leave the coils visible or blend them together.

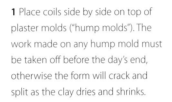

placed at both ends with paper in between to prevent both sticking will dry and shrink along with the form. Paper is useful inside forms to keep walls from caving inward. Try to remove the majority of this paper if possible before firing, since it can create a lot of fumes and this shortens the life span of your electric elements. Different thicknesses of foam sponge are good for temporary support of structures, particularly if you are laying things on their side or turning forms over. This material is good for most areas of support because it remains flexible while the clay shrinks.

Armatures

Clay can be built over and around metal or wooden armatures, but these must be withdrawn before firing because of clay shrinkage. Paper clay is the only clay that defies this rule for removing armatures (see page 38).

Coils laid into a mold
If the coil lines have been left, use a tool to draw along the lines to help join them together. Using a damp sponge will soften any burrs after blending the coils.

SHAPELY VESSELS

BY ASHRAF HANNA

Coil building allows you to gently move forms in and out while retaining very tight lines, compressed smooth surfaces, and control. These forms seem to respond and relate to each other's movement.

FAULTS & REMEDIES

Working edge has dried out too much to add more clay.
Soak newspaper or cloth in water and leave on the edge for 15 minutes to rehydrate. Always try to keep the working edge to the correct consistency to add further clay by wrapping it in plastic.

Work has horizontal hairline cracks.
The edge may have been too dry to accept the additional coil of clay, or not blended well enough. Score and slurry older coils to ensure a good join.

Additions have cracked around the join.
Work dried too quickly. Dry work slowly to let inconsistencies even out.

Areas have sagged and split underneath.
Support structures are needed to support clay while making and drying. Lots of different materials can be used and left in place until dry, providing they allow the clay to shrink.

Base not drying out or getting wetter when wrapped.
Condensation is forming on the surface of the plastic and dropping into the base. This will often happen if a piece has been in sunlight. You need holes in the top of the bag. The form can easily collapse if not partially dried. For large work you could try leaving a work lamp hanging in the middle to dry slowly overnight.

The form's wall is not retaining its shape.
Stop adding coils if there is any flexibility, because the clay is too soft to continue. Partially dry the piece to continue or pack with newspaper to support or plastic sheet to keep damp.

Supporting the form
If the form starts to distort, add temporary coils inside for support. These can be left in place if not visible when complete to aid the firing process.

ESSENTIALS FOR WORKING EDGES

TECHNIQUE FILE **17**

Coil building demands keeping the edge of forms soft and workable to enable further coils to be added during making sessions. They may also need to be hydrated if they have dried out too much.

Use water-soaked newspaper to keep the working edge damp before wrapping or to rehydrate the edge if it has dried out too much. This will soften the working edge, enabling you to add the next coil.

If you are leaving the form to dry out enough to support the next making session, always wrap the top 2 in (5 cm) well to prevent drying. If the clay has stiffened, always score and slurry the edge before adding the first coil.

If you don't want the clay to dry out at all before returning to making, make sure the surface is damp by spraying with water and press the plastic onto both the interior and exterior surfaces. Then cover this in several other plastic bags.

There are two main methods of slab building, which are dependent on the condition of the clay before forming. The sheets of clay may be either fresh and soft (soft slabs) or partially dry (leather-hard slabs). Soft slabs will allow you to manipulate and alter them by bending, folding, pressing, and stretching as you build. Hard slabs allow you to construct complex, angular, sharp-edged forms as though using sheets of wood.

HAND BUILDING: SLAB BUILDING

Slabs are used to create a variety of forms for both function and sculpture. You can make exquisite small boxes that are beautifully carved; simple cylindrical tubes; create monumental-scale forms that stand tall, or tiles that cover vast areas of walls and roofs. All of these are open to the possibility of varying textural surface qualities.

Leather-hard slabs
Slab building using leather-hard slabs is one of the few techniques that enables you to design and make your form completely in card before you touch the clay. You can then use these card templates in the same way a pattern cutter would, to cut out the individual elements before

assembly. This gives you the opportunity to see, assess, and make adjustments to the final form before spending any time making. It will also enable you to decide the type of clay best suited to the scale of work you wish to make.

Soft slabs
Soft slabs are used either to create undulating forms or in conjunction with a range of semihard or hard supporting objects and materials to create a wide variety of forms for both function and sculpture. Smooth, fine clay can be folded and pleated almost like cloth. If you do this, make sure you have not trapped air in sealed pockets. You can always push a pin into areas

SLAB-BUILT SCULPTURE
BY PETRA WOLF
When working with slabs you can explore balance and tension. This sculpture emphasizes the stress of where its weight has produced surface cracks during the making process.

RIBBED SCULPTURES
BY FENELLA ELMS
This pair of skeletal slab forms demonstrates the extraordinary flexibility of working with soft sheets of clay. The making and drying of forms can be assisted by resting on their sides on foam and insulating paper fibers.

you are not sure about to release air and keep the form from bursting during firing. Surface decoration and texture may be left until the form is completed or can be an integral part of the making of the slab.

Appropriate clays

The use of paper clay has changed some of the rules regarding slab working, because you can dry these slabs of clay and then assemble them with slurry. This has eliminated many of the drying, cracking, and wrapping problems inherent in the use of other clays.

Other additives to clay have been used for many years—think of building walls with wattle and daub. Makers have more recently used nylon fibers, fiberglass, cloth, and sawdust to build very large slabbed forms. This means the clay shrinks and warps less and helps with bonding the clay particles during the drying process.

Architectural clay bodies are available from clay

suppliers. These clays have been blended with very high contents of grog and have minimal shrinkage between making and finishing. Crank and raku clay bodies are similar in blend, feel, and texture, creating what's known as an "open body." Take care when using these clays; the more textured the clay body, the more the clay will start to open out and crack as you manipulate it. This characteristic is often used to highlight and create textured cracked surfaces. These bodies have very good mechanical greenware strength (bone-dry stage) and are ideal for medium- to large-scale working. Fine clays like porcelain offer the maker different challenges, but in time you'll be able to use them just as successfully, and they offer their own qualities, such as translucency. The more you use a type of clay, the more you will learn about its particular handling characteristics.

FOLDED SLABS
BY ANN VAN HOEY
These finely made slab forms have been cut and folded like paper while being supported during the making and drying period in plaster molds.

SLAB PREPARATION AND MAKING

This is the main method for forming different clays into slabs. If you intend to work with slabs frequently you may want to use a slab roller.

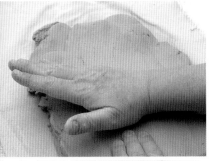

1 Place the clay on a porous surface or canvas and beat it with either the heel or the palm of your hand. Turn it through 90 degrees occasionally and continue.

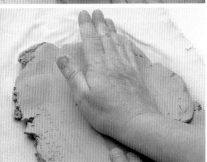

2 Push the clay out using the heel of your hand. Try to keep the clay as even as you can, turning it as necessary to help with this. This method is useful for large pieces of clay.

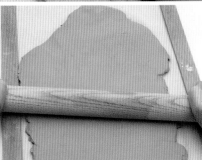

3 Place rolling guides on each side of the clay and roll with a rolling pin. When level, the rolling pin will rest on the guides, creating a perfectly flat slab. With a large slab it can be difficult to roll it all in one direction. Start by rolling from the middle and, once you've reached the end, turn the clay around and continue.

4 If you require a straight-sided slab, use the wooden guide to cut the clay. Before you do this though, always look at the quality of these edges to see if they could be used in some way. They often have an interesting, fresh, ragged softness.

Handling

Any slab should be handled with great care and as little as possible to prevent any stresses and strains being introduced into the clay that may develop later as cracks. These will often remain invisible until the final drying and may only show after the first firing. At both stages they can be difficult to remedy if you are firing to high temperatures. Support the clay whenever possible when lifting or turning until it has been allowed to stiffen to leather hard.

Once you have made the slab, leaving the clay on canvas will help with all the initial moving. Work on clean boards with canvas that will enable you to flip slabs over, lay them in molds, wrap them around forms, or stand upright if necessary. Ideally, move the completed form as little as possible, and if studio space allows, just once to the kiln. You can build complex, small- to medium-scale forms directly onto a kiln shelf. For large slab forms, if possible, build the form on a trolley-based kiln that, once completed, is then rolled into place inside the kiln. If you are making outdoors, bring the kiln to the work and build one around the other. The invention of ceramic fiber has made this a possibility.

The only restriction on the scale of the clay slab will be what you can physically handle without putting too much stress into the clay body. You may need to call upon heavy machinery, methods of transportation, and other equipment if you intend to build large slab walls without sections. Makers can often find ingenious solutions to the problems of construction.

Preparing to make slabs

Prepare your working area to enable you to lay fresh slabs of clay straight down without the need to move things around while you have the slab in your hands. This will prevent unnecessary straining of the slab. You can use new clay straight from the bag without any kneading and wedging if the clay is already at the correct consistency to work with. If not, then you will have to knead and wedge the clay. If you are using soft slabs, you will need the clay (see pages 30–31) to be stiff enough to stay together while you bend and manipulate it. For leather-hard slab work it is better to start with the clay slightly harder, since there is less water to evaporate and you will be able to control the cutting and handling.

Making slabs

While the clay is still in the bag with the top opened, you can throw the bag on the ground to flatten the clay to the desired width. Trim away the plastic bag and cut the clay slab straight from the block using a wire. Cutting from this block or one that has been prepared from reclaimed or blended clays can also be done using a wired harp. Each time you cut through the block by pulling toward you, progressively move the cutting wire down a notch, lifting the slab off as you go down the block. This will produce an even thickness of slab every time.

To make an individual slab you can use a variety of methods including beating, pushing, stretching, and rolling. You may use a combination of these for the same slab. If you are using slab-rolling equipment, don't cut to the exact thickness required, because the slab will benefit from being put under some pressure by the rolling action. It is still better to cut the slab a bit thicker and push or beat the clay to near the thickness of slab required. A medium to large clay slab will benefit from being stretched in different directions rather than just one single direction. For large slabs you will need to overlap them and blend together. Be careful not to trap air when you do this.

Always work on a porous surface such as unvarnished wood or canvas, since this will keep the clay from sticking to the surface. Some makers stretch and tack canvas onto boards to keep it from creasing. If creases are transferred from canvas to clay they will cause the clay to split apart when it is lifted.

For a rolled-even flat slab, use rolling guides placed on either side of the clay. These should be the same thickness as the required slab. As the rolling pin hits the guides, the result will be even. Even slabs are preferable, because any inconsistencies and variations in thickness will dry unevenly and may result in cracks and warping. A slab can be as thick as a brick or paper-thin, but ideally it should be even in thickness. Always check to see whether there are any surface air

CHECKING FOR AND DEALING WITH AIR POCKETS

Air pockets are common in slabs of clay and need to be identified and dealt with before using the slab. Once you start forming the slab they can be difficult to detect and are far easier to spot while the clay is smooth and flat.

1 You may see the air pockets when you are finishing the clay by rolling—they will appear as lumps or blisters on the surface. Smooth over the clay with a wet sponge; this will help when drawing over the surface with any straight edge. The air pocket will be clearly visible.

2 If the air pocket is small, you can prick it with a point and leave it or scrape over it; if it is larger, then "surgery" is needed. Lift the surface with a point and open it out (see detail). You need to reach the edge of the underlying pocket—you will clearly see the edge of the open hole. It will often be larger than it appeared.

3 Once you have reached the edge you can smooth down the area ready to fill with the clay you have picked out. Roll the clay into a smooth, round ball and place it in the middle of the hole (see detail).

4 Press into the middle of the ball and spread out to the edge of the hole. Be careful not to trap any air under the ball, otherwise you will create another air pocket and will have to start from the beginning again.

5 Smooth over with a damp sponge and use a straight edge to compress the surface until it is level with the slab.

Making slurry

Slurry needs to be made from the same clay that you are joining. A quick way to achieve this is to make a small pinch pot, fill it with water, and insert any tool. Twist the tool around until the water has broken down the clay.

TECHNIQUE FILE 20

JOINING SLABS

The method used for joining all edges and separate elements in clay is known as "score and slurry" or "score and slip." It provides the surface "key" or "glue" that holds pieces of clay together. This approach is used when you do not want to disturb the surface of clay as you would when joining coils or pinching.

1 Provide a key to hold the slurry on both surface areas to be joined. Use a fork, needle, knife, toothbrush, or specific scoring tools to rough up the clay surface. Be careful not to score the surface too deeply, since this can create small air pockets that may cause problems when firing.

2 Once you have scored the surfaces, apply liberal amounts of slurry to one or both surfaces with a brush.

pockets. These can be easily spotted by wiping over the surface with a wet sponge and a rubber or metal kidney. They will appear as blisters and must be dealt with (see page 71).

Storing leather-hard slabs

If you are making slabs to use at the leather-hard stage, these will need to be stored or partially dried. If you are storing them, how you do this will depend on your available storage space. Slabs are fine stacked on top of each other. The weight placed on each board will often determine how many you stack. This method requires a layer of paper or canvas in between each slab to keep them from sticking together. This will also absorb some of the water from the slab. First lay down a few sheets of newspaper on an appropriate plywood or laminated board. (Solid wood will warp if damp materials are placed on it for prolonged periods.) Place paper on the board, then the slab, then cover the surface of the slab with paper. Repeat this, sandwich-style,

finishing with a board on top. Wrap the whole thing in plastic sheet. How many slabs you stack together and how tightly you wrap will depend on how quickly you want them to dry—this is something that you can control. If the slabs are tightly wrapped in plastic and kept away from any heat they can remain in usable condition for months before being used with no problems. It is perfectly natural for mold to grow on the surface of the clay and other materials while kept in damp contact with each other. Remember that even slabs are preferable and easy to stack.

Joining slabs

Your main method of joining all clays will be the score and slurry method. This enables you to join flat surfaces accurately without pushing or blending the clay, which would disturb the form. There are several ways to do this.

To join fine, smooth soft clay you can use a toothbrush and water and dab or scrape the join. The toothbrush will key the surface and provide

COLORED SOFT SLABS
BY REGINA HEINZ
Soft slabs of clay are used to create this sharp abstract geometric structure, which successfully combines its form and pattern to explore subtle surface texture and color in an intriguing way.

  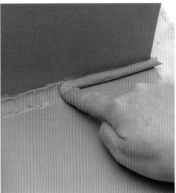 

3 Push the two slabs together, moving them from side to side as you do so. This will key the bond completely. If you can see the slurry ooze out of the join this means you've applied the right amount. If you can't, then you probably haven't used enough.

4 Clean away the excess slurry with a tool or sponge. For much smaller areas, you can use a paintbrush. Pressing the join with a tool will create a firm bond.

5 Large slabs can benefit from a reinforcing coil of clay run along the line of the join and blended in. If you do this, make sure the slab has not dried too much, otherwise the additional clay will crack as it dries and shrinks.

6 Finish the reinforced join by running a right-angle or curved tool over the clay.

WORKING WITH LEATHER-HARD SLABS

Using predesigned and previously stiffened slabs before joining greatly extends the range of forms achievable with this technique.

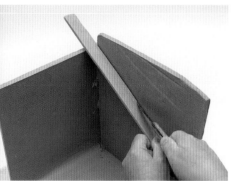

Cutting Sections can be added and cut once joined, or the whole form can be predesigned, cut, and then assembled after.

Supporting 1 When creating enclosed sculptural forms, these can benefit from internal supporting walls, which will help to prevent any distortion during both the making and firing stages.

2 Draping and stretching soft slabs over hard ones can create interesting results. Remember that any fully enclosed space needs a small hole to allow the air to escape.

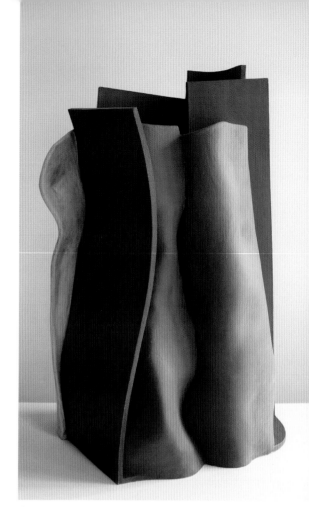

SLIP-COLORED SLAB STRUCTURE
BY KEN EASTMAN
This large slab-built form fully demonstrates the complex vertical structures that can be achieved using a range of soft and hard slabs.

enough slurry to join without the need to apply more. For all leather-hard smooth and textured clay it is essential to score and slurry the join. The slip or slurry should be made from the same clay as the slabs to be joined—simply mix the clay with water. This is the "glue" that will bond the slabs together. Do not try to join slabs that have dried beyond leather hard, because they will split along the joins when drying (unless you are using paper clay). With certain forms, especially those with only two sides, you may find it necessary to miter the joining edges, otherwise there will be a small gap. If this proves too difficult, you can always fill in any gaps with coils of clay providing the slabs are not too dry. All clay work that has been joined should not be left in the open air to dry but instead covered with plastic.

Forming leather-hard slabs

Leather-hard slabs must be made and then partially dried, this is usually done through wrapping and storing or by drying the clay with propane torches and electric dryers. Hard slabs are used to create any form where you require perfectly flat sides or geometric angular forms. They can be self-supporting and are easier to work with than soft slabs.

The surface texture and decoration should

be considered at the start of the slab-making process, since changing the surface will become more difficult as the clay continues to dry.

Any slab that has dried past the point of easily pushing a fingernail into the surface should be recycled and not used. Hard slabs may still require some kind of supporting structure during the making stages, depending on the scale and complexity of the work. Large and complex forms will benefit from temporary supporting sticks with clay at either end while the form is being made and drying. As the form dries, these will shrink away from the form. Generally, the larger the work you are creating, the thicker the slab you will need. However, think of brick walls and their load-bearing potential—the slab may not need to be as thick as you think.

Build hard slabs that are of very similar consistencies, otherwise you will have problems as the form dries. Keep the waiting slabs wrapped up while you are working. Lightly spray your work with water during making, because the room temperature will quickly start to dry out the exposed clay. It's essential that the joins are well scored and slurried. Don't be tempted to add fresh clay to fill in voids and gaps, since these will split during drying. If you do need to do this, try rehydrating the surrounding area before any additions are made and let them dry very slowly.

Forming soft slabs

Soft slabs can be made and used immediately depending on the type of form you wish to create. The form will dictate how much or little support is needed while being constructed.

By using a range of hard or semihard supporting structures, the variety of forms possible is greatly increased. Any support that restricts the shrinking of the clay will need to be taken out as drying

SLAB-FORMED SCULPTURE

BY KATHERINE MORLING

Described by many as sketches in clay, these black and white porcelain slab-formed objects are left unglazed. Together with the drawn black stain lines they seem to help disturb the object's representation of reality.

TECHNIQUE FILE 22

CARDBOARD BOX MOLDS

Choose a strong cardboard box and simply press soft clay slabs into the whole interior. These will shrink easily away from the sides when leather hard. The impressions left on the clay leaves interesting seams and marks as you replicate the box's negative space.

1 Make forms by pressing sections of slabs into selected areas of the box. These are useful to make quick elements that can be left for a time to partially dry and then removed to develop ideas.

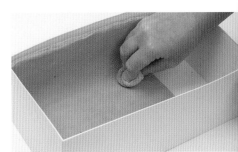

2 A box is an ideal aid to support clay slabs while making and drying forms. It can provide stimulus and suggest ideas while using strips to experiment with structural development.

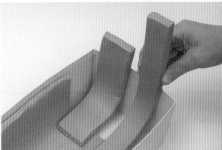

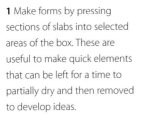

LAYERED SLAB VESSELS

BY SUSAN NEMETH

These porcelain laminated forms are created using layers of very fine different-colored slabs made with stains and oxides. Once the sheets are laminated they are wrapped around tubes. The patterns are created by scraping and subtracting layers to reveal the shapes.

gets under way, because the clay will shrink as it dries. When using support, always consider the quality of the material you are using and whether the clay can be easily separated from it. If not, then you will need to create a barrier between the materials. Commonly used support materials include paper, canvas, cloth, or a dusting of china clay.

Slabs are used widely as part of press molding and may be pushed into or on top of plaster molds. To achieve softer-shaped forms, slabs can be laid into suspended cloth sling molds. They can be pressed into cardboard boxes to replicate both the shape and texture of the box. They can also be folded around cardboard or plastic tubes covered by a layer of paper to create perfect cylinders. (The paper prevents the clay from sticking to the tube.)

The variety of supports possible offers great opportunity to develop the surface texture and the form further by cutting into the walls, and adding sections or separate elements to each other while ensuring the form doesn't collapse.

Large slab forms may incorporate a range of hidden internal clay-slab supporting walls or bars that the clay is draped over or placed on. These will give added strength and support to the shape and prevent distortion and sagging during drying and firing.

Newspaper can be packed into forms to help support soft slabs, and then either taken out or left in place during drying and firing. Sponge and paper supports that are soft enough to flex as the clay shrinks can also be used in this way. If these are left in place to burn away in the firing, your studio must have excellent ventilation, otherwise

CYLINDER MOLDS

Plastic pipes and cardboard tubes are used to make a wide range of cylinder forms— they are easy to use and offer support while you either subtract or add clay.

1 Prepare the slab and cut it to the approximate size of your tube, making sure the tube is at least ½ in (1 cm) taller than the clay slab, because you will need to pull this out.

2 Roll paper around the cylinder, keeping it tight, and ensure that there is at least ½ in (1 cm) of the paper showing at the top of the form to enable you to extract it. Stick the end of the paper down with tape and place at the baseline of the clay.

3 Measure the circumference of the cylinder by rolling it on the slab and make a mark, allowing for a ½-in (1-cm) overlap. Cut off the excess clay.

4 Roll the cylinder while holding on to the clay. Score and slurry the overlapping clay.

5 Roll the clay with the cylinder and, as you come to the overlap, apply more pressure to compress the clay and join it.

6 Finish by applying pressure to the seam with a sponge or kidney.

7 When you have completed the cylinder, you must pull out the supporting tube before the end of your working session, since the clay will quickly start to dry and shrink around it. The cylinder will crack the clay if left in place.

8 The paper will provide more support until the clay is firm enough for you to deal with the interior seam.

9 If the tube is too narrow for your hand to fit, you can draw a stick up the seam of clay and smooth down with a sponge afterward to finish.

MAKING SLING MOLDS

Canvas or cloth can be hung in a simple frame or tied to the legs of an upside-down chair to form a sling mold. This kind of work has the advantage of being able to be manipulated from both sides to create a wide range of undulating forms.

1 Hang a piece of canvas or cloth to form a sling mold.

2 Lay the slab in the canvas or, when dealing with a large slab, you can leave the clay on the canvas on which it was prepared to avoid adding any stress cracks while moving.

3 Alter the clay with a sponge to avoid putting any finger marks into the surface. The sling can be altered at the corners to support the changing shape of the slab.

4 Manipulate the slab from underneath into the required shape; it can be further supported by foam blocks or newspaper and be left in the canvas sling to dry out.

eye-watering fumes will be created that can be unpleasant and hazardous. It will also potentially set off smoke alarms.

Support structures for soft slabs

When constructing form with soft slabs you often need help from other materials in order to create a wide range of shapes, since the soft clay has no inherent structure itself. It will need support while partial drying takes place. If the support is soft and flexible it can stay in place and burn out during firing. Harder materials need to be withdrawn shortly after the drying has started and the form is stable enough to stay in place. If left in place the clay form will crack as it shrinks around the support.

Drying leather-hard and soft slabs

Slow drying is generally the accepted rule for slab building. This allows time for any joins or inconsistencies in the evenness of thickness to dry as evenly as possible. Any joins that are not properly sealed will open up during drying.

Cover slabs under a layer of plastic sheet or loosely wrap completely for at least a few days—longer for larger work. Wrapping work loosely in plastic will let the air inside begin the drying

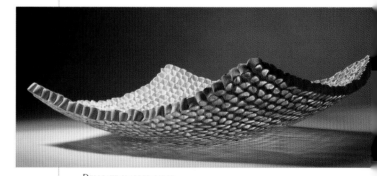

Delicate slabbed piece
by Stine Jespersen
This fragile-looking form seems to hang in the air. Forms like these can be constructed in either plaster molds or in canvas sling molds. Sling molds allow a greater degree of manipulation than plaster ones, because you can access the underside of the form.

CURVED SLAB VESSEL
BY JAMES OUGHTIBRIDGE
*These surfaces are refined by scraping and
sanding to help with the flowing curves. Layers
of slip, stains, and oxides are applied to complete
the form; then it's fired to stoneware.*

process. Small holes in the top of the plastic will let more air in without holding the moisture from condensation on the inside surface. The water caused by condensation can drip inside the form and, if the drying process is under way, this will cause cracking as it hits the dry clay. It can also start to reclaim and crack the clay if it becomes saturated. Avoid drying in direct sunlight or above heaters, which cause greater condensation. There are no problems associated with letting the clay dry over a period of months.

For large slabs, haste with drying can create stress problems due to inconsistent thicknesses and warping. Large bases should be dried on a surface that will allow the base to move while shrinking. Fine silver sand or thick wads of newspaper may help. Industrially, the largest ceramic forms made are bathtubs, which are dried on a series of rollers. Flat tiles are best left to dry wrapped up or loosely covered, otherwise the edges dry first and this will cause them to curl up. Some larger tiles and forms are helped by resting on slats of wood, allowing the air to circulate under and over the surfaces at the same time.

TECHNIQUE FILE 25

ASSISTING DRYING SLABS

All slab work will benefit from drying slowly and evenly under a plastic cover. This can prevent warping from the work drying too quickly. Unwrap work if there is heavy condensation buildup on the inside. This will drip on the work and cause cracking in localized areas. Always check how the work is proceeding.

Slab forms can benefit (in the same way as any other technique) from packing with newspaper to hold the shape during the drying stages. Tight packing may be essential at the start, but then reduced as it dries; you must allow the work to shrink. Newspaper will also help to absorb some water.

Packing the work with plastic will prevent it from drying while you continue to develop the form. Once you have filled the inside, wrap all working edges and cover with plastic. The plastic can be replaced with paper when you want to dry the work. Take all plastic out and remove as much paper as you can before firing.

Try different methods and see what works for you. Because of time constraints and finance, many makers are cautious and stick to tried and tested practice, rather than risk-taking and potential failure. However, development of knowledge only happens when people learn by taking risks or trying something different.

Clay can be an intimidating sculpting material because of the need to adhere to certain core techniques and principles. Even though the clay can be manipulated into virtually any shape, it cannot be fired as a very large solid block. Ceramics is often governed by the hollow form, which for some people can prove too problematic and restricting.

HAND BUILDING: SOLID BLOCK MODELING

Sculptors who do use clay may make the initial form using vast amounts of the material combined with wood and metal armatures as the first part of the creative process. Then multiple molds are made of the work and cast in other materials, using the clay as a waste material to create their final vision.

Firing very thick, solid work is theoretically possible, but demands a much longer drying and firing schedule than usual and will take a period of trial and error as you experiment with slow firing cycles. An average clay working thickness is usually anything up to 1½ in (4 cm)—this

won't cause too many problems. This need not keep you from working with solid masses of clay and then hollowing the form from the inside, though. As the clay surface stiffens enough not to be disturbed and the form begins to support itself, hollowing out can start. Working in this way can be very liberating, because you are free to explore form without the constraint of wondering how it's going to survive the making, drying, and firing process. Making maquettes (see pages 292–293) will also assist with this method, and help you visualize how the form may be developed and cut into sections.

SOLID BLOCK SCULPTURE
BY FERNANDO CASASEMPERE
This powerful sculpture demonstrates the tensions created in the drying and firing of large solid work. Experimentation in the firing process is required when working on thick objects.

CLAY BOOKCASE
BY MAARTEN BAAS
This clay bookcase was individually modeled using a synthetic clay with a metal skeleton inside to reinforce the structure. The use of clay is continually being developed by makers, engineers, and scientists to find new uses and to create new products.

Small forms can be hollowed out from underneath using various-sized loop tools. Depending on the shape and scale of the form, they can also undergo a certain amount of "surgery"; cutting the whole sculpture in half or removing extensions from the main body. These can then be hollowed out separately and reattached using the score and slurry method (see page 72). They may also need to be temporarily supported until dry, using a range of armatures and supports.

HOLLOWING A SOLID-BLOCK FORM

The drying and firing process is much quicker for hollow forms than for solid ones. Cutting the form into sections makes the hollowing more manageable.

1 Take a solid block of clay and manipulate it into your chosen form. Let the surface dry to the leather-hard state, but don't let it get too dry otherwise you won't be able to correct mistakes at the next stage. Cut off manageable sections to allow you to access the inside to subtract the interior clay.

2 Subtract the clay using a variety of loop tools to create an even thickness throughout the form. If you are not sure of the thickness of certain areas you can push toothpicks through the surface—these will act as a guide to how thick areas are and where the clay may need further subtraction. If you go through the surface by mistake, you should be able to patch this up with some of the extracted clay.

3 If some of the sections have been weakened, you may need to add internal walls or pack with newspaper until dry. Score and slurry all edges that are to be joined, and attach them, using temporary supports where necessary.

4 Push the cutoff blocks back onto the main form and blend them back together. The clay should be soft enough to rectify any mistakes and to make further additions. Once finished, wrap loosely and dry slowly.

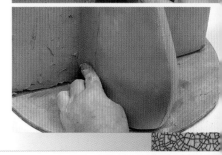

TECHNIQUE FILE 26

For many, wheelthrowing is ceramics. Start throwing in public and a crowd will gather. People are generally fascinated by the activity. For some, just giving it a go once will be enough to satisfy their mild curiosity. For others, it can be the start of a lifelong passion—a source of endless fascination and a place to solve creative problems.

THROWING: AN INTRODUCTION

Why is it called "throwing"? Because you get started by throwing the ball of clay onto the wheel head. It's also suggested that the word "throwing" derives from an Old English word meaning "to twist." Throwing certainly also involves spinning, pushing, lifting, pulling, squeezing, aching, sweating, and frustration.

Using a wheel is a quick way to create form. Successful wheelthrowing involves a combination of speed, pressure, and control.

Following are some of the skills you will need to get started. It is by no means an exhaustive list. There are many variations for how individual people learn to throw. We all feel comfortable with different hand and body positions. Once you have grasped the basic techniques, though, there are many other small, personal variations that can help develop your own expertise—and style—at the wheel.

It will take time, repetition, and patience to gain the skills to produce what you may have imagined your forms to be. As with all skill-based activities, there is no fixed time for how long this will take. You are, after all, seeking to gain control of a speeding, spinning mass. It's rarely an immediately acquired skill. Generally, it takes weeks or months. For some of the less able—but very determined—it can take years. It's all about persistence and determination. Further, it's not a finite competence. As with any other skill, once you have learned to throw competently, it becomes something you can develop, and that poses you the question: What do you do with it? Will it provide you with enough stimulation to generate design ideas and the creativity needed to make highly individual statements with your work? If you're a production potter, will it make you a living wage?

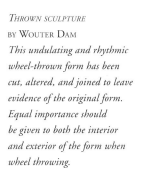

Thrown sculpture
by Wouter Dam
This undulating and rhythmic wheel-thrown form has been cut, altered, and joined to leave evidence of the original form. Equal importance should be given to both the interior and exterior of the form when wheel throwing.

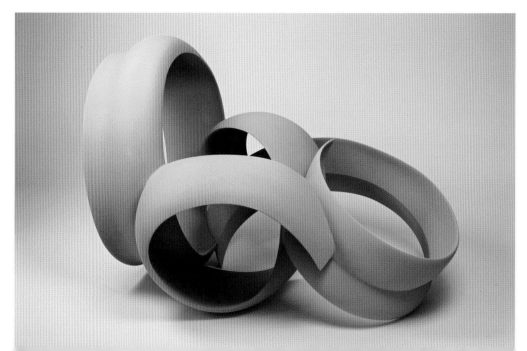

PORCELAIN TEA SET
BY LOUISA TAYLOR
These porcelain vessels demonstrate the ritual of drinking. Made from porcelain and decorated with a range of colored transparent glazes. Wheel work enables you to quickly create a "mix and match" range of work with a similar signature style.

In the West, we throw counterclockwise. In the East, they throw clockwise. Why? No one knows for certain. Perhaps it's like writing. English goes left to right while other languages go right to left. This "handedness" of throwing can make a big difference to some people. While some left-handers can learn to switch hands, others find that rotating the wheel clockwise solves lots of problems. The important thing is that the clay should always come into the dominant hand.

The beginner

When you start out, the consistency of your clay must be as soft as putty. This makes it easier for you to manipulate and begin to develop haptic understanding and confidence. As your throwing develops and your confidence grows, and your forms become more complex, the clay can be prepared to different consistencies—stiffer, generally, to support thinner and even gravity-defying shapes.

To create a wide variety of forms you need to develop an understanding of the correct pressure needed on the clay and the subtlety of the variation in wheel-speed needed at different times in the throwing process. This takes time and repetition, trial and error. Beginners can find it very disconcerting to watch a production potter. They will have developed their own very individual style and shortcuts, which may be very difficult to replicate.

Start with the basics, though, and you will soon develop your very own finger and hand positions. Because forms can develop very quickly on the wheel, there is a tendency to overthrow work. This can cause problems, since

a thin and soft hollow object can only rotate so many times before it collapses. If you are not actually working on the form or trying to figure out what to do next—or simply admiring your achievement—then stop the wheel. When you first start on the wheel, you may want to throw the thinnest, lightest pots possible—an admirable ambition. Yet, while no one wants a teapot that is too heavy to lift off the table, it can be just as disappointing to lift something that feels too light.

Early wheels

As with any world-changing invention or discovery, seeing the very first attempt to make and work a pottery wheel would be fascinating. Imagine seeing the first time someone stuck a lump of clay in the middle of a flat, rotating surface, added lots of water, pushed a hole in the middle, then pulled up the walls of the clay, changing the form as it grew and, finally, admiring the final shape.

We think the person who first did that did so around 6,000 years ago, in Egypt maybe, or somewhere else in what we now call the Middle East. There are tomb paintings in Egypt from around 3,000 BCE that show potters using turntables made from wood and stone. The principle of the wheel itself had been found about 1,000 years earlier, around 4,000 BCE, when it was discovered in Mesopotamia (southern Iraq). The Sumerians were the first to develop carts and chariots using these early wheels.

The first pottery wheels would have had thick, heavy disks (wheel heads) made of stone or wood, which would have been spun by an assistant

DISTRESSED VESSEL
BY JOCHEN RUETH
This form shows all the stresses, strains, and tension that a thick wheel form can be put through, but still be strong enough to retain its shape. Once thrown, wheel work can be manipulated to express other ideas.

LIDDED FORMS
BY TILA AND JAMES WATERS
These functional pieces offer a balance of minimal form and subtle surface glaze decoration. Making work that will stand both domestic use and mantelpiece admiration is a constant challenge for wheel workers.

using a stick placed in a hole. Around the world, many different systems have been used to get the wheel turning: feet, ropes, and sticks. What really changed things was the introduction of the long support shaft to support the wheel head with a flywheel disk at its base. This made for a far more comfortable arrangement for the potter. The other big development was the arrival of mechanical power in the 18th century.

The modern wheel

Three main types of potter's wheel are readily available around the world: the electric, the kick, and the momentum. Which one you choose depends on various factors: cost, the availability of a suitable power source, your fitness level, and certain lifestyle (or aesthetic) choices.

Kick and momentum wheels nod to tradition, evoking self-sufficiency and rural idyll. They have zero running costs, are quiet, and, in design terms, embody a forthright honesty. You throw on them as the wheel slows down. Some potters say they can tell when forms have been made on these simple, nonmechanical wheels. They claim these forms have a different feel and rhythm to

them. Whatever you believe, nonmechanical wheels certainly bring immediacy and a sense of less fuss to a piece of work. They also make overthrowing less likely.

Electric wheels are constantly being redesigned but never really change. New models don't necessarily mean new anything. What you want from a wheel has always been the same: something that will carry weight without stopping, retain a steady speed, deliver stillness without juddering and, finally, offer flexibility for individual comfort and joy. Some wheels are definitely better than others so, before buying one, always ask other potters' advice and try out several. Good secondhand wheels don't come around often—because even if people leave one sitting around unused they remain convinced they will get back on it one day. Ceramic departments in art colleges and adult education institutions often have a variety of wheels to enable students to try different models. Just make sure you try out several—as many as possible, in fact—before you find yourself seduced by that shiny bright red one with an extra button.

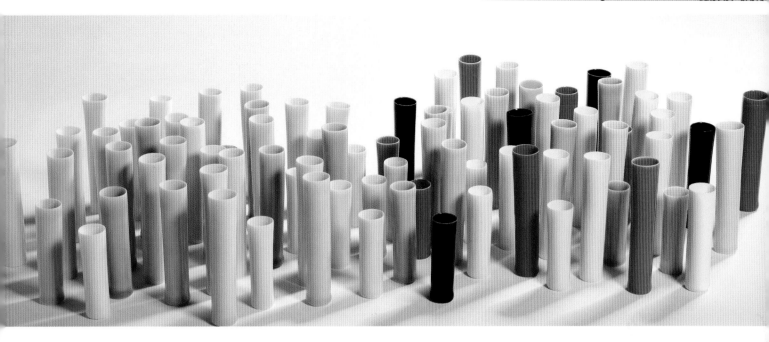

VESSELS FORMED BY REPETITION
BY NATASHA DAINTRY
These wheel-thrown forms demonstrate the individual nature and rhythm of repetition. The pure nature of porcelain is able to show the transparent beauty of glaze color.

THROWN POTS
BY JACOB VAN DER BEUGEL
The repetition of throwing is an ideal technique to create still life. These forms offer an austere aesthetic using only the clay as color.

THROWN JUG
BY RUTHANNE TUDBALL
This free-thrown and altered soda-fired jug reflects the movement of the making process in its final form. It is clearly ready and waiting to be used and poured.

Though dependent on the drying conditions of your workshop and how much time you have available, there is a long-established order for making wheel-thrown work, with all the stages split over two days.

THROWING: THE SEQUENCE

In preparation for throwing you should choose a smooth clay body. Ideally, this should be one specially prepared for throwing, because it will have been blended to give the greater plasticity needed for thrown forms. Any clay can be used, but for a beginner the challenge of the material is large enough, without adding extra difficulties.

The clay must be well kneaded/wedged to give it an even consistency (see pages 30–31). This will also expel any air pockets, which would otherwise cause problems when throwing. If air pockets are left in the clay they will feel like hard lumps and appear as blisters. If left undealt with, they may explode in the first firing.

As a beginner, you want the clay to be as soft as new putty. Stiff clay will be demoralizing. As you fight to control the centering of the clay your hands will bounce off and your shaking will continue until you turn into one big uncontrollable wobble. Therefore, the time you

spend getting the clay to the correct consistency will reap you rewards as you progress through the process.

You will need to prepare as large a lump as you can manage and then cut off the clay into blocks. The size and weight depends on the size of your hands. Generally it should be large enough to force the hands and fingertips apart. Too small and you will be unable to figure out what your hands should be doing. These lumps are then best made into round, smooth balls or cone shapes. Prepare at least five pieces before you start, to allow for making mistakes. If the clay comes off, don't try to reuse it without first drying and reshaping it.

Centering
Centering is the most important aspect of the throwing technique and the one that it may take the most time to be proficient in. Centering is

Hand pressure points

When centering, the main force is applied with the palm of your hand.

Your hand will bend around the form with inward pressure applied.

The area behind your knuckles and finger ends will also apply pressure.

Body position
Sit right up to the wheel tray with your upper arms pressed into your sides and your forearms on your thighs or the sides of the tray. Place your hands at eight and four on an imaginary clock face.

ORDER OF WORK:
THROWING TECHNIQUES
Centering
• water
• both hands pressure in
• build wheel speed to 75 percent
• squeeze don't strangle
• follow clay up
• cone
• dome
• left hand in at top at 45 degrees
• right hand pressure down
• right hand forcing left down

TECHNIQUE FILE 27

CENTERING

This action will enable you to create symmetrical forms. It conditions the clay and expels small air pockets. Unless you conquer this, throwing will be a frustrating activity.

1 The wheel head needs to be clean but damp to help the clay stick. Too wet and the ball will slide off as soon as you make contact. To dry the wheel using your thumb, start at the center and move out to the edge. If the wheel head is completely dry and the clay a little stiff, then this can also cause the clay to slide off.

2 Throw the ball of clay into the middle of the wheel head. Make sure the underside of the ball is completely round and smooth, otherwise you will have trapped air underneath. This will make it difficult to center. Slap the sides with both hands so that you are happy it's stuck and the sides are as even as possible before you start.

3 The next action is referred to as "coning." Start the wheel and wet the clay and your hands (see detail). Place your hands around the clay, applying equal pressure in toward the center or greater pressure with the left or right hand, and increase the wheel speed up to at least 75 percent of the wheel's speed, possibly up to 100 percent. (This will depend on your wheel's motor or flywheel.)

4 As you squeeze in with the palms of your hands the clay should start to rise. You will need to allow your fingers to cross each other. Follow the clay to the top, keeping greater pressure with the heels of your hands while sloping the angle of the hand in at 45 degrees to create the cone shape. Apply water as often as you feel necessary to stop the clay dragging. Let the clay slide through both hands. Ideally, raise the clay during the coning to double the original height of the mass. You need to feel some movement of the clay at the very least.

5 Place and slope your left hand near the top of the cone at a 45-degree angle. Place your right-hand heel over the top and lean into the center with your shoulder pressing down with the right hand while keeping pressure in with the left. It should feel as though the right hand is pushing the clay into the left hand as both go down. The left hand is controlling the cone shape and also the width of the base—don't allow it to spread too far by keeping inward pressure.

6 Repeat this action several times; with each repetition the resistance should decrease until the clay mass is turning smoothly without any sideways movement. Once you have gained this skill you can start the throwing process. Without well-centered clay you will be unable to create symmetrical forms. The experienced thrower will usually repeat the centering action three or four times to make sure the clay is centered, of a similar consistency throughout, and free of air pockets.

FAULTS & REMEDIES

The main problems arise when you are coning the clay up; if the top is too flat and your hands are too vertical, a small dip will appear in the center. As you continue upward, the dip will become a hole.

You need to change the angle of your hands to 45 degrees and not skim the clay up the sides, but instead apply more pressure into the center of the clay to make the whole of the mass rise.

When you push the clay back down, if a mushroom shape forms it means that there is not enough pressure with your right hand pushing in and the left hand on top is too dominant.

Try and keep the clay mound slightly domed at all times. Before pressing down, dome the top and push in hard with your left hand at 45 degrees and push down on the top. Don't ease off pressure with your left hand.

Remember, if you are throwing with the wheel going clockwise, these actions will be reversed.

the process that positions the ball of clay in the exact center of the wheel head. There are many methods for achieving this, and the one you choose will depend on your wheel, body shape, and strength. Observing other throwers will help you to see different approaches. Some throwers do not center and use this to inform the shape and individual nature of their work, but this is not advisable for a beginner!

The principle of centering is to use pressure against the centrifugal force of the wheel. By placing your hands on either side of the clay (at eight and four on an imaginary clock face), pressure is applied into the center from both hands equally or the left hand if throwing as a right-hander (if the wheel direction is

THROWN SCULPTURE
BY BARBARA NANNING
This wheel-thrown form appears to be unraveling. As it does so it releases the tension of the spiral that created it.

CIRCULAR LAYERED FORM
BY MATTHEW CHAMBERS
This wheel-thrown form has been constructed using many individual sections and layers. Oxides have been used to color the clay before the making process.

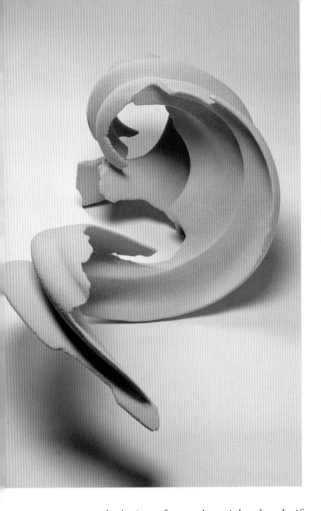

counterclockwise; from the right hand if throwing as a left-hander and the wheel direction is clockwise). Don't let the clay take your hands from this position. Using plenty of water as a beginner, and less as you progress, will allow the clay to slide easily through your hands. The temptation at first is to grab the clay, not allowing it to slide. Bear in mind that by using soft clay and a lot of water you will create a lot of slurry. You can easily reclaim this if you keep it away from your other bits of clay. As you start to understand where your hands need to be and the amount of pressure required, you can use less water. Avoid pressing the heels of your hands onto the wheel head since it is abrasive and they will soon become very sore.

Body position is important if you are going to be sitting at the wheel for an extended period of time. Try to make the majority of movements happen just in front of you. Observing a competent thrower can be misleading, because it's impossible to see how still and rigid they keep their upper body. While centering, you will be keeping your forearms still and stable on either side of the wheel tray or on your thighs,

FORMING THE CENTER HOLE

When creating the center hole of the form it can be easy to disturb all the hard work of your centering efforts. This will depend on where and when you start to press and the speed of the wheel. If this relationship is not right, it can be easy to send the mass off-center.

1 The wheel speed needs to be at least 75 percent of capacity. Any slower and your fingers won't find the center. Place the left hand around the centered clay and put a little pressure against the wall. Place the right hand on top of the left and, with either one finger or two, feel the center of the top. Your fingers should feel still.

2 Press down, keeping your hands together. The clay should start to spread out a little from the pressure of your fingers. You will need to increase the pressure as the speed takes your fingers down into the center. Too fast or too slow and the clay will start to spiral off-center. Remember, you are not drilling the middle out. You can also put one hand on top of the other if that feels more stable.

3 Try to gauge the depth of the base in relation to the wheel head as you press down. The exact depth is easily checked by stopping the wheel and pressing a needle down into the base. Push your finger to the base, keeping it against the needle. Take it out and this will show you the exact depth of the base.

4 Leave approximately ¼–½ in (0.5–1 cm). This will allow you to turn a foot ring into the base at the next stage. Also, when you have finished the form and wire it off from the wheel head, you may leave some of the base behind at first.

FORMING THE BASE

There are many ways to create the base and these have developed for reasons of both speed and ease; also, different forms will dictate how they should be made.

1 Place your left hand in front of you and around the form. Working from the center, place two fingers on the base and link your thumbs or make sure your hands are linked and supporting each other.

2 Draw your fingers across the base toward your body. Try to keep the pressure even. At this stage you are also creating the approximate width of the base. Don't extend beyond the original size of the lump, since you may trap air underneath, but make sure you have gone right into the corner of the base, creating a small undercut in the wall.

3 Once you have reached the edge, push your fingers back into the center to compress the clay in reverse. This will help to prevent any "S" cracks on the base. It will also remove any unwanted ridges and prevent a buildup of clay at the sides.

4 Check the depth of your base once again with your needle. Run your fingers over the clay afterward to close up the small hole. You can smooth over any blemishes with a small compressed sponge. Don't start throwing the wall until the base is finished, because it may be difficult to go back to it.

and you will be bent over your work. A full day's throwing can lead to all sorts of aches and pains if you have not found the right seating and working position.

Once you can center clay you are almost halfway to throwing a form on the wheel. This can be the single most problematic area, though, and the one that puts people off. The textbook form with which to practice technique is the cylinder, since many shapes develop from this. Avoid bowls—the wheel will eventually throw those by itself with its centrifugal force. Once you are in control, then you can start to enjoy the rest of the process.

Forming the base

The base of any form is its foundation. You should create a solid and even base before gaining any height with walls. Once you start throwing it will be difficult to go back down into the base and if you do, you can distort the whole form.

Lifting

Lifting is the main action of throwing and it will take some time for you to learn to lift the clay evenly with control. This process is done in several repeated lifts. With each lift from the base, the walls of the pot will become thinner

FAULTS & REMEDIES

If the relationship between the speed of the wheel turning and the speed at which you are traveling up the form are out of synch then the clay wall will start to spiral.
To prevent this you need to bring your hands up the form together and apply less pressure.

If the clay does not appear to move from the base and remains much thicker after several lifts, it means that the initial push was not firm enough or that your fingers were skimming over the surface.
Push into the form with your outside finger position below your finger position inside. Leave them in that position and don't move them until you feel the clay move above your fingers on the outside fingers. After two or three lifts you will see the roll of clay moving up toward the top.

FORMING THE WALLS: LIFTING

With practice, determination, and repetition you will be able to use all the clay you have prepared and centered. The aim will be to lift an even wall of clay up from the base.

1 Put your thumb and forefinger of your right hand on either side of the wall toward the back of the cylinder at two o'clock and pinch them together; place your left hand over the outside fingers and apply pressure, then pull the roll of clay up. You need strong thumbs for this!

2 Alternatively, with your right-hand forefinger point then bend around your thumb to create a stable pad that will become your main throwing tool. Place it at the base of the form on the outside, initially horizontal to the wall. Push in and wait until you can feel a roll of clay rise above the finger. This is the roll that you will lift up to the top. As you travel up the form, tip your finger

ORDER OF WORK:
THROWING TECHNIQUES
Lifting
• water
• slow down wheel speed to 30 percent
• left hand inside
• right hand outside
• finger pad in at base left hand above
• push in horizontal
• wait for clay movement
• change right finger pad pushing in and up to a 45-degree angle
• finger pad pushing left hand to the top

pad from horizontal to 45 degrees (see detail). Apply greater pressure for approximately the first third of the form, easing off as your hands travel up.

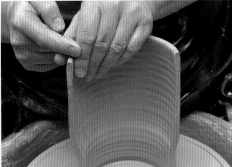

3 The fingertips of your left hand are on the inside, above the outside finger pad. The inside pressure is forcing the wall out and the outside is pushing in. At the same time the outside right hand is pushing the left hand to the top of the form.

4 Whenever possible, link your hands together to create better support. This will be the case with most throwing activity. As you get near to the top your hands should gradually become level. If you don't ease off the pressure halfway up, then the top of the form will become too thin and difficult to control (see Collaring, page 93).

5 The most conventional method for completing the top is to put your left-hand finger and thumb either side of the rim and, with the underneath of the forefinger of your right hand, press down gently. The more pressure you apply, the thicker the rim will become.

OTHER HAND POSITIONS FOR LIFTING

These methods offer alternative ways to lift clay from the base of your form.

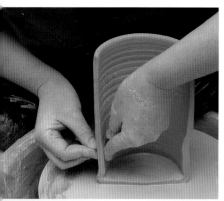

1 With small amounts of clay, you can have just the fingertips of your hands running opposite each other inside and out. This action will simply squeeze the clay up and works well with small forms. Later, to refine your throwing, you will be using just your fingertips together in this way.

2 Take a sponge in the right hand underneath your inside left hand and push this in instead of the thumb pad. This can be very useful if you are throwing particularly rough, coarse, grogged clay or if your nails are getting in the way.

Leveling off the top Imagine that the form is higher than it is as you gently move your hands away. Any sudden movement can knock it off-center. After several lifts, the top of your form may become uneven and you will need to level it off. This is done with a needle. Place your left-hand forefinger and thumb either side of the rim and, with the needle in your right hand, rest the point against your left thumb pointing to the center. Move it into and across the clay until it hits your forefinger on the inside. You can either stop the wheel and lift off or simply move the right hand away with the disk of clay hanging around the needle (see detail).

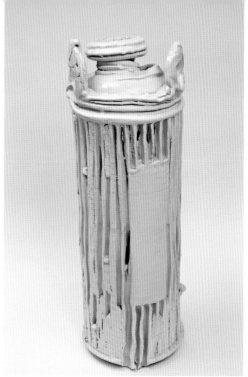

STONEWARE MILK CHURN
BY DUNCAN HOOSON
This large wheel-thrown form used 44 lb (20 kg) of clay and was lifted in several pulls to create the required height. The cylinder was collared after each lift to keep control of the form.

and demand a greater sensitivity to avoid going off-center, twisting, tearing, and collapsing. You can either use the same method throughout the lifting process, or start with one and then change. The speed of the wheel should be about 25–30 percent of capacity. Too slow and the cylinder will spiral, too fast and it will go off-center very quickly. Many throwers use a glass or plastic mirror at the back of the wheel, which enables them to see exactly the silhouette of the form as they work, instead of either bending over or getting off the wheel to check their progress.

Collaring

The collaring technique involves encircling the work with both hands, and will enable you to control the form at all times. It describes the action of taking the clay in toward the top of the form—essential for bottles and spouts. It will also help you gain greater height with forms. A rhythm of throwing for medium and large forms might be that after each lift you collar the clay.

Cutting the work from the wheel

Once you have finished throwing, work can be cut from the wheel using a cutting wire.

ORDER OF WORK:
THROWING TECHNIQUES
Collaring
• at least four points of contact
• wheel speed 50 percent
• reach halfway, increase hand pressure
• as you continue up, increase wheel speed to 75–100 percent
• cut off spiral top

A little water splashed onto the wheel and drawn underneath the work for lubrication will make it easier to slide the work off as you cut. From the wheel, it is transferred to a board and left to dry. If you intend to add to your form, then cover it with polythene or place it in a damp cupboard. You are aiming for a leather-hard consistency, which is perfect for finishing the following day.

Once you are more experienced you will be able to lift the work straight off the wheel head with dry hands. Even so, you still must treat each form very gently as you place it down on the surface of the board, because any sudden movement will affect the symmetry of the form and will cause problems when turning at the finishing stage.

Even with your earliest forms, start thinking about both the quality of surface and what the rim is doing as you work. Often the rim is the visual frame of the form. These will later become fundamental to the type of work you are going to make and your self-expression. Remember that ceramic pieces may be around to be admired for a very long time to come.

Refining haptic skills
Many forms you throw will require slightly different hand movements, pressures, and wheel speeds. It may also be the case that you get too comfortable and stick with particular amounts of clay. It can be very useful to occasionally attempt larger pieces of clay, or to drop down in scale and make some very small, precise work, since this will refine your fingertip control and also your awareness of detail. This is recommended not

COLLARING

Many throwers collar the clay after each lift. This will help with control and lifting.

1 Curve your hands around the form and create at least four points of contact with your fingers and both thumbs (ideally crossed for extra support).

2 Increase pressure as you travel up the form. The wheel speed can start at 30 percent, then, as you travel up the form, increase the wheel speed as the form starts to lift to 50 percent. For very narrow collaring you can increase to 75 percent.

CUTTING WORK FROM THE WHEEL

These steps should help with taking work off the wheel head.

1 Once the form is finished, take an angled wooden or metal tool and clean away the skirt area of the base. Subtract into the cylinder's base by a depth of ¼ in (0.5 cm) before taking your form off the wheel head. This will allow water to flood under the form and, without the mess at the base, allow the form to slide off more easily.

2 Put lots of water on the wheel head. Take your wire and pull it as taut as possible before pulling it underneath the form—if there is no movement, put more water on the wheel head and repeat the procedure. Ideally, dry your hands before pushing with both at the base to slide the pot off onto a wet board or onto your fingertips. The form should aquaplane along the surface.

CHANGING DIRECTION WITH FORM

So many vertical forms start with a cylinder. Once you have gained the skill of lifting the clay from the base you can start to experiment with swelling forms out while keeping control of the top, and then changing direction and taking the clay back in. Mugs, vases, pitchers, teapots, and cups all use the same principles— it will all eventually depend on matching your skill and ideas and keeping your critical eye sharp and your imagination ticking over.

1 Make a basic cylinder, but don't make the wall too thin, because this won't allow you to experiment with changing direction. As you travel up the wall, press with your left-hand fingers on the inside against your right ones to make the form swell out. Don't try to make too big a swell with one push; take at least two or three repeated lifts to create the desired curve.

2 When you decide to take the form in, simply alter the pressure from the inside to the outside fingers. Once you have got to the top, collar the clay to draw it back in to keep control of the form.

3 Both consistency of clay and gravity will play a part in deciding how far you can take the clay out and how long it will allow you to work on it. If you take the clay out and there is too much clay above, this will collapse the wall; this is the reason many forms are made in several individual parts.

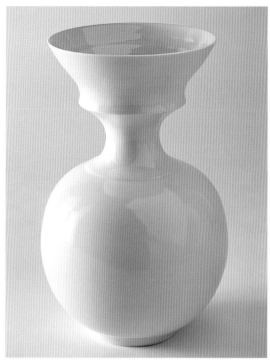

Thrown porcelain vase
by Anna Silverton
This form demonstrates beautifully how you can change direction with clay. Great skill while throwing is required to keep control of this refined form.

just for the beginner but as a creative challenge throughout your ceramic career.

Ribs

The use of different kinds of throwing ribs can greatly help you to refine and shape your forms and create an individual style. They can strengthen the walls of forms and enable larger work to be thrown. Create perfect concave and convex curves on the interior and exterior, subtract unnecessary slurry on surfaces, straighten and angle walls, tidy bases, create rims and galleries for lids…in fact, once you start using ribs you may never throw without one again. The only downside is that they can, if overused, take character out of the form. Each thrower will have their individual collections of ribs, usually made up of ones that are purchased and ones made for very specific jobs. They usually have a hole in the middle to help you grip them while wet. If you are making repeated forms then you could create almost the whole silhouette as a "rib," or a template.

USING TEMPLATES OR PROFILES

Templates and profiles are a great way to start adding details of individuality and quality of finish when throwing. They are very simple to make and use. Throwers will often have a collection of these ready to finish bases and rims—some may even use them for the whole profile of small forms if they throw similar forms repeatedly.

1 Templates and profiles can be used at the wet throwing stage or at the next stage of turning when the clay is leather hard and a crisper, hard-edged profile is required (see page 130). Use wood or plastic for ease of cutting, or metal. Old credit cards are ideal for this. Simply cut your desired profile into the card and sand to refine the edge and remove any burrs.

2 When using with throwing, press the template against the side of the form and the soft clay will take the exact profile offered to it. It is best achieved in several firm but gentle actions with addition of water in between to achieve the perfect result. When used while turning, the clay will be easily subtracted.

3 The template is offered up to the side of the form at different angles while throwing to achieve different profiles. The inside left hand can gently press the clay into the profile of the template. You can apply small amounts of water to prevent dragging.

USING RIBS

Using these will provide great help with refining shape and assist in creating straight, round, concave, and convex forms.

1 Always support the clay on the opposite side to the rib. To straighten a wall, hold the rib vertically against the side at the base and apply pressure from the inside of the form so that you are pushing the clay onto the rib, and travel up the form.

2 To create a rounded form, flex the rib with your thumb in the middle in between your thumb and forefinger and bend. Angle the rib at 45 degrees, pointing the top away from you. Place your left hand inside, opposite the rib, and gently push against the wall into the flexed rib as you draw the clay out.

3 As you get up to the widest point in the swell, start turning the curved rib at 90 degrees. The curve will depend on the amount of flex in the rib. As you pass this point, turn the top more toward you while continuing to flex the rib.

4 As the clay nears the top, the rib and forefinger will be almost pointing toward you. This method of using a flexible rib will enable you to to make much larger curved forms than those that are cut into wooden ribs.

Cultures and civilizations around the world have made and developed bowl forms for many different and specific daily functions and rituals. They have held and mixed the world's lotions and potions, collected and distributed wealth and prosperity, and can help define a culture's rich history and identity.

THROWING: OPEN FORMS

Most beginners will throw an open form more by accident than design. It is far easier to let the clay open out with the help of centrifugal force than to control it and gain height. Thinking about and designing what shape the form is going to take will help before starting to throw. Simple sketches or cutout templates will greatly help you achieve the forms you are aiming for. The action involved in throwing can distract from your initial intention, but sticking to a clear idea of what the open form should look like will prevent a lot of mistakes. It will also make a difference to how you throw it and, practically, what you have to leave for support at or close to the base.

Before you throw the open form, thinking about its function may help you decide on the shape. Is it for cereal, sugar, soup, pasta, salad, fruit, or olives? Or will it be the bowl your keys, a bottle top, and some coins end up in? Or, is it to express an idea or narrative, or to be kept simple to serve as a canvas for decoration, or to compete for admiration on the mantelpiece or inside a showcase?

Technical considerations

Different-shaped bowls will demand different approaches. The base and interior will often dictate how the form flows. As the width increases, gravity will take control and if you've gone out too far too soon, the walls will flop. This will also happen if the bowl is thrown over too long a period, because the walls will weaken. Also, if the clay is very soft and a lot of water has been used in the centering process, then it will be difficult to throw larger and wider. The wider you allow the top section to span out the more difficult it becomes to draw the clay back in or to gain further height. When you are trying to bring clay back in, it will often cause pleating or a crinkled edge. If you are not in contact with the form, stop the wheel. Large, wide-span bowls may be made in several separate visits to the wheel and partly dried in between or left to settle. These would ideally be made on a bat so they can be taken off and put back on the wheel (see page 100), or they can be part-dried while on the wheel with a gas torch or hair dryer and then rethrown.

For small bowls there is no need to use bats, but as you progress they may save you time and cause fewer problems both when taking work off the wheel and at the finishing turning stage. They are useful if you have the space and are throwing very thin, fine clays like porcelain, and

EMBOSSED BOWL
BY RUPERT SPIRA
*An undulating, wheel-thrown
stoneware bowl. The interior
is embossed with text, which
draws your eye in and around
its asymmetrical form.*

THROWING A SMALL/MEDIUM OPEN FORM

Thinking of the bowl's function will help to decide the size and shape it should be. Also think of both the interior and exterior surface quality while throwing.

1 Center the clay as you would for a cylinder, but on the final push down allow the clay to spread to the approximate size of the intended base. This will also give you an idea how much clay you should leave to support the overall width of the bowl. Compression of the base is very important, so remember to always work back into the middle before lifting the walls.

2 Consider what the interior shape is going to be; as you make the base, you will be either creating a flat bottom where the walls spring from the base or a gentle flowing curve where there should be nothing to distinguish the base from the wall. If it's a curved base, then as you pull out, ease the pressure as you near the side to allow the base to naturally curve.

3 Place your left hand inside the bowl and your right hand on the outside and link your thumbs in front of you at five or six o'clock. Push in with your right-hand finger pad and allow the clay to lift, then, with your left-hand fingertips, apply pressure and lift the roll of clay that's been created to the top. You can allow the clay to drift out a little. Compress the rim before moving your hands away slowly.

Support or steady your hands during the process.

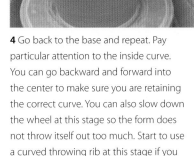

4 Go back to the base and repeat. Pay particular attention to the inside curve. You can go backward and forward into the center to make sure you are retaining the correct curve. You can also slow down the wheel at this stage so the form does not throw itself out too much. Start to use a curved throwing rib at this stage if you like. Always support each hand during the throwing and refining of the form.

5 Do not extend the width too much before you have achieved the approximate height required; you must keep control of the rim at this stage. You can leave the clay thicker for the top 1 in (2.5 cm) to give you the option of forming different angles and thickness for the rim. You can compress the rim with a wooden edge to leave a crisp finish by cleaning away any slurry (see detail).

6 To complete the bowl your last throw may just use your fingertips placed opposite each other to refine the shape. Or you could finish by using a rib to both strengthen the wall and to subtract any slurry that may weaken the bowl and leave a messy surface.

especially when you come to throw larger forms.

You can throw plates without bats, but the clay has to be stiffer to allow you to get them off the wheel. Anything over 6 in (15 cm) in diameter should be thrown on a bat.

If you have used a bat, remember to wire through before taking off. The wider the base the more you risk the wire riding up in the middle. Something that can lessen the chance of this happening is to hold the wire taut and keep your hands as still as you can as if you are pulling against the counterclockwise rotation of the wheel. The wheel speed should be about 25 percent. This will help take the wire under the form without leaving clay on the wheel head.

Open form interiors

An important area for immediate consideration is the interior, and this will depend on the surface quality you want to achieve. Some bowls are completely even, smoothed out using a wood, rubber, or metal kidney; others have the making in evidence, and this gives a particular character to the work. Slip decoration and glazing will also play their part in what you choose to leave or subtract from the form at both the throwing and turning stages. The rim and foot ring of a bowl is a rich area of design possibilities and a chance to stamp your individuality. The rim will become the frame to the inside surface. It will influence how the owner will hold and use the finished piece, and is the division between interior and exterior. Whatever it becomes, give it some thought, even if it's just left to trail off to something fine and then beautifully cuts through the glaze creating a halo.

Foot rings and rims can be made separately and added to the form as composites while still fresh or leather hard. This gives rise to further exciting possibilities and design challenges.

Consider the function of the form. This will help you to decide on some of the details of the surface and the type of rim it's going to have. On such an open form the types of marks made by throwing or the use of tools will be very much in evidence. The slip and glaze will also heighten these to create either intentional surface details or reveal the mistakes.

TECHNIQUE FILE 38

THROWING PLATES AND FLATWARE

Compression to the base of any flatware is essential, otherwise it can develop splits and cracks during the drying and firing.

1 Center the clay as before, but allow the mass of clay to drift out over the last two centering actions to the approximate width of your intended plate. Place your right-hand fingertips in the center and press the left hand on top; apply pressure, and pull in toward you.

5 Once the base is made the next step is to make the small wall and rim. Ideal for this is the right-hand thumb. Place this over your right forefinger and press in at the base. This will lift the clay up, making it easier to then throw as usual.

Profile designs for flatware

 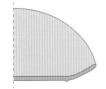 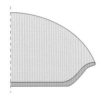

2 You would use the same method if you were throwing wide, flat-based bowls, only leaving more at the side to use for the wall. Try using the heel of your right hand with your left hand cupped on top of the clay, applying pressure to draw the clay out. This is useful for larger pieces.

3 As you near the edge you can put the left hand around the form to keep it from going off-center. This will also condense the mass. Develop the base over two or three of these pulls, gaining greater depth with each pull. Keep the surface well watered with a damp sponge to prevent any dragging on the surface (see detail).

4 Go back into the center with an equal amount of pressure to flatten and compress the base. Once you have made the base you can finish with a rib or leave the incidental thrown marks.

6 If you want a wider rim, gain height in the wall and, with your right hand supporting on the outside, press your fingertips together and pull out in one movement. Don't let the wheel revolve too often, otherwise the rim will drop.

7 To create greater definition with the base and the transfer points in the form, use different curves of a rib. These will not only sharpen the distinct angles but will also subtract unwanted slurry.

8 Always support underneath where you are working. Remember to wire underneath before you lift the bat off. A sponge or piece of chamois leather is useful to compress any rim or plate edge and also to clean away any slurry (see detail).

It's impossible to throw all the forms you will want to make in one single section, and there's nothing to be gained from it, yet for some beginners making things in sections feels like a fraudulent activity. Many forms, even medium-sized ones, are better thrown in sections. These are easier to manage and control, and the result is often lighter.

THROWING: USING COMPOSITES

Throwing in sections will mean using a pair of calipers to measure circumferences to enable sections to fit. A small amount of design and preparation work will prevent you from throwing lots of potential forms only to have to reclaim them when they don't fit.

Another way of using composites is to investigate a more sculptural approach to making forms. This can be a way of developing form in a more intuitive and spontaneous way where the separate elements will suggest how they can be put together and joined and developed to then influence other composites, which in turn will make new forms: an ongoing line of inquiry.

Throwing in sections
If you want to make large work, then composite throwing will be your main activity, because it's impossible to center very large lumps of clay. The two main methods are either throwing measured sections to fit and then join together, or continuous adding of large thick coils onto the rim of the first form and throwing these up, building the form in gradual stages. With both

methods you can add as many sections as you wish. The only restriction to size will be the firing capacity of your kiln and the type of clay you are using (to withstand the weight at the greenware stage before firing). The clay used will usually contain large amounts of grog. Makers are constantly pushing the boundaries of this type of work, often by firing forms in situ or using more than one pair of hands, as the potters of Jingzen in China have demonstrated.

FIXING A PLYWOOD BAT ONTO THE WHEEL HEAD

Spread a 1.5-in (2-cm) layer of clay onto the wheel. Dry the surface with a sponge and draw several rings. This will enable better suction while fixing. Wipe the bat with a wet sponge. Place the bat onto the clay and center. Press down firmly and bang your fist in the center and work around the bat, applying even pressure. Use both hands and try to move the bat; if it slides you will need to wire off and start again.

Composite forms
by Duncan Hooson
Each of these wheel-thrown bottle forms is comprised of three sections, which allows freedom to explore the action of the speed of the wheel and the joining together of the forms.

THROWING IN SECTIONS

This technique will enable you to create a greater range of forms, increase scale, and be more experimental with ideas; opening up new possibilities to explore.

1 Throw a form and dry it either by leaving until leather hard or with electric or propane heat. The clay will need to be stiff enough to hold the extra weight without distorting. Score and slurry the joining edges of the form and additional coil (see pages 72 and 81).

2 Place the coil onto the edge. When making the coil, try to make it as even as you can; this way you will avoid wasting half of it as you center it.

3 Press the coil into position and make sure there are no gaps, and that it is very well attached, before you start throwing. Things can quickly go wrong and are magnified as forms get larger. The wheel speed should be slower than throwing a small form.

4 Use as little water as you can to keep the form from getting too wet, and create definite thrown lines in the surface. This will make it easier to even the wall out.

5 Take off the uneven top, which will always appear as you create an even-centered wall.

6 Compress the rim ready for the next coil to be added.

7 Instead of adding another coil, you could rethrow the additional clay into the final form.

For some throwers the sole activity of wheel throwing can be rewarding, but not fulfilling enough to realize their vision and to keep them returning to the wheel. The challenge for them is where they can take and develop different elements of what the wheel produces.

THROWING: ALTERING FORM BY CUTTING, ADDING, AND JOINING

The starting point for their work may be the action of the wheel. Some may leave trace elements of the action to acknowledge the starting point and then abstract it. Others quietly distort and cut and reform to keep you guessing, mystified, and fascinated as to how a piece has been made. It's an area of throwing that will continue to develop and grow as long as people remain interested in the process of throwing but not necessarily producing form for functional use.

There are numerous ways to develop this approach to working. Once you think of the wheel as a tool of production and have the idea that once an element is thrown it is just the beginning, then you are just starting to engage with this type of work. Cutting away the base of a form and creating a new one by another technique is often the first step. Once you do this you then realize how easy it is to distort the walls with precision and attach a new slab or press-molded base, which need not be symmetrical. Cutting the base of the wall on an angle will change things again. This can be the start of endless curiosity and creative development.

Cut-form tea set
by Margaret Bohls
These wheel-thrown porcelain forms demonstrate how to treat a variety of different forms with the same approach by cutting and altering to create an identifiable set. The overall gentle softness of forms is enhanced by the semi-matte glaze quality.

MAKING AN OVAL FORM

Once you start cutting you may not be able to stop.
It can open up a world of possibilities for both function
and sculpture.

1 Make sure the clay is soft, of leather-hard consistency. The form will require easy cutting but needs to retain its shape. Measure halfway across and draw a line against a hard edge.

2 Draw another line either side of this center line and cut through both of these. Don't try and cut through in one step. Do it gently with several cuts. The width amount you subtract will determine how tight the oval curve will be.

3 Score and slurry both of the edges to be attached very well (see page 72), because you need an excellent join and bond.

4 As you push the pieces back together again, move them up and down to make sure they are well keyed together. Use a sponge to clean up the join and compress the surface (see detail).

MANIPULATED RIM AND BOWLS BY SANDY LAYTON
These porcelain wheel-thrown forms seem to float on a deep translucent blue glaze. The plate has had its rim detached, altered, then reattached again.

CUTTING AND ADDING TO CREATE A TILTED FORM

Once you have started to experiment with cutting, creating even the slightest tilt to a form can be enough to separate it from the crowd.

1 Cut off the base and put it to one side so that you can reattach the wall to it.

2 Use either a taut wire or harp and pull through the form toward you at an angle coming up. This can also be done easily with a knife.

3 This type of work will benefit from playing around with different options first. Once decided, score and slurry all the sections to be joined and reattach them, cleaning with a sponge where necessary.

4 The tilt will depend on how much you have cut off and at what angle. The form once cut and altered will offer different possibilities to investigate.

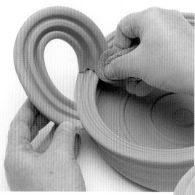

5 Making further additions on the wheel, like this thrown handle, will add character to the form. Experiment with similar details that form a relationship when used together.

6 The base could also be used as a lid if the wall section was attached to a simple slab. You could also add a thrown knob as a decorative detail.

With these forms it can be a number of things that provide interest. The joining, squashing, twisting, pulling, pushing, stretching, tearing, cutting, and the overall surface mark-making potential become really exciting. New forms that emerge from these actions may have no recognizable tradition but may be aligned to Abstract Expressionism.

ALTERED PORCELAIN FORMS
BY SUN KIM
Great technical skill is demonstrated in these porcelain-thrown forms that have been cut and altered. They are precisely considered, inventive, and beautifully made functional objects with simple transparent and semi-matte glazes.

REJOINED VESSELS
BY CARINA CISCATO
These stoneware porcelain forms are finely thrown to create delicate shapes that are cut and altered. The throwing lines and the joining seams have been left as statement scars of decorative detail.

The design, shape, and size of your lid will determine how it is going to be made. Some will be made upside down or the right way up. Some will be thrown off the hump or mound while others are thrown individually. Some will need to be turned when leather hard, while others simply need finishing.

THROWING: LIDS

Lids provide you with an opportunity to start adding your signature style to the work. They also extend the functional possibilities of form. The combinations and styles are endless and present design challenges to find two separate elements that fit, suit, clash, or however you want the viewer or handler to think and feel about them. Are they perfectly matched? Comfortable with each other? Or going through a difficult, scratchy patch? What statement will your lids be making? Will they conflict or be compatible?

Although lid styles vary widely there are four main types of fittings:
• Lids that fit in the form (using galleries)
• Lids that fit on the form (using the shoulder of the form underneath the lid)
• Lids that fit on and over the form (using flanges)
• Lids that continuously follow the line of the form (using a cut through the thrown wall)

As a beginner the best practice is to make a thick cylinder and repeat the actions of forming, then cut off that section and repeat until you understand finger positions and pressure. The one fundamental rule of lid making is that it should be done at the same time as making the form. If this proves difficult, always measure the width with a pair of calipers and make marks in your sketchbook to record it, because the clay will shrink during the drying stage.

A useful design exercise is to throw a single form and make as many different lids as your imagination allows. When making individual pots that you don't plan to repeat, it's always useful to make a few "backup" lids to test ideas with turning at the next stage. This will often help with design development.

Throwing "off the hump"
The reason for using this method is that very small lumps of clay can be difficult and time-

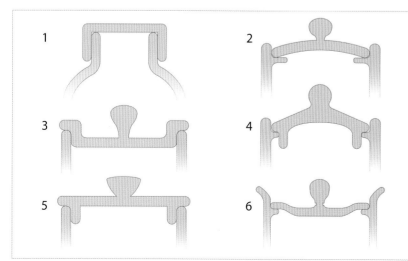

Selection of lid design fittings

1 The simplest lid to achieve, where a pot or bowl sits on top of a neck and shoulder (made upside down).

2 A lid that sits inside the form on a gallery (made either upside down if curved or right way up if flat).

3 A lid that rests inside the form and on the rim (made right way up).

4 A "belt and braces" teapot lid that is made with a flange to sit inside the gallery on the form (made upside down).

5 A lid that has a flange that sits inside the form and on the rim (made upside down unless the inside is solid).

6 A lid similar to number 2, which sits inside the form (made right way up).

consuming to handle when centering. The hump method entails centering a medium or large mass of clay (usually more than 6 lb/3 kg) and using just the top section to create smaller forms. As you work your way down the hump, you recenter the section you are using. This method is commonly used for any small forms like lids, knobs, and spouts. When throwing these smaller forms try not to use too much water, since this will create a lot of slurry and the form will disappear.

Throwing individual lids

There will be times when lids are at that in-between size and difficult to throw off the hump. Your hands will have to work more closely together and on top of each other. You can follow the same principles and steps of each stage of throwing but just by using your fingertips and thumbs of each hand pressed together. Doing this will provide much better support as you throw the form.

LIDDED POTS
BY DUNCAN HOOSON
This series of porcelain lidded forms was based on city living. The towers rise out from the energy and contents of consumerism.

TECHNIQUE FILE **42**

LIDS THAT FIT IN OR ON A FORM

These are the simplest lids to throw, because they require no actual fitting on the lid, just measuring with calipers. They may take the form of a thrown bowl or plate that sits inside the form on a gallery or on the shoulder. These may require a knob or handle depending on the size and design.

1 Center the clay, using at least 4 lb (2 kg). Create a small section at the top by pushing your fingers in, then smooth this into a flat disk to your measurements. You will quickly learn how much clay is required for particular sizes of lids.

2 Press your forefinger and thumb into the middle of the disk, supporting it with your left hand.

3 Push in with the forefingers and thumbs of both hands, and the clay will rise. You can also use a sponge if you feel you do not have enough control.

4 Refine the knob and the rest of the shape using a wooden or metal tool to give greater definition to the design. Think how this will relate to the pot it's going to be matched with.

5 Define where the lid is going to be cut under with a line using a wooden tool. Keep the wire taut and introduce the wire in the line created. Use a slow, gentle wheel speed and pull through letting the wheel motion cut through under the base. This lid should not require turning.

LID WITH FLANGE (FITTING ON AND OVER)

Confident use of your calipers will allow you to make accurately fitting lids. When taking measurements it's important to leave a small amount for tolerance, and remember that the glazing of any of the contact areas will add to their thickness.

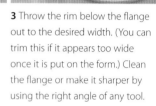

1 Throw a bowl shape, for the lid, on the hump of clay by pressing your right thumb or finger into the middle to create depth, and open out. Leave extra weight and thickness toward the rim. Support the clay with your left hand and take a measurement of the inside of your intended form, and throw approximately to this size.

2 Put your left thumb under the rim with the forefinger inside. With your right forefinger, push the rim at a 45-degree angle; this will split the rim, forcing the inside up and the outside down and out, creating your fitting. Throw the flange up and angle it inward slightly to allow for an easy fit (see detail). Remember that the measurement is taken at the base of the flange.

3 Throw the rim below the flange out to the desired width. (You can trim this if it appears too wide once it is put on the form.) Clean the flange or make it sharper by using the right angle of any tool.

CREATING GALLERIES ON FORMS FOR LIDS

Best practice for a beginner is to throw a thick cylinder until you are confident with finger and tool positions. By repeating the action and cutting off, you will soon understand the pressure required to create the gallery, the amounts and thicknesses of clay needed, and how much you can refine the fitting and wall to support these actions.

Method 1: 1 Throw a cylinder, then put your left thumb and forefinger either side of the rim, and with your right forefinger gently press down to thicken the rim. Supporting the clay will keep any gaps from being trapped between the inside gallery and wall. This is key for hygiene, because no food contents can get trapped. This method can be used on the outside of the form to create a ledge for a dome lid to sit on.

2 Before completing the form, on your second or third lift place your left forefinger inside the rim, and, with your right forefinger, press down on the inside half of the rim. Your left forefinger should then be underneath, supporting the clay that has been pushed down. The gallery can be pushed down the wall as far as your design demands.

3 Press the right angle of a tool into the corner of the gallery to sharpen and clean the area. Make sure you slope the tool at a 90-degree angle away from you. The cleaner this area is, the easier it will be to take an accurate measurement with your calipers.

4 At this stage you can also create the knob. Narrow it at the base by pushing in at either side with both forefingers and thumbs held together, using the sides of your hands as support. Use a tool to indent where the section will be cut. Check that it's lower than the base.

5 Introduce your taut cutting wire and try holding it against the form with the wheel revolving at about 20 percent of full speed. Pull gently into the middle and let the movement of the wheel cut through the clay. Check the measurements with calipers and make adjustments accordingly.

HELP WITH MEASURING FOR LIDS

TECHNIQUE FILE 45

Depending on the form you are making, you will need to measure the inside or outside of the form.

Take the measurement from inside the form. Set the calipers to one side and throw your lid. Transfer this measurement to the outside of the gallery using another set of calipers. This will give you an accurate fit, but remember that the addition of glaze will add thickness to either lid or form, so allow some tolerance for this.

Method 2: Throw a cylinder and thicken the rim as described previously. With the point of the tool, press the point on the halfway line. This will split the rim. Push and flip the inside half over, down, and horizontal (see detail). Sharpen it as before with the right angle of a tool. Some throwers prefer this method for its precision and accuracy.

Method 3: Throw a cylinder and instead of thickening the rim, thin it out. Place your left forefinger on the inside and, with the right forefinger, push the clay over until it is horizontal. Then, with the left-hand second and third fingers under the rim, press in at the top of the rim with a right-angled turning tool to compress the top (see detail). This will produce the gallery. This method can be useful if you have thrown particular forms that are very fine and you don't want to put too much downward pressure on the wall.

Method 4: Collar and enclose the form completely. Once the form is enclosed it will be supported enough to allow for turning and finishing. Cut right through the chosen line of the lid at a 45-degree angle (see detail). Leave on until leather hard, and sponge edges to finish. The 45-degree angle on the rim will be enough to locate the lid.

For functional, sculptural, and decorative purposes, handles present further opportunities for individual creative expression. You should always consider the options of making handles, and how they are going to be attached to reflect your intention. Consider how the glaze will sit in textured areas. Experimentation and play is essential for new ideas and results.

THROWING: HANDLES

Handles can be made using any ceramic-forming technique. The most common methods are discussed here.

Attaching handles

Whichever method of making you use, it is important that the handle's consistency is similar to the form to which it's been added. If they are very different, there may be cracking around the join. This will also happen if the work has gone beyond the leather-hard stage, or if the work is dried too quickly after attaching the handle.

After making you can either leave the handle to dry off a little or use a dryer. Be careful not to dry too much, because this will leave no room for gentle adjustment. If you are using different clays for the form and handle, check for compatibility, since they will have different shrinkage rates. The drier the two elements are when you join them, the more precise they will be. If they are softer, you can be more fluid with your movements and make more adjustments to the design and style.

The key when joining handles is to look at the negative space between the profile of the form and the interior of the handle. How you join the handle to the form will say just as much as the quality of the handle and form themselves. Consider the user's comfort if the piece is to be functional. Hard edges will dig into the fingers when lifting.

Attach the handle using the score and slurry method (see page 72). Depending on the size and weight of the handle, you may need to put in a temporary support. If the piece is going to stay in place for a while you could use clay for this, since it will shrink at a similar rate as the handle dries. A stable, harder material would not allow for this.

• When joining separate elements, wet the form with water and score and slurry both the end of the handle and the form.
• Apply a generous amount of the clay's slurry. Press together so the slurry oozes out.
• Finish off with a sponge, or for a more precise and tidy finish, use a wet paintbrush; this can be drawn around the join and is also useful for reaching into small areas.

Choosing a design

Look carefully at the profile of your form. The handle needs to relate to this in some way. Think about its function and how it will be held and lifted. Make lots of different handles and offer them up against the side of the profile to see which you think best fits. The gray shaded areas represent the cross-section of the handle at that particular point.

CUT AND ALTERED TEAPOT
BY DUNCAN HOOSON
A stoneware, wheel-thrown teapot with a transparent celadon glaze. The handle is made with a simple textured slabbed strap, highlighted by the glaze.

Thrown handles

Thrown handles can add a different quality to the form and are ideal for one-off pieces of work and very straightforward to make. They can be used in different sections and added to a variety of forms in different ways. It's also a quick method to work out possible design ideas for extrusions, since it produces similar results if repetition is required.

Pulled handles

Pulling is seen as a very traditional approach to handle making and attaching. The method involves using 2–4 lb (1–2 kg) of clay to make an elongated cone shape. Hold the end of the cone in one hand and with the other press the forefinger and thumb together to form a negative oval shape between them. It is advisable to have a bowl of water nearby so that you can wet both your hands and the clay regularly.

Start at the top of the cone and draw your finger and thumb down—don't apply too much pressure, since this will tear the clay. Repeat this action a few times to start the process. Keep wetting your pulling hand to prevent any dragging. If any dents appear in the clay it is best to tear it off, because it will become a weak spot.

WHEEL-THROWN HANDLES

You can use the wheel to create a number of different handle options.

1 Center and throw the clay as normal, but as you put the hole in the middle press to the base and draw all the clay out to the edge, leaving your desired width and thickness. This is also a useful method if you want to add much larger rims to forms.

2 This ring can then be finished by cleaning and refining with a tool. Or, for greater definition you can create more detail using tools or templates (see detail). Don't leave until the leather-hard stage, when you won't be able to manipulate it.

3 Once finished the ring can be cut in half and manipulated into shape. It could be cut into further sections and used as small lugs on the side of forms.

4 The handle at this stage can respond to forms in a very direct and spontaneous way. It's easy to manipulate and also to add other clay elements to. These sections can also be placed back to back to create much thicker handles.

PULLED HANDLES

You can use many methods to create a number of different handle options.

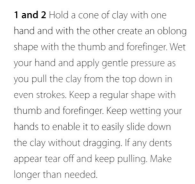

1 and 2 Hold a cone of clay with one hand and with the other create an oblong shape with the thumb and forefinger. Wet your hand and apply gentle pressure as you pull the clay from the top down in even strokes. Keep a regular shape with thumb and forefinger. Keep wetting your hands to enable it to easily slide down the clay without dragging. If any dents appear tear off and keep pulling. Make longer than needed.

3 You can make the handle and leave it to rest until stiffer and then attach it to the form, or, alternatively, once partly made attach it to the form by scoring and slurrying and then continue to pull it to the right length and shape. You can pull the whole handle from the form by attaching a cone of clay and pulling in the same way.

4 Attach using the score and slurry method or, if both are soft, simply blend into the form. When making handles in this way look carefully at the design of the forms you are creating.

Once the clay has started to draw down by sliding down the front and back, start applying pressure from the sides to keep the width of the handle from spreading too much. The shape of the handle will be governed by the shape your finger and thumb make.

You can finish by drawing your thumb down the middle of the handle strap, which will create a gentle curve and a traditional look.

Make all handles much longer than you need, then you can choose the best section. Clip off with your thumb and either attach to the edge of a table or bend into a curve and place on a board to dry. You can then continue to pull more of the cone.

You can also use this technique to pull the handle directly off the pot. Attach a smaller cone to the pot by using the score and slurry method, pull down in the same way, and attach the end directly to the form.

Slabbed handles

Create slabs of clay in different thicknesses. These can then be used in conjunction with a range of precut paper templates.

Draw around the template shape on the clay slab. Dry the clay to a leather-hard consistency so it will keep its shape.

Look at the cut edges to determine the quality of finish, and either leave or smooth as required. The slabs could also have a wide variety of textures impressed into the surface or roulettes run along the length. A metal file can create a range of sharp linear designs when it is pressed into surfaces.

Signature handles

By experimenting and playing with different handle shapes and textures you may discover an element that makes your work individual. Using a range of tools and textures you can try different ways of rolling and imprinting into coils and slab strips, and finish by twisting and stretching. The finished form (far right) demonstrates an exaggerated approach to using handles on forms.

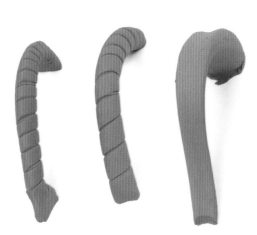

Attach the handle using the score and slurry method. Depending on the size and weight, you may need to put in a temporary support. If this is going to stay in place for a while, use clay for this, which will shrink at a similar rate as the handle dries.

Coiled handles

Roll out or extrude a number of clay coils. You can use these in a variety of ways with texture and other tools to add form and surface. The coils can be rolled over texture, such as rubber mats, carved or cast plaster slabs, and carved lino sheets to impress designs onto them.

To create linear marks you can use the edge of a ruler or stick. By pushing this into the clay and pushing the coil along its surface it will show an imprint of the line. When you reach the end of the length, take off, reposition, and repeat. This will create a barley twist design.

This round, coil shape can be altered by gently lifting and dropping it onto a porous surface.

Press-molded and cast handles

For handles that you want to repeat you could create a two-part press mold from an original clay model (see pages 156–157), or cast an existing form. These are often used for more complex decorative shapes. This is the process used in industrial ceramics.

Sledged handles

Using cut profile templates with the sledging technique (see pages 130–137) can create limitless design options for handles. These can be drawn or

DECORATIVE APPROACHES FOR HANDLES

You can use any number of tools to create interesting and decorative handle options.

 TECHNIQUE FILE 48

Make a flat slab and cut out strips or make some extrusions. Dry the surface off before pressing into wet or fresh clay, since nonporous textures may stick. Use anything with a texture and press this into the surface, which will leave a print. Bend this into the approximate shape and attach.

Press any edge into a coil at a 45-degree angle and push away from you. Once rolled, release the edge, lift the stick, and place back at the end of the line and repeat. This can then be lifted and knocked into different shapes. When bending, push the clay together to prevent cracking.

Once you have made any handle this can be altered by either twisting or stretching. Do this in incremental steps, and when twisting push the clay together or it will start to crack and split. Do this also when bending into the arch shape.

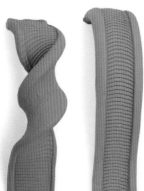

THROWING KNOBS OFF THE HUMP

You can use this method to create a great variety of knobs. Section off a small amount of clay each time.

TECHNIQUE FILE 49

Method 1: 1 Push both forefingers and thumbs together at the base and the clay will start to rise. This will form a solid knob.

2 Press harder and keep control of the top with your other fingers. Keep your fingers clean to avoid too much slurry buildup.

3 By keeping the surface clean and relatively dry you can use a tool to instantly turn the shape to refine the profile without the need to dry before doing this. Keep your other hand around the knob to keep control.

Method 2: 1 Use a small amount of water and press your finger down to create a small bowl. Throw the walls up into a small cylinder.

2 Push in while increasing the wheel speed to cone in toward the top. Continue pushing in to close the top off.

3 Once the knob is enclosed you can play around with the shape to extend the height or width. Clean the surface with a sponge and refine it further with clean tools or fingers. Wire off and dry a little before attaching to your lids.

Attaching lug handles
Using the score and slurry method attach the lug to the vessel. Try and make a lug that has a similar thickness to the pot you are joining it to.

sledged along the precut handle shape or used like an extrusion to create the whole handle form.

Handles using loop tools
You can use loop tools to strip a handle out of a solid block of clay. You could use store-bought tools or create your own profiles out of wire.

Extruded handles
Extruded handles offer both solid and hollow design options and have become widely used because they offer ease of repetition, speed, and precision once the design has been selected. Cutting your own designs into solid plastic blocks offers limitless options (see pages 164–165). This method is especially well suited to large, hollow handles.

Knobs
Knobs can be made as part of lids while throwing, or you can add a piece of clay to a finished lid and throw directly onto this. The advantage of this method is that you can alter as you throw to suit the form perfectly. You can also create a solid while throwing and, during the turning process, discover the form within the block like when using wood or plaster. The other alternative is to throw the knobs separately "off the hump" and join them using the score and slurry method. This can provide endless opportunities for refining and developing finger skills. If you use this method for lids, make several knobs to see which best suits your form.

Spouts are normally thrown off the hump, since they require only a small amount of clay (½ lb/250 g). The throwing is mainly about collaring the clay. They are usually made for teapots, but they can be adapted for a plethora of uses—as long, tall, thin necks for vases and bottles, handles, candlesticks, or doorstops.

THROWING: SPOUTS

For teapots, always throw more than you think you will need, because once you start cutting and adapting to fit the shape of the body, part of the length will be lost. (Unless it's well designed beforehand and a design you will be repeating.) When throwing, try not to twist the clay too much since this will often cause the spout to unravel in stoneware firings. Some potters will put the spout on at an angle to allow for this happening. If it doesn't, then you end up with a twist anyway. Good pouring spouts tend to be the ones that are left sharper at the end. Once you start rounding them off, combined with the layer of glaze, liquid tends to flow easily over the edge of the spout rather than cutting off.

Choosing a design
The shape you decide on for the spout will affect the way in which liquid is poured and how it tapers off. The darker shaded areas represent the cross-section of the spout at that particular point.

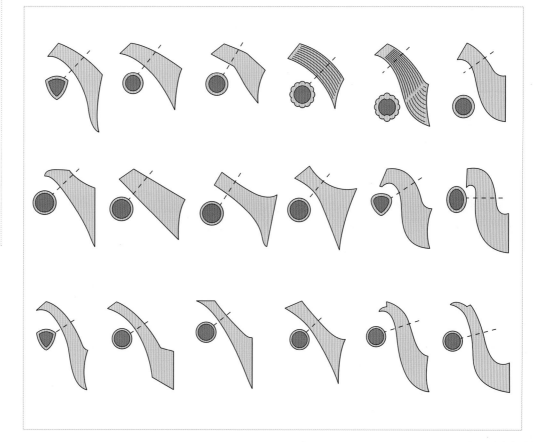

THROWING A SPOUT

The main skill to acquire for throwing spouts will be to get them tall and thin. Your wheel speed should increase as you collar in and up with the clay. Rethrow after each collar to make the spout thinner.

1 Center the clay as usual and concentrate on the section of clay you are throwing. Press with your finger in the center, supported by your other hand. Go down in depth to the length of your finger.

2 Pull up with your fingertip inside and thumb outside and your right-hand fingers and thumb opposite on the outside, tapering in as you near the top.

3 After each pull up, collar the clay with at least four fingers and both thumbs. As you near the top, increase the wheel speed to help draw the clay in. Avoid putting too much pressure on the outside of the clay, because this will twist the inside.

4 When the interior has narrowed too much to put your fingers in, use your needle handle or any stick on the inside to push against as you travel up the wall. Your right-hand fingers should be pinched together, pushing the stick inside up to the top.

5 Refine the shape using as much support from your fingers as possible until your confidence grows. The wheel speed will be approximately 50 percent of capacity at this stage to keep the form in the center.

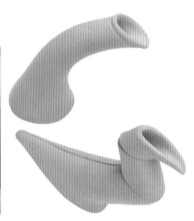

6 Once dried a little you can easily bend and manipulate spouts into a variety of different shapes. Try to throw different widths and heights to give you plenty of options. (The stress of decisions awaits once you start making teapots!)

MAKING A TEAPOT

A teapot is a classic composite form and one you should set yourself as a design challenge. It has all the relevant challenges for a thrower learning the craft. To design and make something aesthetically pleasing, with the right physical balance, and with both good pouring capability and drip cutoff is a significant achievement, even if you don't use it yourself to drink tea!

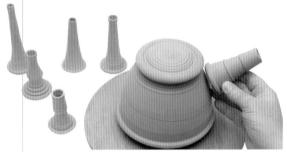

1 Throw the body and lids, providing you with design options. Choose a spout and offer it up to the form to look at the relationship between them.

2 Cut the spout at the correct angle in gradual stages.

3 Cut away the extra thickness at the base of the spout.

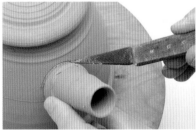

4 Draw around the circumference of where the spout is going to be placed. This can then be cut out just inside the drawn line to create one hole for a teapot that uses teabags only.

5 Alternatively you can use a hole cutter to cut out small individual holes for loose tea leaves. Smooth down any burrs on the inside and outside with a sponge or paintbrush.

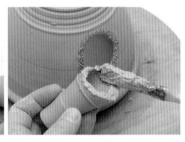

6 Score and slurry the form and the spout and join together (see page 72). Make sure that all the components are a similar consistency before you join, otherwise they may crack when drying.

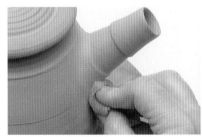

7 Push them together to join, and clean off the slurry both inside and out with a sponge. Make a feature of the join or blend so it's seamless.

8 Make handles before attaching the spouts as you will need them to dry a little before joining. Attach the handle with the score and slurry method.

9 To create a neat join, finish off with a paintbrush. Let the piece dry slowly under cover.

"Turning" or "trimming" describes the technique of putting a part-dried, ideally leather-hard, form back onto the wheel head, recentering it, and then subtracting clay using a selection of metal and wooden tools while it rotates. Before using this technique look carefully at your form and decide on the best way to complete it. Choose the method that will best suit the qualities it already possesses.

THROWING: TURNING AND TRIMMING

It may be that by putting the form back on the wheel and turning with a hard metal tool you will strip away its individual character. Or you could set up an imbalance in the form where one half is very mechanical, smooth, and highly finished and the other ribbed, undulating, and soft, showing the imprint of the maker. Decide what impact you want the turning to have on the outcome of the overall finish. Turning can be used to create highly individual textures and surfaces, very much like drawing. Turning used to be seen by ardent throwers as a way of hiding bad technique, because it's about subtraction. Now, for some, it is seen as the most creative element of the throwing process, where, like a stone- or wood-carver, you are discovering the form within the material. Whatever your beliefs it can certainly refine forms and make their profiles more elegant and interesting, adding to the mark-making potential of the surface and at the same time greatly reducing the weight! It will also give the opportunity to create foot

rings, making it easier to stabilize wide forms and creating an area that defines where the glaze can be wiped back to. Industrially, this is often the only part of the ceramic left unglazed.

Obviously, the more clay you strip away the more recycling you have to deal with. For a production potter this equates to time and money—both the turning and dealing with the reclaimed clay. When throwing, the more you repeat a form the lighter it will become, as your haptic skill level increases, so usually less turning will be required over time. But it may be that you just don't want to spend the time repeating the same form over and over again, making some turning inevitable. If you want your work to have equal weight distribution, then you need an equal wall width throughout. Looking at the inside of the form will tell you where the form needs to be thinner, since this internal shape should be repeated on the outside for good balance. Even though you are subtracting from the form, you should also, in a sense, be adding something to it.

Some makers may finish the form without returning it to the wheel. They may simply roll the base on a smooth or textured surface to soften the edges. They may use a knife to cut into the base to create layers, facets, or texture. They may also use a surform to get rid of rough edges. They could also simply sponge the edge and compress it with their thumb to push back down any grog that has come to the surface. It's

Turning
This technique can be used to create designs on the surface.

Foot ring
This plate has a double foot ring to help prevent distortion during firing.

FIXING WORK TO THE WHEEL HEAD FOR TURNING

A larger form may have more than one natural center. To place your form accurately back into the center may take time depending on how well it was thrown. There are a few methods for this, such as "tapping," but the one described here is the most common and useful for beginners. There are options for the surface of your wheel head, which will depend on your form and preferences. You could use a metal wheel head, a damp wooden bat, or a disk or hump of partly dried clay. If the rim is uneven (in the case of a pitcher, for example), it will need to be placed on a coil of clay to level the base when the form is upside down.

4 Place your form upside down and as central as possible using the rings on the wheel head as a guide. If there aren't any rings, these can easily be drawn on. Position your arm and hand so they remain still and steady. Hold a pin close to but just away from the form, near to where you intend to subtract the clay. Apply gentle pressure on top of the base to prevent the form from moving. Rotate the wheel at 25 percent of full speed. Let the form touch the pinhead. If the pin creates a line all the way around the form, it is centered.

Pin line   Original mark for depth of interior base

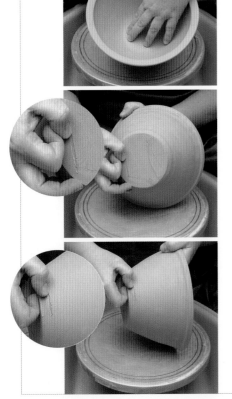

1 Any form needs initial investigation, to decide where to subtract the clay from and the position of a foot ring, if required. By holding the form and looking at the interior, see where the edge of the base becomes the wall.

2 Hold your outstretched finger underneath and draw a line with your nail on the base (see detail). Use this as a guide to where the outside of the foot ring needs to be created.

3 With your fingers either side of the form, run them up and down the wall and make a mark on the outside where the form thickens near the base. Another mark can estimate the depth of the base.

5 If, however, it only makes a line by touching in certain places, stop the wheel. Look at where the line starts and stops. Mark the start and stop with a fingernail, pin, or pencil mark.

6 Place your thumbs exactly in the middle between these. Push away toward the side that is not touching. Rotate the wheel again and repeat this process until the line is consistent all the way around. You may push the form too far, which means making another line so you don't get confused with the first one (see detail).

7 Once the form is centered, fix it down with three small lumps of clay forming a triangle around the rim. Press the clay down onto the wheel head first and then gently against the wall.

Mark indicating break in pin line

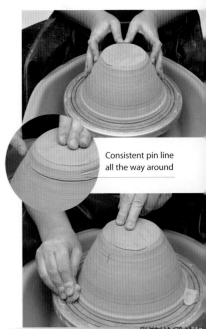

Consistent pin line all the way around

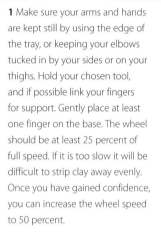

TECHNIQUE FILE **53**

TURNING AND TRIMMING A FOOT RING

Choose the appropriate tools to strip away the clay and consider what type of foot ring is best suited to the form.

Foot ring profiles
The shaded areas show where the clay should be subtracted during the turning and trimming process.

1 Make sure your arms and hands are kept still by using the edge of the tray, or keeping your elbows tucked in by your sides or on your thighs. Hold your chosen tool, and if possible link your fingers for support. Gently place at least one finger on the base. The wheel should be at least 25 percent of full speed. If it is too slow it will be difficult to strip clay away evenly. Once you have gained confidence, you can increase the wheel speed to 50 percent.

2 Apply pressure with the tool, keeping the angle sloping down (not horizontal) in relation to the wall. Do not try to subtract all of the clay in one step. Strip it away in gradual, even layers. Work up the form from your first mark into the mark on your base. You may want to take the form off the wheel to check for when you have an even wall.

3 Once the side is finished, either flatten the base or create the foot ring. The width of the foot ring should balance the width of the rim. If one is much thicker than the other the piece may not look considered. Make a mark to indicate the thickness required. Work from the center, making small rings of equal depth.

4 Creating depth rings will help prevent you from dragging your tool downward and going through the base. It can also help to keep the base level if it is wide. From the center, pull or drag across the base to subtract the rings. By stopping the wheel and gently pressing the base you should be able to gauge the thickness. If there is any give, it's time to stop.

all based on the individual understanding of what the form is about and is not simply about following a set process. Just as the throwing creates something individual, the turning adds to its style and signature. You may even decide in the end that you want to have a form of two halves, for instance.

Clay consistency

Clay consistency for turning will depend on the desired result. Softer clay will allow you to make mistakes and disturb the surface more, allowing for gentle grooves or torn-edged mark-making opportunities. Harder clay will allow you to produce more machinelike, angled, mechanical surfaces with precise, sharp lines. At this stage you can also burnish the surface by compression.

Generally the clay should be firm enough to prevent any distortion during handling. The ideal is the first stage of leather hard, which feels like a mature cheddar cheese, soft enough to move slightly under pressure. Too wet and any subtracted clay will stick to the surface as it comes off. Too dry and it will be difficult to subtract without newly sharpened tools.

Support structures (chucks)

There will be occasions when you will need to use a support for turning your forms, for example, when you are dealing with intentionally uneven or fine rims that you don't want to place back on the wheel head to avoid problems like cracking, or when the form is larger than your wheel head. You will need to use support structures

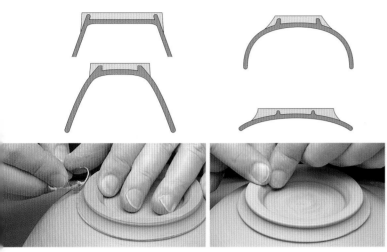

when you are turning anything with a tall neck, like a bottle, or where you have created a more sculptural form. They are ideal for wide bowls or plates when you want to avoid too much weight resting on the rim and can also provide support in the middle. If you are going to turn a lid, then you could use the form it fits on as the chuck.

Throw a thick, hollow cylinder that has a rounded rim to guard against disturbing the surface of your thrown form when turning. This could be thrown on a bat, which is removable. Partially dry the form before using it, then sit it in or on the chuck. You may need to add some fresh clay to stabilize the form. Depending on its size, don't apply too much sideways pressure, since this can force things off.

If you are going to keep changing the shape of the chuck to suit different forms you could cover it in plastic wrap and use it right away. Once used, simply rethrow the shape to suit the next form and reclaim the clay when finished.

You can make a range of different sizes of chucks and bisque fire them so you've always got a selection available. Center the chuck on the wheel head before you start. When using bisque-fired chucks, try soaking them in water before use, which will help when sticking them back on the wheel head with fresh clay.

5 Once you have created the height and depth of your foot ring you can cut an angle on the side to make wiping back the glaze much neater. The whole of the foot ring can also act as an unglazed area, giving the form greater definition. Most forms will benefit from having a turned angle at the base because this creates a shadow underneath, which provides lift to the form, and on a practical level will give you a precise point to wipe the glaze back to.

6 If you have used a grogged clay body then the surface will be rough, so after you have finished turning, and if there is still moisture in the clay, you can compress the surface using your finger or thumb. It's also very easy to burnish work at this stage, which will take away the mechanical, hard-edged feel of the surface. Wide forms like plates may have two or even three foot rings to support the base in stoneware firings.

Using a thrown chuck

You can center and fix any leather-hard form back onto the wheel head and use it as a chuck. It assists in turning a lid or any other form, especially anything with a long neck, such as a bottle.

FAULTS & REMEDIES

Uneven bases
Try holding the tool above the form with no downward pressure and let the form hit the tool. Only use a small part of the tool to create small rings on the surface. The highest part will gradually decrease as you strip away the clay.

Juddering or chattering
There are several reasons for this. Often it's the angle of the tool on the surface, so try changing it. It can also happen when the clay is too hard, or may be due to the tools not being sharp enough. If

you continue to turn, it deepens the grooves. This can create an attractive surface. The best way to get rid of it is to create small rings on the surface and then trim these off.

Work comes off after fixing with clay
The clay work is too dry. The work would be better turned on or in a chuck or on a pad of clay.

The use of plaster of Paris as a forming material has great potential. It is widely used in an industrial context and in batch production because of the smooth surface, accuracy of finish, its ability to pick up detail, and the ease of working. It is also a perfect material for molds because it is absorbent and relatively inexpensive. Plaster is calcium sulfate in powder form that becomes a solid mass when mixed with water.

MODEL MAKING: AN INTRODUCTION

Model making is inextricably linked to the concept of mold making. It is a very useful process to use when reproduction of an object in multiple is the intention. The model is the actual physical object that you would like to make a mold of, and eventually produce in clay. The mold is the negative of the object, and it enables the maker to reproduce the positive object. The main benefits of this process are that the mold will reproduce the model with faithful accuracy and allow the repetition of the object many times. Reproducing the mold will multiply the productivity of your process, in short the more molds you make, the more casts (objects) you can make.

Appropriate model-making materials
In the ceramic context plaster is the primary model-making material, though models may also be found objects or fabricated in wood, clay, or card. Each material has particular qualities that have an impact on the resolution of the model.

Plaster Plaster is a workhorse of the industrial ceramic process; chosen for its rather unique properties of being hard and absorbent with a smooth surface finish. Plaster is supplied in a powdered form and when mixed with water slowly transforms into a hard material. This change allows the maker a number of possibilities to work with it as both a model-making material and a mold-making material. Two defining characteristics ensure its popularity, the first is its ability to mold to objects and pick up fine detail, the second is its porosity, which enables the molds to be used for casting liquid clay or slip.

Plaster is calcined, hydrated calcium sulfate, which is manufactured from gypsum by heating the powdered gypsum until the water escapes. Quite simply the act of mixing it with water is reversing this process to return it to a rocklike state.

Potter's plaster A good general-purpose plaster for both model and mold making, can have a coarse finish if not blended well.

Keramicast This fine powder results in a better surface quality than potter's plaster. Good for both models and molds.

Ceram N1 plaster A good mold-making plaster, with a good surface finish and little wear and tear.

Crystical A very fine powder that takes a long time to blend, but has a very smooth surface quality. Becomes very hard and dense with little porosity. This is only suitable for model making.

The stages of making
The hand-modeled clay maquette is seen here. It informs the creation of the plaster model, which in turn defines the final slip-cast form.

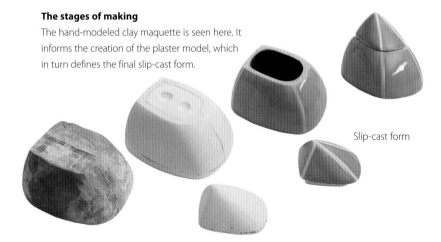

Slip-cast form

Clay maquette   Solid plaster model with lid

ORDER OF WORK:
MODEL MAKING
- prepare cup head, whirler, or sledging tools
- make templates or guides
- mix plaster
- pour plaster
- work the plaster in its required state
- finish the surface with wet and dry paper
- add seams where needed

Clay Clay has great forming qualities; it is really good for adding surface impressions, though it is very difficult to get a smooth and uniform model in this medium. It is, however, possible to form the model in clay and clean the surface of the mold up before casting to attain a uniform surface.

Wood Wood is sometimes used as a model, though the plaster mold will pick up any grain or surface pattern and transfer it to the mold surface and, in turn, the clay object.

Found models The use of found objects as models is perfectly acceptable, though it often requires an innate understanding of the mold-making process, because found objects often lead to complexities and problems. As a general rule, when you have made the object yourself you will have a good understanding of how to mold it. If you do use a found object, carefully study the object. If has been manufactured there is a strong chance it has been made in some sort of mold and will have a seam. Follow this seam when setting up your own mold.

Modeled leaf bowls
by Studio Levien
These elegant bowls have been modeled with skill and accuracy to capture the fluid line and natural taut profiles that make the object look like a natural form rather than a manufactured one.

PLASTER LEXICON
Quench To allow the plaster and water to sit in the bucket so the water breaks down any lumps of powder, helps with the mixing.

To go off This term describes the change of state from a liquid to a solid. During the chemical process the plaster becomes warm, which is an exothermic reaction.

Cottling The act of wrapping a plastic sheet around the cup head or creating clay walls into which plaster will be poured.

Early pour To pour the plaster into the mold or cottle just before the plaster begins to change; this is good for picking up detail.

Late pour To pour the plaster as it begins to thicken considerably, used on the whirler or in some sledging techniques.

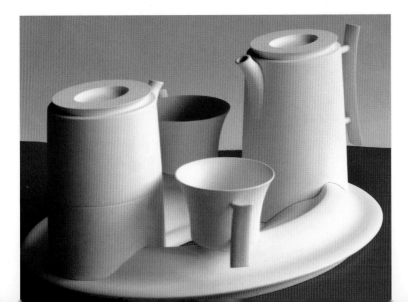

Modeled tea set
by Stephen Graham
This tea set makes good use of the plaster properties in the model-making stage. The models have been formed on top of each other by soaping the lower and creating the higher over the top, to ensure the snug fit of one onto the other.

The lathe makes cylindrical objects, and it makes them well, and the opportunity to manipulate once "off" the machine adds another dimension to this process. Lathes are either bench mounted or freestanding.

LATHE-TURNED VASES
BY ANTHONY QUINN
The lathe was a useful tool to ensure an accurate fitting of the two components of these vases. The dual functions have been broken down; with the water held in a shallow dish and the flower supported by the neck of the object.

MODEL MAKING: LATHE TURNING

The advantage of turning on a lathe is the ability to produce symmetrical, cylindrical objects. It can seem limited as a process, but it takes some time to master the skill, and the resolution of the surface quality once you do can be exceptional.

As with most plaster processes, planning and preparation is key. Most of the processes require a methodological approach. It is important to work in a systematic way, because the process of model generation is a long one, and it is important not to make a mistake that means you need to start over.

The first stage of the process is getting the plaster from its powder state to a solid one that can be offered up to the lathe. In order to get it onto a lathe the plaster must be poured into a cup head or around a spindle. Wrap the cottling material around the cup head or spindle, and mix the plaster thoroughly, paying attention to

the plaster/water ratio. As the plaster begins to go off, pour slowly into the cottle using one continuous motion, trying not to add air into the mix since this will make bubbles in the plaster, which in turn will make the surface difficult to finish smoothly.

When the plaster is hard it is then wound onto the machine. The plaster is turned in much the same way as wood would be turned. Plaster is a relatively soft material, so when turning you must be careful. It is possible to translate your shape design to the plaster model using rulers, calipers, and card profiles.

Making a card profile

To do this you must first create a technical drawing (see pages 294–295). The purpose of the drawing is to capture your design in a format that allows you to transcribe information onto

---

TECHNIQUE FILE **54**

MAKING A CARD PROFILE

The accuracy of the plaster process is ensured by the use of card profiles and templates, which allow you to transcribe the profile from the drawing to your model.

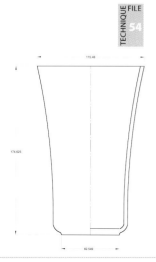

1 From the technical drawing of your object, take a copy and stick to a firm piece of card with spray glue.

2 Firmly cut along the profile in one continuous motion, using a sharp scalpel. If you do it slowly, it is easy to do it freehand.

3 The profile is the area outside of your drawn object. Cut it into a comfortable size to hold. You will use this to check the model against your drawing.

the plaster. Essential tools for this transcription are pencils, rulers, calipers, and a profile made from a stiff card.

Making a profile is simple: stick your drawing onto a stiff piece of card and cut it out using a sharp scalpel. The profile is the area outside of your drawn object. The purpose of the profile is to allow you to compare your object to the drawing by simply placing the profile along the surface of the model.

Using the lathe

When the plaster is hard, after 30 minutes or so, strip the cottle away and wind it onto the lathe. Make sure this is completely secure before you begin turning, and familiarize yourself with the machine before you start to use it.

Switch the machine on, and look carefully at the way the plaster rotates; it may appear to vibrate as it spins. This means you have to center it: take a chisel and press it into the plaster firmly with the flat side up. Working from the outside in, toward the machine, repeat this along the form until the object is completely centered. You can tell when you've achieved this by taking a pencil and making a mark while the plaster rotates. If the line goes all the way around, the plaster is centered. Use calipers to transfer the height from your drawing, and make a mark to show this. Then make a mark for the widest diameter. With the chisel, turn the cylinder down to this widest diameter.

COTTLING UP

This term is used to describe the act of wrapping the plastic sheet around the cup head.

1 Plaster is turned on a converted wood lathe using a specially made cup head or spindle; this is used to fit the hard plaster to the lathe.

2 Use a flexible clean sheet of plastic to cottle around the cup head, securing it with a clip and some string or masking tape.

3 Fill in any gaps between the cup head and the plastic with soft clay "sausages" (see detail) pressed firmly into the join.

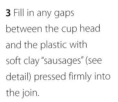

4 Mix enough plaster to fill the cottle to the required height. Pour into the cup head in one continuous motion, taking care not to add air into the mix.

5 Gently tap the top surface with the back of your hand—this will bring any trapped air to the surface.

LATHE TURNING

The lathe is a simple machine to use but a complex one to master. It takes practice to achieve a smooth finish and accurate profile.

1 Study the rotating plaster; if it appears to be vibrating as it spins, then you will need to center it. Work toward the machine, until the object is centered.

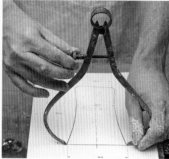

2 Using sprung calipers, accurately measure each of the key dimensions of your object in turn. There is a natural order to this, from widest diameter to thinnest, due simply to the process of removing material.

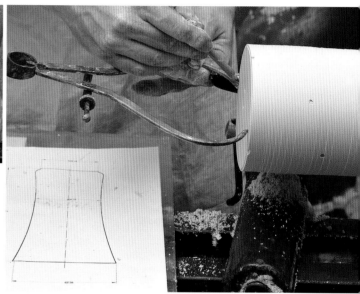

3 Working from your technical drawing, use a ruler to transfer the height to the plaster, and calipers to mark the widest diameter. Take a chisel and trim the cylinder down to this widest diameter.

4 Repeat the process to transcribe the smallest diameter to the plaster and trim the material away to indicate this.

5 Begin to plot the profile with the chisel from the smallest to the widest diameter. Take care not to trim too much plaster away.

6 Use the card template to check your progress. If the profile touches an area but not either side, this tells you that the touching area is high and needs more turning.

Use the chisel to turn between the reference points, taking away as much of the unwanted material as possible. Be careful—it is easy to take away too much material at this stage. When you form the plaster it is important to use card profiles, which allow you to check the shape against your drawing. Always work toward the machine; the plaster is less likely to snap off. As you get close to your required shape, use the card profile to check against the model.

When you are happy that the shape is correct, take a flexible kidney and move this across the surface, gently applying pressure—this will help take any grooves out of the surface. To achieve a final smooth surface, use wet and dry paper, dip it into water, and gently polish the surface. As the wet and dry paper becomes worn it is more useful for this process, so do not throw it away after use.

If the object is not a drop-out shape (it has no undercuts, see page 144) then you will have to make a seam or center line around the form in order to make a two-piece (or more) mold. It is easiest to do this while the model is still connected to the lathe. Place a sheet of glass on the bed of

the lathe, take a surface gauge, and make sure that the point is in the center of the model. Scribe a line around the model on both sides.

The safest way to get the model off the machine is to cut it off with a plaster saw and chisels. Using your chisel, trim the spare material away until you have approximately 50 percent of the material left. Use a plaster saw and the help of an assistant to hold the model while you carefully cut it off. Finish off using a surform and metal scrapers.

INTERLOCKING VASES
BY DAMIAN EVANS
These colorful vases are the result of very accurate turning and measuring while on the lathe. Each colored section is interchangeable, requiring very accurate fittings to be turned in the bottom of each model and an equally accurate casting process.

7 As the profile of the object gets closer to what you want, switch to serrated kidneys to cut the ridges away, then flexible metal kidneys. Gently apply pressure and move backward and forward up the object to make a smooth line.

8 When the profile is finished, turn the foot into base of the object using fine chisels and flexible kidneys. Leave a slight dimple in the plaster that will guide the setting of the surface gauge for seaming on the lathe.

9 Place a sheet of glass on the bed of the lathe, and use a center gauge to fix it to the dimple in the foot. Drag the gauge needle along the length of the object to scratch in a permanent seam line (see detail).

10 To remove the object, use a general-purpose plaster saw. It is important to ask for help to saw the object off the cup head to avoid the risk of damaging the model.

The whirler is essentially a plaster head on a motorized wheel. The plaster head can vary in diameter, though as a rule it is fairly wide and is primarily used for making wide, open shapes such as bowls and dishes.

MODEL MAKING: WHIRLER TURNING

You will need a card profile, prepared from a technical drawing (see pages 294–295), as well as chisels, calipers, and flexible kidneys to use the whirler. There is a tool rest, which is pressed into the shoulder blade and into the wooden board behind the whirler, on which your hand must securely lock your tool to ensure a smooth turning motion. If you do not securely connect to the tool rest then the chisel will vibrate as the plaster rotates. It will probably take a number of attempts to become confident, but over time this process will become much easier. The plaster is turned when soft, so working on the whirler is relatively quick.

Starting to turn

To set up you must first soap the whirler head three times. If the whirler is wide and the diameter of your object is considerably less, you should first turn a shallow retaining disk. To do this, soap the head, then mix some plaster and simply pour it directly onto the head until it is about ¾ in (2 cm) high. While the plaster is still soft, turn the edge of the disk so it is centered and at 90 degrees to the head, then turn the disk flat from the center to the edge until it is approximately 2 in (6 cm) wider than the object. Follow this by turning a recess into the disk for the plaster to lock into.

When the plaster disk is hard, wrap the plastic cottle tightly around it. Mix the plaster and pour carefully into the disk, then wait until the plaster can support its own weight (but is still soft) before unwrapping the cottle. Once unwrapped, it is important to remove as much excess material as quickly as possible. Holding the tool against the rest, trim the material away, taking care not to remove too much. You should already have prepared your card profile and drawing (see page 124). Use calipers to measure the diameter and make sure that you trim from the center out and back again, until the shape of the plaster is close to that of the drawing and profile. Offer your template up to the model to check the accuracy of the plaster model. You can repeat this process a number of times and with less urgency as the plaster goes off, as long as you have removed most of the plaster. Finish the surface with slightly worn wet and dry paper.

Once the model is complete, you can choose to make the mold straight onto the object. Simply soap the model, cottle around it, and pour plaster over the model.

Creamware steamer

BY ANTHONY QUINN

The benefit of using the whirler is that some of the detail on the top rim could be formed before pouring on the plaster, from which the actual model was turned.

WHIRLER TURNING

Turning on the whirler combines the accuracy of turning on the lathe with the skill and speed of sledging.

1 To set up the whirler, turn a flat disk approximately 2 in (6 cm) wider than the object, at 90 degrees to the head, and trim a recess into the disk for the plaster to lock into. Once hard, wrap the plastic cottle tightly around the plaster disk.

2 Having poured the plaster (see detail), wait until the plaster can support its own weight before removing the cottling.

3 It is important to remove as much excess material as quickly as possible. Hold the tool against the rest in your strongest hand and press down with your other hand. Begin to move the tool from the center to the edge.

4 Start to shape the object by rotating your tool in line with your profile; take care not to remove too much plaster. Use calipers to check the diameter and card profiles to check the shape. As the plaster becomes hard it is a good idea to stick it to the whirler head with wet clay (see detail).

5 Use a range of tools, such as flexible metal kidneys, to remove ridges in the surface.

6 Finish and polish the surface using wet and dry paper, the older and more worn the better.

Sledging is essentially extruding with plaster. It relies on thorough planning and preparation, and time spent making tools and profiles by hand is rewarded by this simple and immediate modeling process.

MODEL MAKING: SLEDGING

Sledging is a modeling technique that has huge potential. The name "sledging" describes the act of dragging a profile through wet plaster. Advance preparation of templates and tools allows you to form the plaster with comparative ease. The technique relies on you developing an understanding of the properties of the plaster. Once understood, the process is almost infinite in its potential—sledged models may be linear, formed in a sweep or arc, around a template, inside a gig, or over a hump. Sledging can be used to make solid models for production or shell models for presentation purposes.

Sledging is a very old technique. It was used in the past to extrude long lengths of architectural detailing such as cornicing. (It is said to be called sledging after long pieces of cornicing that required a number of men to complete the job. They would pour a great quantity of plaster in front of the huge profile. It would need two

HOW TO MAKE THE TOOLS

TECHNIQUE FILE **58**

The sledging technique relies on a degree of planning and preparation, but preparing the template and profile will eventually allow you to form plaster with ease.

1 Working from a detailed technical drawing, cut out the shape of your profile in metal using a jeweler's saw. In the same manner, use the jeweler's saw to cut out the template shape in Perspex.

2 Finish both the profile and the template with files and wet and dry paper until they are smooth.

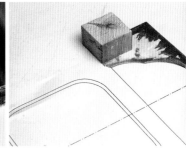

3 Stick the profile to a wooden block at a 90-degree angle to the cutting face. It should stand up on its own.

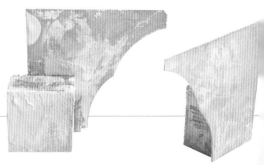

or three men to push the tool and the youngest apprentice would be required to sit on top of it to weigh it down, looking as if he was riding on a sleigh—or "sledge"—through the snow.) Often, architectural details would be sledged in situ.

Making tools for sledging

This technique relies on a degree of planning and preparation. First make a drawing of your object. The top view, or plan, will become the template and the side view, or elevation, will become the profile. This is a general rule—there are some cases where this order is reversed to help with ease of making. When you have this information, make a copy of the drawing, cut out the two views, and stick them to a piece of zinc or metal for the profile and Perspex for the template. You can use other materials for the templates, such as wood or plastic, but whatever you choose you must be able to work the edge into a continuous smooth surface because any bumps, ridges, or texture will be transferred to the model.

To cut the metal, use a jeweler's saw and bench peg. The bench peg will support the metal as you cut into it. The saw blade is very fragile and is fixed in a taut line between the jaws of the saw. Hold the tool at a slight angle, so that the top of the saw is leaning forward toward the metal, and, with a steady up-and-down motion, cut the diagram out of the metal. The metal will be left with a rough edge, which must be filed down and polished. Place the metal in a vise and carefully work the rough edge with a medium-grade metal file. Once the profile is fairly smooth, finish the edge with a range of fine needle files, working along the length of the profile in long sweeps and angling from the front to the back of the tool so it develops a slight angle, similar to the cutting face of a chisel. To finish, use fine wet and dry paper.

Cut out the template using a band saw. Stick the paper plan onto the surface and try to cut around the shape to within $\frac{1}{32}$ in (1 mm) of the line. The band saw has quite an aggressive cut, so you will be left with some work to do to get this smooth. Work through a collection of files from heavy to fine, filing along the length of the edge to smooth it.

TECHNIQUE FILE 59

PROFILING BY HAND

This versatile technique is limited only by the relationship between the profile and the plan on your technical drawings.

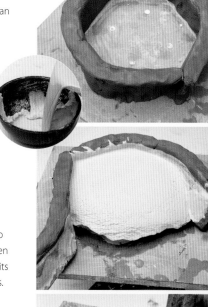

1 Make the profile of the shape in metal, take the plan view, and cut out a template in Perspex. Drill holes into the flat face of the template and glue this to a smooth board or sheet of glass. Place this board onto a banding wheel and secure with clay.

2 Build a strong clay wall around the template, leaving a $\frac{1}{32}$–$\frac{1}{16}$-in (1–2-mm) gap all around, and ensuring that the wall is no more than ¼ in (5 mm) higher than the top of the tool.

3 Blend a generous amount of plaster as usual, but immediately after breaking down the lumps in the mixing process, decant approximately one-fifth of this mix into a clean bowl (see detail). This separate mixture will have the same properties as the first but will go off at a slower rate, therefore creating a repair mixture.

4 When the plaster is ready, pour it into the clay walls. After a few minutes, when the plaster is still soft and will support its own weight, carefully remove the walls.

5 Use a scraper or the back of the profile to clean away the plaster until it is touching the template.

"Profiling by hand" continues on the next page ⟶

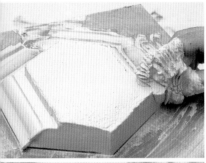

6 Hold the profile perpendicular to the template and press gently into the plaster. At the same time, rotate the wheel with your other hand so the tool cuts away the plaster.

7 Repeat the process, cutting away any excess plaster in a series of "sweeps" until the profile touches the template. When the profile has removed all of the plaster to achieve the final shape, you may need to drizzle water over the model to ease the passage of the profile and smooth the surface. On the first strike through the plaster it is very likely that the surface will contain blemishes and holes (see detail).

8 Use the decanted mix to repair any holes. Slowly drizzle it over the surface, and pull the profile over the model, cutting away the new soft plaster until it has repaired the holes on the model and the plaster hump. This will help create a smooth surface and repair any blemishes or nicks.

9 Use a hand surform to remove any excess plaster as soon as you are able, the softer the plaster is, the easier it is to remove.

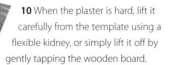

10 When the plaster is hard, lift it carefully from the template using a flexible kidney, or simply lift it off by gently tapping the wooden board.

Hand profiling

"Hand profiling" describes the method of dragging a profile around a template. It lends itself to forms that are wider than they are tall, such as bowls or dishes.

Make a detailed technical drawing (see pages 294–295), and a profile of the shape. Stick this tool to a wooden block that allows it to stand up of its own accord at 90 degrees to the surface. Take the plan view and cut out a template in Perspex or another rigid material; work this until it has a smooth edge. Drill holes into the flat face of the Perspex and glue this to a smooth board or sheet of glass. Place this board onto a banding wheel, securing it with clay so it does not move.

Mix a generous amount of plaster and decant some into a separate bowl. Cottle around the template and pour in the plaster. Once the plaster can support, itself remove the clay walls. Subtract the excess plaster with the back of the profile and then you can begin sweeping through the plaster with the profile perpendicular to the template. Repair any blemishes resulting from the repeated sweeps with the decanted plaster.

You might end up with a slight ripple effect on the surface. This can be removed with worn wet and dry paper rubbed over the wet surface.

Bench/jack sledging

This process results in a linear model. It can be any length, though it should have an inherent

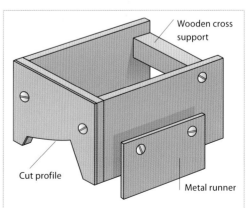

Wooden cross support

Cut profile

Metal runner

Wooden bench/jack sledging frame
This diagram illustrates a simple wooden sledging frame, built to the exact size of the profile. The running edge is created using a second piece of metal screwed to the edge.

Sledged platters
By Stephen Grahams

Two models were used to make this piece. The first was made by the profile, then the profile is cut again into another shape. After soaping the model a second model is sledged over the first.

strength in its depth, otherwise it is liable to snap when you lift it from the surface.

As before, you will make a drawing and cut a profile in metal. The difference here lies in the fact that the profile fits to a jack. This is simply a rigid frame that fits square to the edge of the bench or glass surface. The frame shown here is a steel system for a specialist model maker; it could be as simple as a rudimentary frame made of wood (see illustration). The profile is screwed to the front of the frame with a backing plate of wood or MDF, to keep the thin metal from buckling as the plaster goes off (see page 123). The most important factor is the relationship between the edge of the surface you are modeling onto and the edge of the frame that rests on this. It is of vital importance that this running edge and the adjoining surfaces of the frame are clear of any debris, and both straight and true.

When the frame and profile are built, you are ready to make the model. The first step is to mix the plaster as before, remembering to decant a small amount of the mixture into a bowl and leave it to stand. You will also need a bowl of clean water and a sponge.

You will note that there are no cottling walls to hold the plaster in place. That is because when removing the walls the clay has a tendency to stick to the glass and leave debris behind. Instead of walls this process relies on a confidence and

TECHNIQUE FILE 60

BENCH/JACK SLEDGING

This has many potential uses, as long as the maker is inventive in cutting and assembling the form.

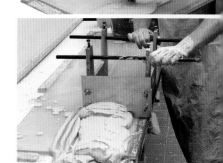

1 Mix a generous amount of plaster and decant; ladle the plaster directly onto the glass, in the general direction of the model. Build up layers with your hand.

2 Grip the front of the frame with your preferred hand and the rear with your other hand; gently push the frame and tool through the plaster.

3 Once you get to the end, lift the frame slowly and return to the beginning. Clean the tool and running edge at the start of each sweep. As the plaster goes off, you will feel more resistance as you try to push. To make it easier, drizzle some water over the model.

4 Repair any blemishes or holes in the model by using the decanted plaster (see detail). Give the mix a vigorous stir until it begins to go off, drizzle water over the damaged area, and liberally apply the soft plaster.

5 To finish the process, clean the tool and push it through the model again. You may repeat this two or three times to achieve a good surface finish. Once the plaster has hardened, polish it with wet and dry paper.

MAKING A SHELL MODEL BY SLEDGING

Using the sledging technique, first make the template and two profiles. The first profile (top left) will be used to make the inside space, known as a hump; the second (bottom left) to make the model itself.

1 Build a clay wall (cottle) around the Perspex and mix and pour the plaster into the walls. Let it stand until it can support its own weight, then remove the wall slowly (see detail).

2 Using a metal edge, work the plaster back to the template and then strike the profile through the plaster, holding it firmly while pressing down to the board.

3 Take care to finish the surface of the hump so it is smooth and free of blemishes—kidneys and wet and dry paper are good for this. When the hump is complete, soap this part of the model and set the first profile to one side.

understanding of the plaster material. The plaster should be blended for a little longer than when pouring into molds or cup heads; as it reaches a cheeselike consistency it is ladled onto the surface and slowly built up to a suitable height.

Taking hold of the front of the frame with your favored hand and the rear with your other hand, gently push the frame and the tool through the plaster. When you get to the end, lift the frame slowly and return to the other end. Be sure to clean the tool and running edge before repeating the process. You can use the plaster cut away by the tool to do running repairs to the model. As the plaster goes off, the smooth running of the tool will become difficult and you will feel more resistance as you try to push. Use your pot of water and liberally drizzle water over the model. This will allow you to push the tool through again to polish the surface.

Any blemishes or holes in the model can be repaired using the second mix; give the mix a vigorous stir until it begins to go off, drizzle

water over the damaged area, and liberally apply the soft plaster. Clean the tool and push it through the model again—you may repeat this two or three times to achieve a good surface finish. Let the plaster harden before polishing it with wet and dry paper.

Finessing your skill

An interesting result of this process is that as you become more attuned to its potential and start to improvise with the orientation or the geometric dissection of the model, the planning and preparation increases in inverse proportion to the plasterwork. In general, where more work has been vested into the tools, frames, and gigs, the plasterwork will be more straightforward.

Wider applications

Traditionally, architectural detailing on cornices, arches, and architraving would have been modeled using the sledging processes described. For curves, the same method of frame and tool

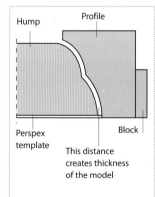

Making a shell model

The illustration shows the relationship between the hump, template, and outer profile. The difference in depth that creates the gap between hump and profile will determine the thickness of the hollow model.

4 Soap the hump thoroughly and build a clay wall around the template, taking care not to overlap onto the template. When this is done, mix enough plaster to cover the hump. During the blending process, make sure to decant some plaster into a second container, as this will be used later. Pour the plaster into the clay wall in a gentle continuous motion.

5 It is important to begin modeling the plaster as soon as possible. Once it begins to set, pull the clay wall away as carefully as you can. When this is done, you will be left with a soft mound of plaster. Take a scraper, press it into the plaster, and drag it around the template so that you can see the edge of the Perspex template at the base.

6 Take your second profile and gently press it into the plaster. Work away the excess plaster by pulling the profile around the template. Work carefully, in a number of sweeps. When finished, repair any blemishes on the surface of the model with the decanted plaster. Stir it vigorously and apply a liberal amount of water to the surface, followed by the decanted plaster. Work your profile tool just across this part of the surface.

7 Smooth the surface with a kidney. You can then polish the surface of the model using old wet and dry paper to remove any scratches from the tool.

is used, but the frame is fixed to an armature, which in turn is fixed to an axis. The radius of the arc is determined by the distance from the axis to the frame—shorten this distance and the arc will get tighter, lengthen the distance and the arc will open out and get longer.

Making a shell model by sledging

A shell model is a thin, hollow plaster model, often used as a prototype or visual model. Using the sledging technique, first make the template and two profiles. The first profile will be used to make the inside space, known as a hump; the second to make the model itself. When the preparation is complete, the first task is to make the hump. Build a clay wall around the Perspex, mix the plaster, and pour it into the walls. Let it stand until it can support its own weight, then remove it and slowly strike the profile through the plaster. When the hump is complete, soap this part of the model and set the first profile to one side. Taking up the second profile, you will

8 Allow the plaster to harden—this usually takes about 30 minutes. When this has happened, you should be able to gently lift the shell model off the hump.

TECHNIQUE FILE 62

SLEDGING OVER A GIG

This is a very effective way of modeling something that would otherwise be rather complicated to model by hand. The templates are fixed to the wood using small screws, which allow you to disassemble the gig when the plaster has gone off.

4 Coat the surface with water (see detail) and add your decanted mix to the surface.

1 This gig makes one half of a model, to be repeated and stuck together to make a whole. The wooden section is the elevation; the two Perspex templates give half of the top and bottom shapes. As the profile is straight, a metal ruler is used as the profile tool.

5 As the plaster expands the profile is more difficult to pull over the surface; continue to add water and pull the profile slowly over the surface.

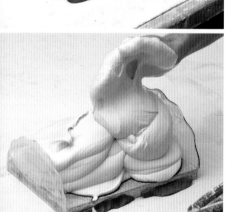

2 Ladle plaster into the gig as it begins to go off; this means it will hold its own form and you do not need to build walls. Decant some plaster into a separate bowl to repair any blemishes later.

6 Let the plaster harden and polish with some wet and dry paper. Unscrew one end of the gig to remove the template.

7 Lift the model out of the gig and repeat the process to make the second half of the model.

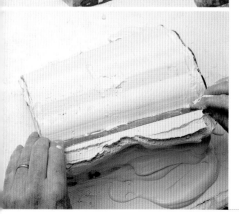

3 When the gig is full, draw the ruler across the Perspex templates to form the plaster—it is likely that you will have to add plaster a few times to reach the highest point in the gig.

start to make the model now. Build a clay wall (cottle) around the template, taking care not to overlap onto the template. When this is done, mix enough plaster to cover the hump.

During the blending process, make sure to decant some plaster into a second container, since this will be used later. Pour the plaster into the clay wall in a gentle, continuous motion. It is important to begin modeling the plaster as soon as possible. Watch the surface of the wet plaster. The reflection will begin to recede, indicating that it is setting. Pull the clay wall away as carefully as you can. When this is done, you will be left with a soft mound of plaster. Take a scraper, press it into the plaster, and drag it around the template so that you can see the edge of the Perspex template at the base. Then take your profile and gently press it into the plaster. Work away the excess plaster by pulling the profile around the template. Work carefully, in a number of sweeps. When the shape is secured, and you cannot work the plaster any more, take the plaster you decanted earlier and stir it vigorously. Locate any blemishes on the surface of the model and apply a liberal amount of water to the surface, followed by the decanted plaster. Work your profile tool across only this part of the surface. Let the plaster go off—this usually takes about 30 minutes. When this has happened, you should be able to lift the shell model off the hump.

Sledging over a gig

If your design is geometric in plan, for example, a hexagon, then the model can be divided up like a piece of cake and made in sections. This is a particularly clever approach to modeling because it does not affect the profile, it is simply an economical way of tackling a complex form. This method requires three components: the gig, which is effectively a stand with the angle of the section cut into it (so if the model is divided into six pieces then the angle will be 60 degrees); the profile, which is cut into two pieces of Perspex and stuck to the gig; and the section of the plan (one-sixth), made in metal.

The process of making the model section is very simple. Ladle a late pour into the Perspex profiles on the gig and pull the tool toward you

SLEDGING A BENCH IN SITU

Studio Glithero's work is concerned with process and craftsmanship. Recording their method of creation is often as important as the work itself.

TECHNIQUE FILE 63

1 Due to the size of the object to be modeled, a wooden frame is built in the shape of the bench for the plaster to hang on. The profile is given a box structure to keep it perpendicular to the floor, and an armature connects the profile to the central axis.

2 The scale of the model requires a team for each stage. Plaster is mixed almost continuously and applied to the frame in a steady rhythm to build up the structure. The profile is pushed slowly through the plaster. After each sweep the profile is lifted off the arm and cleaned thoroughly before repeating the process.

3 The object is built up in layers of plaster formed over each other until the final shape and surface is achieved.

4 The final benches are left in the gallery with the axis remaining in place as a clue to its method of manufacture.

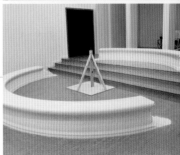

along the length of the frame. You will only need to do this two or three times, then polish the face, and it will be finished. You can either repeat this or make a mold of the section and pour into the mold a number of times to complete the model.

This process can be completed for any combination of pieces—the essential innovation is in dissecting the model in order to make the making easier.

Modeling by hand is essential to making handles, spouts, and asymmetric organic forms. There are a number of different methodologies, though it is easier when making handles and spouts if you try to introduce a degree of accuracy into the process by using template tools and calipers.

MODEL MAKING: HANDLES AND SPOUTS

Handles and spouts are both modeled by hand and require tenacity and patience, since they can be particularly taxing. The most effective way of making both items is by building in geometry and accuracy through the use of technical drawings (see pages 294–295), rulers, calipers, profiles, and templates. Hand modeling of plaster can be very time consuming, so it is a good idea to make card profiles of handles and spouts to assess their design qualities before embarking on making them in plaster. Both require many of the same skills, but they start from different positions.

Making a handle

The most effective way of making a handle model is to cut it from a plaster bat. As a general rule, use a higher-density plaster such as Crystical R to make handles. This will make for a stronger model, which will be important as the plaster is removed. If you find this too difficult to model,

then try mixing it 50:50 with a softer plaster such as potter's plaster.

First prepare a plaster bat (see page 143) to the correct depth for the cross section of the handle. Cut this bat to a perfect square and transcribe the inside and outside profiles of the handle onto the bat. Next, use a saw to cut the body profile along one edge of the bat so that it will fit up against the body. Next, cut the outside shape followed by the inside shape. Draw the handle cross section on either end of the plaster handle profile and model the handle so it is completely square in section, using an engineer's square. Using calipers and a ruler, measure the bat and transcribe the center line of the model all the way around the object. Repeat this action using a card profile and a ruler to create a center line around the elevation view of the handle.

The object will have effectively been divided into quarters—this thorough approach increases

Modeled bowls
by Simon Stevens
These elegant mixing bowls have relied on the same hand-modeling process as used in making a spout. The snip (the spout opening) has been modeled in plaster and fitted as illustrated on page 141.

MODELING A HANDLE

Modeling a handle in plaster is one of the most difficult techniques to master. Using a hard plaster such as Crystical R will help, because plaster can become very fragile as you realize your intended shape.

TECHNIQUE FILE 64

1 Stick your technical drawing to a firm piece of card and cut out carefully using a sharp scalpel.

2 Using a fine marker or indelible pencil, carefully draw around your template, transcribing your handle design onto the plaster bat.

3 Carefully cut the plaster out either by hand using a coping saw or by using a band saw. Try to cut to within under ⅛ in (3 mm) of the handle profile.

4 When the handle shape is cut from the bat the first step is to make the handle square. Use a surform to remove most of the material and follow with a fine-toothed riffler (see detail). Continue to remove until the guidelines have just been scraped away.

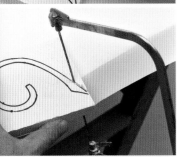

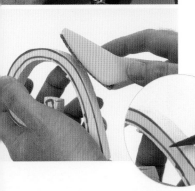

5 Use a ruler or caliper to mark the center point along the inside and outside of the handle. Holding the pencil or marker tight in your fingers, place the point on the mark and your supporting finger against the flat edge of the plaster. Draw your hand in one continuous motion along the plaster, joining the points with one line.

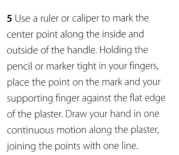

6 The key to modeling the handle is to see it as a series of sections. Using a riffler, work away the corner of the square block to join the edge to the center line. Using a cross-hatch motion you will be able to quickly form your shape along this quadrant. Repeat this process, first completing the back and then the inside.

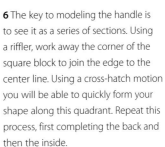

7 As the shape is secured you need to get a smoother surface. First use needle files in a cross-hatch motion and smooth with wet and dry paper (see detail).

8 Check the final model against your drawing, looking in particular at the cross section to ensure a constant thickness. Watch for any change in section thickness that would indicate that the profile had not been modeled properly.

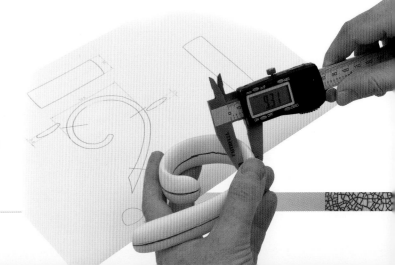

the chances of creating a symmetrical handle. Choose one of the outside quadrants and begin to shape it using knives, rifflers, and needle files. Take care not to cross either of the center lines, because this will mean you are changing the overall shape. When this section is very close to being finished, switch to the corresponding inside quadrant and model it in the same way. When one side of the handle is complete except for the polishing, flip it over and repeat the process. Upon completion of the entire shape, polish the surface with fine and then old wet and dry paper. Check the handle against the drawings and the model to make sure you're happy with it.

Making a spout

Make the spout model in the same systematic way as the handle, beginning with a different technique. Seam your model to obtain a center line at which the spout will join (see step 5, page 139), make two natches (see page 143) in the body, and soap it. Build a clay wall onto the body and prop it at an angle so that you can easily pour plaster into this rudimentary mold. Let the plaster go off before removing the walls, leaving a slightly rough object. The challenge is to achieve geometry and accuracy in the early modeling stages. Cut the spout so it is a square block, add center lines, and model in quadrants, taking care to use a series of profiles as you go. When all of the quadrants are complete, finish with both fine and used wet and dry paper.

MODELED HANDLES
BY STUDIO LEVIEN
This design has a lyric to its shape. The modeling detail on the body of the pot flows into the voluptuous handle. It takes a great deal of finesse to create an elegant line that seems natural.

TECHNIQUE FILE **65**

MODELING A SPOUT

Like the handle, the most successful approach to modeling in plaster is to use a range of devices that allow you to introduce accuracy into the process.

1 First, model two small natches into the surface of the model, these will help you locate the spout at each stage. Soap the model thoroughly and build a clay wall on the side of the pot.

5 Work away most of the material with the surform to achieve a rough shape. Use a riffler to finish the shape until it is close to finished (see detail).

MODELED TEA SERVICE
BY CHAI-YING LIN
The thoroughness and skill of the modeling in this tea service can be seen in the similarity of quality between the large and small handles.

2 Mix a small amount of plaster and pour slowly into the clay walls.

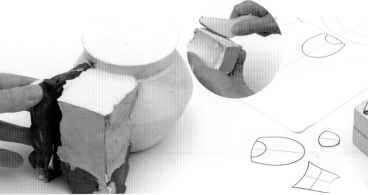

3 Remove the walls after 30–40 minutes and use a surform to square the block up (see detail).

4 As with the handle, measure and transcribe a center line. Using profiles taken from your technical drawing trace the profile (side view) and the plan (top view) of the handle onto the block.

6 Finish the surface until smooth using needle files, and fine wet and dry paper.

Modeled plaster spout

The finished spout model can be seen on the body model, held on with an elastic band. The drawings and profiles are essential in achieving such a symmetrical finish.

Plaster is a great material for molds, because it is poured over the model as a liquid and then becomes a solid, making it ideal for picking up detail. It also has the advantage of being highly porous when dry, making it great for use with clay, particularly for slip casting, when the plaster will draw the moisture out of the clay and create a cast object.

MOLD MAKING: THE SEQUENCE

Molds are used for a number of craft processes, such as press molding and in industrial manufacturing processes, such as slip casting or jigger/jolleying. It is important to take care and spend time at the mold-making stage, following the procedure thoroughly and conscientiously; if you cut corners here, you will undermine all the good work you did in the earlier stages, and probably lose your model in the process.

It is important to design and model the form and then work out how to mold it. If you design the form while worrying about how to mold it, you will diminish the overall success of your design. Once you are confident with model and mold making, you will naturally design things that can be molded.

Using soft soap as a resist
Plaster will stick to plaster, so it is important to use a material as a resist. A number of materials

can be used, but the most effective is soap. The soap process is a very simple one, using a soft—preferably natural—sponge to generously apply soap to the surface of the model and other plaster surfaces, such as bats. Work this into a lather in circular motions, taking care to cover the entire model. Wash it off using clean water until no soap can be seen. Repeat this action twice more. The reason for soaping three times is to ensure that the whole surface is covered and that you get a good barrier in the model. After cottling around the model you may wish to do one more light soap to remove any fingerprints, clay, or debris before casting the mold over the model.

Making a plaster bat
To set up a split mold you will first need a plaster bat—a very straightforward thing to make. First get a hold of two pieces of wood equal in length and depth—approximately 1 in (2.5 cm). Place the pieces of wood on glass, 8 in (20 cm) apart, with wet clay pressed into the wood and the glass to keep them from sliding apart. You will need a long, straight edge—a metal ruler is perfect. Mix a quantity of plaster to fill the space between the pieces of wood. You do not need to build walls at

Molded tableware
BY NICOLE MUELLER
This collection of slip-cast tableware was manufactured using molds. It hangs together well due to the relationships created by details such as color and fluting.

ORDER OF WORK:
MOLD MAKING
• seam the model if
it has not been done
previously
• add the spare
• soap the model
• set in plaster bat or clay
• cottle up
• mix plaster and pour

• clean up seams
• add natches
• soap
• cottle up and repeat
mix/pouring
• finish back of mold for
safety and long life

THE MOLD-MAKING LEXICON

Drop-out mold When set, the model will simply "drop out" of the mold.

Spare This is the reservoir at the top of molds used in slip casting. It allows you to fill the mold up to and above the top of the object, ensuring a good, even cast.

Undercut This describes the area of a model that will not release or drop out of the mold. This usually requires the mold to be split or made up of more than one part.

Soft soap This is the resist material used to create a nonporous barrier on a plaster model so that it does not stick to the mold.

Natches (above) These are the positive and negative locations that help the mold lock together. They usually appear on adjoining faces of the mold.

Plaster bat A flat, smooth slab of plaster that is used to set up molds, it helps make perfect joins and seams in multipart molds.

Seam This is the line along which the mold will split.

---

either end, because this process requires a late pour (see page 123). As the plaster starts to go off, pour it between the bits of wood, gently tapping the plaster with your hand until it levels out. Then, taking the steel ruler in both hands, gently draw it across the plaster until you have a flat surface. It is good practice to have the wood and glass set up whenever you are mixing plaster so you can make a bat out of any plaster that is left over.

How to make natches

Natches are locators that allow one side of a mold to fit exactly to the other. They can be premade in plaster or more often are modeled into the plaster. To model into the plaster, place the first side of the mold onto a wheel, if it is not already on one, and, using a round-ended tool or a good-sized coin, spin the mold while pressing down with the tool. This will cause the tool to cut a recess into the mold face; this is the negative part of the natch. The positive part will be integral to the other side of the mold.

Making a drop-out mold

The drop-out mold is the most simple mold configuration. Its name describes the fact that

---

MAKING A PLASTER BAT

To set up a multipart mold you will first need a plaster bat. This is a very straightforward thing to make, though also very important, as it makes for a clean surface finish to each side of the mold.

1 Place two pieces of wood, approx ½–¾ in (15–20 mm) deep on glass 7¾ in (20 cm) apart, secured in place with wet clay. Use a long straight edge to form the back of the bat; the front is formed on the surface of the glass; a metal ruler is ideal.

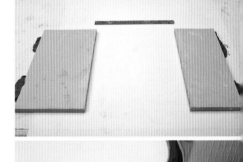

2 Mix enough plaster to fill the space in between the wood. This process requires a late pour; as the plaster starts to go off, pour it between the two bits of wood.

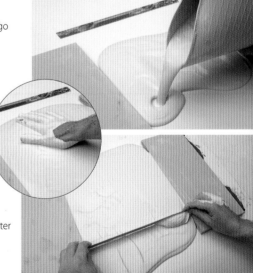

3 Level the plaster out between the pieces of wood by gently tapping it. Carefully draw the steel ruler across the surface of the plaster until it is flat.

---

the model will simply "drop out." This type of mold is made when the object has no undercuts. Making such a mold is very quick but still requires a thorough approach. If your object is round in plan then set it up on a turned disk on the whirler or on a circular bat of plaster. You need to ensure that the disk is approximately 1 in (2.5 cm) wider than the widest diameter of the object. As a general rule, the object will be cast through its widest point, so this surface must be placed face down—the mold will therefore

DROP-OUT MOLD MADE ON A WHIRLER

The model below has been turned on the whirler onto a disk of plaster to define the outside of the mold and the thickness of the mold.

1 With a natural sponge, work the soap into a lather in circular motions, taking care to cover the entire model and bat. Wash this off using clean water until no soap can be seen. Repeat this action twice more to ensure that all surfaces have been soaped.

2 Take a piece of plastic and wrap it tightly around the plaster bat, and secure it with a clip and tape or string.

3 After pouring the plaster (see detail), clean up the mold by centering and turning the back flat (see page 129).

4 To finish the mold, turn the sides straight and true. Chamfer the corner and turn a deep foot into the mold. This will aid the casting of the object by helping the mold to sit stable and flat on the bench.

be made upside down. Stick the object in the center of the disk/bat with a very small amount of glue. Soap the object and bat three times to ensure that all of the surface is covered. Wrap the cottling around the disk, trying to create a good tight join, and fill any gaps with soft clay on the outside of the cottle.

Mix the plaster as before and try to pour in one continuous movement, taking care to cover the entire surface of the model in the first part of the pour and adding weight and depth to the model in the second part. When the mold is poured it is good practice to finish the base by flattening it with scrapers if the object is square, or turning a foot into it if the mold is set up on a whirler. Finishing the outside well means that the mold will sit stably and the cast will be level.

Adding the spare

The spare, also known as the casting ring, is a conical disk that sits on top of the model, from which you will make the top of the mold. The spare is best made from plaster by turning it on the lathe or whirler, though it can successfully be made from clay. The spare may sit inside the model, giving you a cast thickness, or on the outside so the cast thickness is determined by the time spent in the mold.

To finish the mold, turn it over and model natches into the face of the mold. Place the spare on top in the center of the mold with a few dabs of glue to hold it in place. Soap the top of the mold including the spare three times, and cottle around the mold. Mix and pour, then finish the top smooth and take the edges off.

Split mold

This describes the mold for a model that has an undercut—this might be a physical undercut or a surface detail that requires a more complex mold. The description "split mold" describes the splitting of the mold along its seam. In fact, this mold could be just two pieces, or may include a top for three pieces, or a top and base for four pieces.

In preparation for making a split mold you must ensure that your object has a seam that runs along its length, and have a plaster bat. First, stick the spare onto your model. Place the object

SLIP CASTING USING DIFFERENT SPARES

FILLING THE MOLD

The spare is the piece of the mold that creates the hole to cast through and the reservoir for extra slip. It is a very simple thing but very important to the casting process.

Pour in slip

Assemble mold

spare

Fill mold with slip

Clay begins to cast in the mold

Pour out slip

After a specified time tip out the uncast slip

cast

Layer of cast in mold before fettling

TYPES OF SPARE

There are a number of kinds of spare, but in most instances it will be discarded after the mold is made. The cast thickness of your form is defined by the amount of time clay is left to cast in the mold.

spare

remove mold lid and fettle spare

remove mold lid and fettle spare

spare

blade angle

blade angle

after fettling

Outside fitting spare This spare is the simplest for prototyping your object. It sits outside the object and is trimmed off after use by cutting along the top of the main piece of the mold.

Inside fitting spare This spare differs from the outside type in the way it is trimmed after casting. Instead of trimming along the mold you use your blade at an angle to cut down the edge of the spare. There is less to trim using this spare.

Plug When making a completely enclosed form, the spare is retained and used as a plug.

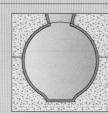

After casting

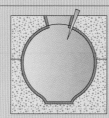

Trim with a blade and sponge the edge

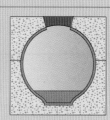

Add a small quantity of slip and add plug spare

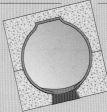

Turn mold over so it casts over spare plug

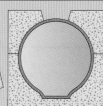

Cut away the plug to leave the enclosed form

onto the bat, supported in two soft balls of clay. Using an engineer's square, check that the top and bottom of the model are at 90 degrees to the bat. Using a soft pencil gently trace the outline of the object, including the spare, onto the plaster. Once this has been transcribed you need to cut the shape out of the plaster bat. Use a band saw or saw by hand. Finish the bat with a potter's knife until it is very close to the inscribed profile. Offer the bat up to the model; when it fits snugly to the outside of the model the bat is finished. Small gaps are acceptable since they can be filled in with clay at a later stage. Cut the outside of the bat to a shape that is approximately 1¼ in (3.5 cm) wider than the widest part of the model.

Prepare a good quantity of soft clay; you will need this to support your model. For best results use a sturdy board and fit it to a wheel. Place the model on two or three lumps of soft clay and check that it is sitting at 90 degrees as before. Use the soft clay to build up support under the model and to either side to create a support for the plaster bat. Build this up until you can support

MOLDED LIGHT SHADES
BY KATHLEEN HILLS
These beautiful translucent bone china lights adhere to the rules about undercuts. They are actually drop-out forms, due to their curved profile.

the bat so that it fits perpendicular to the seam and is horizontal; use a beam level to assess this. Once this is achieved, filet clay into the edges so that the support is sturdy and not likely to collapse under pressure, and trim the clay back so it is square to the bat. Any gaps that might appear along the intersection between the model and bat can be filled with soft clay pressed into the gap and modeled flat with a wooden tool.

Having set up the model carefully, soap the whole thing thoroughly. Build walls around the model using clean cottling boards. The system for building walls with cottling boards is to overlap them in sequence so that they press each other in, with generous amounts of clay fixing the boards to the baseboard, and in the join between the bats. You may wish to further secure it with tape across the top or string around the side.

When this is all complete give the model and the bat a final soap to remove any debris from the setup process. Mix a generous amount of plaster to fill the mold. If you want to calculate the volume of the mold, in this case a square/rectangular one, use the formula: length x breadth x height.

When using a mold it is good to try to pour the plaster slightly early, just as it is about to be ready—the plaster will still be fluid and will pick up all of the detail on the model. Continue to add the mix and tap it gently when it is all in to get the air out of the plaster.

Once the plaster has gone off, you can remove the boards and clean up the back and edges of the mold. Turn it over, taking care that the model does not come loose. Make sure you model in natches, two on each side of the model. To ensure the plaster does not stick to the setup you will need to soap the whole thing and build the walls as described above. Clean the debris with a final soaping, mix the same quantity of plaster, and pour as described above. Remove the cottling boards and clean the back and edges and leave to go off. After a few hours you can split the mold apart and remove the model. If you are having difficulty releasing the model then you can try using compressed air or a gentle tapping on the back of the mold.

MAKING A SPLIT MOLD

TECHNIQUE FILE **68**

In preparation for making a split mold you must ensure that your object has a seam that runs along its length, a prepared spare that fits your model, and a plaster bat big enough to transcribe the object's profile and the mold onto. Setting the mold up using a plaster bat rather than clay leads to a more professional finish.

Model with spare

1 First stick the spare onto your model. Use clay to support the object on the bat. With an engineer's square, ensure that the top and bottom of the model are at 90 degrees to the bat. If you do not have an engineer's square you can use a metal ruler on its end.

2 Using a soft pencil or a fine marker, draw around your object, including the spare.

3 Once this has been done you can cut the shape out of the plaster bat using a band saw, though it can also be done by hand using a coping saw. Finish the bat with a potter's knife until it matches the transcribed profile. Offer the bat up to the model; if it fits snugly to the outside of the model the bat is finished. Any small gaps can be filled in with clay at a later stage. Cut the bat so that it is approximately 1½ in (3.5 cm) wider than the widest part of the model.

4 For best results use a sturdy board and fit to a wheel. Place the model on lumps of soft clay and check that it is sitting at 90 degrees as before. Use the soft clay to build up support under the model and to either side so as to support the plaster bat and withstand pressure. Using a beam level, make sure the bat fits perpendicular to the seam and is horizontal.

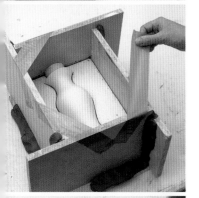

5 Fill in any gaps that appear along the join between model and bat with soft clay. You can smooth the clay with a wooden tool.

6 Soap the whole setup thoroughly. Build walls around the model using clean cottling boards. Overlap the cottling boards in sequence so that they press each other in. In order to secure them, use clay to reinforce the joins and tape across the top or string around the sides.

7 Remove any debris from the setup process and soap once again. Mix enough plaster to fill the mold. By pouring the plaster slightly early, the plaster will still be fluid and will pick up all the detail on the model. Continue to add the mix and tap it gently when it is all in to get the air out of the plaster. It is good practice to try to cover the model first—in the event of a problem you will only have to add plaster to the first mix to retrieve it.

8 When the plaster has gone off, remove the boards, and clean up the back and edges of the mold (see detail). Carefully turn it over, and make sure the model does not come loose.

9 Model in natches, two on each side of the model.

10 Soap the whole setup and build the walls as previously described. Clean the debris with a final soaping, and mix the same quantity of plaster and pour as described above. Remove the cottling boards and clean the back and edges and leave to go off.

11 After a few hours you can split the mold apart and remove the model. If the model does not come out, you can release it using compressed air or a gentle rhythmic tapping on the back of the mold. Always dry a multipart mold together to protect the inner face of the mold—this will take slightly longer, but it is safer. Once the mold has been completed then the model has served its purpose.

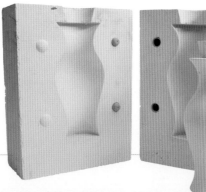

NUMBER OF MOLD PIECES REQUIRED FOR DIFFERENT MODELS

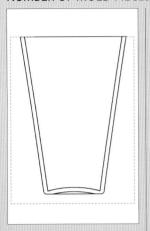

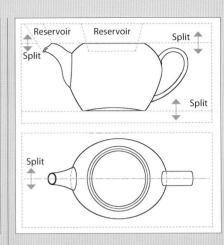

One-piece drop-out mold

A one-piece drop-out mold is the most simple kind of mold. It can be made for any conical or simple shape provided it does not have any undercuts. The diagram shows a conical beaker. The beaker has a foot, but this does not create a problem, since it will appear as a slight recess in the bottom of the mold.

Two-piece split mold

A two-piece split mold is a simple mold for a form that has an undercut. The form is seamed along its length through the central axis. The mold then splits into two pieces. This cast object will have a seam that will need to be fettled away. Note that this has an integral spare or reservoir—this means that it is built into the sides and not made separately. Some forms require a separate spare. Note the flat foot. If this were recessed, the mold would need a bottom.

Three-piece mold

Because of the waisted shape of this form, the three-piece mold must be split along its length to release the cast piece. This mold also needs a bottom, because of the recessed foot. This object has an integral spare; it could be made with a separate spare but this would add a fourth piece to the mold.

Four-piece mold

This a complex four-piece mold, necessary because of the features of the teapot. It must be split along its length and also incorporate a top and a bottom. In this case the teapot has an integral handle and spout, but often the handle will be cast separately. The bottom piece incorporates the foot, and the top piece gives the shape and dimension of the gallery. This creates the diameter of the top opening, giving a hole for air to escape through the spout and a hole to drain the slip out.

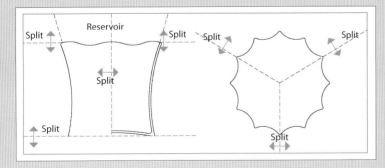

Five-piece mold

The model for this five-piece mold has deep flutes modeled into the surface. This creates a complex rim shape. If you add a domed foot shape you will need a five-piece mold. As with the other molds, the foot detail is captured in the base. The rim is contained in the top, which also creates a reservoir by using a spare. The main body is split into three pieces. It cannot be split in two because it would be undercut and not come apart. Make sure you check your model from all angles, it might be undercut in a direction you did not expect.

Always dry a multipart mold together to protect the inner face of the mold; this will take slightly longer but is safer. Once the mold has been completed, the model has served its purpose.

Hump mold

Using a hump mold is a very low-tech but very effective technique often used to create large open dishes and bowls. This type of mold is unusual in that it stands on a shallow stalk or stand to raise it off the surface of the bench. The model might be sledged around a template (see pages 134–135) or may be built in clay and smoothed with rubber kidneys. When the model of the dish is complete, take the simple mold off it, build a wall around the object, and soap it. Clean up the face, soap it, and pour plaster into the mold. Allow this to go off a bit before making

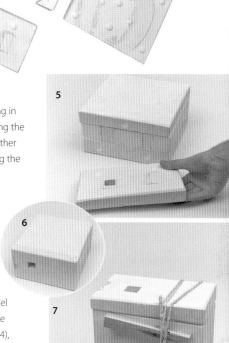

FLOATING MOLD

One of the principal tenets of mold making is that objects cannot be molded if they are undercut, molds have to be split along seams to achieve the cast.

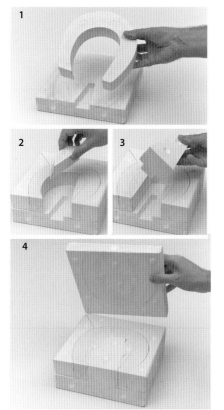

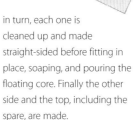

The mold shown here is of a horseshoe model. It is a simple form in itself but with a built-in flaw for the mold-making process, the central core is one huge undercut.

The success of this mold lies in the central core being broken down into parts. The only use of one of those parts is to hold the rest of the mold in place. This is the floating piece, where the mold gets its name from, because it is floating in space and not actually touching the cast.

When molding the horseshoe shape, it is set up on a soaped plaster bat and soaped itself, then the outside shape is molded in three sections: two sides and a bottom. Next, the inside core is treated in the same way with three small pieces of mold being poured

in turn, each one is cleaned up and made straight-sided before fitting in place, soaping, and pouring the floating core. Finally the other side and the top, including the spare, are made.

The images here show the mold and the model inside—post construction—being assembled, to demonstrate how all the pieces fit together. They show the horseshoe model (1), the inside core in three pieces (2 and 3), the top (4), the spare (5), and the mold fitted together ready for casting (6 and 7).

deep score marks in the center of the dish. Build a strong clay wall in an oval shape on the back face of the mold—do not soap it though, because you want the next section of plaster to become integral to the mold. Mix and pour plaster, ensuring that the top face of the stand is completely flat. This will become the base of the mold when it is turned over.

Waste mold

A waste mold makes use of the molding process to create a model. It is usually used when the model needs something added or removed, thus creating another opportunity to work on the model before taking a final mold. The waste mold is a rudimentary kind of mold, because it is

not needed beyond the next stage of the process. When you decide to make a waste mold, set up as normal for the particular model, and calculate where in the process your intervention is needed (either directly on the model or into the mold). Then go through the molding process.

Once you have your mold and have made your alterations, simply soap the inside of the mold and mix and pour plaster into it, creating a new model that has the changes built in.

Indicative mold structures

The diagrams above left explain how a series of particular designs would be molded.

Slip casting is one of the most popular ceramic production techniques. The main reasons for this are the level of accuracy that can be attained and the ability to repeatedly cast the same object over and over again, from short runs through to batches or large volumes.

MOLD MAKING: SLIP CASTING

Slip casting is a natural partner process to mold making in that it relies on some sort of porous mold to form the object. "Slip" is the name for liquid clay. It is mixed in a large blender called a "blunger" and kept in a state of readiness. Most clays can be made into slip; ask your pottery supplier for a recipe, or see the basic recipes opposite. It is important to mix the slip thoroughly before use, at least 30 minutes before you want it.

Most industrial production uses a derivative of the casting process: pressure casting, in which resin molds have slip pumped in under high pressure, such as for sanitaryware; or dust pressing, where ceramic dust is forced between two resin dies under great pressure. Casting gives a very fine-quality result with a constant thickness throughout, which allows for fine rims and delicate handles, and bone china and porcelain to be translucent. Slip casting is an ideal process for any type of batch production.

Making slip

Casting slip is essentially liquid clay in which the clay particles are held in suspension in water by deflocculants, usually sodium silicate and sodium carbonate. Casting slip is made up of approximately 40–45 percent water, and the deflocculant is present in very small quantities. There are two ways to make a slip: either from dry materials all mixed with water to a specific recipe, or by adding plastic clay and the deflocculants to water. Your clay supplier will usually have a standard slip recipe for most of

ORDER OF WORK:
SLIP CASTING
• draw enough slip from blunger to fill mold
• sieve slip from blunger to bucket
• check mold is dust-free
• bind together with elastic bands
• fill mold with slip in one continuous pour
• allow to cast for required time
• tip slip out of mold
• allow to drain
• trim spare
• unmold when cast is strong enough

Nature-inspired slip casting
BY MAREK CECULA
A fallen branch served as a natural model for this tea service. The model was then molded and the slip-casting process picked up all of the detail in the surface texture.

Casting notebook

It is important to keep a record of casting times and thicknesses for each new object/mold. This notebook shows a small diagram of the object with any unusual information, such as casting through the foot. It also records the amount of slip poured in and out, the time allowed, and cast thickness.

the plastic clays it offers. The best method for making slip is to use a dedicated blunger—a big mixing machine. You can also use a portable blunger and heavy buckets.

To make the slip from plastic clay, first measure out the correct quantities of water and clay. Mix the deflocculants together in a jug of warm water until they have dissolved and add to the full quantity of water. Add the clay slowly, in small strips, until all of the material has been drawn into the mix and broken down by the blunger. The slip should be mixed for three to four hours, before being left to stand overnight. Cover the slip if it is to be left for any period of time.

Over time you may have to slightly readjust the slip mixture and add a bit more deflocculant to compensate for water evaporation or absorption.

Standard casting slips

These recipes are very basic; there is a great range of slip recipes available and ready-made slips can be also obtained from pottery suppliers.

White earthenware casting slip
(1830–2100° F/1000–1150° C)
55 lb (25 kg) white earthenware
½ gallon (2.1 liters) water
¼ oz (5 g) sodium silicate
½ oz (12.5 g) soda ash

Stoneware casting slip
(2120–2340°F/1160–1280°C)
55 lb (25 kg) stoneware clay
1 gallon (4 liters) water
2 oz (56 g) sodium silicate
½ oz (12.5 g) soda ash

HOW TO SLIP CAST

Before casting, make sure your mold is dry to the touch, and clean of all dust and debris. Strap or tie the sides, top, and bottom of the mold together before you begin.

1 Draw some slip from your blunger and sieve it as it enters the jug. Make sure you have a large enough jug to prevent needing a second pour of slip.

2 Place the mold on a banding wheel. Pour the slip into the mold in one fluid motion. Gently tap the mold to expel any air trapped inside. Leave the slip to cast for the time stated in the supplier's notes. The water will be drawn from the slip into the plaster mold, leaving a thin wall of clay or cast on the mold surface.

3 When this has attained the correct cast thickness, pour the excess slip from the mold.

4 Leave the mold upturned on a rack so that it can drain. Once the slip has drained from the mold, turn it upright again.

5 Let the slip stiffen a bit, checking until it feels firm but soft to the touch. Now the spare can be cut away. Use a sharp flexible blade to cut the clay away as you turn the banding wheel. Use a soft or natural sponge to fettle the cut edge.

6 Leave the clay in the mold to dry until it is safe to unmold and handle.

ASSEMBLING CAST PARTS

TECHNIQUE FILE
71

When making a cast with multiple parts, such as a cup with a handle, you should cast both parts at the same time. It is good practice to build a location detail into the mold so it is easy to locate the handle on the body.

1 Take the handle mold apart and trim any spares away with a sharp knife. When assembling, gently scratch into both surfaces that will be joined and dab a little water on them.

2 Using a fine brush gently drop some slip onto the handle and press it to the cup.

3 Using the brush, fill in the join with slip to keep it clean and smooth. Use a sharp knife to carefully trim the seam away on the handle.

4 Allow the cup to dry—this can easily be assessed by the change in color from dark to light—then take a damp sponge and using a crisscross motion gently rub away the remains of the seam.

Slip-cast sculpture

by Jeffrey Mongrain

Slip casting has been used to produce this elegant and incongruous sculpture of a moose on a vibrant red branch. Each element has been cast from a found object, but the juxtaposition of each form creates a new narrative for the objects.

Casting slip

Sieve your blunged slip into a jug and ensure that it has greater volume than the mold so you will not need a second pour of slip. A second pour will create a casting ring in the clay—a very fine line that is very difficult to repair or remove. To make the mold easier to manipulate you should put it onto a banding wheel. Once your mold is on the wheel, pour the slip into it in one continuous motion. Do not stop until the mold is full to avoid creating a ripple in the cast surface. Tap the mold to expel any trapped air.

You should leave the slip to cast now for a given period of time. This is dependent on the type of clay—for earthenware approximately 20 minutes, bone china and porcelain 5–8 minutes, but refer to the supplier's notes for timescales. The water will be drawn from the slip into the plaster mold, leaving a thin wall of clay or cast on the mold surface. When the correct time has elapsed, pour the excess slip from the mold. It is best to do this in one continuous movement, since glugging might cause the cast to collapse in the mold due to suction. Next, turn the mold upside down and capture any remaining slip in a jug to be recycled, if needed. When you are satisfied that all the slip has been drained, you can turn the mold upright again.

Allow the slip to harden slightly. Once it feels firm but soft to the touch the excess slip created by the spare should be cut away. Taking a sharp flexible blade, make two vertical cuts on opposite sides of the clay, slide the blade under the cut, and place your spare hand on the clay as if to hold it in place. Slowly rotating the mold with the help of the wheel, cut the clay away in one continuous motion. When you reach the other vertical cut, lift the clay out of the spare and repeat the process.

As the clay dries it will begin to shrink in the mold; at this point you should begin to take the mold apart, leaving the clay to sit in the mold as it dries, until it is to safe to unmold and handle. Allow the cast to dry for a few hours until it is much drier; at this point you should take off the seams using a sharp blade and a sponge. This act of trimming the spare and seams is known as fettling. Take care when fettling, because the cast is extremely fragile.

Fettling and sponging

"Fettling" describes the act of trimming the seams and casting lines with a knife or other tools. It is relatively simple but it takes considerable skill and practice to do it well. The cast object is extremely fragile in its green, or unfired, state. When it is first taken from the mold it is liable to deform through handling. As the cast object dries its properties change; the dry green pot will hold its shape but is very fragile and has a tendency to crack or shatter. It is this property that makes fettling such a skill. You do not want to deform or break all the casts you have just made, so a gentle but confident hand is required.

Drop-out objects can usually be left in the mold until they can support themselves. Often the non-drop-out object has to be removed from the mold to prevent shrinking or cracking. If you have to unmold the object before it is strong, do it in a very systematic way. After a few casts you will begin to recognize how the mold comes apart; often an object will stick in one side of a mold for a little longer for no apparent reason. Mark this side of the mold so you are able to anticipate this. Bring boards close to the model so that the actual handling of the object is minimal. Gently lift the object out of the mold and stand it on the board until it is leather hard.

FETTLING

Fettling and sponging are the processes of removing casting seams and cleaning up the cast surface. If your mold making is effective there should be little fettling to do. After casting, trim the spare away and remove the object from the mold. Try not to handle it too much at this stage, if you leave the object to dry for a few hours it will mean it is strong enough to endure the process. While the object is dry, the fettling should always be done wet to avoid creating dust.

1 The seam is created at the join between two sides of a mold, this may deteriorate over time due to wear and tear.

2 Using a damp sponge, gently work the seam away. You will be able to remove most of the material very quickly. Do not worry about making the cast piece damp because this will help avoid dust.

3 The damp seam is trimmed away first using a sharp blade or fettling knife, pulled forward along the length of the seam.

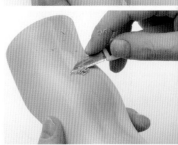

4 The knife is then held perpendicular to the object's seam and slowly scraped along the body to smooth the remainder away.

5 Finally the seam is finished with plenty of water sponged in a crosshatch motion until the seam is removed.

STRATA CASTING

Strata casting is an inventive casting technique that relies on a strong understanding of the casting process. Colored layers are cast in turn, by pouring and tipping each cast and waiting until the slip is at just the right stage before pouring the next layer.

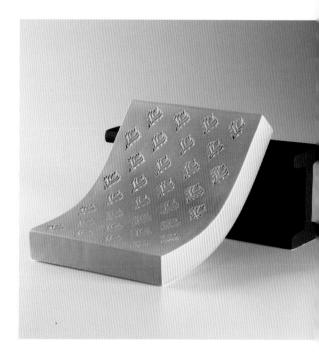

1 The mold is filled with the first color of casting slip. This is then left to cast for a set amount of time, in this case eight minutes. After this time a skin of clay accumulates on the surface of the mold.

2 Empty the mold and allow to drain. Wait for the "shine" of the cast to be dulled before pouring the next layer. Repeat this three times. When the cast is firm, the rim is scraped back with a fettling knife and it should be left in the mold until leather hard. Put a board over the mold and flip it so the vase drops out.

3 When the vase is completely dry you can mark out the pattern with either a tool or pencil as a guide for the carving. At this point it is essential you wear a respirator to ensure you do not breathe in any of the dry clay dust.

4 Carve and refine the surface of the vase to reveal the strata of clay by scraping it back with the curved edge of a metal kidney.

5 Once the vase has been fired it can be rubbed in water with wet and dry paper all over its surface, which will leave a very smooth surface with the colors sharply defined.

6 The vase now has a robust surface with the body stains which have colored the slip integral in the surface of the strata.

One way of knowing whether the object is drying or not is to observe it change color. The cast object will generally look a lighter shade as the water evaporates out of the cast. After about one hour the object should be leather hard. Taking the object in your hand, gently apply a potter's knife or sharp blade to the seam and draw the blade toward you, cutting away the seam line. Set the object down for a while longer, to let it harden some more before sponging. If you have a number of objects, fettle them all then sponge them all—this will generally mean that you don't rush them.

The problem with sponging is that you are reintroducing water into the already soft clay, so letting it dry a bit more first will help the object survive the process. Take a soft, natural sponge and dip in the water. Squeeze it so that the sponge is wet but not soaked and apply to the surface. To remove seams, crisscross the seam in diagonal motions until the line is invisible, then give a final wipe with plenty of water. If the surface is damaged or needs repair, use a generous amount of water and lightly polish the surface.

Strata casting

Strata casting is a technique of casting layers of slip over one another. It is a very simple but effective decorative technique, which relies on the use of body stains in the same casting slip body. Decant a number of bowls from the same batch of slip, mix the required percentage of

Slip-cast sculpture
BY DAWN YOULL
*The perfect surface of
this abstract sculpture is
indicative of slip casting
into a well made mold.
The shallow intaglio motif
can be transcribed onto
the form with accuracy
and attention to detail.*

Slip-cast chandelier
BY JEANNE QUINN
*This vibrant, decorative
installation uses slip-cast
forms in combination
with wire and glass to
create an experience that
is visually stunning.*

stain into the bowls of slip, and let them stand for an hour or two. Remix the slip and pour the first batch into the mold. Let it cast for a few minutes, tip the slip from the mold back into the batch, drain for a minute or so, then repeat the process with another batch of colored slip. This process can be repeated up to five times to create a multicolored slip-cast body. To highlight this process the final object is often cut or changed in some way to show the layers.

Slip trailing into molds

The same batch of colored casting slips can be used to trail into open or two-piece molds. Using a pipette or syringe, draw up a quantity of each batch of slip. Set the mold on a wheel, if it is a single open mold. While slowly spinning the mold, expel the slip from the pipette. The slip will dry very quickly so speed is of the essence. Repeat the process with the different slips as often as you like. Keeping the slip trails damp as you build up can take a bit of practice. You may wish to leave the object as a trailed form—though this will be rather fragile—or you may wish to cast a final layer over it to hold it all together.

Follow the same process to trail into the other side of the mold; joining the two halves can take a bit of practice. Often this technique requires a final binding layer of slip.

Marbling

Marbling is the simple technique of pouring two stained casting slips into a mold at the same time. The real skill lies in getting the two slips to create a marbled effect rather than just mixing into a muddy color. Set your mold on a wheel or a whirler, rotating at a very slow speed. Pick up two containers of colored slip and pour them both at a steady speed into the mold. Let it cast, then pour the slip out. When it is dry, take the object out of the mold and fettle.

Press molding is still used in the manufacture of bricks and architectural faience, as well as for making large open forms, large architectural forms, or forms with a low relief. It lends itself to detailed relief, provided it will release from the mold.

MOLD MAKING: PRESS MOLDING

Pressing is a relatively simple technique, requiring a model made out of plaster, clay, or another material from which you take a mold. If it is a large open form then you can press a large slab into the mold. Alternatively, if it is a more complex form in a multiple-piece mold then you can press small balls of clay into the mold, taking care to smooth them into the surrounding clay until the surface has an integrity of form.

Press-molded forms tend to be rather robust with a generous thickness of varying depths and large rims and edges. With such items, drying is critical, since they will retain more moisture due to the clay thickness.

A press mold is made in the same way as any other mold. The model might be sledged around a template (see pages 134–135) or could be built in clay and smoothed with rubber kidneys. When the model of the dish is complete you take a simple mold off it, build a wall around the object, and soap it. After drying, the mold is ready to use. To make a more complex mold, such as a two-piece split-mold, support the model in clay up to the seam. Soap the model if it is made of plaster, build walls, and pour in plaster. Flip the mold and model over, make four natches in the plaster, soap again, build the walls, and pour the plaster. When the mold is complete, use a sharp tool to model in a "V"-shaped groove around the whole object, approximately ¼ in (5 mm) in from the object.

Press molding a bowl

Roll out a flat slab of malleable plastic clay. Carefully lift it and drop it over your mold. Press the clay into the mold using a constant pressure and a damp sponge. Use a rubber kidney to shape the inside of the bowl and smooth out any blemishes. When you are happy with the inside shape, trim the excess clay from the edge of the bowl, using a clay wire held tightly against the

PRESS-MOLDED INSTALLATION
BY MAREK CECULA
This installation is a tour de force of pressing skills. A collection of press molded objects is buried into a pressed clay dust floor and revealed through a huge crack. The resulting installation is a poignant reference to ceramics' role in recording and understanding history.

PRESSED ARTWORK
BY MAREK CECULA
This kilo of earth has been pressed into a form and sold in a giftbox. It is intended to carry a message about saving our precious earth.

edge of the mold. The wire might leave a slight ripple on the clay edge. Use your damp sponge to fettle this edge until it is smooth (see page 153). Let it dry before demolding.

Pressing into a two-piece mold

A two-piece press mold resembles a slip-casting mold except for two details: first, there is no spare to pour slip in through; second, there is a groove cut into either face of the mold that follows the entire shape of the object. The purpose of this groove is to cut away the excess clay as the mound presses together.

Firmly press soft balls of clay into the mold, building up around the form until you reach the seam. Make sure there is plenty of clay at the top edge to avoid gaps in the object when it is pressed together; the excess clay will either press inward to ensure a good join or will be cut off by the groove. Before pressing, add a soft clay sausage around the entire form and trim back to leave the clay slightly higher than the mold. Wet the clay with a damp sponge.

Carefully press the two halves together and leave for approximately 20 minutes. When the mold is taken apart you will see the excess clay trapped in the groove—remove this and let the object air dry a bit longer before demolding. When the object is leather hard, fettle as before. One of the characteristics of press molding is a very pronounced seam when you take it out of the mold, but this can be removed without too much trouble.

TECHNIQUE FILE 74

PRESS MOLDING WITH SLABS

Press molding can be done in a number of ways. If the object is a big open form then it is possible to press with a large soft slab of clay.

1 Roll out a slab (see page 70), ensuring that it is flat, without bubbles, and big enough to fill the mold. Place the slab over the mold so that it overlaps the edges.

2 Gently press the slab into the mold before smoothing with a rubber kidney.

3 Cut the excess clay from the edge with a sharp blade or a wire held taut.

4 Using a combination of a rubber kidney and an almost dry sponge, clean up the edge of the bowl and set it to one side to dry.

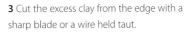

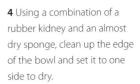

5 To take the bowl from the mold, place a clean flat board on the top of the mold and flip it over. Gently remove the mold, allowing the clay piece to drop out.

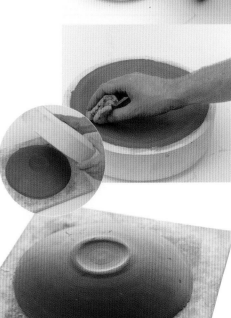

The jigger/jolley is a semiautomatic machine that uses plaster molds, plastic clay, and plastic or metal tools to force clay into a shape on the face of the mold. Jolleyed vessels are usually quite robust, with a nice weight and balance; jiggered plates are relatively thick and chunky with soft edges.

MOLD MAKING: JIGGER AND JOLLEY

Jiggering describes the act of forming over a hump—it is used for plates, saucers, and shallow bowls, where the mold forms the front face of the clay piece and the tool forms the back, or underside, of the object. Jolleying describes the act of forming into a hollow mold and is used for cups and deep bowls, where the mold forms the outside shape and the tool forms the inside. The molds are usually drop-out or single-face with either the inside (jigger) formed by the tool or the underside (jolley) formed by the tool. The molds are manufactured using a ring and frame; this enables each mold to fit onto the machine. This process is at its most successful when there are a number of molds so a piece can be manufactured in runs. Like most of the industrial techniques it takes some time to set up, relying on thorough planning and preparation.

Making molds using the ring and frame
The ring and frame are essentially metal molds that contain the information that enables the plaster mold to fit onto the machine. Center the ring on the whirler and stick it down with some clay. Prepare some profiles from your technical drawing (see opposite). Note that the model is turned in reverse on the whirler within the metal frame, so your profile should be on the opposite side of the line from what you might expect. Once all the pieces are set up, mix and pour plaster into the frame. This process follows the same technique as whirler turning (see page 129). As the plaster is beginning to go off, take your chisels and begin to turn the plaster away, using the profiles to help guide the process in order to complete the front face, then finish with some wet and dry paper. When this is

Jiggered plate
by Andy Allum
This plate has been formed using the jiggering process before being hand decorated. This is a good example of one of the priniciples of manufacturing: simplifying the forming process and creating difference in the surface design.

HINTS

When setting up the molds and profile for the first time, you may find there are some small adjustments to be made. Often there might be a dragging of the profile mold, if you lift the arm you will find an adjustment bolt, this allows you to alter the profile in relation to the clay on the mold. Ideally it should just touch or leave a very small gap of less than 1/32 in (1 mm).

This jolleying mold of a wide bowl has been converted to fit a smaller fitting for the machine. This is indicated by the long thin foot under the mold, which would fit to a cup setting on the machine. This inventive problem solving means that the maker can make wider pieces without needing to buy more apparatus for the machine.

complete, soap the face of the model and use petroleum jelly on the inside of the frame to create a resist, which will help the mold release. Take a moment to study the inside contours of the frame, observing how the details relate to the machine. Place the frame over the ring so that it locks in place. Mix and pour plaster into the frame, vigorously rocking the wheel to dispel any trapped air. Finally, flatten the plaster that appears to be the top, but is actually the base of the mold. Let the plaster harden and, when it releases, repeat the process.

The benefits of batch production

To make effective use of this machine you should make a number of molds, so that you can implement a batch-production process. The preparation of the clay and setup of the machine each time means it makes sense to invest the energy in the molding stage to make a virtue out of both the ring and frame mold and the machine itself.

Making the profile

The profile is made in the same way as described in the sledging section (see page 130). It can be made of plastic or metal and is usually backed by wood. The blade of the tool is chamfered away from the front face at approx 45 degrees; ensure that it is smooth using files and then wet and dry paper. Any ridges or bumps will be transferred to the clay piece. There are two details that are critical to the jigger/jolley tools—the first is the flat edge of the tool that meets the plaster mold. The combination of tool and mold create a scraping edge; as the tool and mold meet they cut away the excess clay. The second important detail is the holes for the screws that fix the tool to the arm of the machine. The cutting of the holes must be accurate so they fit securely and do not allow for any lateral movement; this would result in a variable thickness in the final object.

Jiggering a plate

Set up the machine with your tool fixed to the arm of the machine and your molds placed firmly in the cup head. It is a good idea to check the smooth running of the mold and the tool

MAKING MOLDS USING THE RING AND FRAME

In order to fit the mold to the machine, two metal pieces called the ring and frame are used. These have all of the essential information built in to ensure that the molds fit snugly.

1 Center the ring on the whirler and stick it down with some clay. Take care to soap the whirler head. Mix a generous batch of plaster and pour it directly into the ring.

2 Take your chisels and begin to turn the plaster away, using the profiles to help guide the process in order to complete the front face.

3 Finish the plate front with kidneys and wet and dry paper.

4 When the model is complete, soap the face and apply petroleum jelly to the inside of the frame to act as a resist and aid release. Carefully place the frame over the ring so it locks in place.

5 Mix and pour plaster into the frame. After pouring, vigorously rock the wheel from side to side to dispel any trapped air. Scrape the plaster that appears to be the top but is actually the base of the mold.

6 Allow the plaster to go off before taking the mold apart; the model should remain in the ring and the mold should pop out of the frame. Repeat this process to maximize the use of the machine.

JIGGERING A PLATE

As with many of the plaster-based industrial techniques, the forming of the clay is quick and relies upon the production of a number of molds so that it can become a repetitive batch process.

1 Use plastic clay to prepare a number of flat clay bats by using a bat wheel and tool. Set it at a slight angle to create a thicker clay bat in the center.

2 Take time to set up the machine well, ensuring that the tool fixes to the arm of the machine securely without any lateral movement, and that the molds locate firmly in the cup head.

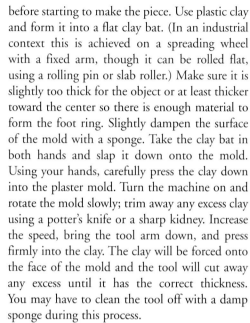

3 Dampen the surface of the mold with a sponge before starting the process; this will help the clay cling to the surface.

4 Carefully lift a clay bat with both hands and press it down onto the mold. Press the clay down into the plaster mold (see detail).

5 Rotate the mold slowly, trimming away any excess clay. Increase the speed, hold the arm and press the tool into your shoulder and down onto the clay. The tool will cut away the clay surface, leaving the removed material on the tool.

6 The tool will continue to cut away any excess until it has the correct thickness. You may have to clean the tool off with a damp sponge during this process.

before starting to make the piece. Use plastic clay and form it into a flat clay bat. (In an industrial context this is achieved on a spreading wheel with a fixed arm, though it can be rolled flat, using a rolling pin or slab roller.) Make sure it is slightly too thick for the object or at least thicker toward the center so there is enough material to form the foot ring. Slightly dampen the surface of the mold with a sponge. Take the clay bat in both hands and slap it down onto the mold. Using your hands, carefully press the clay down into the plaster mold. Turn the machine on and rotate the mold slowly; trim away any excess clay using a potter's knife or a sharp kidney. Increase the speed, bring the tool arm down, and press firmly into the clay. The clay will be forced onto the face of the mold and the tool will cut away any excess until it has the correct thickness. You may have to clean the tool off with a damp sponge during this process.

Take the mold off the machine and leave it to one side to dry or place in a drying cabinet. Repeat the process with another mold, making sure to thoroughly clean the tool before each use, until they are all full of clay pieces. When the clay is dry enough to support its own weight, remove from the mold and clean the mold ready for another production run.

Jolleying a bowl

This is much the same process as jiggering, but the mold is hollow and the clay is formed into a soft ball. The tool will fit to the machine arm in the same way and will have a scraping edge built into the top surface. The main visible difference is that the tool reaches down into the mold. In both techniques it is good practice to try to calculate the amount of clay needed to avoid unnecessary waste.

Taking a ball of clay, place it in the center of the inside of the mold and bring the arm down steadily. Increase the speed to force the clay up the wall of the mold. When finished, set aside to dry until the clay pieces can be removed from the mold.

There is a broad range of tile-making techniques. In an industrial context, tiles are high-pressure dust pressed. In a studio context tiles can be made in a number of ways: cast, pressed, dust pressed, slab made, or extruded.

TILE MAKING

Each process has its own advantages. The key issue to consider when attempting to make tiles is the chosen body. A grogged body will help keep tiles from warping and cracking. How the tile is dried is also very important. If the clay is grogged then it can be air-dried on slatted racks. If the clay is not grogged it will need to be dried very carefully to prevent cracking and warping. Dry the tile very slowly on racks that allow the air to reach both sides of the object.

Cast tiles

Casting is a useful way of picking up very fine surface detail such as pattern or texture. The texture will be captured in the model before molding. The mold will have two spares set apart from each other. It is essentially a drop-out mold with a back section. The slip is poured into the mold through one spare with the mold set at a very slight angle to allow the slip to reach the sides of the mold. Air will escape from the other

SLIP CASTING TILES

Casting slip can be poured into molds so that repeat shapes can be made. The slip should not shrink too much when it dries and should have a good dry strength for handling.

TECHNIQUE FILE 77

1 When the mold is dry, you can start to produce a batch of tiles. First, mix the casting slip to a liquid consistency (see page 150–151). Fill the mold with slip and replenish it from time to time to keep the surface level. Let the slip firm up in the mold until the clay shows no marks when it is touched. This can take any time from 30 minutes on.

2 When the clay begins to shrink away from the edges of the mold it is ready to remove. The clay used here is white earthenware (although it looks buff-colored in its liquid state). It can be cast and removed from the mold in about one hour, depending on the surrounding temperature. This allows several tiles to be cast in a day, although the mold quickly becomes saturated when in constant use and must be dried out thoroughly after each session of casting.

3 To remove the tile from the mold, place a bat over the surface and turn both over before lifting the mold off. Dry the tiles slowly, preferably on a wire rack to allow free circulation of air that will prevent the shape from distorting.

spare. When the cast is solid, open the back of the mold to let it air dry for a short period before demolding. Place a plaster bat on the back of the tile and flip the whole thing over, remove the face, and let it dry.

Pressed tiles

Pressing is a very effective way of making a relief tile, because the clay can be pressed into the detail very easily. Use soft balls of clay to build up the clay body, as in a press mold, until all of the tile mold is full. Clean up the back and let it dry in the mold until it can be demolded.

Dust-pressed tiles

When used in an industrial context, this process ensures an even moisture content and allows little shrinkage, contraction, or warpage. A manual tile press can mimic industrial processes. Using

---

MAKING TILES FROM SLABS

Slabbing is the quickest and easiest method by which to make tiles.

TECHNIQUE FILE **78**

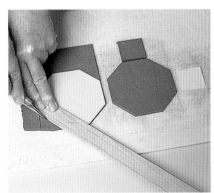

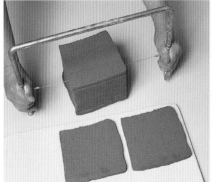

1 Your tiles do not have to be square; you can cut around paper or cardboard templates to make more complicated designs. It is important to measure and cut out templates accurately for a good fit.

2 A clay harp allows you to cut evenly thick slabs of clay. When cutting a block of clay you lower the wire to the next notch as each slab is cut. Although a harp is not essential, it is very useful if you intend to make a lot of tiles. The tiles will still need to be cut to shape.

3 You will still have to roll (see page 70) or harp the slabs of clay, but the tiles will be identical in size when you use a tile cutter. It is a useful tool if you want to make a lot of tiles quickly.

TILE MURAL
BY ROBERT DAWSON
*Tiles are a very effective means of
creating impact across a wide expanse.
With the advent of digitally printed
transfers a mural such as this can be
produced in an industrial context.*

powdered clay obtained from a supplier and gum Arabic, press the dust mixture into the metal die until there is plenty of material. Release the handle and let the die compress the dust under pressure. Press the pedal to release the object from the die and set aside to dry. This is a very effective way of making many tiles of the same size very quickly.

Slabbed tiles

If you would like to make a range of different shapes that fit together, cutting the tiles by hand from a large slab is a very effective method. Roll out a thin slab of clay approximately ½ in (1 cm) in depth. Cut out your desired shapes, using card templates if you prefer. Clean up the edges with a sponge and let them dry.

PRESS MOLDING A TILE

This technique uses small balls of clay rather than slabs. You can vary the effect by pressing different colored clays into the same mold.

1 Take a small ball of clay, about the size of your thumb, and press firmly into the mold.

2 Simply repeat this action, ensuring that you press the balls both into the mold and into each other.

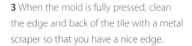

3 When the mold is fully pressed, clean the edge and back of the tile with a metal scraper so that you have a nice edge.

4 When the tile is removed from the mold it has the distinctive, slightly textured surface unique to pressing with balls.

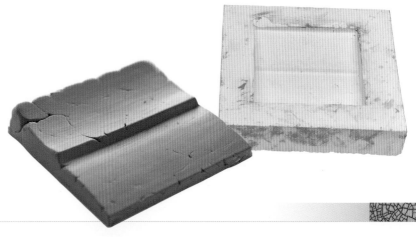

Extrusion is a very direct method of forming clay. It involves forcing soft clay through a shaped die, which in turn will create the cross section of the clay.

EXTRUSION

The die is made in the same way as sledging tools (see page 130), though the shape is completely enclosed in the plate. To start the process the plate must be drilled through and the blade of a saw attached inside of this hole. From this point the die can be carefully cut out before being filed and finished by hand.

Fit the plate to the extruder and press a generous ball of clay into the top. Wind the handle steadily so that the clay is forced through the die. A long sausage of clay material will be forced out with the cross section matching the hole in the plate. This method is ideal for extruding handles.

HOLLOW EXTRUSIONS

Extruding machines are simple to use but can help create forms that appear highly complex. This will be determined by the design and cut of the template profile.

TECHNIQUE FILE 80

Die plates
The die plates are usually made from a thick plastic that is easy to cut. They can also be made from waterproof MDF. Hollow forms are created with smaller plates of the cross section held inside the shape with a metal bar. Holes can be drilled to produce solid coils that can be used for handles, loops, and other additions.

1 To make a hollow form the middle plate is held in place with a metal bar and a wing nut. As the clay passes the metal bar it joins back together. The plate needs to be at least ½ in (1 cm) thick to enable the clay to join as it passes through.

EXTRUDED SCULPTURE
BY REBECCA CATTERALL
Seemingly simple extruded forms are made into complex structures by joining with overlaid repetition. This creates fascinating visual systems.

It is possible to extrude a hollow section. This is achieved by making a die with the middle section retained by a bar either side. As the clay is forced through the die it rejoins after passing the bar. This method is ideal for extruding spouts for thrown ware.

The design of these hollow extrusions can be made as complex as you desire. To make functional forms the extruded section simply needs to be attached to a base. It's a technique that can be used to produce repeated forms quickly. Because of the speed of making they are also very useful in exploring sculptural forms. You need the clay to be quite soft to use in the extruder, but the extruded shape will be easily distorted if handled too soon, so leave them to stiffen for a while before using.

Working with extrusions

The extrusions are better left to stiffen before cutting or using unless you are going to start experimenting with any sculptural manipulation.

2 The die plate is placed under the extrusion box in between a hollow metal square section, which is screwed into the main extruder box to hold it in place. This needs to be tight, otherwise the clay will squirt out of the sides.

3 The clay needs to be well prepared, soft, and air pocket free. Stiff clay will not join back together. If there are air pockets they will appear as holes in the wall of the extrusion. The clay is shaped and pushed into the box and the plunger lifted and placed above it.

4 The lever arm requires a lot of pressure to push down and extrude the clay through the box and die. You will need to have a clean board prepared to lay the extrusions on when you cut them from the machine.

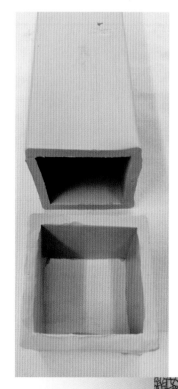

Computer-aided design and manufacture have revolutionized the entire development process, not just in terms of speed of making, but also in terms of the ability to manufacture objects that would previously have seemed impossible to make by hand.

COMPUTER-AIDED DESIGN, MODELING, AND MANUFACTURING

Where once you needed to adhere to the laws of gravity when making objects, they can now be built at the same time as their support material. It is possible to print a finished object in clay from a three-dimensional drawing on a computer screen in a number of hours.

The exciting potential of the process must be tempered with some realism. The software can sometimes be limited, in that you may have to spend many hours working out how to get the software to model something that you would achieve by hand. It can also lack the generative quality of working with your hands; there is a tendency to decide that something is right and have it rapid prototyped without testing its proportions or profile in a more rudimentary way. It is therefore important that any designs made on screen are explored fully before the commitment to go to modeling is made.

Additive and subtractive manufacturing

The computer-aided manufacturing processes are split into two generic fields—additive and subtractive.

Additive manufacturing describes a process in which an object is built by scanning cross sections and adding the material layer upon layer until the desired form is achieved. Subtractive manufacturing describes a process in which an object is milled from a block or sheet of material by removing unwanted material; unlike the additive approach, this does not use cross sections, but instead works from the surface data to create the form of the object. Each approach has its benefits and limitations; when making your choice, you should consider the cost, material quality, finish quality, durability, and use of the model.

Additive processes 3D printing (3DP) is a simple process in which a liquid binding material is printed through an inkjet printer to solidify a powdered plaster-type material. The bed of the printer drops as each layer is printed to allow the object to fill the void.

Stereo lithography apparatus (SLA) is a process in which liquid resin is solidified by a laser beam that traces a section of the object on the surface of the resin. Layer after layer is built up as the bed drops to allow a greater volume of resin to fill the chamber.

Selective laser sintering (SLS) uses a high-powered laser to fuse small particles of material together to create a part or object. Cross sections are scanned in layers and the material fused in a sequence of layers to create the form.

Additive manufactured tureen by Michael Eden
By exploring the potential for additive manufacturing, Michael Eden has been able to play with ceramics conventions of mass, volume, and proportion. His Wedgwoodn't collection uses technology to unpick the historical precedant.

Subtractive processes Computer numerically controlled (CNC) modeling is a system of numerical coordinates that define the cutting or milling of a sheet or block material. The machine uses a range of drill bits and a complicated computer system that plots the path that the tools will mill.

Laminated object manufacturing (LOM) describes the process of cutting and laminating sheets of heat-bonded paper into forms.

Laser cutting uses a laser to cut through a material, creating a highly detailed object and very accurate edge and finish.

Water-jet cutting uses a high pressure and very focused jet of water mixed with a fine abrasive material. It is particularly useful when materials are sensitive to heat that are generated in other cutting processes.

Rapid prototyping bureaus

Rapid prototyping equipment is very expensive, but bureaus offer a modeling service at a range of costs. The files are exported into a generic format (such as STL or DXL), which can be e-mailed to the bureau for prototyping. There are a range of prototyping processes and materials that impact on the quality and cost. It is important that you fully study the quality of surface and finish on your model. As a general rule, the finer the quality of surface, the higher the cost and the longer the time spent generating the model.

PROGRAMS

The software required to generate three-dimensional design is widely available for most domestic computers. These programs create 3D objects within a virtual space, using a basic x–y–z axis to aid orientation and understanding. The programs are split into a range of tools: primitive tools use standard shapes as building blocks; surface tools can generate complex compound surfaces; lines and curves create more complex profiles that can be extruded or lathed. Rendering facilities allow the creation of realistic images with lighting and shadows. The following popular 3D software programs are compatible with rapid prototyping technologies. Some of the rendering elements of the programs use a lot of memory to generate the image, so the RAM is quite important. Check the system requirements of any software before you buy it to ensure that it is compatible with your computer.

- **Rhino** Rhino is a widely used NURBS (non-uniform rational B-spline) modeling program. This means it is very intuitive at creating complex curves and surfaces. Rhino has an easy interface, with a good range of tools, and is fairly inexpensive.

- **Auto Cad** Auto Cad is a high-level drafting and modeling package. It has an extensive and intuitive range of tools to suit a variety of modeling needs.

- **Deskartes** Deskartes is an unusual package in that it was developed specifically for use in the tableware industry; consequently it works in a way that relates specifically to the manufacture of ceramics. It has a very powerful rendering capability.

- **Cobalt** Cobalt is a parametric modeling program with a very simple interface and usability, aided by its intuitive built-in help tool.

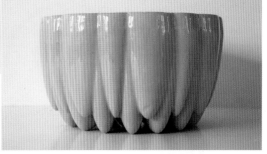

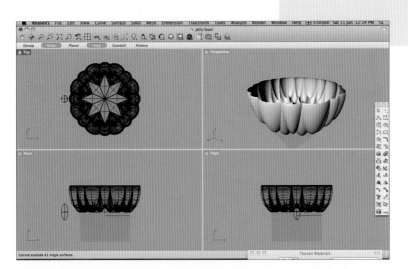

Using Rhino

Rhino's four-view capability is very effective in allowing Emily-Clare Thorn to consider all of the object when developing the form. The ability to flip between perspectives encourages a greater awareness of the form, its proportions, scale, and profile.

HYBRID MANUFACTURING

Roderick Bamford's work is inspired by music and translated by technology into a reality. He has been able to capture musical data in a ceramic form. The development process is an interesting one; it relies on technology to begin with, as a computer program is used to create the surfaces, before using a 3D printer to transform data into a physical model. Following this, the model is slip cast and fired in a traditional manner. The form of the bowl is inspired by sound waves produced on an oscilloscope.

1 The computer image is prepared for rapid prototyping, exported as an STL file and then printed on a Dimensions SST 3D printer. The model is removed from the machine and cleaned of any support materials.

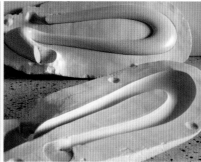

2 The resulting model is in an ABS plastic, which gives a very accurate dimensional geometry and a surface finish requiring little hand finishing. The model is then painted to achieve a super smooth surface suitable for casting.

3 The finished model is then duplicated using the plaster mold to create a number of working models. These models have been repainted.

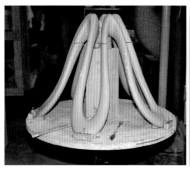

4 The final bowl form is produced by assembling the plaster models in a strict geometry. The plaster models are supported during the process to ensure a perfect join. The remaining lines are filled in and finished until smooth.

5 The assembled model is cast to create a three-piece slip-cast mold.

6 The delicate slip-cast form is supported by a foam-rubber cradle to allow the forms to dry without warping.

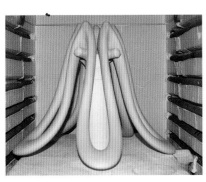

7 A refractory cradle (setter) is slip cast to support each object through the firing. The cradle is cast at the same time as the bowl form.

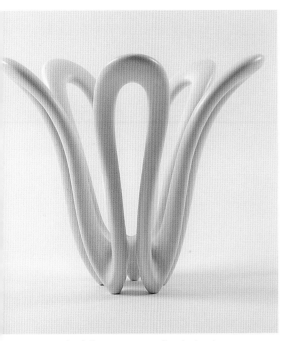

8 The deformation is initially calculated through trial and error, raising the refractory setter by a specific amount so that the fired object shrinks the correct amount to achieve the desired curvature. This way the cradle can be reused and waste is avoided. The high bisque firing of the form allows the piece to be subsequently glaze fired the right way up, so that glaze marks are not visible.

TECHNIQUE FILE 82

SELECTIVE LASER SINTERING

Michael Eden's sculptural forms, Amalthea, are generated using an additive process.

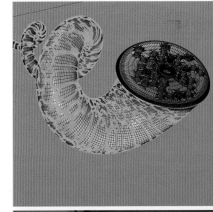

1 Michael uses Rhino 3D software to generate the surfaces of his design, before exporting them into a format to send to the printing bureau. The information is then inputted into the 3D printer and the machine grows the image using a nylon material, building each section of the object in layers until complete.

2 The object is built in the SLS machine and then is placed in a de-powdering unit where the excess powder is removed.

3 The object is gently dusted down until all of the surfaces are clean of the material. Following this the object is coated with a mineral paint to achieve its satin gloss surface. A layer of "Soft Coat" adds a suede-like tactile surface to the piece.

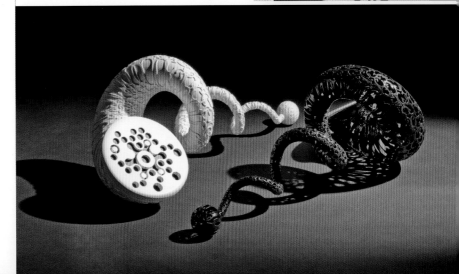

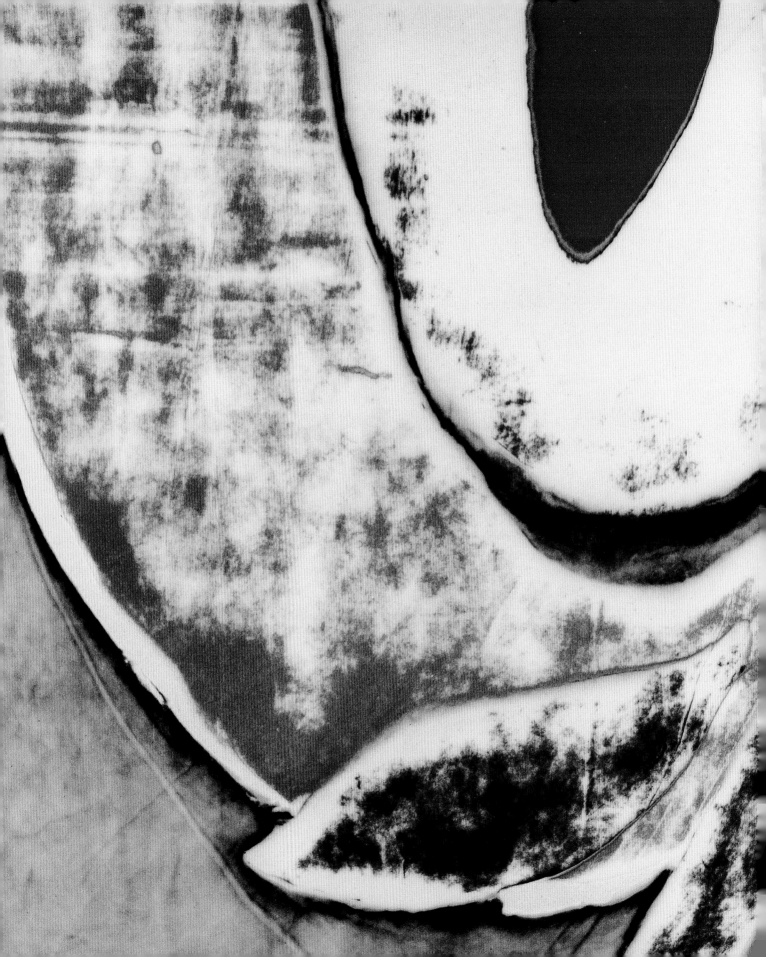

PART THREE

PREFIRING SURFACE DECORATION

COLOR STAINED BOWL
BY SUSAN NEMETH
This detail shows clay that has been colored with oxides and body stains to create a wide-ranging palette. Thin porcelain sheets are laminated together and then scraped and sanded back to create this varied surface color and pattern.
Makers from left to right: Siddig El Nigoumi, Regina Heinz, and Tony Laverick

Slip is simply liquid clay: clay mixed with a lot of water. The simplest decorating slip uses the same clay body as the object. This may be mixed with a metallic oxide or commercial stain to produce colored slip. It can be used to provide the undercoat for glaze or, if left unglazed, to create a matte surface.

SLIP DECORATION: MATERIALS AND MIXING

Slip decoration presents an ideal opportunity to start introducing applied color to your work and is used with a wide variety of techniques to create simple, solid-block color or highly expressive decorative surfaces. Its use is optional, but experimentation with color, brushwork, and surface texture will greatly increase your options when it comes to glazing and will help you create highly individual work.

Slip has been used to create decorative surfaces for thousands of years. The most notable examples of this technique are the Classical red and black figure vases made in Greece between the seventh and fifth centuries BC. Other cultures around the world have examples that date back to this period. The pre-Columbian Mayan culture produced work with slip in the second century, creating some wonderfully expressive designs. Excellent early British examples of folk-tradition slipware include the work of Thomas Toft (1680). Today, Grayson Perry uses slip on the surface of his pots to give depth and richness to his drawings, using a variety of techniques.

Mixing and variations
Slip can be made very simply by breaking down any clay body with water and refining the mixture by pushing it through an 80-mesh sieve.

Slip-decorated pot
by Tony Laverick
This wheel-thrown form has been softened by gentle manipulation. The black crazed lines give the impression of stitching the form together.

TECHNIQUE FILE 83

MAKING AND COLORING SLIP

Mixing and coloring your own clay is a simple process; using one clay as the base and adding different commercially manufactured color stains and metallic oxides means that the clays will be compatible when drying and firing.

1 Start by drying out and crushing your favorite white earthenware or stoneware clay body or by weighing out the dry ingredients of a slip or clay body recipe. It is preferable to start with a dry weight, so that the color is mixed thoroughly throughout the ingredients.

2 Weigh out the powder clay or ingredients so that you can work out how much body stain to add. Depending on the color, 10–15 percent of stain added to the powder will normally give you the maximum strength of color. This will make it easier for you to adjust the proportions in future to obtain the strength of color that you want.

3 Weigh out the relevant amount of body stain or oxide. Depending on how many colors you are mixing at once, it can be easier to place the powder on a sheet of paper, which you can then funnel into your mixing bowl without the need to wash and dry separate containers.

4 Put some of the powder into a pestle and mortar with water to thoroughly mix and blend. If you don't do this then certain stains and oxides may speckle when used.

5 Add more water and mix to a yogurtlike consistency. Blend with the remaining powder in a larger bowl.

6 Prepare two wooden sticks to sit on top of a bowl rim. Place a 60–80-mesh sieve on top of the wooden sticks. Push the mixture through the sieve. A higher-number sieve can be used, depending on what clay body you are using. If the mixture is very liquid, leave it overnight and drain off the top surface water before going on to the next stage.

Identifying clay for slip application

These two tiles demonstrate when to apply slip and when not to. They are made from the same clay. The left-hand tile is leather hard. It still contains moisture so the color is darker. The right-hand tile is too dry to apply slip, because the water has all evaporated.

MAKING A COLORED CLAY BODY

Making your own clay body offers a wide variety of colors, whereas the range of colored clays that can be purchased from suppliers is much smaller. All will require testing to assess their colors at different firing temperatures.

TECHNIQUE FILE 84

1 Pour and spread the mixture onto a plaster bat, using as much of the surface area as possible. This will speed up the drying process. Be aware that this small amount of clay will start to dry within five minutes, so pay attention to ensure it doesn't dry too much.

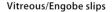

2 Scrape and lift the clay off the plaster bat using a rubber kidney, and knead (see page 31) until it is the correct consistency to use. Leave wetter if you are going to wrap and store it for any length of time.

3 Dark colors may stain the bat. You can obviously use both sides of these, one side to be kept for lighter colors so they do not get contaminated.

Vitreous/Engobe slips

These slip colors are made with commercial body stains. These are different from ordinary slips as they can be used on both leather-hard clay or on bisque ware. Slips can also be made into colored clay bodies to use as solid colored clay, inlay, and agateware.

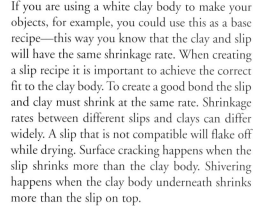

If you are using a white clay body to make your objects, for example, you could use this as a base recipe—this way you know that the clay and slip will have the same shrinkage rate. When creating a slip recipe it is important to achieve the correct fit to the clay body. To create a good bond the slip and clay must shrink at the same rate. Shrinkage rates between different slips and clays can differ widely. A slip that is not compatible will flake off while drying. Surface cracking happens when the slip shrinks more than the clay body. Shivering happens when the clay body underneath shrinks more than the slip on top.

If you are using different clays at different temperatures, then you can make a more general-purpose slip. A ball clay is ideal for this because it will be highly plastic and light in color and will stick to most clay bodies. Ball clays are the base for most slip recipes. They can be used by themselves or with additions of china clay (kaolin) and a small amount of frit. (This amount will be determined by the clay you choose and the firing temperatures you are using.) All makers will develop their favorite base recipe for slip, which they have tried and tested.

Vitreous slips

Slips can also be made with a range of glaze ingredients. These are classified and named differently from general-purpose slips. (These slips are known as "vitreous," or by some as "engobes," sometimes spelled "englobes"; others refer to all slips as engobes.) They contain flux to help stick the liquid slip to the surface of a clay body. They also result in a different surface quality than ordinary slip when left unglazed. When fired at over 2100° F (1150° C), they will often have a pleasant sheen. These can be used, like all slips, on fresh wet clay but, unlike other slips, also on bone-dry and bisque-fired clay. This obviously makes vitreous slips a very versatile medium to use during making and decorating before and after first firing.

Coloring slip

To color slip you can add metallic oxides or commercially prepared stains or a combination of both to the base recipe. Ideally always mix

SLIP-TRAILED PLATE
BY DYLAN BOWEN

The action of loose throwing is perfectly complemented by the flowing movement of the contrasting colored slip across the surface. The beauty and rhythm of the action is seemingly effortless.

these from a dry weight. If using a clay body to make your slip, dry this out first and crush before weighing. This will mean you are not wasting the stains by overcompensating and your results will be consistent.

Oxides and body/glaze stains are highly concentrated and powerful, so always test first to find the intensity of color you require. Most commercial stains will fire at 2280° F (1250° C), others higher, and some lower. The manufacturers' catalogs will always explain the individual firing temperatures and the saturation quantities required.

Improvised slip trailer

Hyang Jong Oh and Dylan Bowen discuss their recent slip-trailing work. Using a plastic bag as an improvised slip trailer they decorated this thrown form. It was made on the kick wheel over two days by Oh and formed part of a series of stage demonstrations at the 2011 International Ceramics Festival in Aberystwyth, Wales, UK.

RECIPES

White Slip		White Slip Base		Vitreous slip		Black slip	
Ball clay	50%	(a good general-purpose base for other colors)		Calcined ball clay	35%	Powdered red clay	70%
China clay	50%			Calcined china clay	25%	Cobalt oxide	15%
		Ball clay	50%	Cornish stone	20%	Manganese dioxide	15%
		China clay	20%	Flint	20%		
		Potash feldspar	20%				
		Flint	10%				

Adding Color

Blue		Green	
Cobalt oxide	4%	Chrome	2%
Copper oxide	2%	Copper	3%

Add the following percentages of stain to the slip recipe to get a range of tones:

	Light	Medium	Dark
Oxides	0.2–2.5%	2.5–5%	5–10%
Stains	2–5%	5–10%	10–15%

Applying colored slip

Slips are ideally used on leather-hard clay to achieve best coverage. They can be used as washes when thinned down with water. Two or three coats need to be applied for full coverage. They are easy to use and create either an undercoat for glaze response or a matte, unglazed surface.

By applying slip you are changing the surface color of the clay. This can have advantages if you prefer using one type of clay over another. Terra-cotta clay, for example, can be given the appearance of porcelain by coating it in a porcelain slip.

SLIP APPLICATION

Applying slip at the greenware stage (before first firing) can make glazing decisions easier because you will be responding to a surface that already has color, marks, or a highlighted texture. For beginners this can provide very useful visual comfort and initial inspiration to respond "to." Being confronted by large quantities of bisque ware recently unloaded from the kiln can either seem a creative opportunity or very intimidating, depending on your point of view: a decorator's dream or a beginner's nightmare.

All slips provide a very inexpensive way to add color and decoration to ceramics. Once applied, all that is required to complete the work is either a matte or shiny transparent glaze. When considering the final glazed color of your work, the initial application of different-colored

INCISED SLIP DECORATION BY SIMON CARROLL *This high-fired red earthenware clay form features energetic brushed and poured slip decoration, which creates a largely matte unglazed surface that enriches the incised texture.*

slip can provide greater options. The slip acts as a visible undercoat and will increase the color range of a single semitransparent or transparent colored glaze. If the glaze is very opaque and laden with oxide the slip will have less impact on the color but may still affect the surface quality. If you want bright colors, always use a white body to make the work or coat with white slip for the background or undercoat.

The benefits of using slip

Slip is easy to apply and control, much easier than glaze. When you apply slip to a clay surface of the correct consistency it will not run, move, or mix unless you intend it to. It does not move during the firing, but fuses with the surface. The decoration will remain exactly the same as when you first put it into the kiln. Once bisque fired and out of the kiln, slip does not come off during handling or glazing. After the bisque firing it will appear lighter in color. (If left unglazed the color will darken with increasing temperature.) Slip will enable you to apply an exact pattern or overlapping colors, unlike glaze, which will melt and mix together. A thick coat of slip will "cancel out" the color underneath. You can use slip freely like paint, or experiment with different application methods and build visually complex surfaces. Any mistakes with slip can easily be wiped away while wet or scraped off when dry.

Some makers prefer to complete their work fully at the making stage with slip. During the decoration stage they would otherwise be responding to, extending, and developing the piece. Using glaze can feel to some like covering the material and intention with something that hides the qualities of the making. The

LAYERED SLIP DECORATION
BY DANIEL WRIGHT
Slip has been used to create
colored horizontal bands
of varying translucency on
this vessel.

justification often heard is that it's difficult to get the life back into the clay once it is dried out and fired. For these makers, the act of making with their chosen material is what makes them feel at their most creative.

When to apply

The stage at which you apply slip is the most important consideration, though the following rules do not apply to vitreous slip. The clay should ideally be leather hard—hard enough to allow for easy handling without losing its shape. The consistency of the surface should be like leather or firm cheese, where you can impress and see a fingernail mark. If you know the clay well then you can also tell if it is ready by its color.

When you apply the slip, remember that the clay will be absorbing a lot of water back into the body. This can cause problems; bowls that are still too soft and not the correct consistency can, in minutes, become plates! If the form is too dry, this will also cause problems. It's the same principle that says you cannot add fresh wet

Slip application effects

These tiles demonstrate the effect achieved by the different slip application methods discussed on the following pages.

clay to dry clay; the two will shrink apart and not together when drying. If you have applied the slip when the form is too dry you will often not see any problem with the fit before or after the first firing stages. It will only be once the glaze has been applied and fired and the work completed that the glaze will flake away from the surface along with the layer of slip. The glaze causes tension and contraction on the surface during the firing and cooling.

How much to apply

The amount of slip you apply is crucial to the success of the work. This will always be dependent on knowing and recognizing the thickness of slip and the consistency of the clay. For a beginner the problem is often not seeing the thickness of slip being applied until the final firing has taken place and the work is complete. Unintentional brush marks and background clay color are often visible until some level of understanding of this has been gained. A single layer of slip when brushed on will be very thin, and when fired it is semitranslucent. If you require complete coverage of a solid block of color then at least three coats should be applied, letting each one dry before applying the next one.

This is why it's important to get the clay to the correct consistency of leather hard before applying slip. You then don't need to wait to apply several layers, because the clay surface will absorb the liquid within seconds. The wetter the clay when you apply the slip, the thinner the coverage will be, as the clay cannot absorb the liquid as quickly. It will also take longer to dry between coats. If, after seeing the results, you want the slip thinner, simply add more water. If you want it thicker, and for some applications this is preferable, you can pour it onto a plaster bat to absorb some of the water. Spread it around the surface with a rubber kidney; you will see it drying very quickly, but you will be able to control the exact consistency required. Take it off before the slip turns into a clay body. An alternative is to add a small amount of a flocculent such as calcium chloride to increase

Brush

Stencil

Inlay

Latex resist

Feather

Slip trail

Wax resist

Sponge

BRUSHING TECHNIQUES

Explore the different qualities you can achieve by using different thicknesses of both slip and brushes.

If you require solid, flat coverage, apply two to four coats of slip with a hake brush. By brushing in different directions the slip will not build on an uneven surface and should remain flat. Allow the slip to become touch dry between each coat.

By using a stiffer brush you will have different mark-making potential. The color of the clay body will show through the slip, and this will be further emphasized once glazed.

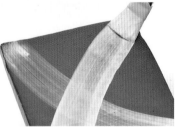

Using different brushes will vary the quality of marks you make. Different thicknesses of slip will help to give further richness and interest to the quality of the surface and, if you use thin washes, they will allow the background slip to show through.

Lightly brushing slip over a textured surface will highlight the textural qualities. Don't load the brush with too much slip because it will start to infill your texture. Wipe the brush on the edge of the bucket to subtract some of the slip before brushing.

If you make mistakes with slip it's easy to wipe it away with a sponge and start again. Using a sponge is also useful for creating a background to respond to with further brushwork.

the viscosity. A deflocculent such as Dispex will make the slip thinner.

Apply with caution

Be careful when applying slip around joins and anywhere there are additions, particularly with slab building and sculpture. It will weaken these joints for a short period as the water is absorbed. If you are concerned, you can add temporary support where necessary. Once slip has been applied, let the work dry slowly. This will give it time to slowly expand and contract. You will need to let the surface dry before wrapping, otherwise the plastic will ruin the slip surface. If you are in a hurry to pack away you can build a tent over the form.

Be careful not to leave certain slips on the base of your work. Those with high oxide content and vitreous ones may stick at stoneware temperatures. Thinking ahead to glazing, if you want to distinguish the exact inside from the outside of a form or any particular feature it is easier to do this by using slip.

Techniques for applying slip

There are many application techniques for achieving specific results with slip, but essentially it's just about how you apply liquid to a surface. You will need to check that the slip consistency is right for the technique you want to use. Many of these application methods will also apply to glazing but with different results. Whatever application technique you decide on, you don't have to be brilliant at drawing to achieve interesting, expressive, and exciting results with slip.

Brushing The first thing to get right when brushing on slip is the quality of the brush for the result required. You will not achieve a smooth, flat, even surface with a small, stiff brush over a large area. But using a small, stiff brush in this way will give you a very particular quality that may be just what you are seeking.

When you look at paintings it may not be the image, narrative, or subject matter that excites but the quality of the paint application. Seeing the dabs or fluid marks on surfaces; how they have been subtracted and reworked; or the overlayering of tinted transparent glazes to deepen the surface quality. It's these details that keep the eyes and mind interested for more than a cursory seven seconds, and it's exactly the same with slip application.

Slip is a heavy material and generally you will be selecting brushes that can hold a lot of liquid. By experimenting with a variety of different qualities of brush you will build your knowledge of mark-making potential, ready for the next fresh piece of clay. Hake brushes are especially designed for covering a large area. These come in a range of widths and are usually wooden with white hair. They will hold a lot of liquid and allow you to make large, broad sweeps without the need to replenish the slip halfway through a stroke. If you are covering large areas it is far better to apply the slip with movement in different directions. This will also help to prevent brush marks appearing.

The liquid slip must not be too thick, since it will not flow as you brush. But neither should it be so thin that it runs away while you apply it; in this case one brushstroke will not cover the clay surface and the layer will become semitranslucent as it dries. Where full coverage is required the slip should cover your finger without dripping. You will need anything from two and four coats depending on consistency, color, and recipe to create a solid color. If the clay is the correct consistency it will absorb the water within a minute. More coats will start to soak the clay so it will gradually take longer to accept further layers.

Some makers will use this semitranslucent quality to their advantage by brushing layers that allow the color of the clay or darker slip to be visible underneath the top coat to create a greater depth of surface. If you are overlaying different colors the effect may be a little like marble, where you can "see into" the material. This is often exploited by makers who use red earthenware clay.

Brushing on slip with a large, flat hake brush can also work very well to highlight any surface texture. You can achieve this by using a small amount of slip on your brush. Lightly brush it over the surface, keeping the angle flat while

*PAINTED AND BANDED VESSELS
BY ELKE SADA
These forms demonstrate the different painterly mark-making potential that can be achieved by using different thicknesses of either slip or underglaze color. The sharp painted lines echo the delicate forms joining seams, which cut through and divide the surface.*

you move across in different directions. The slip will catch on any areas of the surface that are higher and start to build up the texture. The more you brush the greater the depth of surface will become. This way of brushing allows you to control the surface building in front of you. Don't overload the brush with slip, otherwise the surface you have built up will fill in with the liquid.

When you are performing more gestural mark making you will benefit from "warming up" first. Often the difficulty with this kind of work is that no matter how much preparatory painting you may have done on paper, trying to gain the same kind of rhythm, flow, and spontaneity is difficult on a three-dimensional object. You could try practicing on an object that has already been glazed to enable you to easily clean off and keep practicing until you are confident and happy with the results. Looking at negative space is always useful when painting in this manner. The successful flow and impact of this kind of work has a lot to do with the looseness and action of your wrist.

Banding If you require horizontal stripes, bands, or very flat, even coats of slip, use a turntable or a special adjustable freestanding banding wheel. Choosing the most appropriate brush will also help you to achieve the banded effect. Different weights of turntables are available; the ones

BANDING ON THE WHEEL

Bands of slip are made easier to control by using a heavy-duty banding wheel, a turntable, or a throwing wheel. Load brushes to avoid running out of slip halfway round.

1 If you are using a banding wheel, make sure you have centered the object in the exact center of the wheel. You can use the circular marks on the surface to help with this. Either move the turntable with your hand or spin the wheel and allow the momentum to rotate it so you can use both hands to keep the brush steady.

2 If using a turntable, make sure it is heavy. Light turntables will stop turning when you apply anything but light pressure. You may need to lower the form as you develop the pattern. Always have the form at the correct height. Often supporting your elbow or wrist with your other hand will stop any wayward movement. You can always tuck your elbow into your side as well.

made only from metal are heavier and produce a smoother action. A throwing wheel is also often used for this job. The lighter wheels are rotated with one hand while the other applies the slip with a brush. Heavier wheels can be spun and, when the momentum is smooth, the slip is applied using both hands to steady the brush as the wheel slows down. This can also be a useful way to apply oxide, glaze, enamel, and luster at the appropriate stages of making.

Pouring The rule when applying slip by pouring is to make the clay the correct consistency. If you get it wrong and the clay is too soft, your form will start to recycle itself as the clay absorbs the water from the slip and becomes very soft again. If you get it right, this technique will give you a beautiful, even, flat surface.

Start by making sure the clay is leather hard. This will give you the best chance of success. You may need to adjust the consistency of the slip. For total clay coverage, the slip will ideally drip off the tip of a finger dipped into it. If you can feel any lumps in the mixture, the slip should be sieved. (This often happens with slip that has been allowed to dry on the sides of a lidless bucket and flake off into the mixture.) If left, these lumps will show up in the poured surface and will require fettling once dried.

Handle and familiarize yourself with the form you are going to apply the slip to. Decide how you are going to hold, pour, and place it down onto a surface once finished. Otherwise you might get halfway through pouring before realizing you can't place it down without touching or knocking the sides, or ruining the surface because of the angles of the form in relation to the surface it rests on.

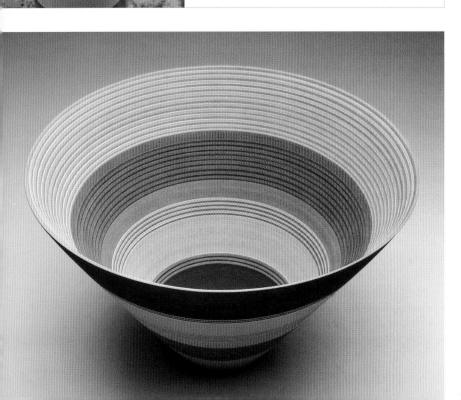

FINELY BANDED BOWL

BY SARA MOORHOUSE
*The magical interplay between
the broader bands on the
outside and the finer interior
ones keep your eyes constantly
on the move.*

Rehearsal should help in particular when you are pouring slip into the inside of a form. You will need to judge the amount you need to cover the whole of the inside in a single pour. Trying to paint missed areas almost defeats the reason for choosing this method, and it is difficult to get to small, awkward areas, which will often require leveling by fettling afterward. Make sure you are able to quickly pour the slip in and not delay the pouring out. Once poured, and while the form is upside down, gently move it around to allow the excess liquid to flow out. If you leave it for any length of time, too much slip will collect at the base and can start to weaken it. It may also crack if it is too thick.

Pouring slip over a form is much easier. Make sure you can either hold the form or, if it is large, suspend it on batons over a bucket or bowl. This will keep the slip from collecting around the rim of the form, which if left will start to quickly soften. It will also mean wiping the rim and reapplying. If the form is anything over 12 in (30 cm), place a turntable inside the container, place the batons on top, and then the form on top of these. This will enable you to move the form around more easily while pouring rather than spending too much time in one area.

Pouring slip can produce flowing designs. Pouring in a variety of different colors, thicknesses, and directions will give richness and depth to a naturally forming pattern.

Dipping When dipping forms into slip it is important to have them at the firm, leather-hard stage because of the absorption of liquid. If the slip is the correct consistency, a single dip will cover any clay or slip color underneath. The advantage of dipping is that you can achieve an even, flat surface, and the lines and edges will follow the curves of the form. Clean, hard-edged lines can crisscross each other.

Make sure when dipping the form that it is comfortable and easy to hold. With wheel-thrown forms you can create a foot ring at the base that is easy to grip and hold while you dip the form into the slip. Dipping is a simple way to define a base.

POURING

TECHNIQUE FILE **87**

It is essential to prepare the clay to the correct leather-hard consistency for pouring and dipping. If not, a bowl will quickly become a plate.

1 The slip consistency can be a little thinner for pouring than for brushing, because you want the slip to flow across the surface as you pour. Make sure you have enough slip in the jug to cover the surface in one step.

2 Make sure you can either hold the form or, if it is large, suspend it on batons over a bucket or bowl. Then simply pour the slip over the form.

DIPPING

TECHNIQUE FILE **88**

Dipping will provide a smooth, even coating of slip if done correctly.

1 Make sure there is enough slip to coat the surface area for your requirements. You should be able to achieve the coating in one dip. Leave the form in the slip for a few seconds; after withdrawing you can gently shake the form to even out any inconsistencies.

2 After dipping it is advisable to wipe any base or surface that will come into contact with kiln shelves during the firing. Because of the amount of oxide and stain in slips these will melt at stoneware temperatures and may stick.

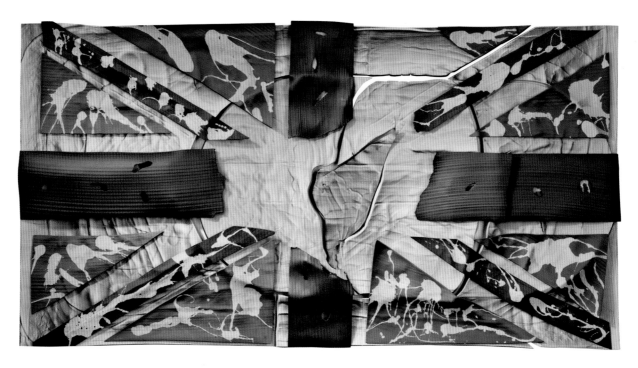

TECHNIQUE FILE **89**

SPRAYING

Spraying slip is a good way of ensuring even coverage over the work.

1 Make sure the slip is thin, so that it doesn't block the spray gun. Angle the gun so that you spray all the surfaces evenly and keep the form moving.

2 Move the spray gun in even sweeps either up and down or from side to side. Allow the form time to absorb the slip, be careful not to saturate the surface. If the appearance is wet, then let it dry for a minute. The main advantage of using the spray gun is that you can control the exact thickness of each coat and blend surfaces.

3 Spraying is also a good way to cover stencils evenly and quickly (see page 187).

SPRAYED-SLIP WALL PIECE
BY NICHOLAS ARROYAVE-PORTELA
This fascinating fractured landscape has been made using cut wheel-thrown forms. The subtle geographical lines have been enhanced by sprayed terra sigillata.

Spraying If you are using a spray gun to apply your slip it will probably need to be thinned out before application. If the liquid is too thick it will splatter and block the nozzle. The main advantage of using a spray gun for any application method is that you can control the exact thickness of the layer you are applying. But, as with all these techniques, it will take practice to achieve consistently good results.

Always work on a turntable so that you don't have to handle the work. When you are spraying, hold the gun at a distance of 12–18 in (30–45 cm) from the work. Too near and the slip will run down because it does not have enough time to be absorbed onto the body. Too far away and the slip will "bobble" in the air as the particles separate before it hits the form.

Keep both the form and the gun moving slowly. Move the gun up and down and from side to side. Don't just spray from one angle, because the underhangs will be left bare—a common bare area is usually toward the base. Change the angle of spray regularly so that the gun is both above

Vessel brushed with slip
BY JOHN HIGGINS
*This stoneware slab-built form creates a
canvas for both subtle surface texture and
varied bold brush decoration.*

ROLLERING

Different roller sleeves can provide a wide range
of surfaces from solid, even coverage to broken
surface pattern.

1 Load your chosen roller in a tray
of slip. Often the roller will absorb
too much slip, so test this out on
a surface before applying to the
clay surface.

2 You can control the amount
of coverage you require through
pressure. For solid, even coverage
press firmly and roll. For a broken
surface press lightly. Rolling in
different directions will start to
build up the surface texture.

3 Further applications will cancel
out the previous layers and increase
the visual interest of the surface.
This can be further highlighted
when touch dry by lightly brushing
over in a contrasting color.

and below the work to achieve an even layer. You
can stop and start the gun instead of trying to
coat the form in one continuous movement. If
an area starts to appear wet, it is saturated and
you must quickly move on otherwise the slip will
start to run down and form drips.

When you have gone around the form once,
make a mark on the turntable so you know
when you have applied one coat. As you come
around again make another to keep track of
how many coats you have applied and where
you started from. The spray gun will only apply
thin layers, so for a solid coat you will need to
apply three or four coats. With spraying you
can achieve perfect graduation of color and very
subtle shading results.

Interesting results can be achieved by spraying
across existing surface texture to highlight its
specific making character. Spraying one color in
one direction and others in different directions
will enhance this. Using different strengths of
the same color, altered with varying amounts of
oxide, will also produce a particular quality.

Rollering A standard small paint roller with
sleeves made from different materials, such as
smooth or rough sponge, short- or long-haired
sheepskin, or cloth, will produce particular
surface qualities. Rollers are interesting to use for
uneven backgrounds, or for rolling thin washes
over areas like watercolor. They can also be used
to highlight surface texture by rolling with light
pressure to pick up fine details. Rollers will
create a texture of their own, which can then be
brushed over to build up the surface details.

SPONGEWARE

A technique that can add a very subtle addition to a surface. Alternatively, you can use a defined printed motif for more of a visual impact.

1 Making spongeware designs is very simple using ordinary kitchen sponges. Cut the sponge to the appropriate size. Draw your selected design onto the sponge.

2 Carefully press into the sponge with a blade. The design can be cut out using several gentle slicing actions. When the negative bulk is subtracted, further refinement can be achieved using scissors.

3 Cut the depth of the design to at least ½ in (13 mm) to allow the sponge to soak up enough slip to produce a clear print when pressed down.

4 Place the sponge into the slip to soak. Test the amount absorbed on a separate surface before printing onto your clay. Often the sponge will absorb too much slip and may distort the image. Trial and error is necessary for success.

Spongeware This is simply work that has been decorated using sponges. Slip is applied with sponges that are cut into specific shapes or by using the texture of the sponge to create a mottled pattern. This is also a term that can be used to describe the application of glaze.

Choose different qualities of sponge and cut them to see how dense the surface must be to achieve the effect you want. Use scissors or a craft knife to cut out the designs. The advantage of using cut sponges to create designs is that you can keep reusing them time and again.

When using sponges with no specific designs to create a pattern you will be able to achieve some very subtle surface effects by overlaying thin layers of one or more colors. Select a range of different sizes and qualities of sponge to vary the repetition as you develop the pattern. If you do not regard yourself as a great drawer or designer, but want to add more contrast and depth of surface to your glazing, using a technique like this is a simple way to make your finished work more interesting.

Slip trailing "Slip trailing" describes the technique of squeezing slip out of a tool known as a trailer. The slip is pushed through a variety of different-sized detachable nozzles onto the surface of the clay. Slip trailers are now mainly made of rubber or plastic and have a bulb or

SLIP-TRAILED VESSELS
BY DYLAN BOWEN

Slip trailing on flatware is one thing, but it is altogether different on a three-dimensional form. This highly expressive slip trailing is often achieved by starting the flow before the form begins and ending after it ends so that it seems to catch only part of the action.

container at the end, which holds the liquid. To get slip into the trailer you squeeze the air out of the bulb and continue to hold it in, invert the end into the liquid and let the bulb out to suck slip up. Gently squeezing the bulb with an even pressure will control the flow of slip out. This is a technique to practice on a table or flat slab of clay before you try it on your work. It does not take long to acquire the skill of controlling the flow. The trailed slip can easily be reclaimed for further use.

The liquid needs to be a medium to thick consistency, since when the slip is trailed it should hold its line and be slightly raised. Too thin and the slip will be flat when trailed and will distort. The raised line made by trailing will also decrease a little while drying, but will still have a surface that can be felt under glaze. The thickness of the slip is something to experiment with and control to suit your needs. If you would like higher raised lines, you can use a technique called tube lining at the bisque-firing stage. The primary aim of this is to separate glazes during the firing process to stop them from blending together.

As with all mark making, experiment with a variety of sizes, speeds, and actions. Different-sized openings are available to create thin, medium, and thick lines. The speed of movement across the surface will create sharp or tentative lines. The quicker the movement, the sharper the line. Different ways of holding the tool and moving it will have different results. Slip trailers are ideal for creating a spotted design or for dribbling flowing, imperfect, meandering lines down a vertical form.

SLIP TRAILING

Slip trailing is a very versatile means of applying slip. Slip trailers come in a variety of different sizes, some of which have interchangeable nozzles that produce different line thicknesses.

1 Apply gentle pressure on the bulb and the slip will flow. Uneven pressure will cause the line to stutter. Stopping in one place will cause the line to thicken. Practice will help you produce the type of line you require.

2 Speed of movement will affect the quality of line that you produce. This line was started slowly and then the speed was increased to create a sharper line. Experiment with different thicknesses of slip and movement across the surface to create different qualities of line, as you would with any other drawing medium.

3 Gentle squeezing of the trailer down a vertical surface will create a soft, meandering line.

4 Slip trailers are commonly used to create dots and spots. It is easy to vary the size by altering the pressure and the length of time spent in one place.

FEATHERING

This is a traditional technique that has been largely absent from the contemporary scene.

TECHNIQUE FILE
93

1 Use a slip trailer to lay down several alternating lines of contrasting slip. Alternatively, you can lay down a single line of color with a space between each line.

2 Simply draw a line through in one direction and then back in the opposite direction to create a feathered pattern. There are very fine, beautiful historic examples of this in many museums.

MARBLING

Mixing colors in this way requires some restraint, since you do not want to overmix the slip.

TECHNIQUE FILE
94

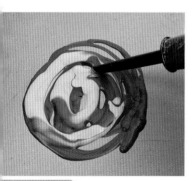

1 Either pour slip on the surface from a jug or, for more control, introduce the slip with a trailer. You can lay one color down and then add another, or add them simultaneously.

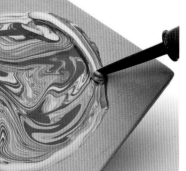

2 Move the form in different directions to start mixing the colors. Try different speeds of movement to vary the size of the blending. You can add more slip to create further marbled effects.

Feathering Feathering is seen as a very traditional technique. Its name is derived from the creation of a delicate, featherlike pattern, which requires a steady hand and good control of trailing. Apply it to leather-hard clay, using one of two methods. Either use two colors and trail alternating colored lines next to each other in rows, or first lay a block of color down using brushing or pouring. Allow this to partly dry, then on top of it lay down trailed lines, leaving spaces in between, in a contrasting color. Traditionally a feather quill was drawn horizontally through the vertical lines in one direction and then pulled through in the opposite direction. The pattern this creates can be very appealing, but it seems that this technique is rarely experimented with in the contemporary context.

Marbling Marbling slip is a technique strongly associated with tradition. It is very easy to achieve and, depending on how it is used, can produce interesting patterns; this will all depend on how much slip you put into the mix at once and how and where you apply it. You can begin with a

FEATHERED POT
BY SIMON CARROLL
This heavy-duty wheel-thrown form demonstrates the potential of what can seem a very traditional technique when used in a more expressive contemporary way. Though it pays homage to the past it is definitely in the present.

LAYERED DECORATION WORK
BY ROBERT COOPER
*This lidded textural form has subtle layers of
print and stencils, which create a complex surface
that seems patinated over many years.*

solid background of slip, which is either brushed or poured, then pour or trail a contrasting color onto this. The form is then moved to make the marbled effect. The speed and direction of these movements will determine the outcome. Some extent of control is possible but, as with all the other slip techniques, the result can be washed off and reapplied if necessary. Some of the fluid subtlety that can be achieved with this technique will not be fully evident until the form is glazed and finished.

Stenciling Stencils can be made from any material that will resist water, either indefinitely or for just a short period. They need to be flexible, and soft enough to lay flat on a clay surface. Different kinds of paper, plastic, and fabric are the most common materials for this purpose. Also useful is anything that has an open texture or gaps that will allow the slip to pass through. Depending on which material you decide to use, stencils can be washed after use and reused to reproduce the same design many times. Precut designs are commercially available, and you can also get custom designs professionally laser cut.

If the clay is a little soft, the stencil can be pushed into the surface to leave a slight impression. This depth will be accentuated once

USING STENCILS

Endless design possibilities await once you start using stencils with slip. A simple design can be repeated to create striking results.

1 Whatever material you have used to create your stencil, either dampen the stencil before placing it down onto the clay or dampen the surface of the clay to help it to stick. Once the stencil is laid down, press gently with a sponge to check there are no areas where the slip can infiltrate and bleed underneath.

2 Start the brushing by applying a small amount of slip over the edges of your design, so that you don't disturb the stencil and to make sure it will stay in place. Alternatively, you can spray the surface with slip.

3 Apply two to four layers of slip for full coverage. The more layers you apply, the greater the depth of the negative space of your design. The deeper this goes the more it will give the appearance of having been carved out of the surface.

4 Once the slip is touch dry the stencil can be peeled away. If the edge is not visible, use a needle tool to lift from a corner so you can peel back in one pull. If you leave stencils in place and allow the surface to fully dry, the stencil can start to lift off other areas of the slip and may not leave a clean edge.

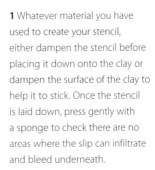
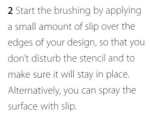
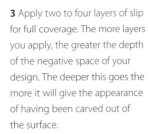

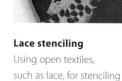

Lace stenciling
Using open textiles, such as lace, for stenciling will produce interesting results with slip.

WAX RESIST

Liquid wax is very versatile and can be used on greenware, bisque ware, and on glazed ware to resist any water-based slips and glazes.

1 Select a brush that will hold enough wax to enable you to lay it down in fluid movements so that you don't need to start and stop to keep loading the brush. One coat should be sufficient to resist the slip.

2 Allow the wax to fully dry. With water-based wax emulsion it will change from wet white opaque to dry transparent in approximately five to ten minutes. Apply the slip with a soft brush otherwise it can scratch the wax from the surface. Once the slip is touch dry you can repeat the process and add further layers of wax and slip.

3 Before the slip is fully dry you can remove any residue from the surface of the wax with a damp sponge, or for smaller areas, a paintbrush. If this slip is left in place it may settle on the clay surface during firing. This should not stick and can be brushed off after first firing.

a layer of slip is applied. Once the initial coat of slip is on and is touch dry, further stencils can be applied successfully on top and developed.

When applying slip onto and through a stencil, make sure the chosen material is lying on the surface with no small gaps that might allow the slip to infiltrate under the stencil. Apply the appropriate number of layers to gain the coverage you require. Once you can see that the slip is touch dry, lift a corner with a needle tool, then peel it away and lift off. If you leave the stencil in place until bone dry, depending on what your stencil is made from, it may start to peel away of its own accord and start to pull the slip along with it.

Wax resist Traditionally, hot wax was used for this technique, but cold liquid brushing wax or emulsion is now readily available and is easy to use. Once applied to the surface of leather-hard clay and allowed to dry for a few minutes, the wax will repel the application of the water-based slip. The wax can then also be applied to further layers of slip to build up the depth of surface

CLEANING BRUSHES
Brushes can be difficult to clean when using all forms of wax and latex.
If left to partially dry, the brush will be ruined. Before dipping your brush into these liquids, try applying liquid soap and rubbing this into the hairs. Gently rinse through with water; this will leave a thin coating on the hairs. It will not affect the application of the wax or latex but should make washing out with soap afterward much easier.

pattern and design. Wax applications can be used at the glazing stage as well.

Applying wax is simple, but think of the quality of line and coverage you require, since this will determine the brushes you use. Try to keep brushes specifically for wax decoration. When you apply the wax it will have a milky appearance, which will become transparent as it dries. Don't apply the slip until the wax has dried fully. It can then be applied using any of the application methods described.

You will often find small speckles of slip that have congealed on the wax surface during application. If these are left they will settle and fix on the surface once the wax has burnt off during the firing process. They can add to the surface interest of wax-decorated forms, but if they are unwanted you can take them off with a sponge or a paintbrush soon after applying the slip.

The problem associated with wax decoration is that it can be difficult to rectify mistakes, because the only way to subtract any unwanted wax is to scrape it off. If you have applied the wax onto another color, you will ruin the surface underneath. The wax is burned off during the bisque-firing stage. If you have used a lot of wax

Forms decorated using wax resist

BY LISA KATZENSTEIN

These highly decorative works fully demonstrate the colorful potential of using a variety of different surface decorating techniques.

APPLYING LATEX

The main advantage of using liquid latex to resist other ceramic materials is that it can be peeled away and further layers of colors applied to develop the design.

1 Apply the liquid latex in a medium to thick layer to enable you to peel it easily from the surface once the process is complete.

2 Allow the latex to dry fully. It will change from wet white opaque to dry transparent in approximately five to ten minutes depending on drying conditions. Once the latex is dry you can apply the layers of slip.

3 Once the slip is dry you can pick off an area of latex with a needle tool. If the design is joined, then as you peel the latex back it will come off altogether. If you have left the slip to dry completely, take care when peeling back to prevent the bits of clay flying around as the latex stretches.

4 One advantage of using latex over wax is that it allows you to overlay the first areas of resist with different colors of slip. Then, as with wax, you can continue the development of the design with further layers of latex and slip.

SGRAFFITO

This is a form of incising. The essential thing to get right is the consistency of clay and slip. If damp and leather hard, the clay should come away cleanly.

1 The slip and clay surface in this illustration is firm and leather hard. This enables the layer of slip to be removed without creating any burrs either side of the cut. The slip is easier to carve away without pulling away any other areas of slip with it. The subtracted bits are also a good consistency to avoid sticking to the slip and can be easily brushed or shaken away.

2 Getting the clay and slip to the appropriate consistency before subtracting will enable you to create precise designs without causing any problems. It will also mean that you can be very exact about how deep you want the line to be, and whether you want to remove just the slip or carve into the clay body as well.

on your work in the same firing, make sure you have very efficient ventilation, since it creates an acrid atmosphere as it burns off.

Latex Latex is a readily available liquid rubber solution that can be brushed on and is easy to use. Once applied to the surface of leather-hard clay and allowed to dry for a few minutes, the latex will repel the application of the water-based slip. Latex can also be used at the glazing stage.

The advantage of latex over wax is that it can be lifted off the surface to assess the design. Futher latex can then be applied to either cover previous or different areas of the design, allowing slip to be added too or overlaid with the same or a different color. This means that mistakes can be rectified and more complex surfaces developed. The latex can be left in place for the firing or lifted off. Don't let the slip become bone dry before peeling the latex off, since it may pull other areas of slip with it.

Sgraffito "Sgraffito" is an Italian word that refers to scratching or drawing into clay. It is derived from the Italian *graffiare*, "to draw." This technique describes scratching through the surface layers of applied colored slip to reveal the color of the clay body underneath. Sgraffito can also be a term that is used at any stage of the ceramic process to describe drawing through any ceramic material. The word "sgraffito" has the embellished sound of a flourish, rather than the short, hard-sounding word "scratch."

INTRICATE SGRAFFITO DECORATION
BY GERRY WEDD
These three jars have been decorated using layers of colored slip and sgraffito. The combination of the contemporary sgraffito drawing is juxtaposed against the traditional shape of the jars.

PRECIOUS BOYS
BY GRAYSON PERRY
The ceramic techniques used here give wonderful depth to the surface. Being able to combine your knowledge of techniques will help to create work that is both personal and individual.

GEOMETRIC PATTERNED PLATE
BY SIDDIG EL NIGOUMI
This plate has been simply decorated using sgraffito through slip decoration and burnishing. It has been left unglazed, which helps it to retain a timeless quality.

What you choose to use to scratch or draw with through the slip and when you do it will very much depend on the type of mark you want to create. The variety and quality of line you can achieve is extensive—from fine, pin-sharp lines to large, soft-edged ones.

Ceramic suppliers offer a wide variety of specific sgraffito tools for this purpose. You'll need to experiment with these to see what suits your requirements. Often makers will choose to adapt them, or custom-make their own tools for a specific task.

Sgraffito can be done at any point, from when you first apply the wet slip layer through to when the work is bone dry. Choosing when you scratch into and through the slip layer will determine the kind of result you will achieve.

If you scratch through the slip while it is still wet with a narrow, sharp tool, large burrs will be made either side of the line as the tool cuts into both the slip and clay. You will need to wait until the form is dry to brush these away. If left in

place, they will be razor-sharp once fired and will often protrude from the glazed surface. Using something softer and wider at this stage, like a rubber tool, a sponge, or your fingers, will push the slip aside and create flowing, soft lines. For deeper, carved lines the slip and clay will be easier to subtract while still damp.

For sharp, accurate, narrow lines, wait until the slip has dried to a very firm leather-hard state, similar to butter just out of the refrigerator. Then, when you scratch in your design, the lines will create only very small burrs that can be easily brushed away without disturbing the surface. Depending on the tool and the dryness of the slip you may not create any burr when subtracting; this is when it can seem the most satisfying.

If the surface is bone dry when you scratch in your design it can, depending on the slip recipe and the clay body, start to chip rather than come away smoothly. This will also depend on the thickness of the layer of the slip.

A technique or action called "combing" is similar to sgraffito. This describes the action of drawing or pulling a comb through the surface of the clay to create equally spaced lines. "Incising" describes another technique similar to sgraffito, where you subtract clay without the covering of slip.

Sgraffito lines can be highlighted throughout the ceramic process by inlaying other stains, oxides, and enamels to add further depth and interest. Depending on the depth of lines, glaze will also settle and pool into these; this will add further richness to the surface and design.

CARVED AND DIRECT INLAY

There are a number of ways to inlay slip: you can carve your design into leather-hard clay and then slip trail into the grooves, or place colored clay directly onto a plaster surface and press a slab onto this (inlay).

Method 2:

1 Apply colored clay directly into the plaster mold to create your chosen design.

2 Prepare a slab of clay, lay it directly on your design, and press it into the mold. As you press the slab of clay, the colored clay or slip will fully inlay or print on the surface.

3 Allow the form to semidry, then take it out of the mold.

Method 1:

1 You can experiment with how deep you want the line to be, depending on how much scraping back at the last stage of the process you plan to do. After carving you can get rid of any small burrs and soften the edges using your finger. This will create a better line to infill with slip (see detail).

2 Use a stiff brush to clear any small bits of clay out of the carved design. This will ensure there are no small blemishes in your final result.

3 Use a brush or slip trailer to infill the design with slip. Let this application partly dry for a few minutes. As the slip dries it will sink into the design. If you want the final inlay to be flush with the rest of the surface you may need to apply another layer of slip. Once dry, the line should be slightly raised above the rest of the surface.

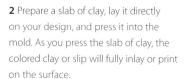

4 To clean any blemishes and finish off the surface, scrape back with a metal kidney to reveal your design. Make sure you fully support the form underneath the area you are working on, since the clay will be fragile at this stage.

4 Leave the clay body and slip to partially dry out before using a flat edge to scrap away the excess slip. If the design has very fine lines you may need to let the clay dry more; otherwise, if the lines are damp they can close up and disappear. Gradually the design will be revealed. You can remove the slip when the clay and slip are completely dry, but if there is any grog content this will cause scratch marks on the surface.

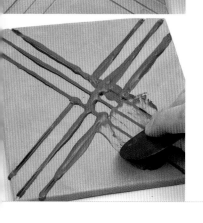

5 Alternatively, use a slip trailer to draw your chosen design on the plaster surface.

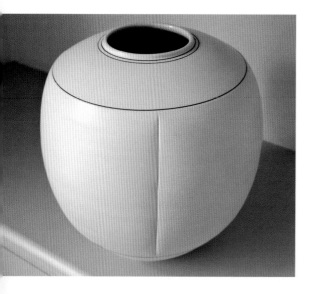

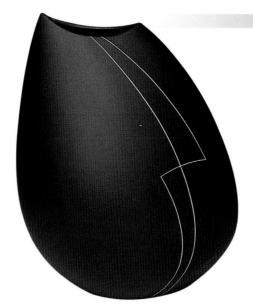

VASE WITH DELICATE INLAY
BY ANNA SILVERTON
*Inlay is often used to add
emphasis and relate directly to
the form, as here. It will bring
the eye directly to any area when
used sparingly (far left).*

INLAID VASE
BY SUE DYER
*Inlaying slips requires a steady
hand and patience. It enables
the creation of fine lines of
contrasting color, and yields
elegant results (above, left) .*

Inlay Inlaying slips has its roots in Japanese techniques. You can inlay any slip into any clay body. The reason for using this technique would be that you want your drawn designs to be perfectly level and flat so that they appear fully integrated into the clay surface. With perfect inlay you will not feel any difference in surface levels under your fingertips. If you require very sharp, fine graphic lines on your work this technique is the most appropriate to use.

Choosing a particular clay body will determine the surface quality and result as you draw the lines into the surface and scrape away the excess slip. Choosing a smooth, fine clay body without any grog content will result in a smooth, flat surface with perfectly flat lines. If the clay body contains a lot of grog the results will be rougher, giving more texture and jagged inlaid lines.

Inlaying is an easy technique, and your patience will be rewarded with satisfying results. Once you have scratched your design into the clay surface you then infill the lines with slip using a brush or slip trailer. You then wait for the slip to start drying, and as the clay shrinks refill or reapply where necessary. Once the line feels raised on the surface, scrape away the slip with the flat edge of a metal kidney to reveal the inlaid lines. It's very satisfying when you start to see the designs appearing out of a mess of slip.

It's important not to scrape away the slip too soon, as this will result in the lines becoming blurred. Fine lines in particular must be scraped back once the clay has had time to dry around the wet inlaid slip, otherwise they will disappear completely. If the scraping back is done when

bone dry and the slip and clay has even the smallest amount of grog it will scratch the surface. This surface will then be very difficult and time consuming to try and repair.

You can inlay very fine lines into existing slip colors using wax resist. Lay wax onto an existing color and, once it is dry, scratch a line into the wax and slip. You can then inlay a different color into this fine line without it mixing in with the underlying color. Wipe away any surface residue of slip; the wax will burn away during firing to leave the inlayed line.

Terra sigillata "Terra sigillata" is a term that has different meanings and definitions; it roughly translates from the Latin as "sealed earth." This does not mean, as is often thought, that the fine slip provides a sealed surface. The term can be a description of a medieval medicinal soil found on the island of Lemnos. Small cakes were made of it and stamped with a seal, the head of Artemis. It's also a general term for Roman red earthenware that has a glossy surface, and is used now by contemporary makers to describe a variety of slip.

Historically we refer to terra sigillata as work produced during the first century by Roman potters in Gaul, known as Samian ware. Before this, Greek potters used this slip on their Classical red-and-black figure vases between the seventh and fifth centuries BC. These contrasting colors were not different colors of slip, but the areas coated with slip that would turn black in controlled, reduced, and oxidized atmospheres in the kiln, due to the heavier iron content.

Terra sigillata is made very simply from fine particles of clay. It's not available to buy from ceramic suppliers but is very easy to make yourself. You can use any application method to apply the slip to your work, and it can be applied to both leather-hard and dry clay. Often the slip will create its own sheen as it dries. If not, you can lightly buff the surface with a cloth or a smooth pad of plastic wrapped around some cloth. This is usually fired once at 1500–1830° F (820–1000° C). The higher you fire the work, the more the sheen decreases. The lower you decide to fire the work, the more fragile it will be; you'll need to find a compromise.

Once applied, the terra sigillata will give the surface of the clay a certain denseness. This will slow down the absorption of water through the still-porous clay body, but will not make it waterproof.

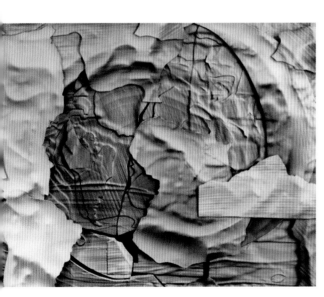

DETAIL OF ABSTRACT WALL PIECE
BY NICHOLAS ARROYAVE-PORTELA
The clay starts as a wheel-thrown form that is cut, stretched, pressed, and marked with geographical representations that remain abstract. The work is often sprayed with terra sigillata, which highlights the varied surface texture.

TECHNIQUE FILE 100

TERRA SIGILLATA

This fine slip cannot be purchased from suppliers. It requires a small amount of preparation, usually from a fine ball clay. The slip can be colored using both commercial stains and oxides.

1 Weigh out all the ingredients and add a small amount of water to prevent too much dust. Add the sodium silicate to warm water to dilute it, and add to the mixture. Sodium silicate is completely transparent. Mix until you have a yogurtlike consistency. Push this mixture through a 60–80-mesh sieve.

The heavier sludge material is easily visible at the bottom. Try not to disturb this when siphoning off the liquid.

2 Decant into a 2-quart (2-liter) bottle and shake, leave to settle for 24 hours. Insert the plastic tube two-thirds of the way into the bottle or just above where you can see the mixture going darker. Above this is the layer of terra sigillata that you need to siphon off.

3 The terra sigillata can be applied to either leather-hard or dry clay with a soft hake brush. The drier the clay when you apply the slip, the quicker it will dry.

INGREDIENTS

This recipe will fit into a clear 2-quart (2-liter) plastic bottle.

Water (distilled if available, but not essential) 3⅕ pints (1.5 liters)
Deflocculant (Dispex/sodium silicate) ⅜ oz (10 g)
2-quart (2-liter) plastic bottle
Plastic tube 1 yd (1 m)

4 Once the terra sigillata has dried, there may be no visible shine. You can easily obtain this by wrapping thin plastic around your finger and gently rubbing the surface.

"Agateware" describes any work that is made from two or more types or colors of clay to create patterns. It is so named because of its visual similarity to the gemstone agate, with its colored mineral strata. Your results will depend on exactly how you put the different colored clays together and how you manipulate them, using a variety of techniques.

AGATEWARE

You can use any clay to make agateware, but the different clay bodies you choose must be compatible. They should be of a similar consistency, otherwise the work will crack and split during shrinking and firing. However, if you are creating more sculptural forms the incompatibility of clays may create interesting results that are worth exploring. If you prepare your own colored clay, you should use oxides and body stains. Choose the most appropriate white clay to add these to for your firing range and glaze requirements.

There are a number of ways to prepare the clay; the one you choose will depend very much on the construction technique you want to use. Once the form is made, the surface pattern will be revealed by scraping the surface with an appropriate flat-sided tool, such as a metal kidney. This can be done once the clay is leather hard, and at further drying stages. First get rid of most of the unwanted excess surface clay, then refine further once it is drier. You can also use wet and dry sandpaper once the form has been bisque fired.

Throwing agateware

A simple technique, used by many to experiment with agate, is to mix red and white earthenware clays. Putting these clays together and blending in different ways will quickly give you an idea of just how striking the results can be. Try creating a layered block by laying thin (½-in/1-cm) slabs of alternate red and white clays on top of each other. Avoid trapping any air between the slabs by pressing from the middle toward the outer edges. This layered block can then be sliced into sections. These can be kept separate and made into balls ready for throwing or may

PRESS-MOLDED AGATEWARE
BY MARION GAUNCE
The clay for this piece was prepared in flat slabs and placed in a three-piece press mold for joining. The top edge was added later to give strength and finish the form.

AGATEWARE

Any number of different compatible clays can be combined to create a varied colored body. You can further explore by blending and cutting to determine the final pattern.

1 Prepare separate blocks of different colored clays by wedging individually to achieve similar consistencies and expel air pockets (see page 30). Use a wire to cut individual slabs, ready to put together.

2 Alternatively, wedge the two prepared clays together, taking care not to overblend them. The way you prepare the clay will affect how the pattern turns out.

3 Place the slabs on top of one another by pressing the middle of the slabs together first and working outward so you don't trap any air between them.

4 Press down with a rolling pin and gradually roll from the middle to the edge. Turn the clay around 180 degrees and repeat. The rolling should be done gradually to compress the block.

5 The slab can be cut in half and either stacked on top or, to create different patterns, turned through 90 or 180 degrees and rolled over again.

6 Thinner-cut strips can be added and blended in to develop the pattern further with a rolling pin.

be mixed further. By slicing and rearranging them in different directions you can create even more patterns. The more you wedge, blend, and rearrange, the finer and more complex the patterning will be.

When centering the clay on the wheel, the more you cone the clay the more you will vary the resulting pattern and strata, although it can be difficult to predict the results. For bold single strips or bands, blend less and try to lift the clay as little as possible. Overthrowing of the form will result in more blending of the colors. While throwing, the slurry on the surface will obscure the pattern; this won't be revealed until the surface of the form is fully turned at the leather-hard stage.

Another simple method for throwing is to sprinkle oxide or stain onto the wedging surface while you are preparing the clay, allowing the lump to randomly pick up and mix the color into the clay. Wheel work will often very clearly show the twisting spiral action of making it.

Slabbing agateware

You can form a slab in a variety of ways. It may be made up from smaller slabs cut from a two-tone or multicolored sandwiched block. These colored clays can be laid down in different configurations using the different cross sections to influence the repeated pattern. The initial block can also be

wrapped in a different color to create a frame around each cut square. If these sliced slabs are thin they can be pressed onto a thicker backing slab without disturbing the pattern. Using slabs in this way is more like inlay, where one clay is pushed into another. This technique allows agateware to be used sparingly and precisely.

You can also create coils of different colors and bunch these together like a rope. This is then twisted tightly together, making sure there are no gaps in between. This coiled rope can then be rolled out to make a slab.

Press molding agateware

Once you have prepared your slabs of clay these can be laid into press molds or laid over hump molds. You can lay fine plastic on top of the clay so you don't disturb the inlay too much when pressing into the molds. Molds also offer many different opportunities to form small slabs of prepared agate joined together with slip. Using cardboard tubes as a mold allows you to create a form without disturbing the surface.

Slip casting agateware

Different colors of thin liquid slip can be poured individually into molds and emptied, allowing each layer to partially dry before the next is added. This will create a fine laminated wall. Once the form has dried sufficiently to be lifted out of the mold, the layers of color can be revealed by slicing or carving through the clay.

Another way to use slip is to press onto the open mold surface different shapes of premade agate. You can then pour in the slip and empty it once you have achieved the required thickness of wall. The agate shapes will be embedded or inlaid into the wall of the form.

AGATEWARE SCULPTURE

BY RAFAEL PEREZ

This form successfully demonstrates the richness afforded by using the agateware method to explore the potential of both clays and glazes.

FORMING AGATEWARE

If the clay surface colors start to become messy through handling, the clay should be left to dry to a very firm, leather-hard consistency and then the surface repeatedly scraped back.

1 Separate, thin coils of clay can be twisted together to form a decorative rim or handle.

2 You could use your twisted coils to construct slabs by rolling them out.

3 Once you are satisfied with the striations you could twist your narrow slab into a more blended handle.

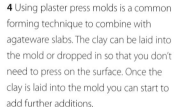

4 Using plaster press molds is a common forming technique to combine with agateware slabs. The clay can be laid into the mold or dropped in so that you don't need to press on the surface. Once the clay is laid into the mold you can start to add further additions.

Ceramics and print have a long historic tradition; the most obvious being the development of the repeatable fired image during the Industrial Revolution. There are many ways to engage with this process at a relatively low-tech level, such as direct printing onto the clay before the first firing.

PRINTING

The following techniques are a good way to start experimenting with printing, which will allow you to see what the different qualities offer and which may interest you to develop with further equipment.

Direct printing

A board is tightly stretched with water-dampened material then painted with oxide and pigments. A clay sheet can be laid onto this and pressure applied with a rolling pin or put through a printing press and the design transferred. Slip, oxide, or pigments can be painted onto the surface of plaster and a sheet of clay laid on top,

which will transfer the design. Or, use a design from a metal etching plate that has been "inked" with a mixture of copperplate oil and oxide or ceramic pigments. This can then be transferred to a sheet of clay. Best results are achieved by using paper clay (see page 38), which is less prone to tearing. There are several books devoted solely to ceramics and print techniques. One simple method you can try onto the surface of damp clay or damp slip is monoprint transfer.

Monoprint transfer is relatively easy to achieve without specialist equipment and facilities and demonstrates how a simple printing technique can develop your surface quality and interest.

Direct-printed work by Steve Brown
This piece was created using complex mold structures. The surface decoration was added while the form was still in the mold and the print was transferred to the porcelain slip using direct printing.

Blossom plates by Heidi Parsons
This work shows how sophisticated tonal qualities, such as duotones, can be printed directly onto the clay's surface, which has first been brushed with a layer of white slip.

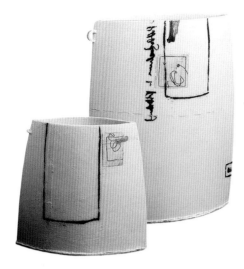

Slip-decorated vessels

BY FIONA THOMPSON

These earthenware forms have been decorated using a mixture of techniques including oxide monoprinting and brushed slip.

To achieve the quality of a drawn line on clay or slip you can use oxide and tissue paper to create a monoprint design. This technique will reproduce the same quality of line in oxide on the surface as the implement that has been used to draw the design, with a sharp pencil being very different from a flat-tip marker or the pad of a sponge, for instance. This is an ideal technique for achieving very fine drawn lines. The lines created in this way allow you to apply one-off drawings quickly without the need for screen-printing and transfers.

Paint a sheet of glass or Perspex with a solution of oxide and water and a small amount of china clay (approximately 1:10 china clay to oxide powder). The oxide will help to give the solution some body and help in brushing evenly onto the nonporous surface. There is no particular set ratio of water to oxide, but you will need enough to lay down a solid block. Do not use any other ingredients or decorating mediums, because these would fix the oxide too well and keep it from lifting from the surface. The strength of the mixture will make a difference to the result when glazed. This is something that you can experiment with to create different weights of line.

DIRECT MONOPRINTING TRANSFER

This technique allows you to monoprint very fine drawn lines onto the surface of damp, leather-hard clay or slip.

TECHNIQUE FILE **103**

1 Coat a sheet of Perspex or glass with a mixture of water and oxide. Adding a very small amount (1 percent) of china clay to this mixture will give more solid coverage. Do not add too much or it will not transfer. Allow the mixture to dry completely.

2 Place a sheet of fine printmaker's tissue on top and fix in position with tape. Use a pencil to draw your design on the surface. The paper should withstand the sharpest, finest drawn line. The pressure will transfer the oxide onto the underside of the tissue paper.

3 Carefully peel back the tissue paper so that you don't disturb the oxide.

4 Make sure that the clay tile to which you want to transfer the design is damp otherwise the oxide will not transfer. Carefully place the tissue paper underside down on the damp clay tile. Gently rub the back of the tissue paper to transfer the design onto the tile.

5 Gently peel back the tissue paper to reveal the design. The oxide is not stable, so be careful not to disturb this. The bisque firing will not completely fix the oxide either, so the tile then needs to be glazed. This technique allows you to draw extremely fine lines of oxide.

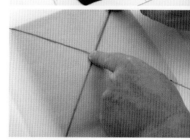

SCREEN PRINTING DIRECTLY ONTO CLAY

Most clay can be flattened to accept a print, although different types of clay may require slight variations in the process. While a black print on a white clay body has a strong contrast and stands out well, a darker clay and lighter-colored ink creates a more subtle effect.

1 If you use a buff stoneware clay such as this grogged crank, applying a white slip first will bring some of the contrast back between the body and the print.

2 Porcelain slip fires to the same temperature as the clay body and gives the surface a slight satin sheen. After painting on the slip, dry the surface until you can place your hand on it without it sticking.

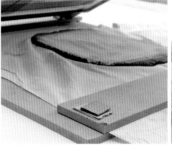

3 To set up the print base you need a pair of hinged clamps, which are designed to hold a screen in position. By screwing these onto a wooden base you can make a simple printing jig. The clamps can be raised up at the back to accommodate differing depths of clay panels.

4 Several stencils can be put on the same screen to save on materials, but you need to cover any unwanted stencils so that only the required image gets printed. Load enough of the underglaze ink onto the screen at the leading edge of the print, being careful not to get any on the open mesh, since this could dry before the print is made.

6 Lift the screen to check the print beneath. If the print is missing areas through lack of pressure or requires a second deposit of the same ink, repeat the process. Be very careful, however, since printing wet on wet ink can result in the ink spreading out and ruining the print.

7 Trim the tile to shape with a sharp potter's knife and carefully remove the surrounding clay.

8 Center the clay on the hump. When the clay is in position, take care not to slide or twist it, as this will result in smudging the print.

9 Gently press down over the curve of the hump mold and work your way evenly around the work. At this stage the mold could be centered on a potter's wheel and a foot ring and the back turned (see page 118) accurately into the lower surface of the clay.

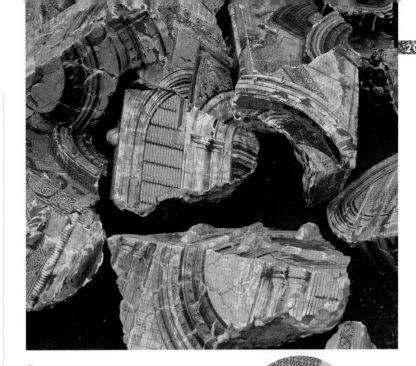

5 Lift the screen slightly away from the clay panel and push the ink down beyond the stencil image. This loads the mesh with ink. Lift the squeegee, place it back down behind the reservoir of ink, and lower the screen. Pull the squeegee slowly and firmly toward you, exerting an even, downward pressure. The screen should break away from the clay as the squeegee is pulled over the image.

10 Allow the clay to firm up a little so that it does not slump back down again when it is taken off the mold. The piece can be returned to the wheel, if desired, in order to turn the top rim cleanly.

DIRECT-PRINTED PIECES
BY STEVE BROWN
The porcelain slip used here has become clear in places. If it is heavily applied, very fine surface cracks form, which reveal the qualities of the grogged stoneware clay beneath.

Once the oxide has dried, place a piece of fine tissue paper on the surface and tape it down using masking tape. You can buy specific ceramic printing tissue, though fine printing tissue is widely available from art suppliers and does a similar job.

If you want to print onto slip you must apply it to the surface of your form and let it dry slightly. Ideally the surface (clay or slip) should be damp to allow the transfer of oxide. Choose your drawing implement and draw onto the paper; the pressure will press the oxide onto the paper. Place this onto the surface of the damp clay or slip and press lightly with a dry sponge on the back of the tissue paper. Peel back the paper and the oxide will have transferred onto the surface. If the surface is dry, the line will not completely transfer. You can add further designs to the surface using small pieces of tissue. Try not to let these come into contact with existing lines. The oxide will remain very fragile on the surface up until the moment when it is glazed and fired.

The oxide solution can be kept for further use. It should be covered to prevent dust contamination, and before reusing wet brushed to get rid of existing lines. Alternatively it can be recycled and scraped off the sheet back into a container.

Complex designs
More complicated printing surfaces can be achieved by using a number of plaster bats. Once you have screen printed onto the bats, you can transfer the design by wetting the surface and pressing clay onto it. When the clay is dry, remove the plaster bats: the print has been transferred onto the surface of the clay.

The inherent human desire to leave a mark on a surface can be given full rein in ceramics. The ability of clay to transform from a soft, malleable, plastic material into a stonelike one enables the maker to leave a permanent mark. Creating textures and making marks in clay can be a lifelong pleasure, delight, challenge, or frustration.

SURFACE TEXTURE

The form is made—now for the surface. What should I do with it? How to make it more interesting? Does it require anything? Should it be left alone to demonstrate how it was made? If I leave it, will this reveal too much about its creation and make it lose its mystery? Should I impress or incise? Make positive or negative marks, or both? The surface should not distract from but rather enhance the two- or three-dimensional quality of the piece. If decisions are too tentative this will be evident. Be bold or subtle, precise or wandering, exaggerated or minimal. Explore ideas on test tiles; these will form a visual library to assist you in making informed decisions later on.

Hands are the critical tools—development of other tools stemmed from people starting to use natural objects with textures. Ceramic mark making has continued apace since and often defines the century and decade. The appeal of surface decoration is still very much in evidence in contemporary work. Perhaps this will develop further with the use of CAD—who knows what marks and surfaces will be written into the digital and technological programs of the future?

Options for surface decoration may seem limitless—the surface can almost become whatever you wish it to be. As you acquire knowledge and skill you can make it replicate many known materials, from extreme textures to subtle, delicate impressions.

Certain forms will require that the texture be introduced at the very start of the making process. Other textures may be added while making, and some can be the final act. This will very much depend on the type of work you are

Slip-cast fruit forms by Penkridge ceramics
These remarkable examples of trompe l'oeil are high-fired earthenware slip-cast forms. They demonstrate great skill and understanding of the craft and how clay and glaze can replicate the real thing.

making and how it is constructed. When you are handling the clay surface, take care not to damage or unintentionally distort it. Often the smallest mistake or blemish on a ceramic surface is highly visible in the final result.

You can start to experiment with textured test tiles to see how slip and glaze will affect the texture—their depth will make a difference. Once you have gained further knowledge of glazes you may find you have to adjust the surface texture so that it remains visible. You'll need to establish whether the surface will benefit from a thick, rich, highly glossed transparent glaze or a thin, matte, dry one, or any possible variation in between.

Tools

Certain tools will unlock creative responses to surface inquiry. They will become the extension your hands have been waiting for. Just as painters trust their brushes, you will start to trust favorite tools, and may even become unable to operate without them. Learning how to use these tools will take time and you will need to experiment to find their full potential and usefulness.

Imitation

Many makers like to see how far the surface of clay can be developed to imitate another material—you may see clay objects that mimic leather, melting ice cream, or fruit and vegetables, for instance. What drives and fascinates some makers is endless experimentation into immortalizing the passing moment of a living thing; to capture it permanently before it disappears. Once you have achieved a formula for imitating a material, what you then do with it is another thing. Do you simply imitate the actual and let the audience marvel at your developmental skill, or do you twist and change it to make them think differently about it? This is the difference between replication and creating a sense of hyperreality, and bringing individuality of expression to a piece. Neither is the "right" answer.

Burnishing

Burnishing is an action that compresses the surface of the clay to create a sheen. It compacts

BURNISHING

You can use numerous tools or objects to burnish with. Usual materials include metal, glass, plastic, and stones. Every maker will have their favorite implement.

1 Start burnishing when the clay is leather hard and firm. Use circular movements to avoid creating ridges. The surface will quickly start to compress and you will see it start to shine.

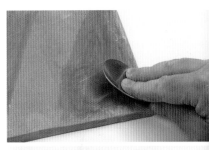

2 This tile features a nonburnished cross design to show the contrast of the surface. The surface sheen may dull after some drying has taken place. A quick rub of the surface with some plastic stretched over your finger will restore it.

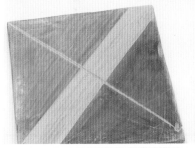

3 You can also create designs in slip and burnish these. You can continue developing the surface by adding slip onto already burnished areas, as long as the surface has not dried too much. Allow additions of slip to become leather hard before burnishing, otherwise it will smear. Don't try to burnish a completely dry surface since it will quickly turn chalky.

the fine particles of clay together so they better reflect light. You can burnish the clay surface with or without slip on it. Any clay can be burnished with varying results. Usually fine clays are used that will produce flat, smooth surfaces. Clays with grog content will burnish, but the surface will be heavily scratched. If you prefer to make your forms with these clays you can always coat the surface in a slip and then burnish this if you don't like the scratch marks.

The clay must be firm and leather hard to achieve successful burnishing. If the clay is too wet the tools will disturb the surface too much and create ridges and marks. If it is too dry the surface will scratch and appear chalklike. It will be very evident if the clay is right because it will compress and create a shine quite quickly.

You can burnish with a wide variety of improvised tools. From the backs of metal spoons to pebbles, slender light bulbs, and wood and plastic objects; basically anything smooth that will compress the surface. You may need different shapes and sizes to get into awkward areas. Simply apply pressure and move the tool on the surface in a range of different rubbing motions and directions to prevent definite patterns emerging, unless this is a quality you would like to explore. The tool should glide easily across the surface, creating a particular clicking noise. Always support the inside of any form and be careful not to apply too much pressure, because the form may start to split.

You can increase the sheen by rubbing the surface with a cotton cloth or making a pad of smooth plastic and buffing with this. As the form dries, the sheen may dull a little. You can continue to buff with the cloth and plastic, but nothing harder, since this will now scratch the surface.

Incising

Incising could be thought of as being the same as carving; however, in ceramics it describes cutting or scratching a narrow line, while carving describes subtracting larger areas. Also similar is sgraffito, but that is a term used specifically to refer to scratching through slip (see page 190).

Historically, the most frequently incised marks were patterns using vertical strips, horizontal bands, zigzags, and diamond formations.

Incising can be done at any time in the making process, from when the clay is soft and fresh right through to when it is bone dry. As with all ceramic techniques you will discover the most appropriate stage of dryness to achieve the quality you require. The dampness of the clay will always affect the quality of the line achieved. You will also find the most appropriate tools for this method, from sharp or blunt pencils to specific incising tools.

If you are interested in incising text, you will probably adapt tools with cushioned padding near the tip so you can hold the tool more comfortably while applying pressure into the leather-hard clay. The creation of burrs (rough edges) and the condition of the clay will be the deciding factor in choosing when to incise and what is the most appropriate tool to use.

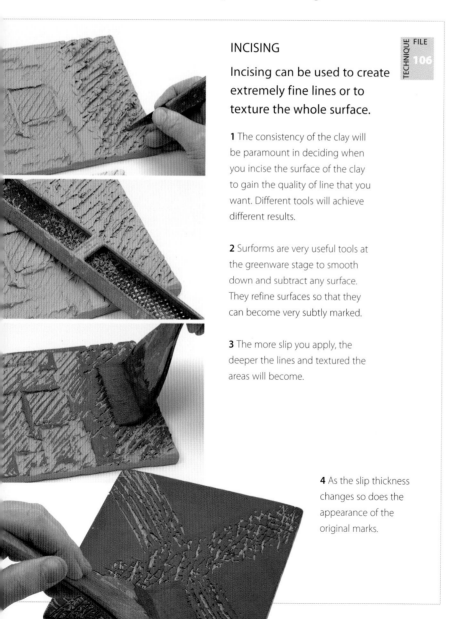

INCISING

TECHNIQUE FILE **106**

Incising can be used to create extremely fine lines or to texture the whole surface.

1 The consistency of the clay will be paramount in deciding when you incise the surface of the clay to gain the quality of line that you want. Different tools will achieve different results.

2 Surforms are very useful tools at the greenware stage to smooth down and subtract any surface. They refine surfaces so that they can become very subtly marked.

3 The more slip you apply, the deeper the lines and textured the areas will become.

4 As the slip thickness changes so does the appearance of the original marks.

Impressing

Makers whose practice is focused on the ceramic surface will have large collections of found objects—both natural and machine-made—that will leave interesting marks when impressed into the clay surface. The impressions may be left for you to relate to that material or object, or be distorted and developed further. These will also be changed through layers of slip application and glazing.

Historically, impressions have been found on the bases of large Chinese pot forms dating from 7,000 years ago. The impressions are from bamboo strip baskets, which enabled the form to be turned around more easily. Others have coarse woven matting impressions created by the same technique.

When impressing objects into clay you will soon begin to appreciate the state of firmness required to achieve the results you are seeking. If the clay is too fresh and soft, the objects may stick, and if it is too dry it will crack. The exact hardness will depend on what technique you are using to make and how much further manipulation of the clay is required after creating your impressions. If you require fresh clay to give the best impression, you may need to leave it to partly dry before using it. If you are pressing into forms that are already made, always try to support them from the inside as well to prevent distortion and cracking. When using rolling pins or slab rollers to impress textures into slabs of clay, always place clean, fine-woven canvas cloths underneath and on top and make sure the roller is totally clean, otherwise you will find unwanted extra impressions.

The full impact and interest of making impressions will only be fully realized once you have finished the work, particularly after slip application and glazing. Certain textures will partially close with slip application, and glazes may pool in deeper lines or areas. Dry glazes will often give a more subtle result, because there will be no reflection on the surface.

Stamping

Stamps in this context are objects that can be used to create an impression in fresh clay. If you

IMPRESSING

All manner of objects can be used to create pattern in the clay's surface. From the most exaggerated to the most delicate, all will leave their mark.

1 Metal files rolled around forms can create strong contrasting bands of texture. If any objects stick then a dusting of china clay can help prevent this. As with all surface texture, it can be either made more subtle or highlighted by the slip and glaze choices you make.

2 Anything can be pressed into surfaces with a rolling pin. Try to develop these to make them communicate something about the form that adds to its visual quality. Find ways to use textures that will intrigue the viewer and don't settle for the obvious replication of a texture that has no relevance to the form.

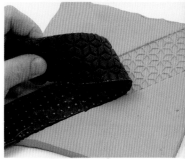

3 Texture can also be developed once the form has been made. Here the form is being gently beaten with a carved wooden paddle to create a rhythm of horizontal lines to contrast with the positive vertical lines. This form has a cardboard tube inside to keep it from distorting, which can be withdrawn once it is finished.

4 By using a range of adapted wooden paddles you can quickly build your own personal surface textures to add to the individual nature of the work you are developing. When you are developing the surface texture always try to support the inside of the form to prevent it from distorting.

USING STAMPS

Stamps may be made from bisque-fired clay, plaster, or rubber. Bisque-fired clay remains porous so is ideal for this purpose. Any letters or words must be carved back-to-front, otherwise they will read backward when printed.

TECHNIQUE FILE **108**

1 Draw your chosen design on either plaster or leather-hard clay. Start by lightly scratching the surface of the clay or plaster with a fine point; this light groove will help you when you draw over the lines further. Mistakes can also be more easily rectified.

2 Different tools can be used to develop the marks and lines when making them deeper and wider. Keep testing the depth and quality of line on a small pad of clay that can be thrown away if contaminated with small bits of plaster.

3 Plaster will be hard to carve when fully dried. Soaking the stamp block in water will make this task a little easier.

4 Make sure you clean any small bits of clay or plaster away before using the stamp. A damp sponge will soften edges and give a rounded look to the line when printed. Be careful not to create undercuts in the design when carving because these will tear the line when lifting the stamp off the clay.

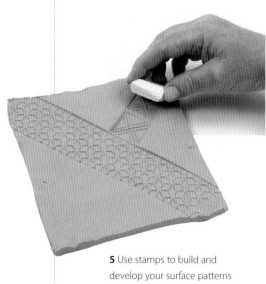

5 Use stamps to build and develop your surface patterns as part of your personal design vocabulary.

6 Making a positive stamp subtracts a larger amount of material which, when printed, creates negative space. This can be time-consuming. A quicker method for this is to carve in your design as before. Fire the result and then take a print of the negative, which will create the positive. This can then be fired to create the stamp.

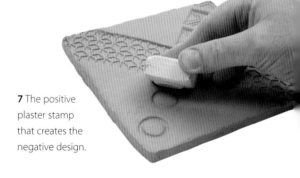

7 The positive plaster stamp that creates the negative design.

8 The flat surface can be distorted to further enhance and articulate the surface.

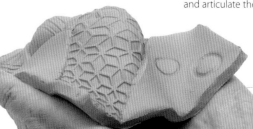

are using text or initials, remember that when they are printed into the clay they will appear in reverse. If you are creating a stamp to identify your work for posterity, carve it backward. The results you can achieve with simple motifs or designs can appear to those without knowledge like a complex method when printed in relief. Experimenting with different strengths and depths of line will produce sophisticated and interesting designs. By using even small stamps you can build quite a complex repeated pattern.

The most common methods for making your own stamps include carving into leather-hard clay or taking an impression off a textural surface and bisque firing to 1800° F (1000° C). Firing to this temperature means that the clay is still porous and will not stick to fresh clay. The third method is carving into a block of cast plaster. Plaster can also be used to cast line drawings or patterns made with latex or wax. You can also send your drawings off to a rubber-stamp-making company who will reproduce them for you.

Rouletting

Rouletting is the process of rolling a cylinder across the surface of clay to create a repeated, impressed, or relief decoration. An ancient technique found on early pottery, there is a a fine collection of Roman roulettes in the Hearst museum at Berkeley university in California. Roulettes can be used with many of the core construction methods—pinch, coil, slab, or wheel throwing. As with impressing, the clay consistency is important. If it's too wet the roulette will stick; too dry and it will cause cracking and splitting. If you are using a nonporous roulette, a dusting of china clay onto the clay surface can prevent sticking. Before making work, think about the surface and how it will be applied. Rouletting can be used at the initial stages of preparation of the form depending on technique, or once the form is completed, depending on its firmness.

Roulettes are obviously easier to use on flat slabs, but will depend on how these are used, because disturbance and gaps can appear when separate elements are joined together. If the rouletted clay has been left to dry too much before being assembled then the bare areas

ROULETTED VASE
BY LES RUCINSKI
This piece was decorated using a roulette while on the wheel. After rouletting a wash of terra sigillata was applied and then wiped back to enhance the varied texture.

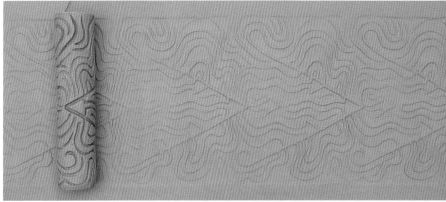

Testing a roulette

To test a design, place a clay slab on canvas. While carving your cylinder you can roll the roulette onto the soft clay to check the depth of the design (above and right).

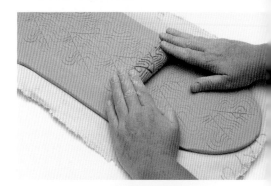

Adapted roulette

An adapted plaster roulette used around the top of a form. Always support the form with your hand and put pressure against the force of the pressure of the roulette action.

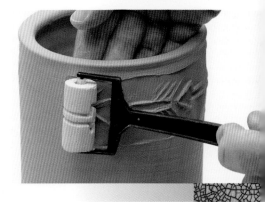

MAKING A ROULETTE

Roulettes can be made easily by carving a design onto extruded coils of clay. Make sure that your design fits the circumference of your coil.

TECHNIQUE FILE **109**

Bisque-fired roulettes

A range of bisque-fired roulettes. These will last a lifetime.

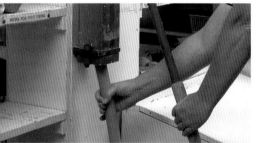

1 Use an extruder to create an even, smooth, solid, or thick hollow cylinder (see pages 164–165). Alternatively, roll out a coil by hand. Leave and dry to a leather-hard consistency.

2 After measuring the circumference, a design has been drawn on tracing paper. The paper design is rolled around the roulette. Because the clay is damp, the paper sticks to it.

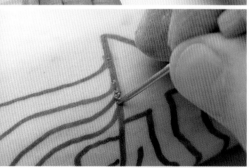

3 If you have used a tracing paper template with pencil or ink, the pattern can be transferred onto the damp clay by rubbing the reverse surface of the template with a sponge. Or you can pierce the design with a pinpoint through the paper template.

4 Remove the tracing paper and choose the appropriate carving tool. Usually everyone has an adapted favorite—if not, you soon will have! Start subtracting the lines of clay. The lines will need to be repeated to create the desired depth. Burrs will appear on the edges. Sponge these off when dry.

cannot be treated. This technique often gives the appearance of being highly skilled and complex to those without ceramic knowledge, but is under-used in the contemporary ceramics field.

Anything cylindrical that can be rolled over the clay surface can be used as a roulette, made or found, large or small, precise or crude. Roulettes can be made using a wide range of materials, such as clay, plaster, wood, metal, rubber, or plastic.

Clay Solid or thick hollow cylinders can be extruded or hand rolled. When soft they can be rolled over any textured surface to imprint its pattern. When leather hard, they can be carved and refined. All need to be bisque fired to 1830° F (1000° C).

Plaster You can mix and cast plaster cylinders. Often when making molds there will be plaster left over. If you have a block of clay with holes pressed into it you can pour and cast cylinders with the excess plaster. Plaster can be hard to carve once it is fully dried. Soak in water before you carve or as soon as cast. Plaster roulettes can give a much more detailed, sharper, defined, and crisp design.

Textured roulette

A simple method of making a roulette without designing and carving is to roll a cylinder or coil of clay onto any texture to replicate its surface. This should then be bisque fired.

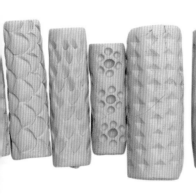
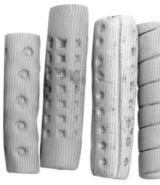
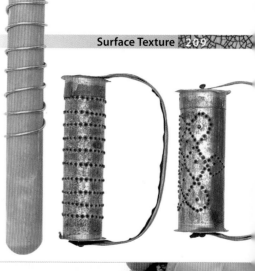

Experimental roulette

A purchased rolling pin with a wire wrapped around (right). Experiment with different wrapping materials.

Aluminum roulettes

These Indian aluminum roulettes (far right) can be used for piercing designs.

Wood Household rolling pins are ideal to adapt for rouletting. Either by wrapping existing texture, string, or wire around them or carving in a texture. Pottery suppliers stock a variety of premade rolling pins, but it is always better to create your own to add your personality.

Metal If you have access to printmaking facilities then you could etch your own designs and textures into metal plates to form round cylinders. Found machine parts, cogs, and wheels are also useful to adapt.

Rubber Rubber-stamp manufacturers will make rubber strips using your designs. These can then be wrapped and glued around any cylinder. Rubber mats can also provide interesting patterns and be used in the same way.

Plastic Found objects like bottle tops or plumbing components provide interesting results. There are many commercially-available rollers from art or decorating stores that can be used or easily adapted for use. Any cylinder can be made easier to use with the addition of a simple handle, purchased or made.

The two plaster roulettes (left) have been made from an adapted paint roller and a handle made from soft armature wire (right).

5 Another tool is used to create an alternative deeper, more rounded shape to the groove. This will affect the shape of the raised line giving contrast within the design.

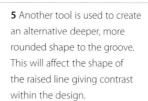

6 Using a wet brush will smooth away any remaining burrs and will define and refine the lines.

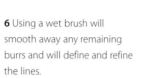

7 To complete the design more refining can be done using a sponge. At this stage, you can decide how light- or hard-edged you want the design to appear. More rubbing with the sponge will soften and make the design more subtle.

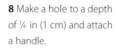

8 Make a hole to a depth of ¼ in (1 cm) and attach a handle.

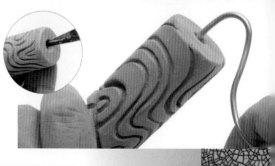

Carving into clay and subtracting are often underused techniques in ceramics. One common method of carving is fluting (cutting the sides) of wheel-thrown work, which creates faceted forms. Most other building techniques are generally additive and not subtractive. Beginners often think that subtracting clay seems almost destructive.

CARVING AND SUBTRACTION

For sculptors, subtraction is key, and is often very time consuming and difficult when working with materials such as marble and stone. Yet nothing could be easier than carving through a large, soft block of clay. However, there are relatively few contemporary makers who exploit its potential.

Wheel throwing uses subtraction in the process of turning to complete and refine the form. This was thought of for some time as a negative thing, as if it was making up for the fact that you couldn't throw the shape you required but had to turn it out of what you managed to throw! But surely subtraction has the same value as addition?

You can start a form with a solid block of clay and begin to carve out by subtracting the clay with loop tools, which are made in a wide variety of sizes for this very purpose. The completed form can then be cut up into sections and hollowed out using the same loop tools. The form can then be joined back together again using the score and slurry method and made to appear as a solid form.

Manipulation from the inside
One advantage with ceramic form is that you can manipulate the clay from the interior as well as the exterior. Once you have created the surface,

CARVED FORMS
BY HALIMA CASSELL
These carved forms (left and right) manipulate planes to create restless and complex surface patterns. The abstract designs play with light, shade, and rhythmical movement.

TEXTURED POT
BY KARIN PUTSCH-GRASSI
This wheel-thrown form has been cut and subtracted on the wheel while still wet. The form is then pushed from the inside to stretch the clay out to create the texture.

you could start to explore further by developing and distorting it, gently pushing and teasing the clay out from the inside. This will open out the texture and, depending on the clay, reveal qualities that can't be achieved any other way.

Often sculptures with other materials are solely about working and reworking the exterior surface, which can become labored and overworked without the opportunity to bring new energy back into the work to freshen the approach and form. In ceramics this opportunity is almost like a surgeon using Botox! Depending on its application this can also give the appearance of something that has happened, or is happening, below the surface.

Surforms
Surforms come in a variety of styles and are very efficient at subtracting clay to create flat and straight bases, edges, and rims.

CARVING AND SUBTRACTION

The clay's consistency and choice of tools will be key factors in the end result using subtraction and carving.

1 Mark out your designs in pencil onto the leather-hard clay to decide on the larger areas to be subtracted. Leather-hard clay is easily carved and subtracted using a variety of tools to create a wide range of marks and surfaces.

2 Makers will often adapt tools for comfort and to create their own individual marks. Any clay can be carved but your choice will be made depending on how fine and smooth you require the final result to be.

3 Try a range of different tools to explore a variety of mark-making potential. Get used to handling them so you feel comfortable when they are needed.

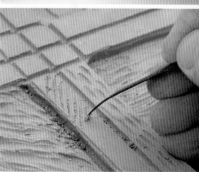

4 A wide range of different-sized loop tools can be used to subtract clay. Very large versions of these tools are also available to subtract large areas.

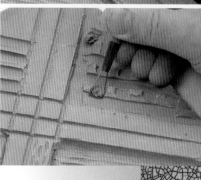

You can create sample tiles to try out ideas on, which can then act as a visual library to call on in the future.

Piercing

Piercing describes the technique of cutting through leather-hard clay to create a decorative design in the clay body. It originated in Persia and was a form of functional decoration usually used to create a pattern in objects that were used for cooking, such as a trivet or colander. Piercing is an interesting and absorbing technique that requires patience, preparation, skill, and an intimate knowledge of the behavior of clay through the making and drying stages.

It's a technique that can either be used to accentuate minimal design features, or the method can be used in a highly decorative way. Today it is mostly associated with one-off pieces or industrial use. Piercing requires specific tools that can be purchased and adapted—often makers will make their own tools specifically for the job in hand and comfortable for their own use.

For a beginner, the most important aspect of the piercing process is choosing appropriate smooth-bodied clay—vital until you have built up experience of the technique. A smooth clay will enable easy cutting. When piercing, the consistency of the clay is very important: too soft and the clay will soon start to collapse; too hard and the clay will crack and crumble. It can be a lengthy process depending on the complexity of the design. It is important, therefore, that the clay is kept at the same working consistency throughout. Once you have made your form, allow to dry to the leather-hard stage.

Design process

The process may start with a predrawn design, working out any potentially critical areas that may cause problems later. The main design challenge is thinking about the positive and negative spaces. Also, how the structure that is left, post piercing, will support itself through the full ceramic process, particularly through stoneware firings.

Some designers choose to draw directly onto

Pierced vase
by Jennifer McCurdy
This is a technically extraordinary pierced form. It has been skillfully carved and pierced in gradual stages. First, the deisgn is sketched onto the surface and then the bulk is removed. The refining process takes place in stages until reaching this delicate skeletal coral form.

DAISY JUG AND PROTOTYPE
BY ANTONY QUINN
This pierced jug was made by hand in the
traditional manner, but it was designed
on a computer with a 3D printed model.

the form using a pencil to develop a more organic approach, seeing the design grow around the form. The difficulty when first trying this technique is visualizing how the form will appear. There is an element of the unknown until the form is finally pierced.

Making maquettes

With cylindrical forms you can cut out the negative shapes on a paper template. Once completed, wrap the template around to form a cylinder to get an idea of how the final form might appear. Once again, depending on the complexity of your design, this could save some considerable time.

Select your favored design method and transcribe onto the form. You can use paper, tracing paper, or a direct method. Choose the appropriate tool and start piercing through the wall at the top of the form. This will allow the base to act as a stable support as your design develops. You may need to repeat the cut line several times, or it may need many sectional cuts through each single piece before the clay comes away. This will depend entirely on the thickness of the clay wall.

It is always important that the form is supported on the other side of the clay. This can be done with your hand or with an internal or external

PLANNING AND FITTING THE DESIGN

The main challenge of your design will be defining positive and negative areas, while considering how to maintain a robust support structure that can withstand the extraction process.

TECHNIQUE FILE 111

1 Roughly sketch out design ideas onto cartridge paper or tracing paper. Think about how the shapes will form enclosed blocks or areas. Look at possible weaknesses in the support structure, and areas that may need further consideration during the piercing process.

2 If designing something to fit a particular form, measure the dimensions or circumference of the shape, then work within that to enable you to link or join up the design to create a continuous pattern. Here, a sketch is being transferred and enlarged onto tracing paper.

3 Check that the design fits the form and adjust areas in the design that do not work. Wet the surface of the form to help the template stick to the surface, and to transfer the design. Wrap the paper around, ink side to clay.

4 Once the paper template is held onto the surface you can simply rub with a damp sponge to transfer the pencil or ink design onto the form. Alternatively, you can keep the template in position and cut or transfer the design using a piercing wheel (see page 214).

PIERCING AND REFINING THE SURFACE

Clay consistency is the most important factor for successful piercing—combined with repetition of surface cleaning to refine the quality of the form.

1 For certain undulating organic forms it may be necessary to mark the design through the paper template using a piercing wheel or repeatedly pricking the surface with a pointed tool.

2 To begin the cutting-out process, starting at the top of the form, push the chosen piercing tool into the clay, making sure your hand is supporting the area behind. Several cuts may be needed for each area to be extracted—these may also need to be subdivided into further sections because it is sometimes difficult to extract whole shapes.

3 As you work around and down the form, you may need to support larger open areas. This can be done with blocks of clay or balled-up paper towels.

4 Once the piercing is complete, start to clean away the serrated burrs with a damp scouring sponge. This will take repeated action and constant cleaning of the sponge.

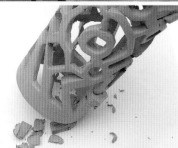

5 Gently turn the form upside down to get rid of scraps—this is easier while the form is still leather hard. If left until later, the form will be more fragile when dry and bits may stick inside.

former. As you proceed with the form, support may be added in between the sections with the scraps of the extracted clay. These will be the same consistency and will dry and shrink at a similar rate. Paper towels are also very useful, as they will prevent any opposition pressure when shrinkage occurs.

You can use a hair dryer to gently dry the pierced sections of the form. Don't overdry since this will cause cracking before you have completed the design. Whatever clay you have chosen, small, serrated burrs will appear on the cut clay. These can be brushed away as you proceed or left until the very end when they are dry.

Cleaning and finishing

Allow to dry to firm leather hard. The form often looks disappointing at this stage, considering all the work that has been done. However, once you start cleaning away the burrs, and sponging, your design will soon be revealed, looking increasingly delicate and refined.

Finishing
Final refining and finishing of both the internal and external edges can be made using a wet paintbrush.

There are many options to add color prior to bisque firing, other than simply using slips: metallic oxides including dioxides and carbonates, underglaze, body and glaze powder pigments, and those with added adhesives such as velvets. These all offer opportunities to experiment with color and provide decoration possibilities. They can also be added after first firing.

USING COLOR

When using these materials care must be taken, particularly in shared workshops, as these colors do not fully fix onto the surface at bisque-firing temperature, and will come off when handled during unpacking of the kiln. This means there is a risk of contaminating your own and others' work. The fixing temperature for the majority of these materials will not be achieved without glaze until 2200° F (1200° C).

The main advantage of adding colors at this stage is that it allows you to blend them with each other and with the unfired clay. If you do not want to use glazes, this work can be fired once to your chosen temperature without the need for bisque firing.

Coloring oxides
Some basic knowledge will help when experimenting with color and glazes. Most ceramic raw materials are naturally occurring and are mined from sites all over the world. They are comprised of oxides—elements combined with oxygen, and may vary in composition depending on where they are mined. Basic oxides are metals and acid oxides are nonmetals. Coloring metallic oxides are industrially ground, prepared, and supplied in different strengths as oxides, dioxides, and carbonates. They can provide color at all stages of the ceramic process. For definition purposes, "oxides" generally refer to coloring oxides in ceramics.

Oxides can be used with water as a wash on top of dry, unfired clay or bisque-fired clay, used under a glaze or on top of glaze, and when used with one containing tin it is known as majolica. They are added to colored clay bodies, to color slips, and color glazes.

Oxides are an extremely powerful colorant. Dioxides and carbonates are generally weaker than pure oxides. How much you will need to use will depend on which oxide and form is being used. Using 0.5 percent will produce a color in any slip or glaze recipe. They are used singularly or in combination with each other and other commercially-produced color stains to produce an infinite range of colors and textures, and are greatly affected by other glaze ingredients, firing temperatures, and kiln atmospheres.

Because of their strength you will need to develop tests to see and appreciate the ratio of powder to water in order to make informed decisions. The thicker you use certain oxides the

Contrasting colored form
by Jane Blackman
The use of a full-color interior and embossed line exterior demonstrates the endless possibilities provided by surface decoration.

COLORED CLAY

COLORED PORCELAIN LAMPS
BY JI-HYUN CHUNG
The high-fired matte porcelain clay has been colored with body stains and the forms are cast in different layers with the colored areas subtracted by fettling or carving. The light then illuminates the thinnest part of the clay wall.

COLOR AND SHAPE DECORATION
BY BARRY STEDMAN
These vibrant surfaces are created by using a mixture of body stains to color slips and as underglaze pigments, which then have a transparent glaze applied to bring out the richness of the color.

SURFACE COLOR CLOSE-UP
BY ANNETTE WELCH
Oxide is used to color a range of slips. These have then been laid on with different resist techniques and have dry glazes applied over them to achieve a varied matte surface finish.

more metallic they are likely to appear, and they will blister. Generally, the thinner the solution, the more variation in color.

You can use washes of oxides and water on top of bisque-fired work to bring out very fine textures. After applying to the bisque surface, wipe back with a damp sponge to highlight the surface texture. This can then be fired to stoneware temperature to fix and produce a matte surface without applying glaze. Or, wait for the body to dry and apply either earthenware or stoneware glazes using a spray gun. This is to avoid contaminating your glaze by brushing, dipping, or pouring (you will disturb the oxide and cause it to come off).

Oxides can be used under or on top of glazes. Be aware that some oxides, if applied too thickly, will lower the melting point of the glaze. Depending on the thickness of application of both glaze and oxide it can cause the glaze to run down the form and cause the form to stick to the kiln shelf.

Historically, Delftware—a type of majolica produced in Delft, Holland—is a fine example of how a single oxide (cobalt) is used with water in different solution strengths to produce different shades of blue. The beauty and difficulty of using oxides on top of glaze comes from the fact that mistakes cannot be rectified. The whole application of glaze and oxide would need to be washed off and started again.

Oxides can be applied using a wide variety of techniques. They, like metals, have different melting points, so some will not fuse and fix onto clay without other ingredients. When using them with other materials you can mix and blend with water or use a pestle and mortar. This will prevent any noticeable speckling in the final application.

Underglaze/body stains/glaze stain powders
Underglaze, body stains, and glaze stain powders are commercially produced from oxides and artificially colored ground powder pigments. They provide stable, reliable, and often predictable color, the majority up to stoneware temperatures. However, they are more expensive. Manufacturers will always supply the information

with the product to tell you the firing range of any given powder, because some will not hold their color in the stoneware range and may fully burn out.

These powder pigments can be mixed with water or a range of adhesives for a wide variety of decoration purposes and techniques on anything from greenware to bisque-fired work. They can be used effectively as washes of color. If applied too thickly they can blister and crawl when glaze fired. They will remain unfixed at the bisque stage until glaze is applied over the top of them and fired. The powders can be used at the bisque stage under or on top of a glaze They can be added to color slips, clay bodies, and glazes. You can use most of these products with each other from the same product range, but they do not behave in the same way as ordinary paint colors when mixed together to form a wider range of colors. When added to a combination of glaze ingredients and oxides, however, they will produce a varied range of colors, tones, and textures depending on the ingredients, temperatures, and kiln atmospheres used.

Velvet underglazes

Velvet underglazes are commercially available in a wide range of colors and contain a binder, which aids their application and adhesion. They require two to three coats for solid coverage. This makes design work easier, since they will not mix together. They harden with bisque firing, but need to be fired to the top earthenware temperatures to fix, when they produce a velvet-like appearance.

STAINS

Contrasting colored form
by Penkridge Ceramics
These pieces use a full range of matte and shiny glazes colored by stains, underglaze pigments, and oxides. Some also have transparent glaze applied that adds to the extraordinarily realistic representation.

Layered and fettled bowl
by Susan Nemeth
The porcelain clay has been colored by body stains. These are then laminated and fettled to allow the patterns to show through the layered surface.

Contrasting colored form
by Regina Heinz
This form has been created using a combination of oxides, body stain powders, and velvet stains with matte glazes. All of these elements together deliver a rich and interesting surface.

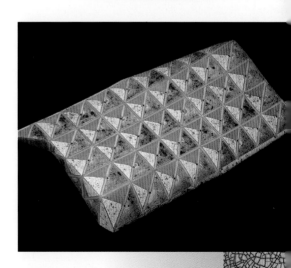

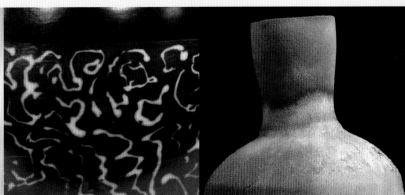

PART FOUR

FIRING

Reduction-glazed vessel
by Karin Putsch-Grassi
*The form and surface of the clay
has been manipulated to create an
interesting textural quality. This
has then been further enhanced by
the glaze, fire and smoke.
Makers from left to right: Jorgen
Hansen, Christine Cox, John
Evans, and David Miller.*

Large kilns

This is the kiln shed at the Leach Pottery in St Ives, England. It shows two of the gas-fired downdraft soda kilns built by lead potter, Jack Doherty.

Your choice of kiln will be determined by several factors: the kind and size of work you want to produce, the space you have available, the type of fuel you want to use, and, of course, your budget. Talk to other makers and manufacturers before you buy to make sure you understand the pros and cons of each type.

WHICH KILN, WHAT FUEL?

Looking into the future of what you are likely to produce is going to be difficult. Choosing something small at first is not wasteful, these kilns can serve a useful purpose as test kilns if your scale of production surpasses it.

Size

Kilns are available in a variety of sizes, to suit everything from a small studio to large-scale factory. Buying the largest kiln that you can afford, thinking that one day you are going to start making large work, may not be the most sensible option, since you won't want to wait until you fill it to fire it and you will end up firing it well below its capacity. Smaller kilns will be fired regularly, making mistakes less costly and allowing you to see results more quickly. Having two sizes of kiln is often an efficient option.

All kilns come with specific information about external and internal dimensions and weight, which is an important consideration if they are going to be sited on upper load-bearing floors. Good suppliers often send a presales questionnaire about electrical supply, location, accessibility, and ventilation, and are always happy to talk through the practicalities and offer after-sales advice. For a fraction of the cost of buying a kiln, you can build your own, and many people who use fuel rather than electric kilns do so.

Small, transportable kilns that can be taken apart after use and reassembled on a different site can easily be made from ceramic fiber and wire mesh. Large kilns tend to be made from various types of firebrick, including HTIs (high thermal insulation) and a metal frame or sheet. They fire accurately at all the required temperatures. Where the kiln is to be sited is another factor, but large kilns can be supplied in sections and built on site.

Fuel

Your choice of firing fuel depends on the type of work you want to explore and create. Electricity provides a stable, efficient, clean, and reliable way of firing ceramics. However, the control and the hands-on physical and sensory experience are missing. All other fuels, which provide flame, offer very different qualities with different surfaces and colors and require greater experience and knowledge to use. All kilns can create fascinating results, but obviously the outcome depends on your knowledge, experience, and what you put into the mix.

You also need to consider your location, the costs associated with fuel availability and delivery, and your personal "carbon footprint." Different countries have different legislation on fuel emissions, and that legislation changes constantly: make sure you are aware of the legal requirements where you are.

CHOOSING A KILN

There can seem an overwhelming amount of kilns to choose from different suppliers, and there are now many excellent products available. As with most things in ceramics, ask other makers what they use. Small to medium top loaders are a common choice for a first "set up" kiln.

Top-loading kilns

Front-loading kilns

Electric kilns

Very few makers design and build their own electric kiln; however, you can commission one to your own requirements.

Construction Electric kilns are constructed from lightweight HTI bricks, which weigh up to 80 percent less than a standard brick. A layer of ceramic fiber blanket goes on top for additional insulation. Both of these materials are easily damaged and so, for protective purposes, they are then clad in metal sheet.

Inside the kiln there are cut channels in the walls, floor, and door, which hold in place banks of coiled wire elements made from a metal alloy called "kanthal." These kanthal elements transfer heat by radiation and no combustion of fuel takes place. Not as common are elements, which consist of silicon carbide rods contained in ceramic tubes. The accurate description of an electric kiln atmosphere is neutral, not oxidized, although most clay makers refer to it as oxidized.

A new kiln will require an empty single firing to oxidize the exterior of the kanthal wire elements. During this firing, a coating of aluminum oxide is created between the metal and oxygen in the kiln. This will protect and prolong the elements' use, because it is this coating that holds the wire together at top stoneware temperatures. If, in future firings, you introduce materials to create a reduced atmosphere inside the kiln, the life of the elements

will be shortened as the carbon atmosphere eats away at the protective surface coating. The life span of the elements in your kiln will depend on how many times you fire and to what temperatures: if you regularly fire to stoneware temperatures, then you may require a new set of elements every few years. Elements can be easily replaced when required, replacing a full set is more cost-effective than changing a few at a time.

Temperature control An electric kiln is fired using a range of temperature gauges; these are usually purchased along with automatic digital program controllers, which switch the kiln off when it reaches the temperature preset.

Electric firings produce a uniformity and evenness of temperature through the kiln, although you may still have "cold" and "hot" spots and differences between top and bottom, depending on how you have packed the kiln. However, the stable atmosphere of electric kilns is not exciting enough for some makers, since it produces results that they consider to be too predictable.

Top-loading kiln Top-loading kilns are available in a variety of sizes; they are efficient, easy to operate, and cheap to both install and use. The work is packed from the base up; in some models, you can add further ring sections to increase the height should you start to make taller work.

Top loaders are relatively

inexpensive for a commercial kiln and ideal for a small workshop since they need as little as 18 in (45 cm) space between the kiln and the wall (more if they are situated in an enclosed room). Because they are designed with the minimum of insulation, they do cool down very quickly, which may present a problem with certain glazes. This can be overcome by setting a cooling program on the controller. Most top-loading kilns will run off single-phase electricity with only the large oval ones needing three-phase.

Front-loading kiln Available in a wide range of sizes from small tabletop "test" kilns to large industrial ones, front-loading kilns are much heavier in construction and far better insulated than top loaders. They are more robust and have heavier external casing, walls, base, and door. The cooling is much slower than that of top-loading kilns, due to the more efficient heat retention. Front-loading kilns are normally three to four times the cost of a top loader of an equivalent size. They usually require a three-phase electricity supply and take up more space than top loaders. The main advantage of front-loading kilns is that they are very hard-wearing and worth the outlay if you are going into production work.

Trolley kiln A trolley kiln has its whole brick base made on top of metal casing with wheels attached underneath. Once the base is packed with work the

whole trolley is gently pushed into the kiln. Now designed in a wide range of sizes to suit smaller workshops, they were once specifically made as huge industrial ones. You will need space twice the size of the kiln in order to accommodate the trolley while you are packing the kiln. These kilns are constructed with metal frame casing all around with excellent heat retention. Small ones tend to be made with HTI brick while the large ones incorporate a high percentage of ceramic fiber in the interior walls and ceilings. Like other kiln types they can be commissioned for individual requirements. These are robust kilns that offer industrial production capabilities and will all require three-phase electricity because of their size. The main advantage of trolley

Costing your own electric firing

A = Kilowatt rating of kiln (taken from the kiln or brochure)
B = Firing times in hours x 0.6 (since the kiln will only be firing on full power toward the end of its cycle)
C = Cost per kilowatt/unit (on your electricity bill)

Cost of one firing = A x B x C

kilns is that large work can be placed or lifted onto the kiln bed, then rolled into the kiln; the only other option with large work is to build a kiln around the object.

Fuel-burning kilns

There are three types of design for fuel-burning kilns: updraft, downdraft, and cross-draft. The design will determine how the flame and heat travel through both work and kiln and finally exit. This will affect how efficiently the kiln works and will depend on what temperature you are firing to, and the type of atmosphere you are creating.

Updraft A kiln where the fire is underneath or at the lower end. The heat moves up through the chamber and exits via a hole or flue at the top. This was a development from early bonfires through pit firing, where the walls were built higher than the pit hole and shards placed on top of the work to retain heat. Updraft firing has ongoing problems with hot spots, depending on how the heat travels through the chamber to the exit hole, which will always be the quickest route. Even packing of work is essential for even firing to take place.

Downdraft A kiln where the fire enters the base or sides and the heat is forced or deflected by a wall (bag wall) up to the ceiling,

and back down through the chamber containing the work and then drawn through by a flue at the back of the kiln. The heat can then be drawn into another chamber or exit via a chimney. These designs enable a more even distribution of heat through the chamber and allow higher temperatures to be reached. They also allow greater control of the internal atmosphere to enable reduction or oxidization. This is the design principle and starting point for many of today's kilns.

Cross-draft A kiln in which fuel is introduced at one side of the entrance via a stoke hole, with the atmosphere (i.e. the heat) circulating in a crisscross pattern before going up to the ceiling and down through the chamber containing the work, finally exiting via a flue at the back of the kiln, on the opposite side to the stoke hole. These kilns were the first to produce wood ash glazes through the ash buildup on the ceilings, which started dripping onto the work. The cross-draft kiln design developed into the tube or bank kiln or into much larger versions—climbing chamber kilns.

Gas kilns

The decision whether to purchase or build a gas-fired kiln will be determined by your location, the space you have available, and local planning

restrictions and regulations. It's also worth checking with your insurance company. Planning of the site will also need to take neighbors into account if they are going to be regularly affected by smoke.

The size of kiln should be determined by what you intend to produce: there is no point in having a large kiln if you are never going to fill it. Makers often have an electric kiln for bisque firing, because there is no advantage to gas firing at this stage. For large work, however, some people prefer to be able to control heatwork (the amount of time something is exposed to heat) in a gas kiln.

Gas kilns can be fired safely both inside buildings with plenty of space around them, and outside under cover in brick- or timber-built buildings, or open or closed corrugated metal-roofed sheds.

Design Having thought carefully about what your likely production and location will be, the next decision is whether to go for updraft, downdraft, or cross-draft. Gas kilns don't necessarily require a separate chimney to draw heat through; this can be the kiln itself in the case of a simple updraft design. The exit hole has to be big enough to allow fumes to escape.

If you are making a downdraft or cross-draft kiln, you require a

separate exit via a chimney that will draw the heat and fumes through. You need to think about the relative sizes of chamber, firebox, and chimney height, since there are basic principles that should be followed with these dimensions to make them work efficiently. Getting the firebox right is key to any flame-burning fuel.

Gas supply and storage Gas can be supplied by mains/town gas, large tanks, or propane bottles. Gas should be stored separately and fed in by pipework. Always seek advice from registered gas contractors who will fit the pipework. All taps should have cutoff valve controls that can be easily accessible in any emergency.

Burners The gas is introduced into the kiln by different kinds of burners, which regulate the amount of fuel flow and air (this air referred to as "primary") into the kiln along with the surrounding air around the burner ports (this air referred to as "secondary"). There is a full range available from manufacturers; they are also available in separate parts so that you can custom-build your own. There are simple gas injectors that rely on primary air pressure, forced air burners relying on pressure supplied by air blowers, and high-end fully sealed injector

Heat direction

These chamber cross sections show heat direction.

Updraft

Downdraft

Bag wall

Cross-draft

Fire box

Chimney

Exit flue

Pierced bag wall

Exit

Chimney

Exit flue

units that have controlled air and fuel. The design of many gas kilns incorporates low internal walls (bag walls), which prevent the flames from coming into direct contact with the work. To select the most appropriate burner, talk to your supplier about the cubic capacity of your kiln, temperatures, and the type of gas you are using.

The number of burners you need will depend on the size of your kiln. All have to be supplied or made with pressure gauges and safety cutout devices that will shut off the gas should there be any failure with the flame. All burners need to be fine-tuned to operate successfully. Explosions

will occur if unlit gas enters the chamber at a low temperature and the kiln is then ignited. The burners are situated at the base just outside the kiln with gaps or holes left around them for the flame and oxygen to enter.

Materials If you are building your own gas kiln, buy the best quality you can, since this kiln will be around for some time. Secondhand materials can be purchased. A kiln for raku only will require low temperatures of 1832° F (1000° C) and normal house bricks can be used for this; for higher temperatures, you will need firebricks. As the heat rating (the maximum temperature a product can withstand) increases, so does the price. Firebricks are less expensive than HTIs.

A metal angle bar frame is often built around the brickwork to help hold the structure in place. The number of times you fire the kilns and to what temperature will determine how long it will last before it needs to be rebuilt. Approximately five years producing 250 firings.

Ceramic fiber is extensively used for its excellent thermal insulation properties (keep up to date with current health and safety regulations, since ceramic fiber is carcinogenic and a skin irritant). As demand increases, new ceramic fibers are being developed that are safer but not heat rated beyond 2282° F (1250° C). Ceramic fiber is a mixture of alumina, silica, flux, and china clay. It is easy to use, but it should always be handled with care and you should wear a dust mask and protective gloves. Always keep the material dry, because it will break down when wet. There is a liquid available that is painted on the surface to provide a bonding coat to help prevent the fiber from breaking down so easily. The fiber comes in a range of different forms: the most useful are the blanket, which is temperature rated up to 2912° F (1600° C) and paper, which is temperature rated to 2300° F (1260° C). All these forms

Construction of a kiln

This is the Leach Pottery gas-fired downdraft soda kiln (1). It shows the HTI bricks with the sides and ceiling covered by a ceramic fiber blanket held in place with foil and metal mesh. The large overhead pipe supplies the mains gas to the double gas-injector burners (3). The diagram shows how simple gas burners can be (2).

can be used in between, over, or inside brickwork to help to retain heat inside the firing chamber. The blanket is also used in many different kilns and especially in site-specific sculpture firings (see page 243).

Timber forming molds and shuttering can be created to help with casting refractory concrete (calcium alumina mixtures) to create structure. For larger kilns, reinforcing bars made from stainless steel can be used, which will not corrode.

Temperature control Gas kiln firings can be fully controlled by a digital program controller, but are often controlled by the maker. The temperature is read by a thermocouple probe inside the kiln, which is attached to and read on a pyrometer (see page 226).

Advantages Two of the reasons makers choose to use a gas kiln are to create a reduced atmosphere and to introduce salt and soda into the kiln (see pages 235–236). Reduction is created by starving the kiln of oxygen for a short period, which changes glaze and clay colors.

Oil-fired kilns

Oil can be used as effectively as gas, especially for large kilns. The choice will usually be decided by fuel availability, supply, and cost. The same reduction and oxidation atmospheres can be created and controlled as with other flame fuels. Different

1

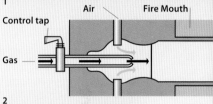

Control tap
Air   Fire Mouth
Gas

2

3

Commercial kiln

A commercial gas kiln with an interior back flue at the base of the kiln and a side bag wall.

Downdraft kiln

This downdraft kiln was built as part of a demonstration at the 2011 International Ceramic Festival in Aberystwyth, Wales. After the festival it was sold for the materials cost of $1,418 (£900.) The base is constructed with heavy-duty firebrick and the main walls in HTI brick. All are held in place by a simple and common system of metal angle bars. The roof bricks were numbered so that it could be reconstructed.

kinds of oil can be used with the appropriate burners and methods. One system that uses thick waste oil is a series of stepped metal plates, where the oil is dripped from one to the other; when it ignites, a fan provides oxygen to combust and enters into the kiln. Forced-air burners produce a fine spray of oil and air and are controlled by compressors and fans; this is known as "primary air." The "secondary air" is that which is pulled in around the burner; this is created by the draft from the chimney. Oil is usually gravity fed, with the supply tank positioned higher than the burner and kept well away from the kiln. As with gas kilns, all pipework should be regularly checked and kept in good order by specialist fitters.

Wood-fired kilns

Wood kilns cannot be purchased: they require someone experienced to build them. As with gas kilns, talk to makers who use them regularly, and inquire about the possibilities of a visit

or assisting in a firing. Attend making and firing workshops to see if this really is the kind of work you want to investigate before making the commitment. There is a range of different kiln designs that are well tried and tested, and information and diagrams are available in specific books.

Materials Often, wood-fired kilns are made from a range of brick types. The fire-mouths should be built of the best-quality firebricks, because this is where the kiln takes the most heat-related punishment, and wood ash is corrosive. HTIs are ideal for the chamber walls and arches, backed up by layers of ceramics fiber in between, inside, or over the top. This may be all kept in place with a metal framework. It may well be clad in clay.

Fuel It takes a large amount of timber to achieve stoneware temperatures, so you will need to prepare your timber supply well before the firing is scheduled, making sure that it is very dry

to produce instant heat. The timber needs to be delivered or collected, cut, stacked, and stored for months, not days, before you are due to use it. Different timbers produce different quantities of heat: soft wood produces a fierce heat and burns rapidly, while hard wood takes longer to burn; a mix of the two is beneficial for different stages of the firing cycle.

Firing Wood firing is typically started very slowly, with the heat being allowed to gently rise through the firing cycle. The quality of glazes is greatly enhanced by wood firing, giving a visual softness created by the gases and composition of the burning wood at high temperatures. This happens when wood is fed into the kiln when

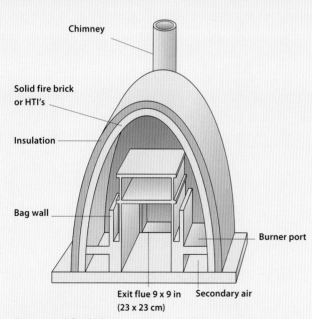

Catenary oil-fired kiln

This has become a classic and popular design. The arch is built using a timber and hardboard former.

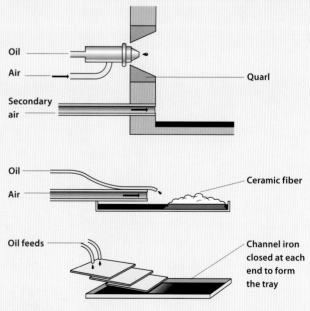

Introducing oil

These burners demonstrate the different ways that oil can be introduced into the kiln.

Updraft kiln

This simple updraft kiln (right) is made using clay, which has been baked hard during the firing. The chamber is exposed by the unpacking of the doorway bricks. The firebox is below the kiln shelf and is fed by timber placed through a hole.

Double-chambered wood-firing kiln

The smaller first arch (left) is the firebox. This is where the timber is fed in during the firing.

white hot, giving off gas, smoke, and ash in a burst of combustion. The ash combines either with the glaze or the unglazed body to give a variety of reactions of rich color and finish.

Glazes Some makers may bisque fire their work in an electric kiln first and then glaze fire with a different fuel such as wood in a flame kiln. Others do one single firing (raw glazing), applying the glaze to damp greenware work and leaving out the bisque stage, which saves on a time-consuming and costly firing using wood.

Solid-fuel kilns

Depending on where in the world you are firing, and local availability, you may be firing kilns with the following fuels. These fuels have enabled some beautiful and exquisite ceramic work to be produced over thousands of years.

Coal, coke, charcoal, sawdust, peat, and animal manure are all fuels that can be used for low- and high-temperature firings. There can be problems with using coal, because the

sulfur in its composition can impart a dry scum to unglazed and glazed surfaces. This is one reason why work was fired inside saggar containers in bottle-oven kilns. Sawdust and peat are used in slow, low-temperature firings to give various reduced, oxidized, and carbonizing effects. This is particularly interesting when used with burnished red terracotta work. Rinsing low-fired work in buttermilk or milk after firing, while it is still hot, uses the casein in the liquids to seal the clay. Mixing 25 percent of coal dust or sawdust into plastic clay assists with the firing of red clay. The fuel ignites and burns inside the clay at around 1652–1832° F (900–1000° C). This method is common when firing handmade bricks.

Paper kilns

These kilns can offer both theatrical and practical firing. Depending on how they are constructed, some designs can be fired up to 2102° F (1150° C). Paper kilns can be built using different paper-folding and -rolling methods to form modules that are woven together

and can be held in place with wire and mesh. Other forms of paper kilns are made with layers of timber and paper coated with wet china clay. These structures become practical firing sculptures that, while burning, can generate enough heat to fire the work as a traditional kiln.

Construction A base foundation is made with a simple layer of bricks with burner/air ports or wire mesh strong enough to support the weight. The work is placed on this, with charcoal in the gaps between the work and the brickwork, leaving enough space for air to ignite the charcoal. Further layers of charcoal and sawdust can be added around the work as you stack. The structure can then be built around this base. You can either insert a small metal tube

Paper kiln

This kiln clearly demonstrates the rolling and folding methods used in making a paper kiln. It is an extraordinary, functional object about to go up in flames.

at the top to act as a chimney or leave a simple exit hole. One method is to create a frame by leaning lengths of hardwood against the work; this is all held in place by wire mesh. On top of this are placed layers upon layers of paper coated with a wet mixture of china clay. If you decide to make the structure with rolled and woven paper, magazine paper is the best option, because it contains the most china clay content; layers of newspaper and china clay are then added on top. These paper structures are set alight at the base and left to burn. Providing the paper is not flaming, small running repairs such as patching holes to prevent too much air entering can be undertaken during firing. It is worth making smaller structures to begin with to gain experience. All relevant health and safety procedures should be observed and put in place.

The control of temperature is central to the success of ceramics: too hot and not only will the glaze run off the work but the clay itself will distort and eventually melt; not hot enough and clays will be fragile and porous and glazes dry and powdery. Kiln temperature is what governs the way things look and feel.

KILN TEMPERATURE

In the past, makers were trained to judge a firing by eye as the color of heat changes inside the kiln from "first red"—a dull red glow around 1110° F (600° C), through orange (1470° F/800° C), and yellow (2010° F/1100° C) to the white heat of 2370°F (1300° C). You can use this as a guide, but makers now rely on other help.

Pyrometric cones

The truest readers of heatwork (the amount of time something has been exposed to heat) inside the kiln are pyrometric cones. Heatwork can greatly affect results. Pyrometric cones are triangular in shape and are made from materials that will bend at a very specific predetermined temperature. They are stamped on the side with a number that refers to that temperature, which varies depending on which make you purchase. The cones may be used periodically to check certain firings, particularly if any problems are occurring. Certain makers use them all the time, especially with flame firings.

Cones are usually placed in a row of three, in front of spy holes in the kiln so that they can be observed, to indicate when a firing is nearing completion, has reached completion, or has overfired. Depending on the size of kiln, they are normally placed at the top and bottom of the kiln to determine an even firing throughout the kiln. If problems such as hot and cold spots are occurring in certain areas of the kiln, then the cones would also be placed there.

Pyrometers and thermocouples

Pyrometers are devices—digital or analog—that show the rise and fall of the temperature on the face of the display. Unlike pyrometric cones, they do not show heatwork. They are connected via a sensitive compensating cable to a thermocouple, which takes the temperature. The thermocouple is a long, thin ceramic probe or tube, which houses two platinum and rhodium wires joined at the tip. These create a small voltage, which is read by the pyrometer.

Pyrometers can be fixed into a permanent position or kept as mobile devices to use in different kilns. They are placed through a small hole in the top, back, or side of the kiln and should protrude in by at least 1 in (2.5 cm). Care should always be taken to identify where this comes through into a kiln, because the

2370° F (1300° C)	2350° F (1290° C)	2340° F (1280° C)

Pyrometric cones

These pyrometric cones are placed with the flat side facing the front in order to lead the bend. These melted cones demonstrate a perfect firing at the Leach Pottery and are a reliable way of gauging kiln temperature.

pyrometer can be easily broken if knocked. Large kilns will have three or more thermocouples for zonal control. The controller will allow the top, middle, and bottom linked element banks to input the correct amount of heat to even out the temperature.

Digital program controllers

These controllers were specifically designed for use with electric and gas kilns. They are very simple to program and use, and offer the convenience of a number of preset firing schedules that allow set stages or "ramps." Generally, the more ramps, the more expensive the controller. Once the relevant program has been selected and the "on" button pressed, the controller will take the kiln through the firing cycle and switch it off when the required temperature is reached and firing is complete. Kilns can also be fitted with a safety "overfire" device so that, if there is a problem with the controller, the kiln will switch off after a certain number of hours. The controller will also control an electronic damper to close at a set point.

Electric kiln controllers

There are two manual dial controllers on the market that operate in much the same system, both regulating the percentage of electricity flowing into the kiln. A combined dial and switch reads from 0–100. The other model dial and switch reads off/low/medium/high.

Electric kiln controllers can be used with both pyrometric cones and with a pyrometer and thermocouple. They work in a similar way to a digital controller and are just as effective; the only difference is that, if you use them with a pyrometer, you need to be on hand to switch off the kiln when firing is complete (unless the pyrometer is fitted with a cutoff switch).

Kiln sitter This is a type of cutoff switch. It operates by means of a trip switch, which is activated by a very small, horizontal pyrometric cone that sits across three bars inside the kiln. When it reaches the required temperature, it bends, and the middle bar, which is a lever, drops and trips the "off" switch: very simple, but effective.

Thermocouple and pyrometer
You can clearly see the thermocouple sticking down through the ceiling and into the kiln (top left). Always identify where this is so that you don't knock it. The digital pyrometer (top right) is connected to the thermocouple and reads the internal temperature.

Draw rings
Draw rings being withdrawn from a salt kiln (left). These show the progression of the salting, and a decision can be made to carry on or stop.

Draw rings

Draw rings are simply rings made from the same clay and glaze that is being fired. Although the color of the kiln interior and the length of time firing provided an indication of the firing's progress, traditionally, draw rings were the only way that the heatwork and temperature could be read inside the kiln; the rings could be withdrawn with an iron rod at any time to demonstrate how the kiln firing was progressing and when it had reached the maturing temperature. These rings are still used by makers who wood fire and those who use salt and soda for their glazes.

Kiln packing and unpacking is an important part of the ceramic process and is always more enjoyable when you are not under any time pressures. It can be thought of as a three-dimensional jigsaw.

KILN PACKING

Kiln packing is very important to the success of a firing and is carried out differently depending on the kiln and type of firing. The main rule is to allow the heat to circulate in the kiln as evenly as possible throughout the rise in temperature. In flame firings where you are controlling the atmosphere with reduction, wood, salt, and soda, it is how and where work is placed that will determine the surface markings and quality of the glaze.

Furniture

To make the most of the space inside a kiln, you will need to use a range of kiln "furniture," also known as "refractories." Made from refractory fire clay and able to withstand high temperatures (2730° F/1500° C), kiln furniture can be refired hundreds of times. The range of items available includes bats or shelves, extruded hollow bats, firebricks for large heavy work, half shelves, hollow tube or square shelf support props, small extension ring props, castellated props, tile cranks, and various designs to keep work off the kiln shelf during glaze firings, such as stilts, spurs, setters, and pins. All kiln furniture comes in a wide variety of shapes and sizes and can be also be made to specific sizes.

For the firing of very large work that needs to be able to move in the kiln as it shrinks during firing, work can be set on a system of rollers. Also used are special heavy-duty metal bars made from silicon infiltrated silicon carbide (SiSiSi) and aluminum oxide; these will support both furniture and work and are specialist and expensive. Also useful is silver sand (silica sand), which can be used as a layer underneath work and will assist in supporting awkward forms and aid moving during shrinkage.

Packing a bisque firing

Packing a kiln (also known as placing, stacking, or setting a kiln) is like undertaking a three-dimensional jigsaw. You need to consider how to make best use of the internal space—and this will depend on the size and shape of your kiln. There are a few basic principles to follow. Assess all the work to be fired and work out what items will fit alongside and inside each other. Similar forms can be stacked together, but take care not to put undue stress on the fragile dry clay. Tiles can be placed upright on their edges against each other or other work. Place very small items inside others, so that they don't get lost. The base shelf can be used for work that takes up the whole shelf space or for heavy work. With a front-loading kiln, place taller work toward the back half of the kiln and put shelves in the front half for ease of handling and packing. With top-loading kilns, you need to judge the height of work with a stick before placing the shelf; allow at least ¾ in (2–3 cm) clearance.

Bat/kiln wash

Mix equal quantities of china clay and flint (or china clay and alumina) with water to the consistency of light cream. This can also be purchased already made from suppliers.

Bisque-firing essentials

• Greenware should be bone dry before first firing: work that is cold to the touch in room temperature is usually still damp.

• Pieces of greenware can touch each other in the firing, since they will not stick together.

• Careful handling of work is essential, because clay is very fragile at this stage—particularly porcelain. Work should always be picked up from the base and not by the rim.

• Three props offer better support for a kiln shelf, creating triangular support. Always place kiln props in vertical lines above each other as the stack progresses.

• Do not place work near the sides close to the kiln's elements; leave a space of 1½ in (4 cm).

• Leave a sufficient gap—1 in (3 cm)—in between flat work and the kiln shelf above.

• Do not pack work too tightly, since this will prevent an even circulation of heat.

• Place very heavy work on the base shelf.

• If your kiln has split shelving (two per base surface area is usual in front-loading kilns) then avoid placing even layers of both shelves as you stack; create steps in shelf heights instead, which will allow the heat to circulate in between the different-height shelves. Circular top-loading kilns also benefit from placing some half (semicircular) shelves in the firing if there is uneven heat distribution.

• Avoid putting too many shelves close together in the bottom half of the kiln with none at the top, since this will retain the heat and can overfire the base due to heatwork because the thermocouple is usually placed near the top. Alternate different heights if possible, placing some taller work toward the top.

• Do not mix greenware and glazed work in the same firing, since this will affect the quality of the glaze.

Packing a glaze firing

Different kilns demand different packing for the type of fuel used. You can follow the same principles as for bisque firing for placing shelves and packing work, but work cannot be touching—otherwise, when the glaze melts, it will stick and fuse the work together as it cools down. In fact, you should allow at least ¾ in (2 cm) all around each piece, both to allow heat to circulate around forms and to prevent glaze migrating onto other work, since glaze materials can move in the atmosphere of firings; copper oxide flashing (where the oxide becomes unstable during stoneware temperatures) is common. Assess how you position the work to make sure it will not distort or bend onto electric elements or onto other work when the kiln is at top temperature. Some work may need props to prevent distortion. Make sure all bases are clean of glaze: no glaze should come into contact with the kiln because the glaze, when melting, will stick. This should be considered during the making stage and is often why makers make a small hidden bevel at the base of work to ensure the glaze is not in contact with the kiln shelf. The bevel also provides a shadow and visual lift to the form. With glazes that are prone to running or if this is something of interest; you can make a drip tray, which can be a simple slab of clay large enough to catch all glaze drips. This will protect expensive kiln shelves; support props can be built on the tray if you require glaze on the whole base surface. Unless you are going to use stilts, there should also be a small glaze-free area on the sides of the work at the base.

Depending on your glazes and results, soaking (holding the kiln temperature at a set point) at the cutoff point for 15 minutes will even out the glaze surface. This also allows the heat to evenly distribute through the kiln. The time for glazes to melt depends on the glazes used and the kiln and firing. Some glazes are better cooled as soon as the temperature is reached.

Coat all kiln shelves with a layer of bat/kiln wash (see page opposite) prior to firing.

Other useful items include ni-chrome wire and alumina. Ni-chrome wire can be tied to clay supports and small objects can either be suspended from it or threaded onto it during glaze firing, enabling work to be glazed all over. Alumina prevents clay and glaze from sticking to shelves and can be used as a powder or liquid. It is the main ingredient in bat wash, which is applied to kiln shelves to provide a protective coating to help prevent objects from sticking completely and enable easier removal if they do so. (Avoid thick layers of bat wash, since this can create a very uneven surface and cause some distortion at stoneware.)

Unpacking the kiln

You can start the "cooling to open" phase by opening the damper around 390° F (200° C) or when "cracking" the kiln door at 300° F (150° C).

It is advisable to leave the door open by 1 ft (30 cm) for one hour to allow the kiln to cool further. You can then, wearing kiln gloves, start unpacking the kiln, but it is advisable to allow the kiln to cool even further. Once the work is out of the kiln, it will cool rapidly. Faults that could not be seen before firing may show once the piece has been bisque fired. Any work that has handles with hairline cracks should be immediately thrown away. Bisque work should be handled with clean hands. It is strong enough to be stacked together.

The firing of greenware (dry clay) is called a "bisque" firing. Once the work has been fired and unpacked, it will have changed color; depending on the clays used, it may be mainly beige, light terra-cotta, or white in appearance. Handle all work with clean hands and keep your work and working environment as dust-free as possible until glazing.

FIRST FIRING: BISQUE

During bisque firing the clay goes through a cycle of changes that transform it into a permanent material called "ceramic." The firing temperature for bisque depends on the type of clay that has been used and how it will be glazed: generally, it is 1760–1830° F (960–1000° C). It is higher for bone china and low-fired earthenware; glaze is applied and fired at a lower temperature. The reason to bisque fire work to this temperature is to make the work stable and easier to handle when applying glaze; also this temperature will not vitrify the clay, leaving it porous and able to absorb liquid glaze easily onto the surface. Another reason is that, during firing, carbon deposits and gases in the clay are burnt out; this prevents many glaze faults such as pinholing and bloating from happening in the second glaze firing.

Once the kiln is packed and the door or lid locked, the bung holes in the kiln must be left open to allow steam and gases to escape. They can be closed when the kiln has reached 1290° F (700° C) since this will help to retain the heat. They may be left until the end of the firing and then the kiln should be fully closed.

The firing schedule (length of the firing) also depends on what kind of work you are firing—its size, shape, and thickness. An average bisque firing will take between eight and eleven hours. Some makers fast-fire in four to six hours. Once you are confident with your own work, you can experiment.

4 360–480° F (180–250° C)

3 280–360° F (140–180° C)

2 170–210° F (80–100° C)

1 0–280° F (0–140° C)

FIRING CYCLE: WHAT HAPPENS TO CLAY

The changes that take place during the firing of clay are complex, but you only need to know a few basics to fire clay successfully. The following is a summary of what happens. The hourly rise in temperature of between 170 and 210° F (80 and 100° C) is noted for even-walled work up to a thickness of ¾ in (2 cm). A more cautious approach and longer firing cycle should be taken for thicker, larger, and more complex work.

Where two temperatures are given, the first denotes the temperature at that particular stage of firing and the second indicates the maximum rise per hour.

1 0–280° F (0–140° C)
2 170–210° F (80–100° C)
Work must be fired slowly at this temperature even though the work will look dry, water is held in between the tiny clay particles and will be driven off as vapor in the firing. Water boils at 210° F (100° C) and, as the water turns to steam, it expands; pressure builds in the clay and if the water is heated too quickly, there is a risk of the work exploding as the steam escapes. The less grog the clay body contains, the more dense it is, which increases the chances of the work exploding. A dull thud can be heard from inside the kiln

when this happens; localized damage may occur or the whole piece may shatter. Cracking in thick work happens because of the tension differences between the interior and exterior of the work, as it takes longer for the heat to penetrate. Much slower firing is essential to even out this tension and prevent cracking.

3 280–360° F (140–180° C)
180–210° F (80–100° C) per hour rise to first set point of 1110° F (600° C). If you have thick work, then soaking the kiln for a few hours (see 8, opposite) will lessen the risk of the work cracking. This gives the clay wall the chance to even out in temperature to reduce the tension.

TYPICAL BISQUE-FIRING SCHEDULE

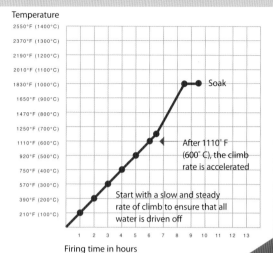

Temperature

Soak

After 1110° F
(600° C), the climb
rate is accelerated

Start with a slow and steady
rate of climb to ensure that all
water is driven off

Firing time in hours

Quartz inversion

Silica takes different physical forms—quartz, cristoballite, and tridymite—but remains chemically the same. Silica has a crystalline structure and through firing changes occur known as phases. At 1063.4° F (573° C), any unbound silica in the clay goes through a physical change known as the alpha–beta quartz inversion. During this phase, the alpha silica molecule becomes 1 percent larger; this changes back when cooling. This rearranging of the structure by the movement of the particles is what makes the structure increase in size. It's important not to pass this point too quickly since, in thick work or areas of thickness, this can cause cracks due to this tension. Beyond this point, the clay has gone past being able to be recycled.

12 Beyond 2280° F (1250° C)

11 2280° F (1250° C)

10 2190° F (1200° C)

9 2010° F (1100° C)

8 1830° F (1000° C)

7 1200–1830° F (650–1000° C)

6 930–1200° F (500–650° C)

5 480–930° F (250–500° C)

4 360–480° F (180–250° C)
During this period, organic materials in the clay start to oxidize.

5 480–930° F (250–500° C)
During this period the chemically/crystal bound water (held in between the tiny particles of clay) is being driven out. Firing too quickly in the early stages does not allow time for enough of the carbon deposits to burn out.

6 930–1200° F (500–650° C)
The temperature can increase more quickly between these points. From 1120–1290° F (600–700° C), depending on the kind of work, there can be a rise of 300–480° F (150–250° C) per hour. This is when you can program the kiln to go quicker. This is the point of quartz inversion (see box above).

7 1200–1830° F (650–1000° C)
During this phase gases (fluorine and sulfur trioxide, which combines with moisture to form sulfuric acid) are released due to the oxidation of limestone, organic matter, and iron sulfides. Held water (see page 26) is still being driven off. The kiln bungs and damper can be closed after 1290° F (700° C) to help the temperature to rise. Some makers leave the small top spy hole open to allow all the gases to escape.

8 1830° F (1000° C) Soak for 30 minutes to 1 hour. Soaking means holding the kiln temperature. It is optional to soak, as it does not seem to affect all clays. However, by soaking you will ensure that the gases and carbon deposits are burnt out of the clay, which will benefit the glazing stage. This is an average bisque temperature, where the work is stable enough to be handled and all clays are still porous.

9 2010° F (1100° C) At this temperature some clays, especially ones that are iron rich and high in calcium and magnesium, will start to melt. This is why you should always test any found clays.

10 2190° F (1200° C) This is the end of the earthenware range. Many clays start to distort and melt before this temperature is reached; others may fire higher.

11 2280° F (1250° C) At this stage, sintering (where the clay particles have fused together) has taken place in most stoneware clays. Some of the clay materials melt and start to fill in the spaces between other particles; this encourages others to join in, which compacts the structure. Another binder, aluminum silicate, is formed, which also knits the particles together. At this temperature there is a wide range of glazes achievable and the clay is not pushed too far in its structural capabilities. Vitrification is the point at which the clay body has become sealed.

12 Beyond 2280° F (1250° C) Vitrification and maturity will continue for other clays and individual materials. A porcelain body made from kaolin might not melt until over 3270° F (1800° C).

Cooling

1380–1110° F (750–600° C)
Materials that have fused into a glassy state become rigid. Very large work will need controlled cooling from here to below 300° F (150° C) to avoid problems such as cracking.

930° F (500° C) The kiln will have dropped quite quickly to this temperature and will now slow down from this stage. Insulation bricks cool considerably slower than ceramic fiber. Quick cooling may have an effect with certain glazes and cause crazing.

480–350° F (250–180° C) Care should be taken around the cristobalite inversion phase around 440° F (230° C). The high temperature firing has created more crystalline silica through the fusing of the silica molecules, which requires slow passing of this transition phase. Do not open the kiln door above this temperature, since this may cause the work to crack. Cooling the work too quickly can cause this cracking known as "dunting." When the temperature reaches 300° F (150° C), the bungs can be taken out and the damper and door partly opened to speed the cooling process.

Once the bisque-fired work has been unpacked from the kiln and has cooled down, glaze can be applied using a variety of techniques (see pages 258–261). The work is then put back into the kiln for glaze firing at the appropriate temperature. It can be fired as soon as the glaze has been applied and is dry or can be left indefinitely.

SECOND FIRING: GLAZE

If the work is damp, leave it for a few hours to allow it to dry sufficiently for firing. Glaze firing differs from bisque firing in how you pack and fire. Electric kilns offer even distribution of heat from the kiln elements, which should provide reasonably predictable results; again, this will depend on your personal knowledge and experience. Kilns that use other fuels are more unpredictable. Glaze firings take different lengths of time, depending on the type of kiln and the temperature.

Earthenware glaze firing

If the clay body has not been taken to near its vitrification point during the bisque firing, and the glaze firing is only going to 1940° F (1060° C), the body will remain porous. Earthenware may require glazing all over to help with this porosity. Props or stilts should be placed underneath the work to prevent contact with the shelf. These will need to be knocked off after firing. Be careful not to leave a piece of the prop or stilt behind, because they are razor sharp: grind them off with a small abrasive block. On industrial work, if the foot ring is glazed you will notice three very small pinholes on the base where they have been stilted underneath.

The schedule for the glaze-firing length can proceed more quickly than the first firing since many of the changes that take place with clay have been dealt with during the bisque firing. Still, the thicker the clay, the slower you should fire due to heat penetration and tension.

Stoneware and porcelain glaze firing

Stoneware firing poses more demands, which you must take into consideration when making the work. Any wide unsupported areas are prone to distortion. Ideally, it is far better to build the support into the form than to try to fire work on props and stilts, since these will cause much deeper marks on the surface and be harder to remove than at earthenware temperatures, and will require more grinding.

Unglazed porcelain clay will form a glassy surface and can fuse to the kiln shelf, creating a fault called "plucking"; small pieces of the base or foot ring break away and are left stuck to the shelf. To prevent this, you can place a layer of dry alumina on the shelf (be careful not to get this onto any glaze, which will spoil the surface) or make and bisque fire small disks of the same clay, coat them in thin bat wash (see page 228), and place underneath the work. Flame firings will require more attention as the maturing temperature is approaching, since it's important to allow the clay and glaze to fully fuse together to achieve the desired color and surface results. The average time for a stoneware firing is nine hours, but it can take up to two weeks in a wood-fired anagama kiln.

The stages of the glaze firing can proceed more quickly than the bisque firing: 210–250° F (100–120° C) per hour to 930° F (500° C) and then 480° F (250° C) or full to top temperature.

Raw-glaze firing

Small work can be fired once, leaving out the bisque-firing stage and applying the glaze at the greenware stage. Form-making processes will need to be considered in relation to how you will handle the work during glazing. How you hold the work will be critical because as soon as you apply glaze the work will soften. Makers will often spray-glaze the work to prevent damage. A slower firing schedule of 120° F (50° C) is required but then proceed as normal.

Reduction firing

The principle of reduction firing is to reduce the amount of oxygen in the kiln. In so doing, the clay and glaze react differently and produce varied results, introducing a greater degree of unpredictability to the work.

In a fuel-burning kiln, the fuel is burned within the chamber itself and carbon is produced. If the carbon is fed with air, or oxygen, then an oxidizing atmosphere is created. The gas that is given off is carbon dioxide. When the supply of oxygen (but not fuel) to the area of combustion is restricted through the use of a damper, the fuel gives off the unstable gas carbon monoxide (or free carbon) which, when hot enough, takes oxygen from the metals present in the clay body or glaze, which greatly affects their color. The prime example of this is copper and iron oxide in a glaze. In an oxidized neutral firing, copper oxide usually produces greens (unless the glaze contains tin), but in a reduction firing it will produce an extraordinary range of beautiful reds. Pale blue to green celadons are achieved with the addition of 2–5 percent iron oxide.

The reduction procedure is started toward the end of the firing, between 1830–2010° F (1000–1100° C), by observing a single appropriate cone bending. It can last for a short time or for the whole period up to top temperature. Some makers switch between oxidizing and reduction as they reach completion. The periods of reduction are approximate: some for 30 minutes; others for 90 minutes up to five hours and beyond. As with most procedures in ceramics, there are many variables on how long makers reduce their work to achieve a particular glaze and clay quality.

The process To put the kiln into a reduced state, the oxygen flow to the burner is gradually reduced until a yellow flame replaces a blue one. At the same time, pressure in the kiln is increased by partially closing the damper in the chimney, which reduces the exit flow. A passive damper can also be used; this may be a small brick that enables finer tuning to the reduction process. After a few minutes, the kiln atmosphere will start to reduce. Visible signs, depending on the strength of reduction, include black smoke

Reduction firing
The flame of reduction firing searching for air outside the internal kiln atmosphere.

REDUCTION-GLAZED VESSEL
BY EDDIE CURTIS
This wheel-thrown form demonstrates the beautiful deep rich red of a copper reduction glaze.

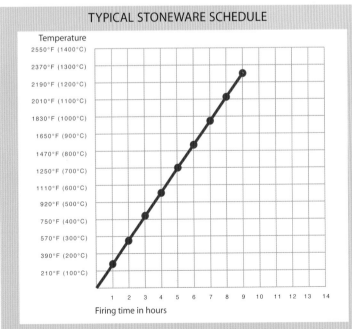

TYPICAL STONEWARE SCHEDULE

Temperature
2550°F (1400°C)
2370°F (1300°C)
2190°F (1200°C)
2010°F (1100°C)
1830°F (1000°C)
1650°F (900°C)
1470°F (800°C)
1250°F (700°C)
1110°F (600°C)
920°F (500°C)
750°F (400°C)
570°F (300°C)
390°F (200°C)
210°F (100°C)

1 2 3 4 5 6 7 8 9 10 11 12 13 14
Firing time in hours

Wood firing
Adam Buick's large wood-burning kiln going into reduction during the evening darkness. The opening of kilns have become event gatherings and celebratory occasions. This has become an extremely good way to both market and sell new work.

Wood-fired kiln
This diagram shows how the firebox is incorporated into the design of a wood-fired kiln.

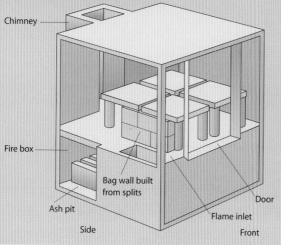

Chimney

Fire box

Bag wall built from splits

Ash pit

Door

Flame inlet

Side

Front

Porcelain moon jars
by Adam Buick
The small wheel-thrown forms show the range of glazes that come out of a single wood firing. Some of these have local clay embedded in the surface, which melts and drips, adding to the surface quality.

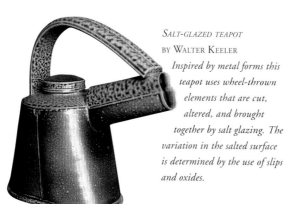

Salt-glazed teapot
by Walter Keeler
Inspired by metal forms this teapot uses wheel-thrown elements that are cut, altered, and brought together by salt glazing. The variation in the salted surface is determined by the use of slips and oxides.

coming out of the chimney and a yellow-to-orange flame appearing out of the spy hole or any gaps in the brickwork. The flames coming out of any available space are searching for more oxygen to burn more efficiently. A green or blue flame indicates that no reduction is taking place.

Do not look into the kiln too closely once you have put the kiln into reduction, since this flame is fierce and extends some distance. The greater the distance from the kiln's spy hole and any gaps, the stronger the reduction. As the kiln reaches the desired temperature, the damper can be opened for a short period to clean the reduced atmosphere and glazes. Once the kiln has reached your top temperature, turn off the burners and close the damper and block any holes, leaving the kiln to cool down naturally.

Wood firing

Firing kilns with wood takes place worldwide and historically is strongly associated with ceramics in the East, with large hillside kilns and the Japanese multichamber noborigama and single-chamber anagama kilns. Whether you are able to undertake this way of firing, more so than with gas, will be determined by where you live, because of the need to conform with local planning regulations.

Wood firing is hard, physical, and time-consuming work, not only with handling the timber to feed the kiln but also with the firing, which demands constant attention. Wood firings can take from one day to two weeks, depending on the kiln size and the quality of work the maker or group is hoping to achieve.

Packing Stacking work in a wood-fired kiln follows the same principles as those for any other firing, but you need to give greater consideration to how the heat, gases, and particularly ash will flow and fall in the kiln (fly ash).

The way the kiln is packed will affect the potential quality of interesting marks on the surface. As for soda and salt firing (see pages 235–236), the work should be placed on three small pads of wadding to form a triangle of support. Wadding is a mixture of alumina hydrate and china clay. It prevents bases from sticking to kiln shelves as the wood ash settles on everything in the chamber.

Wood ash as a glaze Wood ash by itself can be used to create a glaze; it contains among its ingredients calcium, potassium, and some silica. The longer the work is fired, the greater the buildup of ash in the chamber, creating a buildup of glaze on the work. Some makers glaze only the inside of work, allowing the full effects of the ash to control the outside appearance.

Firing Wood is introduced into the kiln via a fire mouth, and heating the kiln is started slowly. Makers talk about getting into the "rhythm" of the firing: when you introduce the wood and how much you put in is important. Maintain a slow and steady rate to begin with, to allow the heat to be drawn up from the fireboxes and into the kiln chamber via the chimney. Too little fuel and the firing will stall; too much and the airways will choke and the heat-rise will also stall. Too many embers in the firebox will restrict the air intake and will require raking out. The primary and secondary airways need to be kept clear at all times. For efficient heat increase, you need a balance between the amounts of oxygen and fuel for complete combustion, enabling the heat to rise. The longer the firing time, the more the heat and ash buildup affects the quality of the surface. Once the firing is finished, the kiln will cool and the bricks of the door can be unpacked. You can then assess the results to determine the success of the firing.

Salt-glaze firing

The orange-peel surface of salt-glazed stoneware has been continually explored since its early development in Germany in the 15th century. Classic examples of this were from the Westerweld pottery in Rhineland, Germany, and Doulton in England from the early 1800s.

Salt and process Damp common salt (sodium chloride) is introduced into the kiln toward the end of the firing cycle between 2010–2190° F (1100–1200° C). Salt is active between 1470–2550° F (800–1400° C). It vaporizes in the

heat and reacts with steam to form chloride and sodium. The sodium reacts with the silica in the clay body and the salt glaze is formed on the surface of the work. The chloride then forms hydrogen chloride and chlorine gas, which is released through the chimney.

It is possible to create a variety of surface effects and color ranges, which can highlight fine detail without covering the form like a thick glaze. Colored slips with oxides can be applied to greenware and provide the surface color, which interacts with the salt. A common base slip recipe is 50 percent china clay and 50 percent fine ball clay, with the addition of oxides. You can also use commercial colored stains, but check their temperature range. For domestic purposes, work is glazed on the inside. All stoneware clays can be used; the bodies will react differently depending on the silica content. Suppliers will advise you on which clays will create different surfaces and salt reaction.

Kilns The kiln is specifically designed and built for salt glazing; once used, it is kept solely for that purpose. The materials used to build salt-glaze kilns are the same as for other flame kilns. The whole of the interior is coated with sodium glaze during the firing, which will reactivate during the next one. A newly built kiln will require more salt than an older one. These kilns have a shorter life span than other flame kilns, due to the corrosive effects of salt. Salt-resist slip (two parts alumina to one part china clay) can be painted onto kiln furniture to prevent the corrosive effects of salt vapor.

Fuel The fuel for salt firing can be supplied by any of those previously mentioned. Gas, wood, or oil will produce different qualities to the surface of the work, particularly when firing with wood ash.

Firing The salt is put into the kiln in dampened paper packets or held on long-handled implements and tipped into the kiln via the burner openings or salting ports. It can also be sprayed in as a liquid solution with water. Work needs to be individually placed on wadding

Salt kiln before and after firing

Each form has to be placed on three pads of wadding to prevent the salt from sticking everything to the kiln shelves. These areas are clearly visible when knocked off after firing.

Soda firing

A mixture of water and soda being sprayed into the kiln at the reduction phase demonstrated by the flame. This will take place several times during the firing.

SODA-FIRED POT

BY JACK DOHERTY

This porcelain form shows the subtle and varied colors that are achievable with soda firing.

pads, because the salt glaze will cover and stick to everything. A reduction atmosphere is used for the firing cycle and started after the first salting of the kiln. The amount of salt used will vary depending on the size of the kiln and what surface you hope to achieve, but 9+ lb (4.5 kg) is required for an average-sized kiln.

Draw rings are always used so that they can be periodically withdrawn from the kiln to access how the salting is progressing. There are obvious health risks with salt firing, and an appropriate mask rated for chlorine gas should be worn when salting takes place. Salt firing can only happen outdoors and kilns should be placed well away from people and other buildings. Consult local planning regulations to see if you are allowed to do these firings. More makers are now exploring soda firing, as these are believed to be less toxic than salt.

Soda firing

Soda (baking or washing) is sodium bicarbonate. It produces similar surfaces to salt glazing, with a less harmful impact on the environment. The most common method of introducing soda into the kiln is to mix it into a solution with warm water and spray it through the spy holes for the whole of the reduction period. Pack and fire the kiln in the same way as with salt. How and where you pack work in the kiln will influence the results, which range from soft, varied surfaces to ones with a heavy, orange-peel-like surface.

Raku firing

Raku is the name given to the technique of fast firing and cooling of clay and glaze, which throws out the usual rule book of producing glazed ceramics. The cracking and crazing of the glaze (sometimes the pot) is admired for its aesthetic and not its functional qualities.

Raku originated in the 16th century in Japan, with tea bowls for the tea ceremony. A tea master in Kyoto named Sen Rikyu admired the work of a potter called Chijiro, whose individual handmade bowls were taken from the kiln while glowing hot and were put either directly into water or left to cool. Sen Rikyu was presented with a gold seal with the ideograph for "Raku," and this became the family title. The family is still making work in this tradition, and the current master is Raku Kichizaemon XV. Raku translates as "happiness" or "enjoyment," and makers are certainly still enjoying the activity today.

The techniques have been modified since then, particularly starting in America from the 1960s. The work is usually bisque fired as normal to 1830° F (1000° C) and then glazed with either earthenware or specific glazes that will melt between 1800–1940° F (980–1060° C). These glazes are usually made from low-melting, high-alkaline frit with oxides and commercial stains. The work is placed inside a range of specifically designed kilns fired by different fuels and rapidly fired up to approximately 1830° F (1000° C), which takes between 30–45 minutes depending on the fuel and kiln type. Once the glaze has melted, the work is taken out with long metal tongs and placed red hot and glowing into a metal trash can or pit containing sawdust. The lid is placed on and left for 15–30 minutes, during which time the sawdust reduces the atmosphere and the created carbon turns the unglazed areas black. The area that was glazed will have crazed due to the rapid cooling and

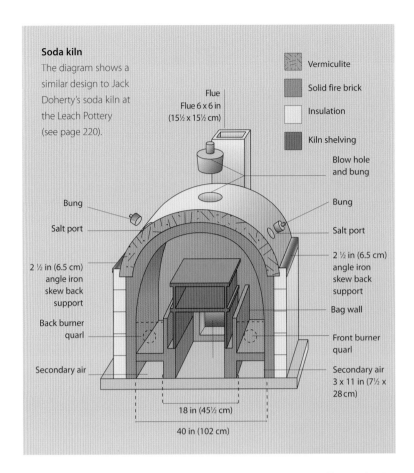

Soda kiln
The diagram shows a similar design to Jack Doherty's soda kiln at the Leach Pottery (see page 220).

Vermiculite

Solid fire brick

Insulation

Kiln shelving

Flue
Flue 6 x 6 in
(15½ x 15½ cm)

Blow hole and bung

Bung

Bung

Salt port

Salt port

2 ½ in (6.5 cm) angle iron skew back support

2 ½ in (6.5 cm) angle iron skew back support

Back burner quarl

Bag wall

Secondary air

Front burner quarl

Secondary air
3 x 11 in (7½ x 28 cm)

18 in (45½ cm)

40 in (102 cm)

RAKU-FIRED POTS

BY DUNCAN HOOSON
These raku bowls have been made as tests with different rims and bases to demonstrate the variety of decorative possibilities.

thermal shock; the carbon will have infiltrated the lines, highlighting the crazed pattern.

Kilns You can raku fire using any type of kiln, but the kiln must be placed outside due to the smoke that is produced when the work is put into the sawdust. You can purchase very light metal and HTI brick kilns that are available in sections; this means you can stack and build as high as you need. Many clay makers now choose to build very simple ceramic fiber versions, either cylindrical or square, which are contained in thick wire mesh or a metal trash can for stability; this has added to the popularity and affordability of raku firing. The kiln has to have a hole or vent in the top to allow the heat to circulate upward and out, which is a simple updraft design. Other designs can be built from any of the previously mentioned bricks and materials, especially Durox blocks (temperature rated 2010° F/1100° C), which are larger than HTIs.

Burners and fuel The most popular choice for raku firing now seems to be commercially supplied atmospheric gas burners, which are fitted with all

Kiln brick door
The door is almost unpacked (above) and starting to display the delights that make the effort worthwhile. The U-shaped shelf on the wall (right) is an intuitive solution by Jack to packing and unpacking a brick door.

Top hat kiln design

A simple and cheap raku kiln can be made using metal wire and ceramic fiber. The ceramic fiber is held in place with ceramic buttons tied to the frame with ni-chrome wire. These kilns can be static with a separate lid that lifts off. If you want to make large work, which can be difficult to lift out of the red-hot kiln, you can make a top hat design like this one. The whole kiln is lifted from the base and away, then a hollow drum is placed over it for reduction purposes.

HTI block kiln

This simple raku kiln design uses HTI blocks to reach 1830° F (1000° C). The gap at the top acts as an exit flue and draws the heat up through the work. It can be fired with a single burner that should be placed a little away from the burner port and at a slight angle. The work should be placed on a raised shelf so that it's away from the direct flame path.

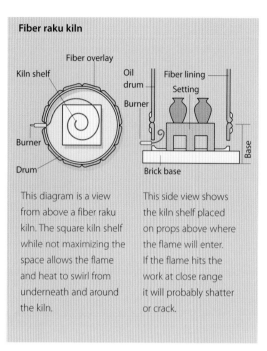

Fiber raku kiln

Fiber overlay

Kiln shelf

Oil drum

Fiber lining

Setting

Burner

Burner

Drum

Base

Brick base

This diagram is a view from above a fiber raku kiln. The square kiln shelf while not maximizing the space allows the flame and heat to swirl from underneath and around the kiln.

This side view shows the kiln shelf placed on props above where the flame will enter. If the flame hits the work at close range it will probably shatter or crack.

the relevant fail-safe devices; these can also be made from individual parts. They are placed a little away from the burner port and directed at an angle and not head-on to allow the flame to circulate around the kiln. The fuel is supplied by a propane gas bottle connected via rubber pipework and kept at a safe working distance of 10 ft (3 m). This system provides a very quick, clean, and efficient way to fire raku. A 42-lb (19-kg) bottle of propane will fire at least 15 firings. All other types of fuel and kilns can be used.

Packing You only use one shelf on the base; this should be put on props and made especially stable, because you don't want it to move when you are taking out red-hot work. The shelf should be placed above the burner port hole, so that the work is not in the direct flame path. Choose the most difficult pieces to hold first, since these can be placed in by hand as the kiln is cold. Plates can be tilted on their rims and leaned on the sides of the kiln. Ideally, pieces should not touch each other, since the glazes will melt together; if they do, they can be pulled apart when lifted out.

Firing Preparation is key for safe firing with raku: you should be appropriately dressed and covered, wearing gloves, goggles, and a mask.

All types of clay can be used, including porcelain, but experimenting will be necessary. Grogged "open"-bodied clays offer the least challenge, with work that has even thickness of walls and additions very well joined. For the first firing, warm the kiln for ten minutes by igniting paper inside or by lighting the burner on a gentle flame for the first five–ten minutes. The burner connection should be fitted with a pressure gauge, which reads the amount of gas flowing into the kiln. The heat rise should be gradual and can be turned up in two stages during the firing; by how much will depend on the size of the kiln. The first firing, before the kiln has warmed up, will take longer than subsequent ones. Once you see the glaze surface go shiny, turn the gas down for a few minutes to allow the kiln to soak so that there is an even melt. Turn off the gas supply and lift off the lid, ideally placed to one side on the kiln shelves. While the inside of the kiln is red hot, lift out the work using long-handled metal tongs and place it in the pit or trash can, which should have a layer of sawdust in it. Once the trash can is full of work, throw in large handfuls of sawdust and replace the lid, making sure it's a tight fit. Cover the can with a soaked blanket to prevent a lot of smoke.

Once you have placed the lid on the trash can, do not take it back off to check: the flame will burst back into combustion with the oxygen and create a large, high flare. Wait until the sawdust has had a chance to burn down and then gently take off the lid. By placing work in a pit, you will have greater control over the reduction and coverage of the developing black. The work that is controlled in this way will usually have much lighter and more subtle tones of grays and blacks. All work will still be very hot, so use small metal tongs to take it out of the pit. Work can be quenched in water and cleaned off. Assess the work as you gently clean away the sawdust, since there is a temptation to scrub vigorously away at what might be interesting surfaces and marks. There may be a certain number of cracks when you first start firing, but these should become less frequent the more experienced you become. Don't allow your kiln gloves to get wet, because they then have no protection against heat. Repack the kiln with your long-handled metal tongs while it is still hot and refire. Those clay makers who work with raku explore a wide range of glaze and post-firing techniques, continually advancing the possibilities of this type of firing.

Fuming

This very simple technique, which can produce a wide variety of interesting patterns and colors, is often done as part of a raku firing. It uses a copper oxide recipe that is coated onto the bisque clay body and fired as standard raku to 1830° F (1000° C). The work is then reduced by being placed on a small amount of sawdust in the trash can, with the lid placed over the work, enabling fuming to occur inside.

Other types of firing

These type of firings are considered less common in ceramics, but not by those clay makers whose whole creative output is based around them. These firings use smoke and carbon to help create varied surface patterns.

Saggar firing A saggar was, and is, a ceramic lidded container made from coarse, grogged clay, which will withstand refiring many times far better than finer types of clay. Once it has been bisque fired, it is filled with work and put into the kiln, which protects the contents from burning bits that fly around the kiln during any flame-fuel firing. Saggars can be stacked on top of one another as high as the kiln will allow.

Today, makers use saggars to protect the kiln's brickwork or electric elements and keep fumes in. They also use them to explore the effects of heatwork from combustible materials, which create surface markings and colors on bisque work. A specific climate is created in the saggar by trapping the smoke and fumes that bring about local reduction and carbonization.

Ideally any work that contains combustibles should be fired in a gas kiln since damage to electric elements can occur even from combustion inside a saggar. Too much use of these materials

FUMED RAKU: VELVET EFFECTS

TECHNIQUE FILE 113

This technique creates very fine iridescent surfaces with a great deal of variation. These surfaces are purely decorative.

1 The fuming mixture is painted on, but it could be applied by any of the usual methods. Spraying is a favorite, since it gives an even and controllable coating—but the mixture is heavy so it can block the spray gun.

2 Similar to the firing process of raku, the form is fired in an outdoor kiln and taken out between 1690–1830 ° F (920–1000° C) with metal tongs and placed on a bed of sawdust. The sawdust will ignite immediately.

3 Place a lid over the container immediately, and then leave for a few minutes.

4 Remove the lid. At this stage the pots will cool rapidly in the open air because, unlike raku reduction, there is not enough sawdust to act as insulation. Cool the pot in water, washing off any sawdust residue. Quenching in water is optional.

Fuming mixture

Copper oxide	90
Alkaline frit	10
+ Bentonite	10
+ Wallpaper paste	1

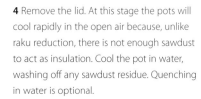

Velvet-effect vessel
by Tony Blenkinsopp
Fuming produces extraordinary varied surface colors that develop while cooling.

SAGGAR FIRING

How you place the objects with the materials will affect the marks that can be created. Objects can be wrapped up in foil parcels to localize effects.

1 Decide on which materials you want to use to surround your object. Many tests have been done with coal, charcoal, sawdust, salt, soda, vegetable skins, seaweed, oxides, copper, and a variety of metals and sulfates. Iron and salt can produce a range of orange, and copper carbonate can produce reds and pinks.

2 Once everything is inside, roll out a coil of clay and place it on the container rim. Press the lid on top to seal the saggar, making sure it is airtight: you don't want any of the released fumes escaping and damaging the kiln or setting off alarms. Excellent ventilation is required for indoor firing.

3 The saggar can be placed into any kiln and fired with other work. Experiment with different firing temperatures from 1650–2280° F (900–1250° C). Be aware that many effects may burn away at the higher temperatures. Once fired, you need to break away the coil of clay; you may need to use a hammer and chisel to prize off the lid.

4 It is worth taking a photograph of the contents before and after firing, so that you can keep a record of what was and wasn't successful.

Saggar-fired protective suit
by Brian MacKenzie
This work has been left with subtle shades and markings. The copper nail in the chest has created a slash of green across the suit.

inside an electric kiln will cause a great deal of smoke, which can also set off alarms. Excellent ventilation and extraction is essential.

Smoke firing A lot of makers use smoke to enhance the surface quality of their work, as with raku.

Any kiln that uses a combustible fuel and material will produce smoke. The technique uses the carbon produced by smoke to create a varied decorative surface on work previously bisque fired to a maximum temperature of 1830° F (1000° C); the carbon is absorbed into the porous clay. The smoke can be produced by lighting paper in a container and the degree of color controlled by how much smoke is created and the amount of time it is in contact with the work. The more smoke and the longer the contact time, the deeper the color. Smoke firing can be used alongside other decorative techniques such as terra sigillata, burnishing, and different resist methods (see pages 193, 203, and 187–190). The patterns that are created can be highly individual and varied, with a subtle surface quality.

Slip resist method The slip resist method is sometimes referred to as "naked raku," in part because it has no glaze to produce the black crazed line patterns on a white surface typical of raku firing, and in part because the method is also used during the raku firing process. You can burnish or apply terra sigillata to the surface at greenware stage and then bisque fire to a temperature of 1470–1830° F (800–1000° C), which creates a soft sheen to the surface of the finished work.

The slip is applied to bisque-fired work and acts as a temporary surface resist, which is easily removed after firing. Before the slip has dried, you can scratch designs through it where the carbon will infiltrate to create strong black lines. You can create precise line-drawn designs or a varied painterly surface. The slip can be applied thickly or thinly to the bisque surface. Depending on how the slip has been applied, the carbon will penetrate the surface to different degrees.

The slip will dry quickly as the bisque absorbs the water. The work can then be placed

SMOKED VESSEL
BY ASHRAF HANNA
Slip-resist techniques offer elements of control and randomness as the effects of the smoke infiltrate the drawn or applied marks. Forms are often firstly coated with terra sigillata or are burnished.

in a metal trash can with paper or sawdust and set on fire. Cover with a lid and leave for 10–20 minutes. Alternatively, you can burn paper around the work without a lid for more subtle smoking. Wash the surface with water: the slip will fall away, revealing the smoke-patterned surface. Once the work has dried and been assessed, further smoking can be repeated until you are satisfied with the results. This same method can be used by applying masking tape to the bisque surface, used with or without slip to create hard-edged resist designs.

Pit firing Dig a hole in the earth (always a worthwhile activity: you never know what you

SLIP RESIST WITH SMOKE

The technique of slip resist can offer great mark-making potential, which produces finely controlled surface detail.

1 Coat the form with different thicknesses of standard slip. These varying layers will produce a varied tonal surface when the smoke penetrates it to differing degrees.

2 While the slip is still damp you can draw very precise or random lines with your chosen drawing implements. Here the lines are being created with wire. Don't allow the slip to dry before you do this because it may flake off as you draw.

3 Once the form is dry you can put it into some sawdust or on some newspaper and set it alight. You can control the degree of smoke that will penetrate where the lines or marks have been made.

4 Once the form has cooled the slip can be washed off to reveal where the smoke has left its marks.

SMOKED VESSEL WITH SLIP-RESIST DECORATION
BY JOHN WARD
The sharp, contrasting, and defined imagery that can be achieved with slip resist is perfectly demonstrated on this simple bowl form.

PIT FIRING

This is an exciting way to spend a day digging and firing. In addition it is a very direct approach to finishing a form's surface.

TECHNIQUE FILE 116

1 The pit contains sawdust in the bottom and is lined with timber. The pots are made from white stoneware clay and coated with terra sigillata before bisque firing in an electric kiln to 1920° F (1050° C).

2 Once the pots are stacked, wood has to be carefully placed, not dropped onto the pots. The last layer of wood is laid on top, with a layer of newspaper and tinder to help get the fire started (see detail). The packing can take several hours. When it is complete, the pit is covered with corrugated sheeting before the wood is set on fire.

3 For eight hours the pit is fed with wood and covered, but opened at intervals to allow the fire to travel evenly over the pots throughout the kiln. Here the wood has burned down and the pit is a mass of embers, but the pit is not opened for 36 hours.

4 Two days later. The sides of the pit have collapsed, but luckily the pots remain undamaged, the earth being very sandy. At last the pots can be removed, cleaned up, and evaluated.

5 The tactile quality of the pots is enhanced with a coating of beeswax, and the flame marks and colors give each its own personality.

might find—maybe clay!). It should be big enough for your greenware or bisque work and a proportionate amount of timber to the hole and the work to be fired. The minimum size requirement is at least 2-ft (60-cm) deep to allow sufficient timber to be placed on top to burn for long enough to create the required effects. Fire with a mixture of different kinds of hard and soft woods (slow and fast burning) to enable the fire to continue over a longer period—approximately 6–16 hours.

Alternatively, dig a larger trench of any size. Place down a layer of sawdust and some combustible materials and place the work on top of this. Pack a range of materials (as per the saggar firing) tightly around it, cover with more materials, and place the timber gently on top with even distribution. Light a fire on top of the pile; and once it is well lit, place a metal cover over it and allow it to burn down. You can check the firing by lifting the cover periodically and placing further strips of timber on the embers to ignite and keep it alive. This will produce a reduction atmosphere around the work. Like saggar firing, pit firing will produce purely decorative work that is not functional. You can seal the surface with wax as with all smoke-fired surfaces. Note that the effects can fade if left in direct sunlight.

Sawdust firing This is a very simple, but visually rewarding, way to fire either greenware or previously bisque-fired work that is for decorative and not functional use. Buy a metal trash can and make a series of holes in the side, or build a square design of your own, using Durox or HTI bricks and leaving gaps in between for air vents; alternatively, buy an incinerator.

There are many ways to pack your "kiln," depending on the color variation you wish to achieve. If you pack the sawdust densely, the fire will burn slowly, creating darker areas; if you pack it loosely, then the color will be lighter.

When you place the work inside, you can separate layers with expanded metal to prevent breakages caused by work collapsing inside as the sawdust burns away. When the sawdust is well lit, place the lid back on; this will put out

SAWDUST-FIRED POT
BY GABRIELE KOCH
The simplicity of sawdust firing can be controlled to some degree or left to create random subtle carbon markings. How you pack the work and sawdust will affect the outcome.

Built brick box kiln

This is the simplest of designs to contain a sawdust firing. Notice the small vents, which allows air in to aid the burning.

the flame. If the sawdust is burning too rapidly, block some air holes with clay to slow it down. The sawdust will burn down very slowly until it has completely burned away; depending on the density of the packing, this may take several hours. The temperature reached will be around 1470° F (800° C).

Allow the work to cool before you take it out and wash it; be careful not to scrub. Some makers cover the work with wax to seal the surface and create a sheen. Using terra sigillata with this sawdust firing produces a beautiful natural sheen on the surface.

FIRINGS AS THEATER

There are many ways to build kiln shapes and structures that use the same materials as mentioned before—fired bricks, clay and natural material mixtures, and ceramic fiber. The making of a kiln as spectacle has been developed by makers such as Karin Putsch-Grassi, who creates kilns with glass bottles, while Jorgen Hansen and Nina Hole make kilns that are often built with fresh clay to remain on site as semipermanent or permanent sculptures once fired.

The technique of making varies widely, but these kilns are often constructed using a module method with clay coils and slabs. They use the simple principle of the updraft design, fueled by wood introduced at the base and fired over a period of one or two days. Once the sculpture is made and dry, it is wrapped in a ceramic fiber blanket held in place with ni-chrome wire. This covering is taken away at top stoneware temperature and the outline of the silhouetted sculpture is revealed in all its blazing glory. The drama is enhanced by throwing paper packets of sawdust, salt, and oxides at the structure, which ignite to produce sparks and colors. All relevant health and safety procedures for a public event must be observed.

FIRED STRUCTURE
BY JORGEN HANSEN
This large clay structure is made, dried, and then wrapped in ceramic fiber. The kiln is fired by wood fed in at the base. When stoneware temperatures are reached the blanket is taken away to reveal the glowing beauty of fire and clay.

BOTTLE KILN
BY KARIN PUTSCH-GRASSI
Bottles are stacked and packed in between sand, soil, and clay to create a kiln. The internal bottlenecks close and drip in the firing but don't explode! When fired, the kiln becomes an evening spectacle.

PART FIVE

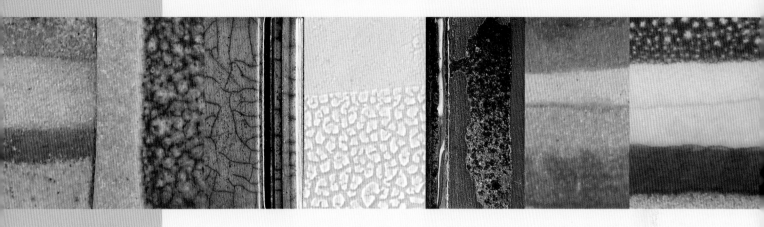

GLAZING

LAYERED GLAZES
BY PIPPIN DRYSDALE
*These beautiful, smooth, colored
surfaces are created by spraying
several layers of glazes and stains
on top of one another. These are
covered in Liquitex resist, which
is then cut into so that further
layers of glaze can be sprayed to
create the inlaid lines.*

Understanding glaze, its formulation, application, and its final quality, are essential to creating a successful final piece. The sheer breadth of quality and decoration that can be achieved through glazing is arresting. However, this area of ceramic practice is potentially the most volatile and impactful on your work. A thorough and conscientious practice is required to ensure the glazed object comes out of the kiln as expected.

INTRODUCTION

Glazing is often considered an art form in itself. It can take years to become proficient, but the endeavor is rewarding in the quality of the finished objects.

In its simplest form a glaze is a thin coating of glass that fuses to the clay body during the firing process. Raw materials are weighed to a recipe and mixed together in water before being applied.

The act of glazing is important on a number of levels. In functional pieces, glaze is used primarily to finish the fired ceramic surface, making it smooth, nonporous, and hygienic. In a more artistic context, glazing is a means of expression in its own right.

Glazes can be bought from pottery suppliers either as a ready-mixed liquid or as a powder to which you add water. Alternatively, many artistic glazes can be obtained as "ready to paint" in jars.

Whatever the medium you still need to observe the conventions of glazing and health and safety requirements, even a paint-on glaze may contain toxic materials.

A glaze is made up of three constituents: silica or silicon dioxide (SiO_2) is the main ingredient to form the glassy surface; a flux such as zinc oxide (ZnO) or calcium oxide (CaO) to control the melting point of the glaze; and alumina or aluminum dioxide (Al_2O_3) to stabilize the glaze and bind it to the clay body. Many materials may be mixed together, but they must still make up these three separate parts. Decorative qualities or colors are introduced to the basic glaze through the use of pigments or metallic oxides such as cobalt oxide (CoO).

The glaze constituents can be further subdivided into the following categories:

Glass formers

Feldspars Feldspars include potassium feldspar, sodium feldspar, and Cornish stone. Fluxes and frits are used to help the feldspar melt.

Frits Frits are ground glasses with a low melting point of 1380° F (750° C); they are formulated to aid glaze fit, facilitate melting at different temperatures, and give color variation.

Clays Clays aid the suspension of the glaze, help adhere the glaze to the body before firing, and help stabilization of the final glaze. China clay is widely used for this purpose.

Silicas Silicas such as flint and quartz form a hard glass at a high temperature and harden the surface of the glaze against abrasion.

Modifiers

Fluxes Whiting, magnesium carbonate, and lithium carbonate are all potential fluxes. The

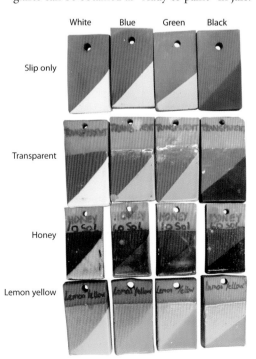

Earthenware slip and glaze test samples

These samples show the effect and value of using underlying slip to change glaze color. The application of different slips means that you can achieve a wide tonal color range from a single glaze. The slip color runs vertically and is placed on the right-hand corner. The glaze runs horizontally over both clay and slip.

White   Blue   Green   Black

Slip only

Transparent

Honey

Lemon yellow

Carbonates decompose during the firing and interact with the glass formers to become a glaze.

Colorings Metal oxides, carbonates, and prepared stains give color to the glaze while adding flux, stabilizing or opacifing the glaze.

Opacifiers Opacifiers such as tin oxide or titanium oxide give opacity to a glaze by resisting full integration into the glaze and resting on the surface as dispersed fine particles.

Testing glazes

A glaze quality can be judged on a number of levels: it may be the glassy quality or the depth of color, the gloss of the surface or the way it has run over the surface or crawled away from details. Adding particular materials, even in small amounts, will have an effect. You can also vary the outcome of glazes by layering them over different slip colors. This will increase the color range of many glazes.

To understand the variation and potential of a glaze, it is important to experiment with it. There is a range of tests that can be undertaken.

It is a good idea to design a test tile that carries as much information as possible. A completely flat test tile is something of a missed opportunity: it needs a good surface area so that you can see the depth and quality of the glaze; it should have some ridges or sharp edges so that you can see if the glaze crawls from the edge; and it should have a sense of three-dimensional form to allow you to understand how the glaze flows across an object.

Recording your tests

Experienced makers keep a detailed record of all glaze experiments. They develop a system of analysis and notation, making sure they record the firing range and soak time, the position of the test tile in the kiln, the thickness of glaze application, how the glaze has reacted to the form, and any visual effects such as crawling or cracking. If you do this from the start of your career, you will be able to successfully reproduce glazes made many years before. A glaze notebook that is kept well can become something of a bible that you carry for years to come.

You will also need to have a system for recording your tests. A simple number-and-letter system

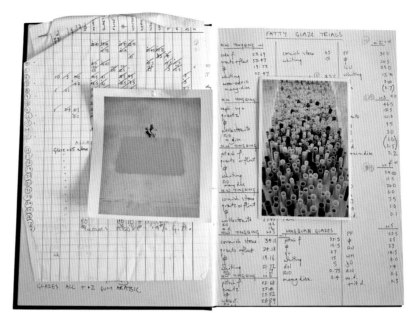

works well, with the number representing the base glaze and the letter denoting the percentage of oxide that has been added—1a + 2 percent cobalt, 1b + 4 percent cobalt, for example. Use an underglaze pencil to inscribe the number on your test; alternatively, paint the number on with an oxide and fine brush.

Glaze tests

50:50 blend This is a good test to carry out as you become first involved in glaze formulation, as the simplicity of the mix gives you a good understanding of the properties of particular materials. It is one of the simplest tests to undertake: glaze materials are simply mixed in water to a 50:50 ratio, sieved, and poured over the test tile. A shallow box is a good test vehicle, since it helps to contain the fluidity of the glaze. Fire the tests to an earthenware temperature; make comparative notes against each test first. Any of the tests that do not melt should be fired at a higher stoneware temperature and the analysis repeated.

Line blend A line blend is a simple but effective test to understand the effect of adding one material to a glaze in increasing amounts. It is often used to test an oxide addition to a glaze.

Mix your base glaze and divide into equal proportions, enough to carry out a systematic test, add the oxide in increasing amounts—1 percent, 1.5 percent, 2 percent, and so on. Fire

GLAZE NOTEBOOK
BY NATASHA DAINTRY
Keeping a detailed record of your glazing experiments will help you to reproduce effective glaze recipes in the future. You should record information such as firing range, thickness of glaze application, and the outcome.

all the tests together to the required temperature, then assess and record the results.

Glaze—useful terms

No glaze recipe is infallible. The idiosyncrasies of firing cycles, kiln models, and dry materials supplied create a high degree of potential variation from written recipe to actual result. It is very likely that you may need to adjust glazes for optimum performance. Having a good understanding of the chemistry of a glaze and the characteristics of particular materials is important to understanding the glaze and any potential adjustments you might have to make. Developing this knowledge will be key to successful glaze experimentation.

Crackle/crazing This is the effect of a glaze cracking over the surface of a pot and is caused by the glaze not fitting to the body. This is seen as a fault in commercial industrial context but can be desirable in a craft context.

Earthenware/porcelain/stoneware A shorthand way of describing a firing range is:
Earthenware 1760–2160° F (960–1180° C)
Stoneware 2190–2370° F (1200–1300° C)
Porcelain 2260–2460° F (1240–1350° C)

Matte A nonshiny glaze with a dulled-down sheen. A matte surface can often be quite soft, and so can wear and scratch in functional ware such as plates. However, high dolomite content can produce these soft, lovely surfaces for domestic-ware exteriors or for sculpture.

Oxidation This is the atmosphere of an electric kiln and describes the circulation of the air during firing.

Raku This describes the process of removing a glazed object from the kiln just as the glaze is melting and placing the object into a bin of combustible material such as sawdust or wood shavings. This causes a post-firing reduction atmosphere, which can create a range of effects.

Reduction This is the atmosphere in fuel-burning kilns such as gas or wood, where the circulation of the air is controlled, thus reducing the oxygen.

Salt/soda This firing process introduces salt into the kiln at 2265° F (1240° C), causing the salt or soda to fuse with the silica in the clay and cause the distinctive orange-peel surface.

Satin This is similar to matte but the addition of flux creates more sheen on the surface. It is a better choice for functional ware if a matte surface is required, but will still scratch.

Transparent A clear glassy glaze that allows you to see the clay body through the glaze. This is useful if your clay has a particular quality of material.

Opaque The opposite to transparent, which means you cannot see through the glaze to the clay body. Opacifiers will make the glaze opaque.

Crater There are different surface qualities achievable with this glaze. Ones that are harsh and sharp with cutting peaks while others have softer edges. The recipe will contain varying amounts of silicon carbide and may have a specific slip to achieve the required surface. Application thickness plays its part as with all glazes.

Dry A glaze that historically was described as "sculptural" due to its very dry surface. It is not appropriate for functional work for reasons of hygiene, especially where it contains lithium and barium. These ingredients are often present to produce an interesting range of colors.

Crawl This is a glazing fault that is now used in contemporary ceramics to create interesting surface effects.

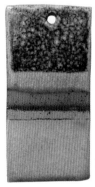

Stoneware glaze tests
The tiles above show the effect of using two glazes, one on top of the other (glaze on glaze). Each tile has a single-dipped application of both glazes on each end. Changing which you apply first will affect the color response.

Glaze samples
The tiles below show the levels of strength created using a single versus a double dip.

Single dip

Double dip

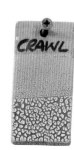

Shiny   Crackle   Crater   Crawl   Satin   Matte transparent   Dolomite

Oxide compounds

These compounds of metallic oxides, dioxides, and carbonates are the pigments that provide the basic color palette in glaze making. They will be used singularly or more often in combinations with each other.

Copper compounds These strong fluxes produce apple green colors in normal conditions but in alkaline glazes give rich turquoise. In reduction atmospheres, they produce the characteristic copper red glazes.

Cobalt compounds The most powerful of all the coloring oxides, cobalt compounds produce strong blues even when used in low percentages. If manganese is present, cobalt may form purples.

Iron compounds Iron oxides give a wide range of honey yellows, brown-reds, blacks, and yellows in oxidized firings. They produce blues and greens in reduction, as in celadon glazes.

Manganese compounds Manganese gives a brown color but can produce purple colors in alkaline-based glazes. When mixed with cobalt it will give violet.

Opacifiers Oxides such as tin, zirconium, and titanium make transparent glazes opaque—a characteristic feature of the white tin earthenware glaze. These materials are known as "opacifiers" and will also react with other oxides to produce a range of glaze colors.

Rutile An ore containing titanium dioxide and iron that is used to produce soft browns and mottled surfaces.

Coloring glazes with oxides

The table below describes the quantity of oxide required to achieve a particular color. This is only a generic guide and a range of variables such as base glaze, firing temperature, kiln atmosphere, and glaze thickness will all have an effect on the final quality. The metallic colorants vary in strength, with carbonates always weaker than the pure oxide form.

When used in glazes, the oxides should be finely ground to give even distribution of color. Stains are commercially manufactured pigments. They are relatively stable and will always give a good color response, making them ideal for staining clay bodies and coloring slips.

Single and double-dipped test tiles

The intensity of color varies according to the clay base and application thickness.

Single dip

Double dip

Fleck iron buff   Grogged white   Smooth white   Porcelain

Oxide	%	Color
Black cobalt oxide	0.1–2	Gives a deep blue; it tends to blacken in higher amounts.
Chromium oxide	0.5–2	Opaque green.
Cobalt oxide	0.5–3	Smooth blue, vivid in some glazes.
Chromium oxide	0.5–3	Normally gives a green color. When used in combination with tin oxide, it can produce pink.
Copper carbonate	0.5–4	Red in reduction, green in lead glaze.
Copper oxide	0.5–5	Strong fluxes that produce greens, in alkaline glazes rich turquoise. In reduction the classic copper red glazes.
Manganese dioxide	0.5–8	Gives pinks to browns but stronger than the carbonate form produces.
Red iron oxide (ferric oxide)	0.5–10	Gives honey yellows to dark browns; this is the most popular form of iron oxide.
Cobalt carbonate		Gives a blue glaze.
Nickel dioxide	1–3	Ice blue, yellow, muted greens.
Nickel oxide	1–3	Produces brownish greens or grays. When added to high-zinc glazes, a yellow color is produced in oxidation and blue in reduction.

Oxide	%	Color
Manganese carbonate	1–5	Will produce pink to brown.
Manganese dioxide	1–8	Pink, mauve, brown.
Iron oxide black/red	1–15	Pale blue, brown-black, pale honey.
Titanium dioxide	2–10	Matte creamy white, rich blue.
Antimony oxide	2–10	Produces a yellow color when added to a high-lead glaze.
Tin oxide	2–10	Gives the best-quality white.
Vanadium pentoxide	2–10	Gives a yellow or orange in most glazes.
Rutile	2–15	Buff, brown, deep blue-gray.
Copper carbonate	3–7	Produces a more even color than the oxide with less risk of speckling.
Yellow ocher iron oxide	3–8	Produces yellow to light brown due to the oxide containing clay.
Black iron oxide	4–8	Gives darker shades than red iron oxide.
Purple/crocus martis iron oxide	4–8	Produces speckled effects due to its impurity.
Titanium dioxide	5–15	Produces a creamy color. In its impure form, known as rutile, it gives a pale brown color.
Zirconium	6–15	Produces a milkier white than tin oxide and requires greater concentrations.

COMMON RAW MATERIALS

The raw materials listed here are the common ones in everyday use. By understanding these materials you will be better equipped to use them in glaze recipes.

Alumina hydrate or calcined alumina A refractory additive for glazes. Alumina's reaction in glazes is complex. It can aid stability in a mobile glaze but by itself will not melt until it reaches a temperature of 3630° F (2000° C). The melting temperature is considerably lowered when small amounts are used in combination with silica. When added to clay, alumina will increase the fusing temperature of the body, making it less likely to melt. It is also used in a grainy sand form for embedding into fine bone china to act as a support during firing. Alumina can also be sprinkled onto kiln shelves or combined with china clay in a 50:50 mix and applied as a wash to the kiln shelves to protect them from glaze runs.

Ball clay A highly plastic clay that is generally added to other clays to increase their plasticity. It improves the mechanical strength of clay bodies and casting slips and is excellent for use in glazes. In its powdered form it is good for making slips. Usually it is pale ivory in color, making it a good base for decorating slips where a good color response is required.

Barium carbonate A secondary flux used in stoneware and porcelain glazes to produce a matte, vellumlike surface. It is poisonous in its raw state.

Basalt A ground volcanic lava used in glazes that melt at stoneware temperatures. It is useful as a base for tenmoku glazes.

Bentonite Weathered and decomposed volcanic ash that is a highly plastic material. It greatly improves the plasticity of clay bodies when added in amounts up to 5 percent. Bentonite is also highly colloidal and absorbs large quantities of water to form a jellylike substance that is excellent as a suspension agent in glazes (up to 3 percent additions), especially for the heavy particles in a raku glaze.

Bone ash A secondary flux in glazes prepared from the calcined bones of animals ground into a fine powder. Bone ash contains calcium and phosphorous, which is a glass former, and is the essential constituent of bone china, giving translucency to the body. Bone china typically contains up to 50 percent bone ash, and when fused with china clay and Cornish stone, forms one of the thinnest and hardest ceramic bodies. It is sometimes used as a glaze opacifier to reduce the amount of tin needed.

Borax An extremely vigorous low-temperature flux for glazes that contains boric oxide and soda. On its own, it is soluble in water, so it is introduced into glazes in a fritted form with silica to render it food safe. Otherwise, it is poisonous.

China clay A pure white, residual primary clay, ideal for making white earthenware and stoneware bodies. China clay is also used in glazes to provide alumina and silica. If larger quantities are added, it will act as a matting agent.

Cornish stone A decomposed granite used as a secondary flux in glazes. It is composed

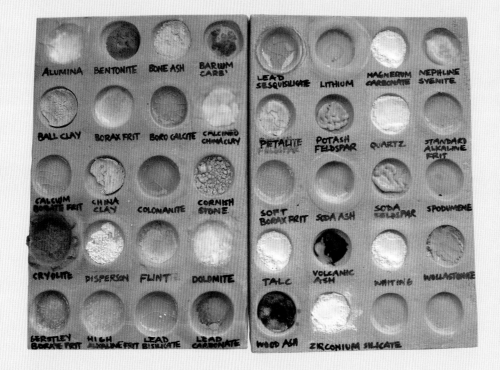

Button test

The button test is a very good way of understanding how certain materials react to firing. Each of these raw ingredients has been fired to 2280° F (1250° C). By studying their fired state you will begin to understand how mixing one with the other might produce a smooth or runny glaze.

of feldspar, quartz, mica, and fluorspar and contains fluxes such as soda, potash, and calcium. Cornish stone is also used to give whiteness to clay bodies and glazes because it is almost free of iron. It is used as an alternative to feldspar in clay bodies and glazes but is not as fusible as feldspar because of its higher silica content.

Cristobalite A powdered, fired form of silica used to improve craze resistance in slips. It is hazardous when inhaled.

Dolomite A combination of calcium and magnesium carbonate that occurs naturally and is used as a secondary flux in high-temperature porcelain and stoneware glazes. When used in high quantities of between 10–20 percent, dolomite will produce a beautiful silky matte surface.

Feldspar The major flux in clay bodies and high-temperature glazes, some of which contain up to 70 percent feldspar. Feldspar tends to be milky due to fine bubbles in the glaze body. There are three main feldspars, each name referring to the principal, but not the only, flux present. Potash feldspar (orthoclase) is the one generally used and recommended, but soda (albite) and lime feldspar (anorthite) are also common.

Fire clay A refractory material used as an additive in stoneware clay to produce a more open texture and speckling in reduction. It is also commonly used as a mortar in building kilns.

Flint A highly refractory material that provides silica in clay bodies and glazes, increasing the firing temperature but reducing the plasticity and shrinkage of the clay. It also increases craze resistance in glazes. Prepared from calcined flint rock, it is

ground into a fine powder and is the form of silica preferred by most potters. It is hazardous in dust form if inhaled.

Fluorspar A vigorous flux in glazes. At low temperatures, fluorspar can cause bubbling in the glaze surface as it volatizes.

Frit Certain forms of materials such as lead, have a low melting point and are also highly soluble in water, making them poisonous for use. Fritting involves the melting of these materials together with glaze ingredients such as silica to produce a compound that is either insoluble or has a low solubility. The constituents of frits are melted together and poured into water when molten. This causes the frit mixture to shatter and makes grinding it into a fine powder easier.

Seldom used in their pure state as a glaze, frits need the addition of alumina, usually from china clay or a similar compound. The common frits are lead bisilicate, lead sesquisilicate, standard borax frit, soft borax frit, calcium borate frit, and high-alkali frit.

Grog Prefired clay that is ground down into various particle sizes (categorized by the size of sieve mesh they will pass through) and added to clay bodies. The addition of grog to clay bodies reduces shrinkage and warping because the grog has already been fired and is inert.

Lithium carbonate An alkaline flux used as a substitute for soda and potash when craze resistance is needed. It gives a typical alkaline color response to oxides.

Magnesium carbonate A secondary high-temperature flux that produces a satin matte surface when used in quantities of up to 10 percent. If used to excess, crawling and pinholing

may occur. At lower temperatures of up to 2120° F (1160° C) it acts as an opacifier, but above that it becomes an active flux. On cooling it may cause crystals to form, creating an opaque matte finish.

Molochite Calcined china clay used as a pure white grog, commonly in white-firing clays. Fine grades can be used in vitreous slips as a substitute for the clay to reduce shrinkage.

Nepheline syenite A similar mineral to feldspar but containing less silica and more alkaline flux. It is used in both earthenware and stoneware glazes. It is more fusible than feldspar and can therefore be used to reduce the maturing temperature of glazes.

Quartz A pure form of silica that can be used as an alternative to flint in glazes. It is hazardous if inhaled.

Silicon carbide Used to achieve local reduction in glazes in electric kilns. As a glaze constituent, it creates bubbly, lavalike finishes.

Soda ash (sodium carbonate) Used in the making of casting slips, it is combined with sodium silicate.

Talc A secondary flux high in magnesium that is used in both glazes and clay bodies. In glazes it improves resistance to crazing but can form opaque surfaces. In clay it acts as a flux and is especially useful for making flameproof pottery for cooking.

Whiting A mixture of chalk, calcium carbonate, and limestone. It is the main source of calcium in glazes and is used extensively as a flux. It is prepared by finely grinding chalk originating from shells. It helps to increase the hardness and durability of a glaze and in

larger quantities produces a matte finish.

Wollastonite (calcium silicate) An alternative to whiting in glaze formulations, containing both calcium and silica. It is a good source of lime in stoneware glazes and is useful where pinholing is a problem.

HOW TO MIX A GLAZE

Mixing a glaze is straightforward, but your measurements must be accurate.

1 Find a suitable glaze recipe and make sure that you have all the base materials listed. You will need two plastic bowls, accurate scales, a fine sieve, a brush, and a rubber kidney. Using the scales, measure the ingredients one by one into a container. Take care to weigh any receptacle for the ingredients and to zero the scale before continuing the weighing process. Add each weighed powdered ingredient in turn to an adequate-sized bowl or bucket.

2 Cover the ingredients with water and allow to slake down (see page 29) for a period of time; this can be up to 30 minutes or more, and makes mixing much easier. The quantity of water is something of a guess; add it in small quantities, a cup or jugful at a time. Using a stick, mix all the ingredients together and allow them to soak for a short time.

3 Pour the glaze through the sieve into the other bowl, using a brush and a rubber kidney to force the materials through the sieve. Try to ensure almost all the material passes through the mesh.

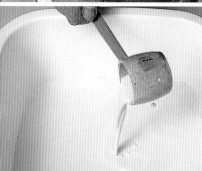

4 The consistency of the glaze should be that of a thick cream. If it needs it, add more water; if it is too thin, leave to stand for three or four hours and it will separate, at which point just decant some water from the top before mixing again.

The principles involved in mixing a glaze are universal: you need to mix specific quantities of powdered material with water. This holds true whether you are using a commercial ready-mixed glaze or creating an experimental glaze.

MIXING GLAZE

Mixed glaze should be stored in airtight containers. Do not use any food storage containers or bottles as this might cause confusion, and glaze must not be accidentally ingested. For large quantities, bins with lids or airtight drums can be useful. You should clearly label containers with the glaze name and its firing information, because it is very difficult to recognize one glaze from another before firing.

The biggest problem with glazing is the dust. It is important to follow good workshop practices at all times. Dry glaze materials can be hazardous or poisonous. Use extraction if it is available; otherwise wear a dust mask. Rubber gloves are useful, since some glaze materials are an irritant to the skin.

Glaze ingredient proportions

When you look at a glaze recipe, it will give a list of materials and the proportions required to make up the glaze. The quantity may be recorded as a weight, as a percentage, or simply as a number; this is known as "parts" and will often add up to 100. Unfortunately for the beginner, there is no prevailing convention. Many respected glaze books have different glazes shown as weight, percentage, parts adding up to 100, and parts adding up to all manner of numbers.

Glazes don't necessarily have to add up to 100, although it is easier to formulate your own if you work in parts per 100. In many instances if the total number of parts adds up to a little over 100, the base glaze will add up to 100 and the oxides that are often added in small amounts for color will bring the total slightly over—for example, to 102.

Glazing is something of a soft science and these slight discrepancies derive from the idiosyncratic practice developed in different pottery studios. With a range of potential recipe approaches, it is important to understand what to do depending on how the glaze is written.

Percentages/parts per 100 If the glaze is written in percentages or parts per 100, then you simply measure material to a quantity that relates to each percentage or part. For example:

Ingredient		Mix x 10
A	35 percent/ 35parts	350 oz (350 g)*
B	40 percent/40 parts	400 oz (400 g)
C	25 percent/25 parts	250 oz (250 g)

Parts adding up to a figure that is not 100 In this case, simply multiply each part by the same factor, so that you are increasing each quantity by the same amount.

Ingredient parts = 86		Mix x 10
A	12	120 oz (120 g)*
B	21	210 oz (210 g)
C	53	530 oz (530 g)
Total		860 oz (860 g)

Conversion equation As a general rule, glaze is easier to measure in parts per 100. If the glaze recipe does not add up to parts per 100, you can use the following conversion equation:

$$\frac{\text{known part value} \times 100}{\text{known part total}} = ?$$

In the example below, the original recipe has the following parts:

Original glaze		New recipe**
50	$\frac{50 \times 100}{77} = 66$	66
20		26
4		4.5
3		3.5
Total 77		Total 100

*These are not direct conversions. Please choose either the imperial or metric measurement.
**Figures have been rounded up/down to simplify the explanation.

GLAZE RECIPES ▶

Here are some simple glaze recipes to get you started. In the recipes that follow, the glaze categories have been split into: earthenware, stoneware, porcelain, majolica, and raku. The glazes in each firing category have been selected to give you a varied but systematic palette. Unless stated otherwise, the quantities of raw materials are given as proportions of dry weight. So, if a recipe calls for 4 parts china clay and 6 parts ball clay, you could decide that 1 part is equal to 1 lb (1 kg)* and therefore measure out 4 lb (4kg) of china clay and 6 lb (6 kg) of ball clay. The basic weight unit will depend on the quantity of glaze you wish to produce, and you will need to experiment to get this right.

LEAD WARNING

Potters who use these glaze recipes on functional ware should always have them tested for lead release. This is because variations in materials from different areas, or the individual firing method used, could affect the levels of lead release.

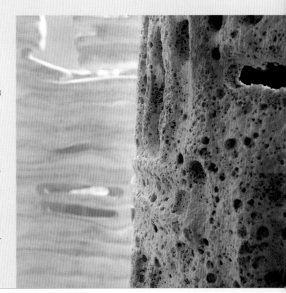

GLAZE TEXTURE
BY JOHN-ERIC JOHNSON
These coil-built forms have been greatly enhanced by using different glaze surfaces; the horizontal dolomite glaze lines in the background contrast with the vertical crater glaze in the foreground. Both glazes soften the forming technique.

EARTHENWARE

The glazes at earthenware temperatures are generally a brighter, more vibrant color than glazes at a higher temperature. This is due to the ease of reaching the low temperatures and the ingredients in the glaze remaining stable; they are usually more volatile at higher temperatures and often "fire out." Most brightly colored ceramics will be an earthenware temperature firing.

Transparent
Oxidized

Description: A satin/gloss transparent with mottled red/brown areas, on red terra-cotta clay.
Uses: Decorative and sculptural.
Firing range: 1940° F (1060° C).
Parts dry weight:

Lead bisilicate	57
Feldspar	31
China clay	7
Whiting	5
+ Red iron oxide sprayed	

Vellum white
Oxidized

Description: Matte vellum white/cream on white earthenware clay.
Uses: For decorative and sculptural work. A good base for on-glaze colors.
Firing range: 2010° F (1100° C).
Soak time: 30 minutes.
Parts dry weight:

Lead bisilicate	47
Potash feldspar	25
China clay	16
Whiting	12

Glossy transparent
Oxidized

Description: Glossy transparent white on white earthenware clay. Good general-purpose earthenware glaze for use with colored slips, over- and underglaze stains and colors.
Uses: Decorative.
Firing range: 2010° F (1100° C).
Parts dry weight:

Lead bisilicate	62
Cornish stone	30
Whiting	5
China clay	3

STONEWARE

Stoneware is a vitrified body and as such is not porous, which can sometimes make glazing quite difficult. The clay body and the glaze fuse together at the high temperature and materials in the glaze tend to burn out to leave a more subdued color palette than at earthenware temperatures. The use of commercial stains does allow the potential for brighter colors.

High gloss black
Reduced

Description: High gloss, solid black when applied thickly, breaking to rust red-brown on edges.
Uses: Domestic and decorative.
Firing range: 2300–2340° F (1260–1280° C), with reduction starting at 1830° F (1000° C). Firing has a 12-hour cycle.
Parts dry weight:

Potash feldspar	60
Quartz	20
Hvar ball clay	10
Whiting	10
+ Red iron oxide	8

Shiny white
Reduced

Description: Hard, glossy white.
Uses: Decorative and domestic. This glaze works very well over cobalt oxide decoration.
Firing range: 2340–2370° F (1280–1300° C), with reduction starting at 1580° F (860° C).
Parts dry weight:

Feldspar	35
Flint	23
Whiting	23
Zircon silicate	10
China clay	9

Pale blue
Reduced

Description: Satin/gloss, pale blue, breaking to white on edges. Apply thinly for "china" blue.
Uses: Domestic, decorative, and sculptural.
Firing range: 2300–2340° F (1260–1280° C), with reduction starting at 2830° F (1000° C). Firing has a 12-hour cycle.
Parts dry weight:

Cornish stone	41
Flint	27
China clay	16
Whiting	11
Dolomite	5
+ Zinc oxide	1.5
Cobalt carbonate	1
Copper carbonate	0.4

Parts dry weight:
Each list adds up to 100 parts. "+" means that additional material is added to the base recipe, usually to create a change in color or effect.

Glossy blue
Oxidized

Description: A glossy dark blue turning to black where glaze was more thickly applied on white earthenware clay.
Uses: Decorative.
Firing range: 2010° F (1100° C).
Parts dry weight:

Lead bisilicate	62
Cornish stone	28
China clay	6
Whiting	4
+ Rutile oxide	2
Cobalt oxide	2

Satin
Oxidized

Description: Satin, smooth, dense metallic, hint of green on white earthenware clay.
Uses: Mainly sculptural.
Firing range: 2010° F (1100° C).
Parts dry weight:

Lead bisilicate	62
Cornish stone	30
Whiting	5
China clay	3
+ Rutile oxide	3
Copper carbonate	3

Glossy yellow
Oxidized

Description: Glossy golden yellow on white earthenware clay.
Uses: Mainly decorative.
Firing range: 2010° F (1100° C).
Parts dry weight:

Lead bisilicate	62
Cornish stone	30
Whiting	5
China clay	3
+ Yellow "body" stain	5
Yellow iron oxide	5

Matte green
Oxidized

Description: A smooth, matte green, with warm red terra-cotta clay body breaking through.
Uses: Decorative and sculptural.
Firing range: 1980° F (1080° C).
Soak time: 30 minutes.
Parts dry weight:

Lead bisilicate	47
Potash feldspar	25
China clay	16
Whiting	12
+ Chromium oxide	3

  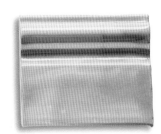 

Semitransparent brown
Oxidized

Description: High gloss, semitransparent mid-brown with crazing, breaking to white/beige on rims and edges.
Uses: Decorative.
Firing range: 2350° F (1290° C).
Soak time: 1 hour.
Parts dry weight:

Cornish stone	28
Quartz	20
Dolomite	18
Whiting	16
China clay	12
Bone ash	4
Tin oxide	2
+ Manganese dioxide	2

Chun
Reduced

Description: Glossy "chun"-type glaze, pale green with crazing.
Uses: Decorative.
Firing range: 2300–2340° F (1260–1280° C), with reduction starting at 1830° F (1000° C). Firing has a 12-hour cycle.
Parts dry weight:

Potash feldspar	45
Quartz	25
Whiting	17
China clay	9
Bone ash	2
Dolomite	2
+ Red iron oxide	1

Glossy light yellow
Oxidized

Description: Glossy light yellow. Can be used on porcelain and stoneware bodies.
Uses: Domestic and decorative.
Firing range: 2260–2340° F (1240–1280° C).
Parts dry weight:

Potash feldspar	34
Quartz	23
Standard borax frit	14
China clay	11
Whiting	11
Dolomite	5
Bentonite	2
+ B 100 yellow glaze stain	5

Speckled white
Reduced

Description: Satin/matte, white with mottled and speckled gray areas.
Uses: Decorative ware and could work on sculptural pieces.
Firing range: 2300–2340° F (1260–1280° C), with reduction starting at 1830° F (1000° C). Firing has a 12-hour cycle.
Parts dry weight:

Potash feldspar	34
China clay	30
Whiting	21
Flint	12
Talc	3
+ Titanium dioxide	6

  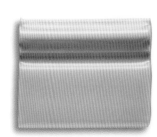 

PORCELAIN

Porcelain is a high-fired vitrified body usually associated with very fine and beautiful items. The temperature range results in a subtle or softer color range. Porcelain is often associated with beautiful sensuous blues and greens of celadon, although commercial stains are helping potters obtain brighter colors at the higher firing range.

Smooth matte
Oxidized

Description: Smooth matte, cream/off-white.
Uses: Domestic.
Firing range: 2340° F (1280° C).
Parts dry weight:

Potash feldspar	35
Quartz	20
China clay	20
Dolomite	20
Whiting	5

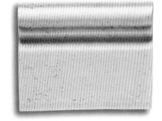

Satin matte
Reduced

Description: Satin/matte with good crystals of gray/green.
Uses: Domestic.
Firing range: 2370° F (1300° C).
Soak time: 30 minutes.
Parts dry weight:

Potash feldspar	36
China clay	21
Whiting	17
Quartz	10
Talc	10
Ball clay	6
+ Tin oxide	3
Rutile	3

Deep red
Reduced

Description: Derek Emms red. Apply medium to thick for the fullest cherry red, but beautiful serendipitous pink blushes can be achieved where applied thinly. Fluid where thick.
Uses: Domestic and decorative.
Firing range: 2300–2370° F (1260–1300° C).
Parts dry weight:

Soda feldspar	42
Flint	19
Whiting	14
High alkaline frit	14
China clay	5
Tin oxide	5
Copper carbonate	1

MAJOLICA

Majolica describes decorated tin-glazed earthenware. The object is first covered with a white tin glaze (see below, left); when it is dry to the touch, the color is painted onto the surface in layers, with each being allowed to dry before the next is applied. The recipe describes the order of layers painted onto the piece. The more layers applied, the stronger the color. To help the color blend with the white glaze, the glaze stain is mixed with clear glaze (see below, right). This mix is one part powdered glaze stain to three parts liquid clear glaze. This is then diluted with water to a working consistency.

Orange through to reds
Oxidized

Description: Left: orange/yellow blending with dark brown; Right: red/yellow/orange blend.
Uses: Decorative.
Firing range: 2010 °F (1100° C).
Parts dry weight: Base: white glaze on red earthenware clay.
Left: clear glaze
+ yellow glaze stain
+ red glaze stain
+ brush dipped into a mixture of crocus martis and cobalt carbonate.
Right: as left, without crocus martis and cobalt carbonate.

Copper green and metallics
Oxidized

Description: Left: copper green to dark metallic blend; Right: as above.
Uses: Decorative.
Firing range: 2010° F (1100° C).
Parts dry weight: Base: white glaze on white earthenware.
Left: clear glaze
+ iron oxide
+ copper oxide
+ brush dipped into a mixture of crocus martis and cobalt carbonate.
Right: as left, without crocus martis and cobalt carbonate.

White glaze
Parts dry weight:

Lead bisilicate	60
Calcium borate frit	10
China clay	10
Tin oxide	10
Flint	5
Zirconium silicate	5

Clear glaze
Parts dry weight:

Lead bisilicate	68
Calcium borate frit	12
China clay	12
Flint	8

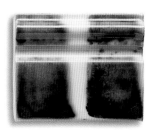

Parts dry weight:
Each list adds up to 100 parts. "+" means that additional material is added to the base recipe, usually to create a change in color or effect.

Celadon
Reduced

Description: Satin—celadon type. Best if used thick to enhance "buttery" quality.
Uses: Domestic and decorative.
Firing range: 2370° F (1300° C).
Soak time: 30 minutes.
Parts dry weight:

Quartz	26
Potash feldspar	25
Whiting	21
China clay	15
Molochite	13

Satin matte turquoise
Oxidized

Description: Satin/matte turquoise. Can be used on porcelain and stoneware bodies.
Uses: Decorative.
Firing range: 2260–2340° F (1240–1280° C).
Parts dry weight:

Potash feldspar	49
Barium carbonate	27
Whiting	14
HP71 ball clay	9
Bentonite	1
+ Copper carbonate	2.5

Blue-green celadon
Oxidized

Description: Blue/green celadon over hamada celadon. Layered glaze. A pleasant glassy pale green, darker in pooled areas.
Uses: Domestic and decorative.
Firing range: 2300–2370° F (1260–1300° C).
Parts dry weight:

Cornish stone	27
Whiting	27
China clay	23
Flint	23

Hamada celadon

Potash feldspar	75
Whiting	15
China clay	5
Flint	5
+ Red iron oxide	5

Pure white
Oxidized

Description: Smooth satin. Pure white. Very even surface.
Uses: Domestic.
Firing range: 2340° F (1280° C).
Parts dry weight:

Soda feldspar	45
Quartz	17
Borax frit	15
Whiting	13
China clay	5
Tin oxide	5

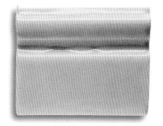  

RAKU

Raku firing is a visceral and exciting glaze technique. Objects are removed from a kiln just as the glaze has melted and placed in a bin of combustible material such as sawdust. This causes a post-firing reduction atmosphere, which can create a range of effects. Raku glazes are frit-based to help them melt at a low temperature, this allows them to become smooth and glassy.

Gloss white fine crackle
Reduced

Description: Smooth gloss glaze, white crackle (small).
Uses: Decorative and sculptural.
Firing range: 1740–1800° F (950–980° C), plus at least one hour post-firing reduction.
Parts dry weight:

Alkaline frit	68
Borax frit	25
Tin oxide	5
Bentonite	2

Turquoise crackle
Reduced

Description: Gloss, turquoise/green crackled surface.
Uses: Decorative and sculptural.
Firing range: 1740–1780° F (950–970° C), plus one hour post-firing reduction.
Parts dry weight:

Alkaline frit	90
China clay	5
Tin oxide	4
Bentonite	1
+ Black copper oxide	3

Metallic luster
Reduced

Description: Matte metallic/lustered surface with yellow tinges.
Uses: Decorative and sculptural.
Firing range: 1800–1830° F (980–1000° C), plus one hour post-firing reduction.
Parts dry weight:

Alkaline frit	50
Borax frit	20
Ball clay	15
Flint	10
Tin oxide	3
Bentonite	2
+ Manganese oxide	4
Copper oxide black	4
Uranium substitute	2
Vanadium oxide	2
Red iron oxide	2

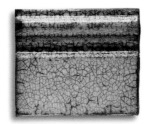 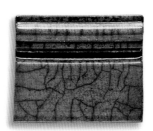 

Dip tests
These quartered dry-glaze
tests show the variation gained
from different thicknesses of
application. The top triangle
has been dipped once, the two
middle triangles twice, and the
bottom triangle three times.

Experimentation is the key to developing original and personal ways of working with glazes. An infinite variety of surfaces is possible, and there are countless techniques for achieving them. The following are some of the most frequently used.

GLAZE APPLICATION AND DECORATION

These methods can be used individually or in tandem; for example, it is appropriate to pour the inside of a teapot but spray the outside. The combination of different application methods can create a very interesting quality in the final object. There is a breadth of glaze application methods and each one brings with it a particular technique to master and a particular glaze finish or quality.

Glazing the base
The bottom of your object is a crucial area in terms of glaze. If you do not deal with this correctly, then your piece will stick to the kiln shelf. If your object has no foot ring, then its base must be wiped clean of glaze or suspended on saddles in the kiln. If your object has a foot ring, then you must glaze the base but wipe the base of the foot clean.

Correct thickness
Obtaining the correct thickness in a glaze takes practice. Due to the nature of developing a glaze, some flow, crawl, or craze differently. It will take some experience to get the glaze thickness correct every time. If your glaze is the same color in its liquid state as the clay body when dry, it can be very difficult to assess the depth. A good solution is to add a small quantity of colored food dye to the liquid glaze. This will give the glaze a pastel green, pink, or blue color but more importantly will help you see the glaze against the body.

Dipping
Make sure that the glaze bucket holds enough glaze for the object to be immersed fully. Hold the vessel by the foot or the rim and simply immerse it in the glaze for a few seconds. Try to consider the effect on the area that you hold it

by and select the area with the least impact on the final glaze quality. You can use other devices to hold the pot, such as metal tongs, or you can drop glaze into the blemish created by holding the form.

Brushing and painting
These methods are used for artistic or decorative glaze qualities. You can use any type of brush or sponge to apply the glaze in a freehand design. It is a very good technique for using small amounts of glaze and for applying different qualities or colors to the same object. The possibilities for creating different effects are almost endless: you can paint, sponge, stripe, create motifs, and work in layers.

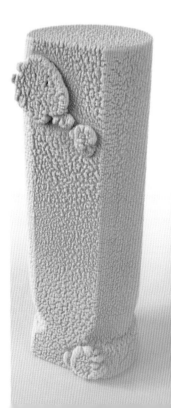

*Sprayed Cornish stone
by Alex Huber
This altered wheel-thrown
and part-slabbed form
demonstrates how the
testing of materials can
achieve fascinating results.
The surface was built up
by patiently spraying layer
upon layer of Cornish
stone. It was extremely
fragile until placed in
the kiln and fired
to stoneware.*

GLAZED SCULPTURE
BY RICHARD DEACON
The remarkable craft and technical knowledge necessary to create a sculpture of this scale cannot be underestimated. The volume, mass, and seemingly folded nature of the material are heightened by the contrasting richness and beauty of the glazed surfaces.

EXPERIMENTNG
BY ZOE CLARE
This lyrical, experimental, free-styled form consists of a body of steel wire coated in slip with an underglaze color and a transparent glaze. The detail below shows the exposed wire skeleton of the piece.

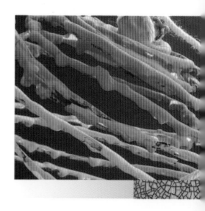

Pouring

This is a very simple application method that takes only a little practice to achieve good results. Simply hold the pot over the glaze bowl so that any excess glaze is caught, and pour glaze into the pot until about half full, rotating the pot until the glaze has covered the entire form evenly. Pour the remaining glaze back into the bowl. Pouring is primarily used on the inside of vessels, though it can be used on the outside for a more artistic effect. Pouring is often used in conjunction with dipping.

Spraying

This is the main method of glazing for slip-cast functional ware, because it uses a very small amount of glaze and covers the body with a constant thickness. Glaze for spraying needs to be slightly thinner than with other glazing methods. The spray-glaze particles will be airborne, so it is very important that the area has good extraction. Place the object to be glazed on a turntable in an extraction unit; a waterfall unit is a very good method. Hold the spray gun 12 in (30 cm) from the object and rotate the turntable slowly, sweeping the object with glaze. Repeat until the glaze has a good, even thickness. Understanding the actual thickness of the glaze is quite difficult, but you can add a food dye to the glaze to help you see the depth of glaze; this will burn out in the firing.

Raw glazing

This describes the process of applying glaze to an unfired clay piece. It is best to glaze the object between the leather-hard and dry stages. Glaze can be applied in the same ways as it is for bisque-fired ware, though the object is unfired so it must be handled carefully. This is used as a standard technique in the sanitary-ware industry. With raw glazing it is important to test the work first since this is not a shortcut. Raw glazing is a very risky process, because the clay is very porous so prone to dunting (when pottery cracks due to a too rapid cooling after firing) and other faults.

Glaze resist

There is a wide range of materials that can be used as a glaze resist. The word "resist" describes the role of the material in preventing the glaze from touching the bisque body. A resist is often painted directly onto the bisque-fired object, though it is possible to use a stencil to define the design. The resist material itself will have an impact on the quality and definition of the design.

Wax resist Probably the most widely used glaze-resist material is wax, which comes in either hot or cold form. Working with wax takes some practice, because it has a tendency to dry very quickly. If your design is intricate it is important to plan and test it first; you can mix a vegetable dye into the wax to help it to be seen once on the body.

Hot wax needs to be melted before use. A wax pot is the best device for melting since it is thermostat controlled, which means the wax can be kept at a good working temperature for the duration of the application. A small amount of paraffin added to the wax will help it flow more readily from the brush. Cold wax emulsions take longer to set than hot wax; they must be dry before the glaze is applied, otherwise they will smudge and smear across the object.

Whichever type you use, the wax burns away in the kiln to reveal the unglazed surface if applied to bisque or the undecorated surface if applied to a glazed object. If the object is glazed, the edges of the resist area will blur or change in the firing as the two glazes react with each other.

It is a good idea to keep brushes and tools specifically for wax, because they become clogged with the material over time but continue to be workable for wax techniques.

Latex resist Latex is a liquid rubber solution that cures in air. When dry, the latex has a rubbery feel and can easily be pulled from the object using a scalpel or pin. The material has a stretchy quality when removed from the object. This is a very good material for making intricate designs with, because it can be painted or trailed onto the body.

Glaze can be sprayed, dipped, or painted over the latex resist. When the glaze has dried, peel the latex away. As before, the glazes will react with each other to add interesting effects.

Paper resist Cutting out a design in paper allows you to make a paper stencil. This can be held over the object and painted or sprayed with glaze, thus giving a motif or design in clay. The edges will be slightly feathered, because the glaze has a tendency to bleed under the stencil even when stuck down.

Glaze on glaze

Glazing over a glaze has a rather exciting and rich potential. When glazes are applied to other glazes the resulting serendipity and chance in the final surface quality can be astounding. This approach relies on testing, especially on early maquettes, to ensure you understand the potential results before you commit to the final object.

Glazes with different properties, such as shiny and matte, are more likely to produce interesting qualities as their different properties react with each other in the kiln atmosphere.

The most effective use of this technique is pouring one glaze over the other; you can also splash or flick designs with a paintbrush. Simply allow the base glaze to dry before applying a second or third over the top. Fire as normal and enjoy the results.

Sgraffito

Scratching through from the top glaze to reveal the glazes below is known as sgraffito and often produces quite spectacular fired results. While the scratches are intentional, the reaction of the glazes to each other is somewhat uncontrollable.

Tube lining

Tube lining is a very beautiful technique that requires a little planning before arriving at the glazed stage. The name describes the process of using a slip trailer or pipette to draw a design onto the clay body in the green state. This design becomes a fired-on raised line on the object on which glaze is applied in a thick suspension, which will run and pool in the raised line during the firing process. A characteristic of this technique is very colorful motifs with a distinctive line-drawing effect.

Adding ball clay to the glaze will ensure that the thickened glaze has some fluidity and

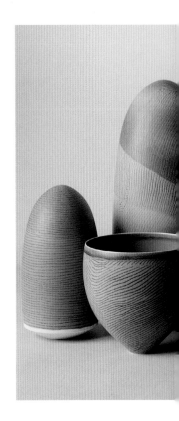

Glaze on glaze
by Chris Barnes
This plate has slip-trailed lines of different-colored glazes applied on top of a base of white glaze. This technique will produce a varied surface quality because the glaze thickness will create different tones of color and bleed into the underlying glaze.

movement for the painting. The surface of the pot must be damp before application. so that the glaze does not dry on contact; if it starts to dry or crack, simply add water to the surface and paint in with a soft, fine brush.

Majolica

Majolica describes the process of painting colored glazes directly onto a dry but unfired white tin-glazed earthenware object. Historically, this was inspired by and intended to mimic the quality of Chinese porcelain. Over a period of time, the process took on a life of its own and was known also as "faïence" or "Delftware,"depending on where it originated.

The distinctive characteristic of majolica is of a brightly colored, expressively painted surface motif on a gray-white background. The color is usually an oxide mixed with water and a little of the base glaze and painted directly onto the dry unfired glaze. The glaze should be left for some time (overnight) to dry and harden in the air. Designs can be roughed out on the glaze with a soft pencil before committing to painting. Color is built up in layers, with outlines applied as bold lines and color applied in a wash, to achieve the distinctive majolica finish.

MIXING AND SGRAFFITO
BY PIPPIN DRYSDALE
These smooth, simple forms demonstrate the variety and subtlety of colors it is possible to achieve by mixing colored stains and glazes. The surface complexity is added to with incised lines that are filled with more glaze.

MAJOLICA
BY MICHE FOLLANO
These forms show an expressive approach to majolica where the oxide washes have been freely painted to create different densities of blue from cobalt oxide.

PART SIX

POST-GLAZE SURFACE DECORATION

*Mixed motif flatware
by Peter Ting
A playful and inventive
decorative process has
resulted in a vivacious
collection of plates. The
motifs and patterns break
with the formal boundaries
of the object and grow
across multiple objects.
Makers from left to right:
Studio Glithero, Felicity
Aylieff, and Jason Walker.*

The opportunity to further enhance your work through post-glaze decoration opens up all kinds of visual opportunities. On-glaze processes can produce vibrant motifs and colors, using a breadth of skills and techniques.

INTRODUCTION

The breadth of processes and vibrancy of color and motif make post-glaze decoration very rewarding. The ability to interchange the processes and create complex surfaces and images requires a number of firings to fix the layers, but the time invested is repaid with beautiful detail and a rich color palette. For the most part the beauty of these processes is their stability; colors, if fired correctly, appear exactly as expected.

Probably the most popular method of post-glaze decoration is making transfers either by the traditional method of screen printing or by digital printing direct from a computer file. The use of stencils is widespread and immediate, proving particularly useful for direct printing onto objects such as tiles and for printing glazes. Enamels are widely used in the production of back stamps, for directly spraying onto the glaze, or for stamping and banding. Lusters add a final sheen and quality to the surface.

Transfers or decals

Transfers are sometimes referred to as "decals," an abbreviation of "decalcomania," a term used to describe a design that is produced on a special paper to be transferred to another surface.

Originally surface design, an area in which the development of transfers was pivotal, was used to hide blemishes in the glaze, such as pinholes or oxide spots. This practice began with hand painting and continued in this way until the development of the on-glaze printing processes.

The use of transfers is widespread both in industrial and studio production. Transfers are easy to make, robust, easy to apply, and permanent once fired. The beauty of using a transfer is the ability to repeat the decoration over and over again with certainty of purpose and economy of labor. Transfers are created by a number of methods using ceramic inks and printed onto specially coated ceramic papers. The ink used is an on-glaze enamel mixed with

FLOWER DECORATED VASES
BY STUDIO GLITHERO
These vases use a direct photography technique to expose beautiful surface designs that are unique to the vessel they adorn. Due to the nature of the process, each design will be different.

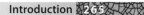

Slip-cast sculptures by Christopher Headley *These sculptures use slip-cast forms made from found objects that are assembled before firing. The intense surface quality is achieved using open stock transfers that are applied in a context that challenges the motif itself.*

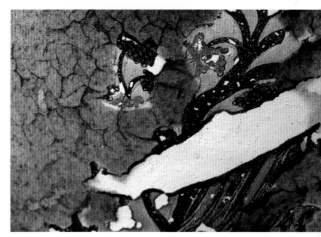

an oil-based medium. The most widespread method of producing transfers is screen printing, which is relatively cheap and simple.

It is possible to buy transfers from suppliers, known as "open stock transfers." This can be a good place to start, though you risk creating work that is not completely original, because these transfers are available for anyone to buy.

Alternatively you may send your artwork off to be printed as transfers, or you can create them yourself (see pages 267–274). Like many of the more industrial processes, there is a lengthy setup period, which is then offset by the speed of the run once you are able to begin production.

Bio fireplaces by Alexandra Mazur-Knyazeva *The patterned transfers used in these fireplaces are only revealed once the ceramic surround begins to conduct heat. The image will slowly disappear when the ceramic begins to cool. The effect of the transfer dropped into the cracked glaze surface creates a very beautiful revelation over time.*

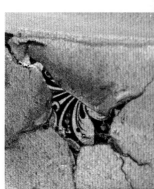

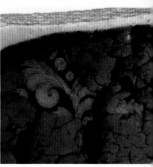

Screen printing is a relatively low-tech process ideal for studio and batch production. The term describes the process of forcing ink through a mesh screen. The real benefit of such a process is the relative cheapness of setting up and the ability it gives you to print sophisticated, multicolored images.

SCREEN PRINTING

The screen is a rectangular frame with a fine mesh stretched across its length to create a taut mesh canvas. Mesh is measured in threads per inch or centimeter. The ideal for ceramic printing is between 100 and 250 mesh, depending on the detail required in the image. The lower the number of threads, the more open the mesh, resulting in a heavier deposit of ink. A more open mesh does not support a highly detailed image as well as a fine mesh. Artwork is transferred to this screen using a photographic exposure process. Ceramic inks are then forced through the screen using a rubber blade (known as a squeegee) onto specially coated ceramic paper, and then covered by a plastic coating to allow the print to be lifted from the paper when immersed in water. The resultant transfers are applied to the glazed surface using a rubber kidney and usually fired at approximately 1360–1560° F (740–850° C).

When the transfers are fired they become fused to the surface of the glaze and are permanent. A characteristic of the inks used is a bright and vivid flat color. Transfers allow for a detailed resolution of any design and, due to their method of manufacture in layers of color, they allow for very complex patterns.

Screens may be bought or made by hand. Some artists make their own screens from ad hoc materials such as picture frames,

TRANSFER-DECORATED PLATE
BY ROB KESSELER
The tableware has been inspired by research into pollen under a powerful electron microscope. The various pollen grain cells have been transcribed with a color and produced as a range of transfers before applying to plates.

ORDER OF WORK:
MAKING A TRANSFER
- create artwork
- separate color layers
- make screens
- screen print each color in turn and dry
- apply covercoat layer and dry
- apply to object and fire to 1360–1560° F (740–850° C)

mosquito nets, and pantyhose. This improvised approach creates a breadth of quality and engenders an experimental approach to what is normally a rather fixed linear process.

Creating artwork

Artwork for transfers can be made from a range of sources. You may wish to use sketches or drawings made in a range of media, or artwork from the computer. It is important to recognize that each method will have a different printed quality.

The type of artwork you create will impact the method of printing you will use. For a traditional surface pattern design that has been drawn and painted by hand, screen printing is the perfect

TYPES OF ARTWORK

Simple lines

Simple line images can be drawn by hand into artwork for screen printing. You might decide to misregister your designs to give a freedom to the design (right).

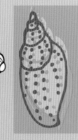

Complex lines

More complex line work would be suitable for the single-color photographic transfer method (see page 282).

Full color

Full color illustrations or photographs would be digitally reproduced (see page 278).

TECHNIQUE FILE **118**

MEASURING TO FIT A TRANSFER

To produce an image that wraps around the rim of a form such as a bowl, it is first necessary to find out which shape "fits" to it.

1 Cover the rim of the bowl where the decoration will be positioned with several layers of masking tape and draw a line around the rim.

2 Up-end the bowl on a flat surface and rotate it with one hand, while holding the pen firmly against the bowl with the other hand. This will leave a drawn line parallel to the rim. Change the position of the pen and draw more horizontal lines around the bowl; these will act as guides.

3 Finally, divide the rim into eight equal parts using a flexible straight edge, such as a palette knife, to mark the vertical divisions. Then cut through at one of the divisions.

4 Carefully peel the tape away in one piece. Flatten it and stick it to a piece of paper. This is the "map" of the area on the rim, around which the decoration will wrap. An alternative way to add imagery is to break the rim down into "leaf" shapes, as shown on the left side of the map. Divide the shape into eight leaves. These can then be flattened out and a print made to fit the shape.

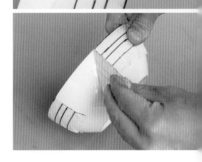

MAKING A DESIGN FIT TO A FORM USING CAD

Once the flattened guide is made, this can then be used to produce a surface design pattern. While an image can be drawn by hand to fit to the curved shape, the use of a CAD program can do this more effectively.

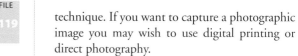

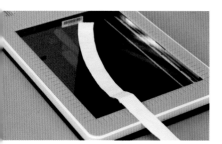

1 Scan the image into the computer. (This may have to be done in sections.)

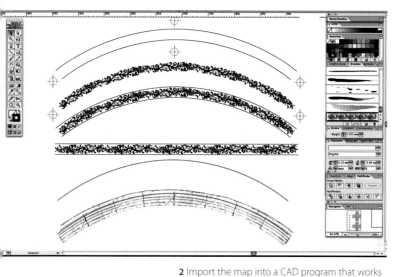

2 Import the map into a CAD program that works with Vector drawings. Create a path that matches the mapped lines. The decoration is designed and turned into a brush and then the software applies the design to the path. The lines are separated from the main decoration since they will be printed in another color. This separation allows a two-color print to be made.

3 The resulting image with its registration marks is printed out onto acetate or transparent film.

technique. If you want to capture a photographic image you may wish to use digital printing or direct photography.

Traditionally a photographic image would have been printed using a halftone screen, which reduces the artwork to a series of dots much like an old newspaper image. This process has largely been replaced by digital printing, though it is still used where this particular quality is desired.

Creating the artwork

Your image will be used to create a stencil. The stencil is essentially a mask that allows only your design to be printed onto the transfer paper; the squeegee spreads the ink across the entire screen but only allows it to print through the nonmasked area.

To convert your image into artwork ready for the screen it must be transferred to a sheet of acetate or film. This is because the exposure of the screen requires the light to pass through all areas except the design itself. If you created the artwork by hand, simply photocopy it in black and white onto an acetate sheet. If you created the artwork on screen, print it using an acetate or film sheet that is compatible with your printer.

Color separation

Once the artwork has been created it must be converted for printing. If the design has two or more colors, each color needs to be captured as a separate design. A universal convention of printing is that each color must be printed separately, one at a time. This is true of T-shirts, posters, and ceramic transfers. To achieve this you must separate your artwork into different layers of color, in a process known as "color separation." If your design uses four colors you will need to produce four screens, one for each color.

If the design is produced by hand you will have to separate each layer of color by hand. This is relatively simple; you just have to create a series of artworks that each represent one color only. The simplest method of color separation is to trace the area of a color by hand on a lightbox. This image would then be photocopied or scanned so that it appears as a black image, and then printed from the computer or copier onto an acetate film. If your design was created in a program such as Photoshop, then you can separate each color as a layer. The easiest way of doing this is to use the Color Picker tool. From each of these layers, a screen will be exposed.

It is important to be aware of the firing temperatures of certain colors. For instance, you might make a design of blue, gold, and red. Each color will fire at a different temperature, so you'll need to work out the correct order of firing.

Registration

The most important aspect of multicolor printing is the registration marks. If you go through the lengthy process of creating a number of screens to produce one image then it is really important to ensure that they line up. Registration marks should be built into each layer in exactly the same position. The purpose of these marks is to allow you to check the alignment of the layers.

If you print one screen over the other, the colors should all line up over one another. However, if one color creates a "ghost" image, the screens are misregistered.

Preparing the screen

The screen is prepared by coating the mesh with a light-sensitive emulsion (this must be done in a darkroom with a nonultraviolet safelight). The emulsion is applied evenly across the surface and allowed to dry for a short time before exposure. The film artwork is placed carefully in the center

COATING A SCREEN

A photographic stencil is created by exposing a screen coated with light-sensitive emulsion to ultraviolet light.

1 Apply a coat of photo emulsion using a coating trough. Holding the screen at an angle, place the trough firmly against the nonprinting side of the screen and tip it up, so that the liquid touches the mesh.

2 Draw the trough up the screen, exerting an even pressure to leave a deposit of the photo emulsion on its surface.

3 When you reach the top of the screen, turn the trough back until it lies horizontally so that the emulsion flows back into it. Then lay the screen flat so that the liquid can dry evenly. You can apply gentle heat with a fan heater to speed up this process.

COLOR SEPARATION PROCESS
BY NAOMI BAILEY
This vibrant design for a collection of plates uses a three-color printing process. The final design shows how the separate color layers have been combined.

EXPOSING A SCREEN

Films suitable for exposing photo stencils can be produced by hand drawing and photocopying the imagery onto acetate, or by printing from a computer onto acetate or transparent film.

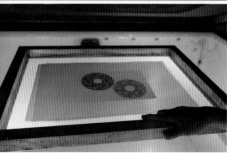

1 Place the positive film on a UV light bed, using the safelight to position it.

2 Place the screen printing side up on the film, taking care to position it centrally.

3 Place the UV exposure unit on top. UV exposure units have a special vacuum blanket that comes down over the screen and presses it down firmly. It is vital that the glass, film, and emulsion side of the screen are pressed together, so that no UV light can come through.

4 Expose the film for the required length of time. Different emulsions, images, and UV units require different exposure times, so you will need to experiment to establish the correct exposure for the materials and equipment you are using.

of the front of the screen and placed face down on a UV light bed. If the image depends on a particular orientation, such as lettering, you must place the artwork so it reads through the back of the screen, so it will appear correctly when printed onto the sheet.

The light bed is a dedicated exposure unit that uses mercury vapor lamps to expose the emulsion to ultraviolet light. When switched on, the vacuum pulls the screen and the film artwork close together and it is exposed for a particular amount of time.

After exposure the screen is washed using warm water to reveal sections of open mesh through which ink is pushed to produce a positive printed image. If your image does not completely adhere this might be for one of two reasons: either it is too fine, which will require you to redesign or print by another method, or it was not exposed for long enough.

Printing a transfer

Transfers are printed using a vacuum table. The transfer paper is held in place by a vacuum sucking air through holes in the table. The screen frame is held in place on a hinged frame and the squeegee given better control through using a movable print arm. Clamp your screen to the vacuum table.

The screen frame can be raised and lowered in relation to the surface of the print table. The gap between the screen and the transfer paper beneath it is called "snap off" and allows the screen to break away from the paper once the squeegee makes a pass and deposits the ink.

Use masking tape to cover the area of the screen stencil that is not to be printed and position a sheet of transfer paper directly beneath your design. Multiple color prints can be produced in large batch quantities by carefully positioning small card tabs along the two leading edges of the sheet of paper. These will ensure that the paper falls in the same position each time over the whole print run.

To ensure that the vacuum table is working as efficiently as possible, you should block out the uncovered holes so it holds the paper down better. Clamp the squeegee into position in the

Burnished gold tableware
by Peter Ting
This richly decorated tableware uses a range of decorative transfer qualities. Patterns are taken from other collections and combined with new designs and burnished gold.

print arm and make sure that the clamp is in place so that, when the squeegee is pulled, the stroke covers the stencil area. Put your chosen ink in front of the squeegee and, using the arm, apply downward pressure while evenly moving the print arm forward. When finished place the transfer sheet in a print rack to dry.

The final stage of making a transfer is to add the covercoat layer; this encapsulates the ink and when dry, and immersed in water, the covercoat will separate from the paper taking the ink with it. A coarse blank screen is used to print the covercoat layer. A typical thread count for laying down a heavy deposit of ink would be 86 threads per in (34 threads per cm). A rectangular section

Continued on page 274 ⟶

TECHNIQUE FILE **122**

WASHING OUT THE SCREEN

After the screen has been exposed for the correct amount of time, turn off the UV unit and take the screen straight over to the sink to be washed. All of this should be done under darkroom conditions.

1 Spray both sides of the screen with water so that you begin to see your design.

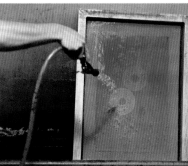
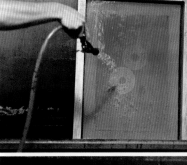

2 Once both sides have been rinsed, leave the screen for a short while so that the water can loosen the unexposed emulsion.

3 Now use a higher degree of water pressure to wash out the image. At this stage you can turn the main room lights on to see what areas you have washed out. Less UV light will have come through the print side of the screen to expose the emulsion, and so any of this unexposed residue needs to be washed away.

4 Keep working on the image area until the mesh is completely clear of emulsion and open. Dry the screen thoroughly and get rid of any pinholes by painting on a small amount of emulsion with a brush. If you feel that the emulsion is underexposed, leave the screen in daylight for a short while to further harden.

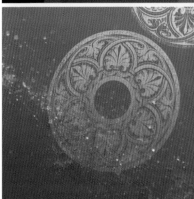

PRINTING THE FIRST COLOR FOR A TRANSFER

A transfer is a print that is encapsulated in a flexible gelatine-like layer, which enables the image to be returned to the form and fit perfectly to it.

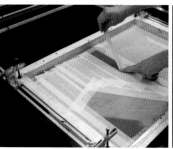

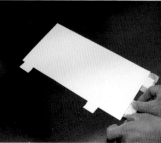

1 Clamp the hinged frame containing your screen onto the vacuum table.

2 Adjust the screen frame so that the screen will be able to break away from the paper once the squeegee makes a pass with the ink.

3 Tape the parts of the screen that you do not want printed. In this case, the black lines with their registration marks are printed first because they are the easiest to see when setting up the second color.

4 Place a sheet of transfer paper directly beneath the area of the screen stencil that will be printed and secure it with tape.

PRINTING THE SECOND COLOR

The screen-print process lays down one color at a time, each new color requires a new stencil. This stencil needs to be positioned so that it fits together with any other colors in the way that a jigsaw puzzle does.

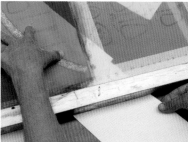

1 Remove all the tape, clean the first color off the stencil and tape it out in readiness for printing the second color.

2 Reposition one of the dried transfer sheets from the first color printing under the screen. To help with alignment, attach a piece of paper to the transfer to act as a handle, the transfer paper can be "wiggled" into position.

3 Look through the screen to check the fit by aligning one registration mark over another.

4 Then print the second color—blue, in this case. Once finished, place the transfer in the print rack to dry.

5 Block out the uncovered holes on the vacuum table to make it hold down the paper more efficiently.

6 Clamp the squeegee into position in the print arm. Ensure that the stroke of the squeegee will cover the entire stencil area.

7 Load your ink in front of the squeegee and, using the print arm, apply downward pressure while moving the print arm along.

8 Dry the transfer sheets with the first color in a print rack.

PRINTING THE COVERCOAT LAYER

The covercoat layer is printed over the image encapsulating the ink. When immersed in water the covercoat will separate from the paper taking the ink with it.

TECHNIQUE FILE **125**

1 A coarse blank screen is used to print the covercoat layer. Tape off the areas you do not want coated.

2 The covercoat is a thick, viscous ink; some have a color added for visibility, although the one shown here does not.

3 Angle the squeegee steeply to put down a heavy layer of ink. This should be done in a well-ventilated space, since the covercoat is a solvent-based substance.

4 Place the finished transfer on a drying rack and leave it to dry overnight.

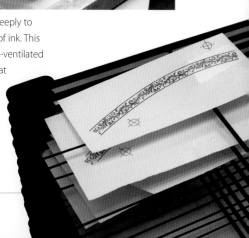

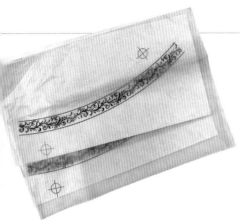

Separate layers

The covercoat layer can be tacky; so, to ensure the transfers do not stick to each other, you need to keep them between sheets of tracing paper.

APPLYING THE TRANSFER

The printed design is now ready to be returned to the original object. Care is needed to get the transfer to fit back exactly to the form.

1 Trim away the excess from the transfer. This will make it easier to apply as there will be less transfer film to manipulate into place

2 Immerse the transfer in demineralized water. After a few seconds, lift the covercoat away with the ink on it.

3 Before applying to the bowl, wet the rim, this will aid moving the transfer into place. The transfer is quite flexible so take care to accurately position the design. The top line should follow the rim, as this was the position originally chosen. This will ensure that the pattern will join correctly. When you are satisfied with the position you can use a rubber kidney to smooth it down.

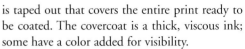

is taped out that covers the entire print ready to be coated. The covercoat is a thick, viscous ink; some have a color added for visibility.

Print the covercoat layer slowly, with the squeegee at a steep angle to put down a heavy layer of ink. This should be done in a well-ventilated space, because the covercoat is a solvent-based ink. Leave this layer to dry. In normal conditions the oil-based ink that is used to print ceramic transfers and the covercoat both dry overnight, after which the transfers are ready to use.

You then need to immerse the transfer in water. Sometimes water from the faucet contains minerals from old pipes that leave unsightly marks at the edge of the design after firing; to avoid this, use demineralized water. After a few seconds the water penetrates the transfer paper, lifting the covercoat away and taking the ceramic ink with it. This layer can then be applied to the ceramic form. Slide the transfer onto the glazed surface, using a rubber kidney to force any air bubbles out by smoothing the image outward from the center. When all the air and water has been expelled the image will be firmly adhered to the surface.

Transfer application

Transfer application is a very simple process that can be mastered relatively quickly. It is important to apply your transfers in a dust-free environment since it is very easy to trap dirt behind the image and this will cause it to blister during firing. Transfers are usually applied to a glazed surface and fired at around 1360–1560° F (740–850° C) depending on the color. Some colors, such as reds, are quite volatile and can burn away if overfired by a small amount. When fired, the covercoat will burn away to reveal the final image. The image will fuse with the glaze and become permanent. The firing temperature must be such that the glaze begins to soften but not run, so that the ink fuses to its surface.

Stencils

The simplest and oldest method of screen printing is to print using paper stencils. The stencil may be rudimentary or sophisticated depending on what you are trying to achieve. It

Paper stencils

Paper stencils can be cut into positive or negative shapes or even a combination, as seen in the botanical image (left). The imagery can be based on realistic subjects or geometric designs.

can be cut by hand using scissors or a craft knife, or may be torn. Stencils are fixed to the face of the screen using masking tape or a water-soluble glue and are drawn to the screen by the ink once you start printing.

The beauty of the process is its immediacy and simplicity. It allows for a very quick and inventive approach and is a good choice for experimentation when you do not really know what you are trying to achieve.

Handmade stencils also allow for the combination of different qualities. An image can be made up of a number of colors and components; you may produce one layer through strips of torn paper and lay a second color on top by printing through a found stencil such as a paper doily. This process of layering can create a complexity of image that it difficult to achieve by other means.

If you are trying to achieve a more sophisticated and accurate surface you can produce a design on a computer or take the time to draw it by hand. Take a copy of it and fix it to rigid fine card using spray adhesive. Using a craft knife, cut out the design carefully, taking care to ensure a smooth cut line. If this is still not accurate enough, you can design a pattern on a computer and have this made into a vinyl stencil commercially. These are very effective for accurate design resolution.

One rule of stencils is that you cannot have enclosed areas, such as the center of a zero. To make this work on a stencil the inside shape would need to be connected to the outside by two "bridges," which creates that distinctive, broken-up stencil-style imagery.

USING A PAPER STENCIL

While photographic stencils are the most effective way to make a screen print they require access to special equipment. Other stencils can be produced more immediately by cutting out a design that has been drawn onto paper, or you could even just tear some paper.

1 Roughly tear a sheet of newspaper, so that it has an interesting edge.

2 Clamp a screen, with no stencil on, into the vacuum table and tape out an open rectangle. Position a sheet of transfer paper directly beneath the open rectangle and place the torn newsprint on it. Lower the screen and pull a print.

3 Upon lifting the screen, you will notice that the torn newsprint has masked out the print and has also stuck to the underside of the screen because of the ink sticking to it. The newsprint is now fixed in place as a stencil that can be used over a small run of prints.

4 An alternative to the simple paper-cut stencil is to use adhesive tape to block the screen. This is best done on the underside of the screen, but in this case a second color rough line has been torn from masking tape and positioned over the first color print.

5 Pull a print in the normal way. This is a simple and immediate way to build up multicolor prints.

6 The finished print shows how the two colors can be layered.

Printing directly onto the form using ceramic inks is a very simple and immediate process. It is used widely in the manufacturing of modern tiles, but it also produces great results in the studio.

DIRECT PRINTING

This technique is primarily used with flat objects such as tiles. The ink is mixed to a stiff, fluid condition and printed through a larger meshed screen than the one used for transfers. By screen printing directly onto the object you are able to avoid the lengthy process of having to create a transfer.

The screen is produced in the same way as for making transfers (see pages 267–274), but it is set up to print directly onto the object. It is vitally important to create registration marks so that each tile lands in the right place; one method for this is to cut a square in a sheet of foamboard to hold the tile, or you can fix corners

of card to the table to hold the tile in place. Flat sticks are used to raise the screen slightly above the tile, allowing the screen to lift off the tile once it has been printed.

Mix the ink before printing and apply to the frame with a palette knife, then draw the squeegee along the screen, forcing the ink through the design. The image is transferred onto the tile. As it is printed directly onto the object the print is quite fragile before firing. You may wish to lift the printed objects onto a tile rack to reduce handling before firing.

PRINTED AND PAINTED TILES
BY CARLY WEINSTEIN
A strong graphic image of a boy or girl has been printed onto each tile while a wash of purple is painted over one eye; making for a very unsettling image.

TILE MOSAIC PATIO TABLE
BY JO CONNELL
This willow-pattern table has been constructed using cut tiles. The tiles were printed using on-glaze enamels mixed with a water-based medium.

SCREEN PRINTING DIRECTLY ONTO TILES

Because tiles are completely flat, they provide a great surface onto which to print directly. They are already glazed, so the ink that you should use is an on-glaze enamel mixed to a thick but fluid consistency with a water- or oil-based screen-printing medium.

Hinged unit
The tile can be printed in the same simple hinged unit that was described for directly printing onto clay (see page 200).

1 The tile needs to be held in place, so that it doesn't slip during printing. To do this, cut a card frame of the same height and tape it down. This also allows the squeegee to run on and off the surface and print the whole tile. In the example shown here, the image doesn't reach the corners of the tile and so the tile itself can be taped down.

2 Add the ink to the far side of the print (see detail). Draw the squeegee toward you, applying firm, even pressure. Note that it was not necessary to load the ink into the mesh in this case, because the tile's surface is harder than for the plaster or clay printing methods. If you put down too much ink, the image could bleed out.

3 Leave the printed tile to dry before applying a second color. The length of time this takes depends on what medium you have used to mix with the ink: a water-based print medium will dry slowly; an oil-based version will only take a short time, but will require washing up with a solvent.

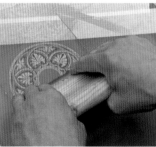

4 To register the second color stencil over the tile, fix the screen into the hinged clamp and move the tile into position. This can be done by taping a piece of card onto the tile and shifting it slightly until it fits perfectly. Because the screen should be set to about ⅛ in (2–3 mm) above the tile surface, the tile will move freely.

5 Print the second color in the same way as the first.

6 Once you have printed the second color, carefully lift the screen and check that it has printed correctly.

7 Finally, check that the image on the positive film matches the original image and that all the information has come out on both the screen stencil and the screen-printed ceramic version.

Yellow stencil

Two-color printed tile

Blue stencil

A relatively recent innovation in ceramic on-glaze decoration is the advent of digital printing. This is a process in which the designs are printed direct from the computer screen using ceramic inks onto special coated paper.

DIGITAL PRINTING

Designs can be created on screen in Illustrator, Photoshop, or a similar program, or they can be drawn by hand or photographed and then scanned and manipulated on screen. The resulting artwork can then be saved in a format such as JPEG or TIFF and e-mailed to the print bureau. The print is usually produced in an A3 format and covercoated at source.

A big advantage of this process is the low setup cost, with no need to create screens or stencils, and so it is very easy to make short print runs. This method is perfect for testing ideas or limited editions and is particularly useful for large-scale murals where each tile has a different print on it. (It is important to note that traditional screen printing is a more economic decision if your print exceeds a certain volume, as the high setup costs are offset by the low cost per printed sheet.)

The main benefit of the digital printing process is the ease with which photographic images can be produced, essentially replacing the more complex halftone printing. One of the problems of this process is that the colors lack a certain vibrancy, especially the reds, which often appear dull.

Digital transfers are applied to the ceramic surface in the same way as their screen-printed equivalents and can be fired between 1360–1560° F (740–850° C), though it should be noted that it is usual to fire at the higher end of that scale to ensure permanence and durability.

INK-BLOT PLATE
BY KAORU PARRY
These plates use a very simple hand-printing process to create beautiful artwork which is then scanned into Photoshop and sent to a printing bureau for digital printing. The plate is also gilded with 18ct gold to create a formal quality to the ink blot design.

LAYERED SURFACE DECORATION
BY MISS ANNABEL DEE
Each pot retells a personal narrative through underglaze paints, digital transfers, and lusters. The effect is an arrestingly dense surface with new motifs to discover each time you study it.

The use of on-glaze enamels in inks for printing has been covered (see pages 266–277), but there are a number of other methods in which enamel color is used.

ENAMELS

The popularity of enamels stems from the vibrancy of color that can be achieved—something that is very difficult to achieve through glaze, which is less stable, or underglaze colors, which tend to be more subdued.

Enamels are effectively low-fired glazes that require a third firing as they are applied over the body glaze. Some enamels fire at different temperatures, meaning that you may have to do a third, fourth, or fifth firing. If this is the case it is important to fire to the highest temperature first, and then drop down accordingly.

The main issue encountered when using enamels, is getting them to stick to the form. In each of the following techniques slight tweaks have been made to address this problem.

Spraying enamels

Enamels can be applied using the same spraying method used for glazing (see page 259). Spraying enamels is particularly effective at picking out areas of a form such as facets or rims. Achieving a crisp line using a spray gun requires a bit of extra work. You can try to do this by using a sponge after spraying, though this will take some practice and can be a bit indiscriminate.

To achieve the desired crisp edge to the color you can mask off areas using masking tape, masking fluid, or a vinyl stencil. With any of these processes the effect is achieved by masking the surface beforehand, so that the exposed area is the only part that receives the application of color. When the color is dry you can peel off the masking using a craft knife. The enamel is not very robust at this stage, so you must be extra careful not to damage the design as you remove the stencil—it will be almost impossible to reapply.

Perhaps the most difficult part of spraying enamels is the application to the surface. The enamel must be mixed to a runny consistency to pass through the spray nozzle. It can be helpful to warm the object beforehand, which helps to prevent runs, because the enamel will dry more quickly once it hits the surface. You may also mix a little PVA glue with the enamel to help it stick to the surface.

Ensure that the spray gun is clean before use. If this is the same gun used for glazing you could contaminate the enamel color with glaze or oxides. The enamel may also require a finer nozzle than the one used for the glaze.

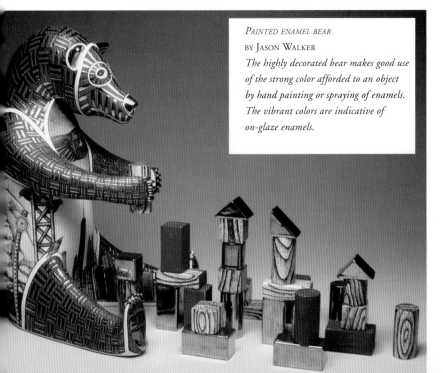

PAINTED ENAMEL BEAR
BY JASON WALKER
The highly decorated bear makes good use of the strong color afforded to an object by hand painting or spraying of enamels. The vibrant colors are indicative of on-glaze enamels.

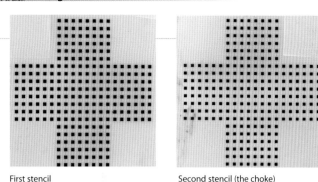

First stencil   Second stencil (the choke)

MAKING A RAISED WHITE PRINT FOR A TRANSFER

This technique is predominantly used in larger-scale productions where industry has refined the technology and materials. It is possible, however, to produce raised prints in the studio.

1 Mix the enamel pigment and oil-based print medium, adding powder until it is a paste.

2 Adding food coloring will help you with registration (see detail). This will color the ink but burn away in the kiln without changing the fired white enamel.

3 Set up and screen-print the first layer as described on page 272 using a coarse mesh screen. Be sure to load the ink into the stencil by lifting the screen away from the paper and pushing it forward into the mesh of the design.

4 The second stencil is slightly smaller than the first one, which is known as "choke" (see top right). This means that the second print has a little more of an ink "platform" from the first layer to sit on. Print the second layer.

5 If you run your finger over the completed print (right) when dry, you will feel the pronounced step. Print the covercoat and apply the transfer (see pages 273–274).

Hand painting

Enamels can be hand painted onto the surface; a process that is particularly evident in the commemorative plates manufactured by companies such as Royal Crown Derby and Wedgwood. Hand painting onto white ware is often referred to as "china painting" and it takes practice to become good at it. Some ceramics companies will mix techniques such as hand painting, transfers, spraying, and burnishing. The reason for mixing the processes is to create a unique decorated surface and also to make optimum use of process.

To hand paint you will need a soft paintbrush and to mix the enamel with turpentine and an oil-based medium. Mix the powder with the turpentine, then add the oil to achieve the right consistency. The colors will appear dull before firing but should become vibrant and glossy afterward.

Banding

Banding on the rim of a plate is a good way to use enamels because it is easier to get the material to rest on a horizontal surface, rather than a vertical one. The plate is placed centrally onto a banding wheel. A broad, soft brush is dipped in the enamel color and the wheel is slowly rotated by turning it gently with the other hand. The brush is gently pressed to the rotating surface, which receives the color. This seemingly simple process—as with many things of simplicity—depends on skill to do it well.

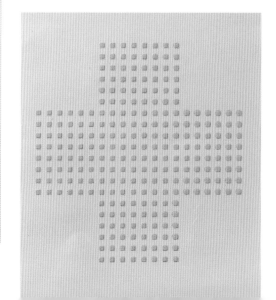

"Banding" can also refer to the delicate painting of gold, silver, or platinum on the rims of plates. This tends to be used sparingly, primarily due to the cost of the gold, platinum, and silver; the paints actually contain the precious metals and are therefore expensive. It could also be argued that the small amounts used are an aesthetic consideration, since a thin band of silver, for instance, creates a sophisticated accent. This use of precious metals to highlight decorative objects was historically referred to as "gilding." Banding in this instance is applied in the same way as enamel, but using a finer brush and less material.

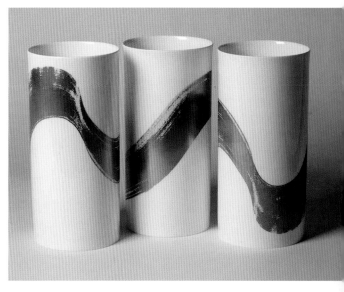

BONE CHINA WITH BURNISHED GOLD BY NAOMI BAILEY *This energetic and vibrant mark making has been printed in 18ct gold and burnished to create a voluptuous and flowing pattern.*

Burnished gold

Gold can be quite a difficult "color" to achieve because it is rather temperamental and requires an accurate firing temperature. It will also appear very dull when it comes out of the kiln.

Applied gold requires another process known as burnishing to bring out the brightness of the material. Burnishing is essentially the polishing of the gold to draw out its material qualities. When burnished it has a satin finish.

Bright gold

Liquid bright gold has a brighter finish than the burnished gold. It can be applied using the same techniques, though does not require any more work once it is removed from the kiln.

Raised white

This is a very old printing technique. The name describes the process of printing an opaque white enamel as a transfer; this is then applied to the surface of a white glazed object. The effect is very sophisticated because the design can disappear and reappear under certain lights.

Traditionally the enamel was printed thickly to produce a raised motif, giving an embossed, tactile quality to the final object. Subsequent developments have used printmaking techniques to produce finer imagery quicker.

BACK STAMPS

The back stamp is the little motif that appears on the underside of an object. This traditional maker's mark denotes who made the form and where it comes from. The back stamp is of interest to collectors and gives provenance to the object.

The design of a back stamp is important, since it is effectively the logo or brand motif for an object. Try to develop a distinctive mark that relates to you. Traditional back stamps are often loaded with symbolism.

Back stamps can be produced in a number of ways. Perhaps the most popular is the transfer back stamp. This is easy to produce, because it can be added to the edge of a screen and printed almost "by accident" when printing the actual transfer. However, a screen print may struggle to pick up really fine detail.

Digital printing can be an economical way of producing a large number of stamps, as you can fit many onto one page.

Another way of producing a back stamp is to print it using a physical stamp. This can be done using either underglaze or on-glaze enamels, though if you choose underglaze you must glaze with a transparent glaze.

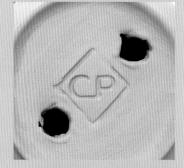

The process of using photo stencils is very exciting and something of a hybrid process. Using technology from photography, images are exposed directly onto the ceramic surface, creating dramatic, photorealistic imagery. The "stencils" here are designs copied in negative onto an acetate sheet.

DIRECT PHOTOGRAPHIC STENCILS

This process uses light-sensitive emulsions applied to the ceramic surfaces, which are allowed to dry before being exposed to light and developed. This is a very simple process; after coating the surface with the emulsion, apply your stencil and expose to ultraviolet light in the same way as with screen printing (see pages 269–270). The exposed areas will harden; wash away the unexposed areas with water, leaving the image on the surface ready to be fired at 1470° F (800° C).

The photographic emulsion potassium bichromate is mixed with gum arabic, water, and ceramic pigment to create what is known as gum bichromate. This is painted onto the fired surface with a soft brush and exposed for up to ten minutes.

The beauty of this process is its immediacy, and though it can be somewhat hit and miss judging the correct exposure, this does come with practice.

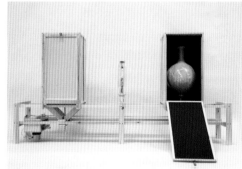

STENCILED VASES
BY STUDIO GLITHERO
These vases are painstakingly manufactured, using an alternative direct process to the one detailed here. The vases are coated in a light-sensitive emulsion before carefully taping plants to the surface. The objects are carefully placed in a darkroom box on an exposure machine built in the studio. After exposure the plant stencil is removed and the photo emulsion cleaned off to reveal a ghosted design on the surface.

A luster is a thin metallic layer usually applied to the glazed surface, though it can also be used on the bisque body. Lusters are made up of precious metals, resins, and oils. The complex chemical mix creates a localized reduction when fired in an oxidizing kiln. During firing, the resins and oils burn away and the luster is fused to the glaze surface as it begins to soften.

LUSTERS

LIFE-SIZE LUSTER SCULPTURE
BY KIM SIMONSSEN
Luster is used to great effect in this piece to help convey a sense of movement. Luster's mercurial surface finish means that it continues to change and move under the light.

Due to its mixture of resins and oils, a luster always appears on the surface as a brown sticky fluid. It is important to work out the color before application since it is only revealed after the firing.

Lusters can be applied in a number of ways: brushed, sponged, stamped, or sprayed. The choice of application relates to the overall effect required. The supplier of the luster will recommend which mediums to use to thin it down to the correct consistency. Probably the most common application is by painting it on with a brush, though this takes some skill because the luster can be difficult to control and should be applied sparingly to the brush and the surface. Using a brush will give a fine sheen to certain areas. If you want to create an overall surface effect you can spray on the luster, but do ensure that this is carried out in a spray booth. Sponging, resists, and stenciling are also very effective; they create a patterned effect rather than an overall finish, sometimes only glimpsed in the correct lighting.

It is important to wear masks and gloves when working with lusters, since some of the metals they contain can be dangerous if they are inhaled or come into contact with the skin. Fumes will be released during firing so good ventilation is essential.

PART SEVEN

DESIGN

COMBINING CONTEMPORARY
AND TRADITIONAL METHODS
BY EMILY-CLARE THORN
A hybrid manufacturing process allows
Thorn to develop her forms on Rhino,
3D print the models and then make plaster
molds and cast them in the traditional way.
This method means that complex forms can
be modeled on the computer, but are simple
to manufacture.
Makers from left to right: Emily-Clare
Thorn, Shin Azumi, and Nuala O'Donovan.

Tulip project studies
by Miranda Holms
Inspired by vibrant, colorful tulip fields, Miranda has developed a thorough and engaged study of her source material. The potential of the buds as forms has been explored by looking at surface quality, color variation, and glaze quality.

Getting started can be one of the most difficult parts of a project. To guard against getting a "creative block," it is important to be open to influences from a wide range of sources. Inspiration comes in many different forms, from many areas—architecture, nature, fashion, art—and the possibilities are endless.

VISUAL INSPIRATION

Try to select the area you will explore as early as possible in the process, because this will help you to move forward. Do not worry about committing to a particular source of inspiration—this is just the beginning, and the work is likely to evolve through a number of different subjects before you arrive at the final form. It is fine to have varied source material as long as the study is in-depth, and useful.

Inspiration can come in a flash, a "eureka moment," but more often it is the result of the painstaking study of options, from many different perspectives. You need to delve deep into source material, turn it upside down and inside out, and study it using different media and under different conditions. Consider alternative thematic approaches, and explore the material in a varied and expressive way. A sustained period of research will result in a multifaceted collection of references, which will, in turn, inspire the design process. Drawing, photography, sketching, and

painting are part of primary research: they are your firsthand research techniques. Secondary research refers to items you collect, such as articles, clippings, postcards, samples of materials showing different textures, and other objects. A good body of visual stimuli will be made up of both primary and secondary research material.

Inspiration comes from looking at the world with a new perspective. Use diverse methods to create, and collect, ideas—photography, drawing, listening, writing, painting, collage—to gain a broad understanding of your source material.

A mood board can provide a very successful way of translating visual inspiration into a format you can use. The benefit of creating a mood board is that you must filter your ideas and select imagery on the grounds of its relationship to your idea, thus you see the images from a different perspective.

Collecting and displaying the results of your research on a selection of mood boards is an

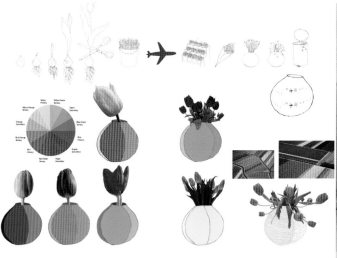

RESULTS OF INSPIRATION
BY CJ O'NEILL
The inspiration process can be witnessed here; from the initial sun-dappled photograph, to the guide for the water-jet cutter to form the final object from recycled tableware.

important part of the design and development process. This can be achieved with wit and personality to make the presentations a visually interesting and stimulating source of inspiration in themselves.

The process of selecting images and drawings as a source of information is important and something at which you will become more skilled with experience. Using discretion in your choice of images is important, so that each one is loaded with meaning, especially when presented on a mood board to represent some aspect of the character of the intended work.

It is a good idea to group visual information into broad categories, linked by a particular theme. For example, you may have a number of images, or samples, to represent texture on one board, and another group of drawings and photographs as a source of architectural inspiration on another board. These boards play an essential role in clarifying and separating different strands of your inspiration. It is most important that each mood board clearly communicates the potential highlighted by the sources of inspiration displayed. It must also continue to be visually inspiring each time you look at it. If you can achieve the latter, then your mood boards will be a successful part of the creative process.

WHERE TO LOOK FOR INSPIRATION

Make your search for inspiration as wide as possible. Visit museums, galleries, and exhibitions, but also look in other spaces, such as parks, zoos, department stores, city streets, and public transport. Carry a camera and look for the unusual in the everyday.

Plan and prepare Try to assess what you want to see before setting off on a trip around a museum. Ask for a map of the layout and visit the rooms you are interested in first. Take a notebook and pencil with you and jot down anything that you find inspirational.

Museums Visit museums and study the ceramics, brass and copperware, agricultural and industrial tools, and anything else that you find stimulating. Remember that small local museums can be fascinating and will give you an excellent feel for the topography of an area.

Galleries Find out where your local galleries are. Visit their exhibitions and ask to be put on their mailing list so that you can find out about suitable upcoming events.

Exhibitions and studios Read local newspapers or listings in magazines for news of other exhibitions. For example, your town may have a festival where

local artists open their studios to the public. Take the opportunity to see other artists' work and talk to them about what they do. Some exhibits and fairs may feature artists actually making their work.

Magazines There are specialist ceramics magazines; ask at your local library or book store.

Books Books about ceramics provide a fantastic insight into the way ceramicists around the world work. Research these sources of inspiration in your local library, or look up ceramic-related books online.

The Internet Use the image option in a search engine to find inspirational and informative photographs, drawings, and graphics related to any subject you can think of from a huge range of sources. As with any source material, don't copy other artists' work, but do use it to inspire you.

A sketchbook is an invaluable device for the artist or designer, acting as a recording device, a continuous design development tool, and an aide-mémoire. There is no right or wrong way to use a sketchbook, the main objective is simply to fill it with drawings, photographs, rubbings, useful information, and anything else that you find interesting.

SKETCHBOOKS

The most successful sketchbooks are highly personal, beguiling objects full of interesting notations, unfinished drawings, and initial ideas. The only way to achieve this is to be confident and open to the process of filling the book. Do not worry about making mistakes, because often a mistake will open a new avenue of inquiry or carry the DNA of the final design that may take some time to evolve.

The process of building the sketchbook can seem a bit daunting when you open a new one. You may like to adopt the following techniques to overcome this. On the first page, draw the first thing that comes into your head, without taking your pencil off the page. Now completely color the first page in with a random color. Roughly rip it out. Once you have overcome the first page you can get on to make good use of the book.

The sketchbook is part of an important process for your personal design development, and its beauty is its portability. The choice of format (size, paper, binding) allows for a range of activities, as does the quality of the paper. Watercolor paper is textured and is great for paints and other water-based materials; cartridge paper is a versatile surface for general use. Layout paper is very useful for iterative design drawing. A simple sketchbook method for design development is to draw from back to front of the layout pad, which means each time you turn a page you lay it over the previous drawing; this allows you trace or build upon the previous drawing with a degree of accuracy.

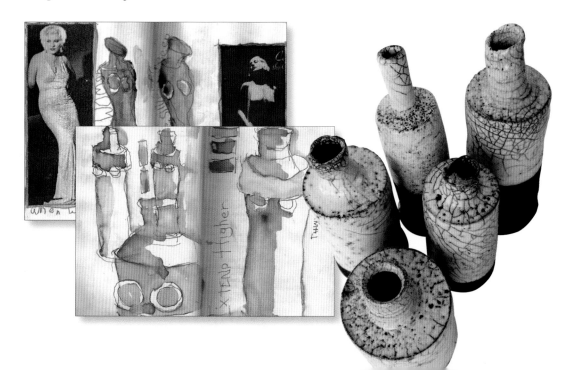

Silver-screen inspiration by Miche Follano
With female Hollywood icons as inspiration, this sketchbook shows the benefit of working in an immediate and expressive manner. Figures are abstracted quickly before a metaphorical transformation to a bottle takes place.

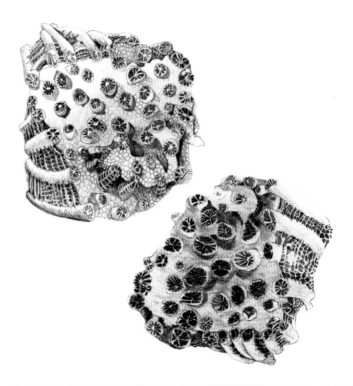

EARTHENWARE FORM
BY CLAIRE PRENTON
The preliminary studies contained in the pages of this sketchbook can be clearly tracked into the final object. Inspired by sea life and coral, the ceramic object uses shells, sea urchins, and tentacles as a decorative palette.

PINECONE WALL PIECES
BY NUALA O'DONOVAN
This work draws inspiration from nature. The initial drawings and observations are abstracted into organic forms and brought together into this collection.

DRAWING COHESION

BY ELLEN HORNE

The computer is a very useful tool for understanding the implication of your design decisions. Here line drawings can be filled with color quickly to allow a sense of variation over a collection.

Drawing as a means of expression has been written about endlessly. The reason for this is quite simply that drawing is the most effective and immediate method of capturing the ideas in your head and translating them onto the page. As with using the sketchbook, the key to successful drawing is confidence.

DRAWING

A blank sheet of paper can fill even the most skilled artist with dread, but being confident at drawing is the only way to overcome this. At some point you will have to make a mark on the page—so pick up your pencil, think of an idea, and go for it. As you become more confident, and skillful, your drawing will improve. The trick to gaining confidence in your drawing ability is to stop worrying about what other people might think, and just do it. Experimenting with a wide range of materials will help you to develop confidence. Pencils are the most obvious and readily available material and have the benefit of immediacy. But you can also use charcoal, pastels, markers, drawing pens, and paints. Each material has advantages and disadvantages, and you will become more proficient in certain methods of expression; it is important to stay open to the variety of materials and techniques, because each will have its own qualities. For example, a long brushstroke might lack accuracy but embody the spirit of your idea, whereas charcoal may allow you to give a sense of volume through shading and smudging with the fingers.

Exploratory drawing

Drawing is a means of recording what you see, but it does not have to be painstaking or photographic. The beauty of drawing is that it is for yourself, and, as such, the requirement first and foremost is that you are able to explore your ideas. Your drawings will convey the line, proportion, movement, emotion, and atmosphere of the work and, over time, help you to develop a visual communication of your ideas.

As your project evolves, you will move from expressive drawings that capture the essence of the idea to exploratory ones that help you understand the object or form. Consider the form from every angle and try to draw it from as many views as possible. The more you do this, the more you will understand it in three dimensions. This analytical approach may illuminate new ideas that can be abstracted into bodies of work.

Computer programs such as Photoshop and Illustrator can be used to manipulate, repeat, or group images. Drawings can be distorted, scaled, squashed, or stretched. The filters in these programs can be interesting abstraction devices, since they have settings that transform the image at the click of a button. Playing with these devices may help you explore the form further.

Drawing in ceramics can be used simply as a way of visualizing your ideas for the form, or as a means of devising the surface pattern or visual quality of the surface.

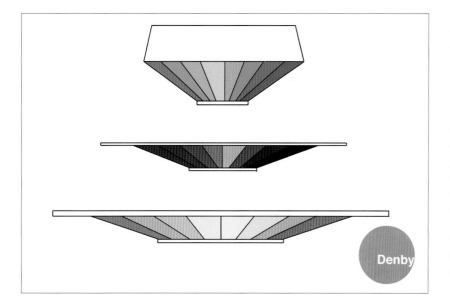
Denby

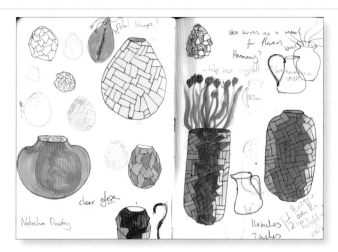

Thumbnail sketches

Quick sketches are often made on table napkins, receipts, and even the back of travel tickets, but they capture the essence of an idea as the inspiration strikes, which is usually unexpected. This example of thumbnail sketching comes from Miranda Holms. Remember, a thumbnail sketch is not about accuracy. Instead, the function of this type sketch is to get ideas out of your head and onto the paper.

Exploratory sketches

These sketches by Ellen Horne explore scale, line, and the proportions of an object before you make a model or maquette. Notice how the lines have been drawn a number of times, trying to find the right ones.

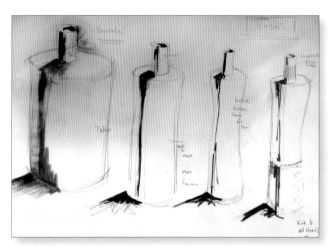

Iterative drawing

This form of drawing evolves an idea through iteration and has been used here by Miche Follano. Repetitive drawing of the same form or idea will lead to it evolving in an incremental way, in small steps. This is a particularly valuable approach to developing designs with an attention to detail.

General arrangement drawing

A general arrangement drawing is a carefully considered three-dimensional drawing that seeks to explain your object in an annotated and representational format. This drawing by Chia-Ying Lin is very useful for describing how something works.

PAPER MAQUETTES
BY SHIN AZUMI
Shin Azumi's paper models are used to explore the nuances of proportion, scale, and profile. He prints drawings from the computer and sticks them to foamboard before assembling them. The resulting finished form is featured beside the maquettes.

An important part of the development process for any ceramic work is the ability to visualize your ideas in three dimensions. Many artists, makers, and designers use a maquette to think their ideas through. Becoming proficient with maquettes will help you to evolve as a designer and make idea generation exciting and valuable.

MAQUETTE MAKING

A maquette is a rudimentary scale model. It is ideal for helping you to realize how an idea will work. By definition a maquette is a three-dimensional "sketch": it does not have to be highly finished, or detailed, but it is important for bringing an idea to life. The spirit that goes into its making, and the confidence to be adventurous in the choice of materials used, have an impact on the success of the maquette. Similarly, sometimes a very simple, well-made maquette will capture all of the details as you think through your designs. A successful maquette can be used to present an idea to clients, colleagues, and teachers.

The material used to make a maquette must be easy to manipulate—clay and children's modeling clay are perfect, but you can use papier-mâché, card, anything that comes to hand. You can use a range of techniques, including pinching clay into a form, cutting out and assembling paper into a shape.

A maquette will usually evolve from a sketch—its primary service is to help you understand what you have drawn—though you might jump straight into thinking through an idea in maquette form in order to understand it. In this instance, you may make a number of models that remain unfinished as they cease to be useful through a "trial and error" approach. Do not be afraid to stop making the maquette when it has fulfilled its purpose, these are not meant to be finished objects. There is something very satisfying about having a suite of maquettes as a three-dimensional visual record of the iterative design process. Sometimes it can be more difficult to draw a form than it is to just model it; other times you might find it helpful to alternate between sketching and maquette making.

There is a school of thought that maquettes are pieces of work in their own right, and in certain fields such as sculpture or architecture the maquette is considered a valuable object that is preserved for many years. It is advisable to keep maquettes safe, as a record of your thinking process. It is useful to review these objects in the context of new projects because they might inspire new forms and can illustrate your intellectual development process to new clients or curators when they visit your studio.

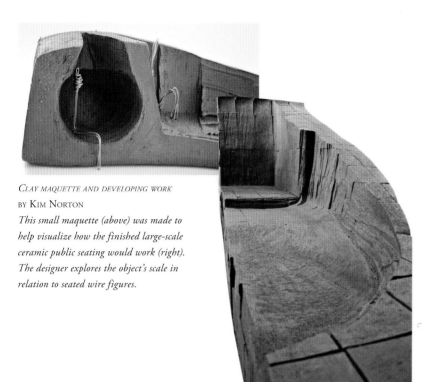

CLAY MAQUETTE AND DEVELOPING WORK
BY KIM NORTON

This small maquette (above) was made to help visualize how the finished large-scale ceramic public seating would work (right). The designer explores the object's scale in relation to seated wire figures.

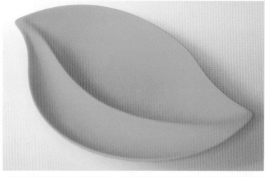

SLIP-TRAILED MAQUETTES
BY ZOE CLARE

These expressive maquettes use clay in an immediate and intuitive approach to capture ideas in a free-form process. The slip-trailed clay in a wire form relates directly to the surface of the clay bowls, illustrating the transformation of ideas across the maquettes.

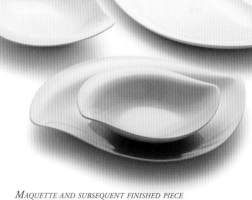

MAQUETTE AND SUBSEQUENT FINISHED PIECE
BY STUDIO LEVIEN

Studio Levien is a design studio that works primarily in ceramics designed for the bathroom and the table. The designers have become skilled at forming their thinking through blue foam maquettes. Blue foam is used because it is an inert, light material that can be modeled quickly.

A technical drawing is an accurate drawing that contains all of the essential information for making a piece, such as dimensions, scale, profile, and material.

TECHNICAL DRAWING

The technical drawing has three important roles to play. First, it provides an accurate drawing from which to work. Second, it will lead to a rationalization of the actual design. Third, it will act as a set of directions to pass on to an assistant or manufacturer in order for them to implement your design successfully.

You should prepare technical drawings when your design development and maquette making result in a clear idea of the end product. The maquette is invaluable to this process, supplying data such as proportion, scale, and measurements. Examining them closely will enable you to resolve any problems that the maquette highlighted.

The aim of a technical drawing is to provide a detailed design record, so that the item can be produced to the correct scale. To do this you must try to draw your idea with accuracy. You need a few essential pieces of equipment, such as a metal ruler, a set square, a protractor, a set of four French curves, calipers, a mechanical pencil, an eraser, a pair of compasses, and some sprung dividers. It is possible to make such drawings using computer software, but the experience of drawing by hand can be helpful to start with. In short, you can't really make a drawing using the software if you don't already know how to make such a drawing.

After you have tried hand drawing you might like to try the following software: AutoCad, Corel Draw, Ashlar Graphite, or Adobe Illustrator. Each has its own merits and features, though it must be said that Illustrator is not a dedicated drafting program so it lacks some of the benefits of the other drafting applications such as dimensions, radius tools, and the ability to export files to three-dimensional modeling programs such as Rhino, Graphite, or Solid Works.

CONSTRUCTING A TECHNICAL DRAWING

TECHNIQUE FILE **130**

This vase form is rather simple, though it still needs a drawing to record all of the accurate information.

1 Take your rough maquette and analyze which information is correct or useful to your drawing. Using rulers, dividers, and calipers transfer this information to your drawing.

3 To draw the profile, place a French curve on the paper on your intersection points and move through the points until the curve sits on the page in a position that you like. Extend the curve and then rub back, which ensures a neat junction.

2 Using rulers and a set square, draw a base line, then a center line. Using a ruler, measure the height of the object and draw a line at this point. It is customary to draw one side of the object first.

4 Using a ruler, measure the correct diameter on the opposite profile. With a pair of compasses or dividers plot the points for your French curves.

5 Flip the French curve over and locate the marks you made against the points. Draw the other side of your drawing.

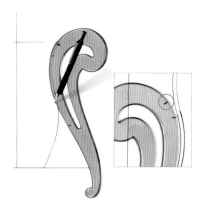

6 Decide on the thickness of the wall of the piece, and then draw the inner profile on one half of the drawing. Line up the marks on the French curve with the marks on the original outline, then pull the curve back to make the required wall thickness.

• Use the original junction point on the outer edge and line it up with the mark on the French curve, then move the curve inward to make the required thickness of the wall. Draw the inside line so that it is smooth and an equal distance from the outer edge.

7 Work your way around the drawing, considering the final object. You will need to incorporate the cast thickness, the dome of the foot, and the rounded lip of the rim.

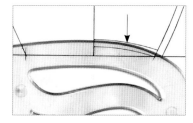

• Draw a dome on the inside of the foot. This allows the object to be glazed later on in the process. If this was not on the drawing, the final object would have a flat base.

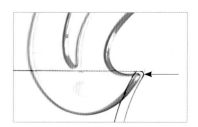

• This inside, rounded curve denotes that the object is cast. A cast object adheres to the shape of the mold on the outside but creates a softer form on the inside.

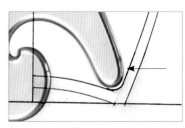

• If clay was left sharp on the rim it would chip and create a hole in the glaze. With this in mind it is good practice to have a rounded rim.

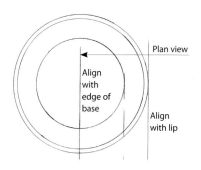

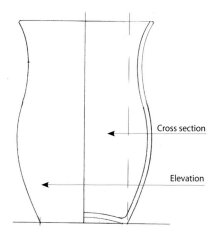

8 The convention is to make one side of the drawing the view from the front, known as the elevation, and to make the other side an interior view, as if you have cut through the object. This is called the "cross section." When this is complete, plot the view from above—this is known as the "plan view"—then add any relevant dimensions.

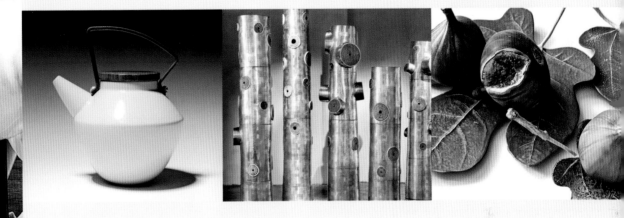

PART EIGHT

PROFESSIONAL PRACTICE

INDUSTRY COLLABORATION
BY CHRIS KEENAN
This collection was created in conjunction with Habitat. The challenge for the maker was to produce a collection of objects which exhibited the same quality of form and exquisite surface finish while working for a manufacturer in the Far East. Makers from left to right: Joseph Bird, Fausto Salvi, and Penkridge Ceramics.

A photograph is a very important tool in the communication and recording of ceramic work. The advantage of a photograph is that it can communicate relatively simply across thousands of miles and give a context and concept to the work that may otherwise be difficult to express.

PHOTOGRAPHING YOUR WORK

Creating images of your ceramic piece is crucial if you want more people to see it, whether producing business cards, brochures, or material for a web site. Many ceramicists will have their work professionally photographed, but this section explores some of the effects that can be achieved with basic photography equipment. The use of lighting and backgrounds can help to communicate different aspects of your ceramics.

With a few key items of equipment, it is possible to take clear images of your work or other relevant subjects. Most of the equipment can be sourced for a reasonable price; you will only need the basics when starting out.

Photographic equipment
The most important piece of equipment is the digital camera—cameras can now be found to suit every budget, but if you will be using photography

a great deal, you should try to spend as much as you can afford to ensure that the image quality is satisfactory. Make sure that the camera has a macro function, which allows the camera to focus close-up on small objects, and use the highest image-quality setting. Computer and image editing software, such as Photoshop, may be desirable, but this will not be within everybody's budget; digital prints can easily be ordered online or from your local photography store.

A small tripod that supports the camera will be useful for taking close-up shots, especially when camera-shake is an issue.

It is possible to find small light cubes or tents for sale inexpensively. These are folding fabric structures with a steel frame that have a removable front cover with a slit through which to insert the front of the camera. They are particularly useful for taking shots of pieces with a high-shine

Rim light
By using a rim light with a soft box at a 45-degree angle between the object and background, the edge detail is revealed. The remaining light is bounced back with the use of a large piece of white card giving the object some roundness. Shadows are soft.

"Natural" light
This image is lit in the classic window-light method with your soft box at a 45-degree angle between camera and subject. This suggests natural light from a nearby window. Fill in the shadows with white card. Experiment and modify angles, since there is no fixed formula.

Flattening light
This is lit using direct lighting with a soft box from above (or anywhere near) the camera lens. This will flatten off your ceramic considerably. However, this is a handy technique for objects with rims or bowls, because it leaves soft shadows underneath.

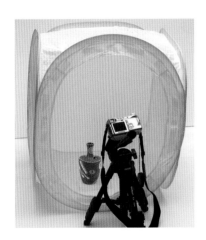

Typical setup

This image (right) shows the position of each piece of equipment in a typical setup.

Light cube

A light cube (right) gives an evenly diffused light, softening reflections to give a more professional result. It is especially useful for glossy glazes.

Flash unit and soft box · Digital SLR camera · Seamless paper background · White card reflector

surface, because the interior is completely white, eliminating all unwanted reflections. The fabric cover diffuses the light source, softening shadows to give a more professional look. You might also find a soft box useful; these fit over the light and produce soft, neutral tones.

Getting good results

Give yourself plenty of time; take far more shots than you think you need and vary the camera angle and the lighting—take close-up detail shots as well as wider-angle ones. Digital cameras make it easy to take a large number of shots, which can then be compared and edited down. You should keep a spare battery and memory card in case you exceed capacity. Clearly label your images and store them so that they can be found easily; keep a high-quality master copy of each image in one folder and smaller copies in another.

Highlighting contrast

This image shows light on the forms' surface that eliminates short shadows and brightness around the base of the ceramic, while retaining contrast, dimension, and depth.

Side light

This is side lit with a metal reflector bowl on the flash head (not a soft box). It is a naked and very hard light source similar to the midday sun in a cloudless sky. It will leave a smaller highlight on shiny surfaces and is great for contrast.

Graduated light

Graduating the background using one light should separate the subject from the background while adding some drama. Your soft box should be pointing from slightly behind the ceramic toward the camera lens. You will need a lens hood over the lens to eliminate flare. A lower camera angle helps.

Metal reflector light

This accurately shows how much more drama you can achieve with a different object when using the metal reflector bowl instead of a soft box. In this shot the light is above and to the side of the object, pointing down to give a stouter shadow.

Developing promotional material for your work is an important part of a professional approach. Photographs of your work (see pages 298–299) might be applied to business cards, portfolios, or catalogs that you put together. You may also be requested to supply images for web sites, magazines, or books.

PROMOTING YOUR WORK

Today's artists, designers, and makers are required to be publicists as well as craftspeople. The need to keep one's practice exposed to a 24/7 world is vital to the development of a strong creative practice. Various tools are at your disposal to help you with this plight.

Software such as Photoshop is vital for image manipulation, giving you the chance to improve the lighting, color, contrast, or the background to ensure perfect photographs for whatever purpose you require. It is also a good idea to keep press-ready photographs stored in a range of formats such as JPEG or TIFF. As a general rule, a print-ready image is set at 300 dpi and should be still small enough to e-mail. If the request is for a high-resolution image (too large to e-mail) you can either mail a disk or use a Web-based FTP service, such as Dropbox. (FTP stands for file transfer protocol; these sites allow you to upload large files to a server and e-mail the recipient instructing them to go to the web site and download your file.)

If you are asked to supply images for a magazine, it is also advisable to supply a press release, written in the third person, with any images. If the release is good enough, the magazine will often simply copy your information into their article. The ability to quickly supply print-ready images and text can make the difference between being included in an article or not.

Digital printing has made it easier to produce your own promotional material relatively cheaply. You can design the artwork using your preferred software, then upload a PDF, and have business cards returned complete in a matter of days. The production of catalogs in short runs (around 100 copies) is also very simple and cost-effective.

Designing a web site/blog

Arguably the most important promotional tool is the Internet. Having a web site, blog, or e-folio is a very effective device for self-promotion, and its role as a permanent public presence cannot be underestimated. It is always on and ready to promote, it can be accessed by many more people than you can meet face-to-face, and it communicates a professional front to your practice. It is important to have an online

WEB-SITE CONTENT

BY CHARLOTTE HUPFIELD

A web site should be simple and accessible. It's a good idea to have a gallery of your work up on the front page. This will ensure the viewer is engaged with your work and does not get lost looking through pages of information.

presence that you can tailor to your own personal style; even if you buy a generic web-site-building template it is possible to make it personal by thinking through what you are trying to achieve.

Start by buying a domain name. This is a straightforward task: simply search for a domain name sales service, type in your desired web-site name, and, if it is available, buy it. You will be asked how long you would like the name for. It is a good idea to buy it for three years or more, since you will have to renew it at some point.

There is dedicated software that can be used to build a Web presence from scratch. Web-site template software may be the better option if you are a beginner.

Another solution is to start a blog (short for "Web log"). Blogs were originally intended as Web pages to be updated almost every day—a kind of diary. However it did not take artists and designers long to recognize the benefits of using a system where you do not need to be a Web designer to add regular updates to your online offering.

Blogger and Wordpress both offer a very good service where you sign in and choose a style for your page (known as a theme) and simply build the pages from there. This is a very user-friendly solution—it's free, easy to update, and can be built up periodically. Blogging is increasingly becoming the chosen method by which makers build their web sites. You can even assign a private domain name to the blog if you prefer.

Design and layout are key to the success of a blog. Consider the viewer, keep layouts simple, and add only relevant information. It is a good idea to develop a narrative that helps the viewer understand the site and how it will work.

BRANDING

BY MAARTEN BAAS

The key to self-promotion is the notion of your brand. This may mean designing a logo or symbol to represent you, or developing a body of work that is uniquely yours. Maarten Baas does both of these—his idiosyncratic ceramic furniture is branded with his own chunky metallic logo. By using the same typography and logo on his web site, Maarten projects a unified brand identity.

One of the key aspects of running a professional studio is understanding how to make sales. Knowing how to price your work and where to find the right audience for it are essential areas of your practice. They impact on how you are understood professionally and, more importantly, on your ability to make a living.

SELLING AND EXHIBITING YOUR WORK

Choosing the correct arena for selling your ceramics will depend greatly on the price range of the work you make.

How do you price work?
Pricing work can be a complex and often troubling process. How can you work out the cost of something you have spent many hours thinking about and producing?

Exhibitions
Craft and design exhibitions are an ideal place to both promote and sell your work direct to the public. They are also attended by international gallery owners and buyers for independent and department stores.

It is relatively straightforward to calculate the manufacturing cost of an object—simply add up the cost of the materials (clay, glaze, color, etc.), the cost of the firing, and the time it took to produce. It is a good idea to work out a basic hourly rate for your labor. Once you have worked out the production cost of the work, you can also build in a profit margin. The simplest method is to add a percentage (usually 50–100 percent).

Whatever figure you arrive at, try to view it realistically. For instance, you may have had to invest more time due to trying a new process; this should not be factored into the price.

Wholesale or retail?
If you will be selling your work through a third party—a gallery, a store—then your prices are wholesale. This simply means that your stock is to be sold by others. Therefore, your costs are not the final cost; the final cost includes the price set by the person actually selling the work, and this difference is called the "markup."

The marked-up price is the retail price. If you do an open studio event or a retail show, then you should also add a markup so that there is a consistency in the pricing of your work.

One of the things you must consider is the amount of markup the gallery/store will add to the work. The markup can be anything from 100–250 percent. Put simply, a 100-percent markup means if it cost $10 to produce, it will sell for $20. This is why it is vitally important that your costing is accurate and realistic. If your costing process means that after markup you have a ludicrously expensive product, you need to consider if you will be able to sell enough work.

Your work can be sold in a number of ways:

Sale or return This is when the gallery/store takes your work for free and offers to showcase it in their space. They will endeavor to sell the work and pay you the agreed fee upon sale of the item. This is often a good way of selling when you are starting out, though it has its limitations. It tends to favor the gallery, which can have work on show without paying for it. The process means you have to make work without guaranteed sales, and thus you begin to carry a stock. If you enter into a sale or return agreement it is a good idea to set a time limit on the process and agree on a recall date if the work has not sold. This prevents the gallery from becoming complacent.

Pro forma This means that the gallery places an order and pays in advance. Upon receiving an order you will produce a pro forma invoice, which clearly specifies to the gallery that you expect payment before the work is shipped to them. You will then begin to make the work but not send it out until payment has been made. This process favors the maker a bit more and encourages the gallery to commit.

If your work is expensive to produce you may ask for an advance fee in order to buy materials for making, though when you are established you should have stopped working in this way.

Where to exhibit?
There are a variety of ways to showcase your ceramics and you should pick the settings that are most suited to your work.

Galleries Solo or group shows are the bread and butter of a ceramicist's practice. Each exhibition should be assessed on its merits; as a general rule any exhibition is worth doing but you must check up on the gallery before committing. A popular first exhibition space is an artist-led gallery, which can be hired and managed by whoever holds the exhibition. If you host your own exhibition then

HANGING INSTALLATION BY LEO RICHARDSON
Leo's huge sculpture was an ambitious and well-executed installation. Hung down the center of a seven-story stairwell, her planning, organization, and implementation were paramount to the successful resolution of her project.

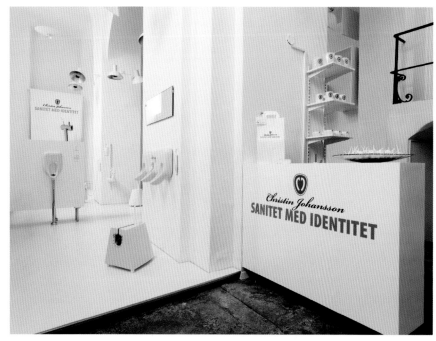

you need to plan for publicity material, a private view, press packs, and gallery attendants.

Craft fairs These events are great for showing your work and networking with colleagues, gallery owners, buyers, etc. It is important to understand whether the customers will be retail or public, and price your work accordingly. Being a member of a craft organization is useful because they provide essential information and support for exhibiting. Often they will take larger stands at bigger events, offering members the opportunity to exhibit in a group that would otherwise be very expensive.

Trade fairs Trade fairs are by definition for trade, so they are wholesale events. Often there are government subsidies available for fairs abroad to encourage the export of unique design objects. They are excellent opportunities to showcase your work in new markets. It is really important to do your homework about an event before committing to it, because they can be expensive to attend. Exhibiting at a trade fair exposes your work to a mainly retail or manufacturing market.

Commissions

Receiving a commission is a very rewarding experience and can take on many forms: it may be to design a bespoke gift, or a sculpture in a public space. Regardless of the type of commission, and even if the commissioner is a friend or relative, it is good practice to draft a simple, direct contract.

If the commissioner is a friend or colleague, then you may temper the tenor of the agreement, whereas if it is for a public body or hospital, you should seek legal advice. It is standard practice to expect part of your fee in advance, and this arrangement should be clarified in the contract.

If the commission is for the public domain, then obtaining the correct insurance is vital. Part of your negotiations should relate to the maintenance of the work. Sometimes a contract might require the artist to be responsible for this upkeep, which should be approached with caution.

Whether you are a craft maker or designer, the opportunity to collaborate with the ceramics industry is an exciting prospect. Consider the industry as a commercial opportunity for your work. As companies are always looking for something new, there may well be an opportunity to sell your designs to a company for manufacture.

WORKING WITH INDUSTRY

If you have an inquiry from a manufacturer when showing at an event, this potential opportunity should be considered carefully. Many craftspeople talk of turning down these opportunities early in their career, while some established makers or artists never turn down such a chance. If you get such an opportunity you should think of it as the chance to expose your work to a wider public. As a general rule there are three different models of working directly with industry:

In-house designer Working in the design studio of a manufacturer and designing products for its catalog is a good way of gaining vital hands-on experience and knowledge of developing a product from studio to marketplace.

Freelance The freelance role is to develop individual projects with a range of clients, enjoying a variation of project opportunities. You may work thoroughly through the entire design process or just at the initial stages, depending on your agreement with the client.

Collaborator This involves working with a manufacturer to develop an individual collection or project, usually based on your own work or a collection you have developed. The challenge here is to develop unique work that is reminiscent of your own style but not so close that you are just developing a cheaper version of it.

There is another aspect of working with industry that might be helpful to your practice. Industrial processes might be the only way to realize a particular product or project. It is possible to commission the manufacture of short, or bespoke, production runs through an industrial partner. Your idea might be impossible to fulfill without the capacity for manufacture that comes with a factory, or there may be a technique or quality that can only be achieved by a particular manufacturer.

Outsourcing the production of designs is an intelligent business solution for some small, studio-based companies. The maker may develop the initial object in a prototype form before commissioning a company to produce the final piece. The advantage of this is that it frees up the maker to move onto other projects while somebody else is concerned with delivering the existing body of work.

MANUFACTURING QUALITY
BY KAORU PARRY
Kaoru Parry commissions the production of her collection from a number of small manufacturers. She personally manages the quality control, ensuring that the manufacturer is meeting the standard required for her to supply the design-led stores that her work is sold in.

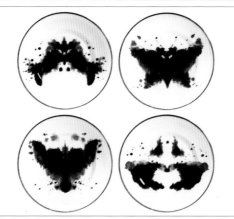

Whether you are a potter, sculptor, or designer, the collection of your work into a presentation format such as a portfolio is of vital importance. The portfolio can be achieved in a number of ways, and just like the work itself, it is important that the portfolio is personal to you with a style of its own.

PORTFOLIO PRESENTATION

When developing your portfolio it is a good idea to think of it as two tasks: the first is a pragmatic formatting challenge—size, orientation, format, quality of paper, etc.; the second is a visual challenge—how to make it different, engaging, and interesting. It's not an easy balance to strike and it can take a few tries to get it right, but the way to succeed is to try things out and ask friends or colleagues to offer opinion.

There are some key rules to adhere to but beyond that the portfolio can do anything. Above all a portfolio is about the communication of your work to an interested party. With this in mind it is a good idea to make your portfolio easy to read and legible. This does not mean that it cannot be visually interesting, just that you need to have considered the experience of the viewer in the design presentation. Another key idea is that the portfolio should be portable. Occasionally you may be asked to send a portfolio to someone, so you might consider having a smaller format that is relatively easy to send in the mail. The choice of paper, card, or mounting material will also have an impact on the overall portfolio experience.

Portfolio sequence
by Pacharapong
Suntanaphan
By using professional-quality photography, a well-designed layout, and consistent typography, this portfolio shows it has been carefully considered and executed.

A relatively recent development is the idea of an e-folio. This is often produced in the form of a blog. Once mastered, blog software is easy to update, allowing you to add images and text at will. The benefit of this is that you do not need to reprint documents, and you can refresh or redesign with relative ease.

It is a good idea to include the breadth of your practice in your portfolio, from sketches, drawings, tests, and images of maquettes through to finished pieces. This will help the viewer to understand your work fully, and appreciate the quality of your thinking and workmanship.

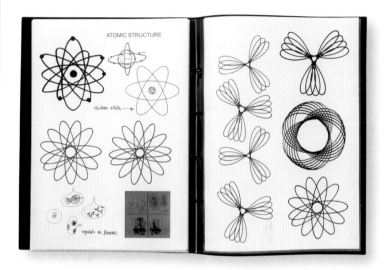

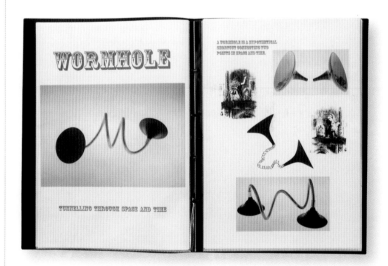

ATTENTION TO DETAIL

BY TAMSIN VAN ESSEN

This portfolio very effectively conveys the concept of the project. Tamsin designed a collection of forms based on the laws of physics and decided to make this the design philosophy of the portfolio. A collection of imagery, photographs, and type creates a presentation that clearly communicates the essence of the work, presenting complex information in a graphic way so that we understand it as a graphic rather than as a diagram or equation.

GLOSSARY

Agateware Clay patterns and structures formed by laminating, mixing or inlaying different colored clays, to give an effect like agate stone.

Airbrush A device operated with an air compressor used for spraying on colors, either in overall coverage or decorative form.

Antiquing A method of applying color and wiping it back to accentuate the detailed surface.

Ash Useful ingredient as the fluxing agent for a glaze. Wood ash is usual, but coal ash, and any plant ash is also usable. Ash also may have a high silica content, and combined with clay it will form a simple stoneware glaze.

Ball clay Clay of high plasticity, high firing and pale in color. An ingredient of throwing clay and other bodies, as well as glazes.

Ball mill An enclosed, mechanically revolved cylinder containing flint or porcelain balls which are used to grind ceramic oxides or materials mixed with water.

Banding wheel A turntable operated by hand, used for decorating purposes.

Bat A plaster or wooden disk for throwing pots on, moving pots without handling, or for drying clay.

Bat wash Also a term for kiln wash.

Beating Also a term for paddling.

Belleek A village in county Fermanagh, Northern Ireland, and famous for the fine translucent porcelain produced at the Belleek pottery, the oldest pottery in the country, founded in 1857 by John Caldwell Bloomfield. The first examples of this porcelain were made using local kaolin and feldspar deposits. It became famous worldwide and some people will refer to it as a shorthand to describe fine translucent porcelain regardless of where it is made.

Bentonite A plastic volcanic clay used in small amounts for suspending glazes or increasing the plasticity of a clay body.

Bisque (biscuit) Clay ware after the first firing, usually around 1830°F (1000°C). First, low-temperature firing to which a pot is subjected. Moisture within the clay is driven off slowly in the form of steam, along with other organic compounds—clay becomes converted to "pot," a chemical change that is irreversible. Biscuit firing is usually between 1562°F and 1832°F (850°C and 1000° C) but can be higher if less porosity required. Work is often biscuit fired before being decorated in other ways.

Bisque firing The first firing of pottery to mature the clay, rendering it permanent. In a bisque firing, pots may be stacked on or inside each other because there is no glaze to stick them together.

Blunger High-speed mechanical mixer for slip, usually casting slip.

Body The term used to describe a particular mixture of clay, such as a stoneware body and porcelain body.

Body/clay body Term potters use for clay, especially when it is a prepared mixture and may contain other non-plastic materials such as grog and sand.

Bone china A clay body with a quantity of bone ash in the recipe.

Burnishing Compacting a clay surface or slip coating by rubbing in the leather-hard state with a smooth, hard object to give a polished finish.

Calcine A form of purifying by heating oxides or compounds to drive out carbon gases or water and to reduce plasticity in powdered clays.

Carborundum stone A hard, dense stone that is used for grinding away rough patches on fired ceramic.

Casting Making pots by pouring slip into a porous mold to build up a layer of clay.

Casting slip A liquid clay used in the process of forming objects with molds. Also referred to simply as slip.

Cavity (of a mold) The inside section of a mold where the casting is formed.

Celadon Green stoneware and porcelain glaze colors, which contains iron.

Cement clay This is a mixture used mainly for industrial and construction purposes. There have been successful experiments with 50/50 combinations of clay and cement for self-setting external sculptures. Testing should always be carried out and technical data sheets read to access the compatibility if firing.

Ceramic Any clay form that is fired in a kiln.

Chattering An irregular surface caused by blunt turning tools or a coarse grog in the clay.

China A term associated with vitreous white wares and porcelain.

China clay A pure non-plastic primary clay, used in bodies and glazes.

Chuck A hollow form made in clay or plaster that holds a pot securely during trimming.

Chum A metal turning lathe attachment for placing leather-hard hollow ware over to hold it while turning. Also applies to a turned dome of clay, over which leather-hard articles are placed, prior to turning.

Chun Chinese glaze which gives a milky blue coloring when fired.

Clay ($Al_2O_3.2SiO_2.2H_2O$) Essentially the product of weathered granite and feldspathic rock; a hydrated silicate of aluminum. The purest "primary" clay, china clay (Kaolin), is found where it was formed. Transported "secondary" clays become contaminated, are colored and due to the variable presence of fluxes have a range of lower firing temperatures.

Clay body A balanced blend of clay, minerals, and other non-plastic ingredients which make up the pottery structure.

Cobalt oxide/carbonate (CoO and CoCO$_3$) Powerful blue colorants. Used widely in ancient China, cobalt is said to have been first found in Persia. Blue and white decoration is one of the strongest traditions in ceramics.

Coiling Making pots using coils or ropes of clay.

Collaring The action of squeezing around a pot in order to draw the shape inward.

Cones See Pyrometric cones.

Copper oxide/carbonate (CuCO$_3$) Strong colorant in ceramics giving green to black and brown. Under certain reduction conditions it can give a blood red.

Crank Refractory support for tiles, plates, etc. Crank also refers to a type of heavily grogged clay body.

Crawling Movement of glaze over the clay body during the glaze firing, due to dust or grease on the surface.

Crazing The development of fine cracks caused by contraction of a glaze.

Decal Pictures or text printed onto special transfer paper and used to decorate pottery.

Decorem Photographic method used to apply images to a fired glazed surface, before refiring.

Deflocculant An alkaline substance, commonly sodium silicate or soda ash, which when added to a slip, makes the mixture more fluid without the addition of water. The clay particles remain dispersed and in suspension, an essential quality required for casting. Also see Flocculant.

Deflocculation The dispersion of clay slip or glaze by the addition of an electrolyte—e.g., sodium silicate or soda ash—thereby increasing fluidity and decreasing thixotropy.

Delftware Also known as Majolica and Faience, this tin-glazed ceramic ware was named after the town of Delft in Holland.

Dipping Applying a glaze by immersion.

Downdraft kiln One in which heat and flames are drawn downward and out through flues at the base or floor of the kiln.

Dunting Cracking of pottery due to a too rapid cooling after firing.

Earthenware Pottery fired to a relatively low temperature. The body remains porous and usually requires a glaze if it is to be used for containing water or food. Low temperature ceramics generally fired between 1832°F and 2156°F (1000°C and 1180° C). Earthenware pottery is fused but not vitrified and remains porous unless covered with a glaze. Naturally occurring red terracotta clays have a relatively high iron oxide content that acts as a flux and therefore will not withstand high temperatures. White earthenware is a manufactured clay body used widely for industrial production.

Egyptian paste A highly alkaline body with low plasticity and alumina content. The alkali comes to the surface in drying, leaving crystals that flux in firing to give a glazed surface. Coloring oxides are also added to the body.

Enamels Low-temperature colors containing fluxes, usually applied on top of a fired glaze. Enamels require a further firing to render them permanent. Also known as on-glaze colors or china paints.

Engobe A white or colored slip applied to pottery before glazing. Usually the slip contains an amount of flux to fire it onto the bisque pot.

Fettling The process of cleaning up slip-cast pottery with a knife or sponge, especially when removing seams left by a mold.

Filter press Machine into which slip is pumped under pressure so that water is extracted, leaving a stiff plastic clay.

Finger-sand The gentle rubbing of a glazed surface with the fingers to remove ridges.

Firing The process by which ceramic ware is heated in a kiln to bring glaze or clay to maturity. Process that changes clay to ceramic (see Biscuit). The usual firing ranges referred to are raku, the lowest at around 1472°F (800°C), followed by earthenware, then stoneware, and finally porcelain, which can be fired up to a maximum of 2552°F (1400°C).

Firing chamber The interior of the kiln in which pottery is fired.

Firing cycle The gradual raising and lowering of the temperature of a kiln to fire pottery.

Flange The rim on the inside of a lid and the ledge around the inside of a pot's opening that are used to locate the lid and hold it securely in place. The ledge on which the lid sits is sometimes called a gallery.

Flocculant An acid or salt, which when added to slip has a thickening effect and aids suspension, delaying settlement. Calcium chloride and vinegar are commonly used flocculants.

Flocculation The aggregation of suspended particles by the addition of electrolytes—e.g., calcium chloride to give a proper consistency for dipping, casting, etc. Flocculation decreases fluidity and increases thixotropy.

Flux An ingredient in a glaze or clay that causes it to melt readily, helping silica to form glaze or glass.

Food-safe Pottery or glaze that has been tested and determined to be safe for use with food or drink.

Foot The base of a piece of pottery on which it rests.

Footring The circle of clay at the base of a pot that raises the form from the surface it is standing on.

Frit Glaze ingredients that have been fused to give a more stable substance and to render harmless any dangerous material. Most lead compounds have been fritted to prevent the release of lead into food or drink.

Fused Melted together, but not necessarily vitrified.

Fusion When the fluxes in a body cause the clay to melt and form a solid composition.

Gallery See Flange.

Glaze A thin, glassy layer on the surface of pottery.

Glaze fit How well a fired glaze adheres to the clay body. Ideally, the glaze should have a slightly lower thermal expansion than the body, so that on contraction the body puts the glaze into compression. This avoids glaze crazing due to stresses.

Glaze stain Commercial color added to a glaze.

Glost Alternative word for glazed, more commonly used in industry.

Greenware Unfired clay ware.

Grog A ceramic material, usually clay, that has been heated to a high temperature before use. Usually added to clay to lessen warping and increase its resistance to thermal shock.

Ground-laying Applying an even coat of enamel with an oil medium to a once-fired glaze surface and refiring to a low temperature of approximately 750°C (1350°F).

Gum arabic and gum tragacanth Water-soluble gums, used as adhesive in glaze or colors.

Hardening on Heating decorated bisque pottery to a temperature of approximately 1200–1290°F (650°C–700°C) in order to burn out the organic media of the decoration and to fix the color prior to glazing.

Heat work Energy input during firing, normally represented in terms of temperature and time.

Hot spot A section of a kiln that fires to a hotter temperature than the rest of the kiln.

Incise The process of carving a design into a raw clay surface.

Inglaze To apply pigment, stain, or glaze to an unglazed or glazed surface so that in subsequent firings the color melts into, and combines with, the glaze layer.

Iron oxide The most common and very versatile coloring oxide, used in many slips and glazes and often present in clays too. Red iron oxide (rust) is the most usual form but there are others (black iron, purple iron, yellow ocher).

Jasperware A type of stoneware first developed by Josiah Wedgwood. It is made from colored clay and is always un-glazed. This produces a matte surface finish and is produced in a number of different colors— green, black; known as basalt ware, and (best known) the pale blue that has become known as Wedgwood blue. The decoration is usually made from relief white sprigs. The term jasper describes the name of a quartz mineral.

Jigger and jolley Plastic clay is formed on or in a rotating plaster mold with a metal profile. Jolleying produces hollow ware, jiggering produces flatware. Mostly an industrial process, but sometimes used by studio potters.

Kaolin China clay. Primary clay in its purest form ($Al_2O_3.2SiO_2.2H_2O$).

Kidneys See Ribs and Scrapers.

Kiln The device in which pottery is fired. Kilns can be fueled with wood, oil, gas, or electricity.

Kiln furniture Refractory pieces used to separate and support kiln shelves and pottery during firing.

Kiln setting The way in which a kiln is packed for firing.

Kiln wash A coating of refractory material applied to kiln furniture to prevent it from sticking during firing.

Kneading A method of de-airing and dispersing moisture uniformly through a piece of clay to prepare it for use. Sometimes referred to as wedging.

Luting The blending of two clay surfaces, using slip.

Lead release The amount of lead that can be dissolved from the surface of a glaze that has been in contact with acidic solutions.

Lead sesquisilicate A high lead content frit with low solubility in weak acid or water.

Leather-hard Clay that is stiff but still damp. It is hard enough to be handled without distorting but can still be joined.

Lug Side projection of a pot which acts as a handle for lifting.

Lusters Salts of metals fired at low temperatures, giving a lustrous or iridescent metallic sheen to a body or glaze surface.

Macaloid Brand name for a superior and very plastic form of bentonite.

Matte A soft finish with little or no shine.

Matting agent Ceramic compound used to give matte surfaces when added to glazes.

Maturing temperature The temperature at which a clay body develops the desirable hardness, or glaze ingredients fuse into the clay body.

Majolica Decorated tin-glazed earthenware with the color decoration being applied on top of the raw glaze surface.

Meerschaum An opaque clay-like material, white, gray, or cream in color. Meerschaum is a hydrous magnesium silicate. It is incredibly light and will float in water. Most of the meerschaum used today is extracted from the plain of Eskisehir in Turkey and is found in irregular nodular masses in alluvial deposits. When first extracted, meerschaum is soft and can be easily scratched with a nail, but it becomes hard when exposed to heat. Meerschaum has occasionally been used as a substitute for soapstone and fuller's earth, but its main use is for making smoking pipes. When smoked, meerschaum pipes gradually change color, and old meerschaums will turn incremental shades of yellow, orange, and red from the base up.

Melting point When a clay, in firing, fuses and turns to a molten glass-like substance.

Mini bars Pyrometric bars used to measure the firing temperature of a kiln. They are usually used in a kiln sitter, a mechanical device that shuts off power to the kiln when the bar has bent enough to release a weighted switch.

Mochaware Type of decoration performed at the wet slip stage when a mixture of alkaline liquid and pigment rapidly disperses into the slip giving a fine lattice pattern.

Mold A plaster former in which clay can be pressed or slip cast to create forms. Molds can be made up of only one section or multiple pieces.

Mold strap (mold band) A band made of cloth or, more commonly, rubber used to secure parts of a mold together during the pouring process.

Muffle Refractory chamber inside a fuel-burning kiln which contains the pottery and protects it from direct contact with the flames and gases.

Nesting Stacking pottery in a kiln for bisque firing. Pots can safely be placed inside one another.

Once firing Firing ceramics without a biscuit firing, usually with a raw glaze or pigment applied at the leather-hard or dry stage.

On-glaze color See Enamels.

Opacifier Material used to make a glaze more opaque, often tin oxide, titanium oxide, or zirconium silicate.

Opaque Glazes that do not allow other colors to show through, as opposed to transparent glazes.

Oxidation Firing pottery in a kiln with sufficient supplies of oxygen.

Paddling Tapping a wooden tool against a piece of clay to alter its shape.

Peeling A defect in glazed pottery where the engobe or glaze separates from the body in flakes, usually due to high compression stresses in the layer.

Pinholes A glaze or body fault caused by trapped air erupting through the body or glaze during firing.

Plaster of Paris/plaster (2CaSO$_4$· H$_2$O) A semi-hydrated calcium sulfate, derived from gypsum by driving off part of the water content. Used in moldmaking.

Plastic clay Clay which can be manipulated, but still retains its shape.

Porcelain Highly vitrified white clay body with a high kaolin content. Developed and widely used in ancient China, its low plasticity makes it a difficult clay to work with. It can be fired as high as 2552°F (1400°C) and when thinly formed, the fired body is translucent.

Pour hole The opening of the mold used for pouring the slip into the mold cavity.

Primary clays Those clays which have remained in their forming grounds, such as china clay or kaolin.

Prop A refractory clay pillar used for supporting kiln shelves during firing. Also known as posts.

Pugging Mixing and extruding clay from a pugmill.

Pug mill Machine for mixing and extruding plastic clay.

Pyrometer An instrument for measuring the temperature inside a kiln chamber. Works in conjunction with a probe (thermocouple) placed through a hole drilled through the top or side of the kiln wall.

Pyrometric cones Small pyramids made of ceramic materials that are designed to soften and bend when a particular ratio of temperature and time is reached during firing.

Raku A firing technique in which pots are placed directly into a hot kiln and removed when red-hot.

Raw glazing See Single fired.

Reactive glaze One that combines with a harder glaze when fired under or over it.

Reducing atmosphere Deficiency of free oxygen in a kiln atmosphere that causes the reduction of compounds rich in oxygen, which affects the glaze and clay color.

Refractory Ceramic materials that are resistant to high temperatures. Kiln bricks and shelves are made from refractory materials

Resist A decorative medium, such as wax, latex, or paper, used to prevent slip or glaze from sticking to the surface of pottery.

Ribs Wooden or plastic ribs are tools used to lift the walls of thrown pots, while rubber ribs are used for compacting and smoothing clay surfaces. Some ribs are kidney shaped and may be referred to as kidneys.

Salt glaze A glaze formed by introducing salt into a hot stoneware kiln.

Saggar A box made from fire clay used for holding glazed pots in a fuel-burning kiln to protect the pots from direct contact with the flames and gases.

Sawdust firing Sawdust is the fuel most often used for smoking or reducing ceramics at low temperatures.

Secondary (residual) clays Primary clays which have been carried away by erosion and earth movements and have combined, in the process, with mineral impurities.

Scrapers Thin metal and plastic tools used to refine clay surfaces. They may be either straight or kidney shaped, and are sometimes referred to as ribs or kidneys respectively.

Seam lines Small lines on pottery produced where two sections of a mold join or where sides come together in slab construction.

Semi-matte A satin-like surface that has a slight sheen to it.

Semi-opaque Colors that generally allow only dark colors to show through.

Semi-transparent Slightly colored and/or speckled colors that allow most colors to show through with only slight distortions.

Sgraffito The cutting or scratching through an outer coating of slip, glaze, or engobe to expose the different colored body beneath. From the Italian word graffito, meaning to scratch.

Silica/Silicon Dioxide (SiO$_2$) Primary glass-forming ingredient used in glazes and also present in clay. Silica does not melt until approximately 3272°F (1800°C) and must always be used in conjunction with a flux to reduce its melting point to a workable temperature range.

Silk screen Nylon mesh screen used for printing an image onto a flat ceramic surface or onto transfer paper.

Single fired The making, glazing, and firing of pottery in a single operation. Also known as raw glazing.

Slab building Making pottery from slabs of clay.

Slip Liquid clay.

Slip casting Casting slip is made from clay and water, but also contains a deflocculant, allowing a reduced water content. Poured into a plaster mold, casting slip is then left to build up a shell on the inside of the mold before pouring out the excess. Remaining moisture is absorbed by the plaster.

Slip trailing Decorating with slips squeezed through a nozzle.

Soak Keeping a predetermined temperature at the end of the firing cycle to maintain the level of heat in the kiln to enhance many glaze finishes.

Spacers Hollow sections of a thin-walled clay cylinder, used to glue pieces of pottery together.

Spare The section of a model that will form the pouring hole when casting a plaster mold.

Sponging Cleaning the surface of pottery before firing or a decorative method of applying slip or glaze.

Sprigging Plastic clay applied to an article to form a relief decoration.

Spyholes (vent holes) Small holes in the door or side of a kiln used for viewing cones and ventilating the kiln during firing.

Squeegee A rubber-edge wooden tool, used to force printing ink through a mesh screen in silk screen printing.

Stains Unfired colors used for decorating pottery or a ceramic pigment used to add color to glazes and bodies.

Stilts Small shapes of bisque clay, sometimes with metal or wire spurs, used for supporting glazed pottery during firing.

Stoneware Vitrified clay, usually fired above 2190°F (1200°C). Any glaze matures at the same time as the body, forming an integral layer.

Terra-cotta An iron-bearing earthenware clay that matures at a low temperature and fires to an earth-red color.

Terra sigillata A very fine slip used as a surface coating for burnishing or other treatments.

Thermal expansion The expansion that occurs in glazes and clays during firing.

Thermal shock Sudden expansion or contraction that occurs in a clay or glaze and causes damage, usually through sudden heating or cooling.

Thermocouple The temperature probe in a kiln that transmits information to the pyrometer.

Thixotropy The ability of clay suspensions to thicken up on standing. See also Deflocculation and Flocculation.

Throwing Clay is placed on a rotating potter's wheel and formed by hand in conjunction with centrifugal force. Wheel designs vary from momentum "man-powered" wheels, through pedal type "kick wheels" and belt-driven, hand-turned arrangements to the modern highly powered electric version. Throwing is said to have been developed first in Egypt c. 3000 BC.

T material Highly grogged white plastic clay.

Toxic Any ceramic material, raw, gaseous, or liquid, that is injurious to health.

Transparent Clear base colors that are free from cloudiness and distortion.

Trimming (turning) Trimming thrown pots in the leather-hard state to refine their shape and to create footrings.

Tube line To decorate on a fired or unfired clay body, giving a raised line. The tube line is a

mixture of clay, flux, and other ceramic compounds.

Twaddell Degrees (°TW) Units used to measure the specific gravity of solutions and suspensions.

Updraft kiln A fuel-burning kiln in which the smoke goes into and through the kiln and up the chimney.

Underfiring Not firing hot enough or long enough, or both.

Underglaze A color that is usually applied to either greenware or bisque-fired pottery and in most cases is covered with a glaze. A medium, such as gum arabic, is usually used to adhere the color to bisque but needs to be fired on before glazing.

Vitrification point The point at which clay particles fuse together.

Vitrified Usually refers to porcelain and stoneware that are fired at a high temperature. The clay begins to become glass-like.

Volatilize To become vaporous. Certain oxides, such as copper, do this at high temperatures and are deposited onto other pots and kiln shelves.

Volume calculations The volume of an object can be measured using displacement. When immersed in water, a solid object will displace its own volume in water. With the help of measuring cylinders you will be able to calculate its volume.

Volume (v) of a cylinder
Volume $= \pi r^2 h$ (in which $\pi =$ pi or 3.142; r = radius; h = height)
Volume $= 3.142 \times r \times 2 \times h$

Volume of a block
Volume $= l \times b \times h$ (in which l = length; b = breadth; h = height)

Volume of a cone
Volume $= \frac{1}{3} \pi r^2 h$ (in which $\pi =$ pi or 3.142; r = radius; h = height)

Wad box A manually-operated machine for extruding cross sections of clay.

Wedging A method of preparing plastic clay by distributing clay particles and additives such as grog evenly throughout the clay mass.

Wheelhead The circular revolving flat disk, attached to the potter's wheel, and on which the pot is thrown or formed.

RESOURCES AND FURTHER READING

COLLECTIONS

Museum of Arts and Design
40 West 53rd Street
New York, 10019, USA
www.madmuseum.org

British Museum
Great Russell Street
London, WC1B 3DG, UK
www.britishmuseum.org

Cooper Hewitt Museum
2 East 91st Street
New York, 10128, USA
www.cooperhewitt.org

Design Museum
Shad Thames
London, SE1 2YD, UK
www.designmuseum.org

Gardiner Museum
111 Queen's Park, Toronto,
Ontario, Canada, M5S 2C7
www.gardinermuseum.on.ca

The Potteries Museum and Art
Gallery
Bethesda Street, Cultural Quarter
Stoke-on-Trent, ST1 3DW, UK
www.stokemuseums.org.uk

Powerhouse Museum
PO Box K346, Haymarket,
NSW 1238, Australia
www.powerhousemuseum.com

Victoria and Albert Museum
Cromwell Road
London, SW7 2R, UK
www.vam.ac.uk

Yingge Ceramic Museum
200 Wenhua Rd, Yingge District
New Taipei City 239, Taiwan
www.ceramics.tpc.gov.tw

CERAMIC WORK CENTERS

Design Centrum Kielce
ul. Zamkowa 3
Kielce 25-009, Poland
www.designcentrumkielce.com

European Keramic Work Centre
Zuid-Willemsvaart 215

5211 SG 's-Hertogenbosch
The Netherlands
www.ekwc.nl

International Ceramics Studio
H-6000 Kecskemét
Kápolna u.11, Hungary
www.icshu.org

John Michael Kohler Arts Center
608 New York Avenue Sheboygan
Wisconsin, 53081, USA
www.jmkac.org

EVENTS

100% design, London, UK
www.percentdesign.co.uk

British Ceramics Biennial,
Stoke-on-Trent, UK
www.britishceramicsbiennial.com

Ceramic Art London, UK
www.ceramics.org.uk

Collect, London, UK
www.craftscouncil.org.uk/collect

Earth and Fire, Nottinghamshire,
UK
www.nottinghamshire.gov.uk

European Ceramic Context,
Bornholm, Denmark
www.europeanceramiccontext.
com

International Film Festival on Clay
and Glass, Paris, France
www.fifav.fr

Origin, London, UK
www.originuk.org

New York Gift Fair, USA
www.nygf.com

SOFA, New York, USA
www.sofaexpo.com

FURTHER READING

Adamson, Glenn
The Craft Reader
Berg, 2009
Adamson, Glenn

Thinking Through Craft
Berg, 2009

Cooper, Emmanuel
Contemporary Ceramics
Thames & Hudson, 2009

Cosentino, Peter
*The Encyclopedia of Pottery
Techniques*
Sterling, 2002

de Waal, Edmund
20th Century Ceramics
Thames & Hudson, 2003

Del Vecchio, Mark
Postmodern Ceramics
Thames & Hudson, 2001

Greenhalgh, Paul (editor)
The Persistence of Craft
A&C Black, 2002

Gregory, Ian
Alternative Kilns
A&C Black, 2005

Hamer, Frank and Hamer, Janet
The Potter's Dictionary
A&C Black, 2004

Hanoar, Ziggy
*Breaking the Mould: New
Approaches to Ceramics*
Black Dog, 2007

Jones, David
*Firing: Philosophies within
Contemporary Ceramic Practice*
The Crowood Press, 2007

Jönsson, Love (editor)
*Craft in Dialogue: Six Views on a
Practice in Change*
IASPIS Stockholm, 2005

Lefteri, Chris
*Ceramics (Materials for
Inspirational Design)*
Rotovision, 2003

Mattison, Steve
The Complete Potter
Barron's Educational Series, 2003

Quinn, Anthony
Ceramic Design Course
Barron's Educational Series, 2007

Reijnders, Anton and European
Ceramic Work Centre
*The Ceramic Process: A Manual and
Source of Inspiration for Ceramic Art
and Design*
A&C Black, 2005

Rhodes, Daniel
The Clay and Glazes for the Potter
Pitman, 1973

PERIODICALS

Blueprint
www.wdis.co.uk/blueprint

Ceramics Art and Perception
www.ceramicart.com.au

Ceramic Review
www.ceramicreview.com

Clay Times
www.claytimes.com

Crafts Magazine
www.craftscouncil.org.uk

Icon
www.icon-magazine.co.uk

KeramikMagazinEuropa
www.keramikmagazin.de

WEB SITES

www.100percentdesign.co.uk
www.designboom.com
www.designnation.co.uk
www.designobserver.com
www.matrix2000.co.nz
www.studiopottery.co.uk

INDEX

CREDITS

· ·

Quarto would like to thank the following artists for kindly supplying images of their work for inclusion in this book.

Allum, Andy, p.158bl
Arroyave-Portela, Nicholas, www.nicholasarroyaveportela.com, Photographer: Sophie Broadbridge, pp.182t, 194bl
Aylieff, Felicity, Photographer: Derek Au, pp.17tr, 263tc
Azumi, Shin, pp.285tc, 292b
Baas, Maarten, www.maartenbaas.com, Photographer: Maarten van Houten, pp.15tr, 81l, 301
Baid, Joseph, www.jbird-design.co.uk, p.297tcl
Bailey, Naomi, www.naomibailey.co.uk, p.269b, 281
Bamford, Roderick, www.rodbamford.com, Photographer: Helene Rosanove, pp.168, 169tr/br
Barnes, Chris, www.morvernpottery.co.uk, p.260bl
Blackie, Sebastian, p.225
Blackmann, Jane, p.215br
Blenkinsopp, Tony, p.239br
Bohls, Margaret, www.margaretbohls.com, p.102b
Bowen, Dylan, www.dylanbowen.co.uk, pp.175tl/tr, 184t
Brown, Rowena, http://rowboatlondon.co.uk, p.38tl
Brown, Steve, http://steveroystonbrown.com, pp.198bl, 201t
Brownsword, Neil, Photographer: Guy Evans, p.12b
Buick, Adam, http://adambuick.com, Photographer: Greg Roland Buick, p.234tl/bc
Carroll, Simon, pp.176b Courtesy of Craft Potters Association, 186br
Casasempere, Fernando, www.fernandocasasempere.com, pp.35tr, 80b
Cassell, Halima, www.halimacassell.com, p.210bl
Catterall, Rebecca, www.rebeccacatterall.com, Photographer: Prodoto, pp.53tc, 165t
Cecula, Marek, www.marekcecula.com, pp.150b, 156b, 157tl
Chambers, Matthew, http://matthewchambers.co.uk, p.88br
Chung, Ji-Hyun, http://chungjihyun.wordpress.com, p.216tl
Ciscato, Carina, www.carinaciscato.co.uk, Photographer: Michael Harvey, p.105b
Clare, Zoe, pp.259cr, 293bl
Connell, Jo, www.jjconnell.co.uk, p. 276
Cook, David, pp.136, 149
Cooper, Robert, www.robertcooper.net, p.187tl
Corby, Giles, p.26t/c
Cox, Christine, www.chriscoxceramics.com, p.219tcl,
Cummings, Phoebe, pp.13tl, 21tc
Curtis, Eddie, www.eddiecurtis.com, p.233tc
Daintry, Natasha, www.natashadaintry.com, pp.5, 53tl, 85t, 247tr
Dam, Wouter, www.wouterdam.com, pp.2–3, 82b
Dawson, Robert/Aesthetic Sabotage, www.aestheticsabotage.com, p.162–163t
Deacon, Richard, www.richarddeacon.net, Photographer: Charles Duprat, p.259t
Dee, Miss Annabel, www.missannabeldee.co.uk, p.278br
Doherty, Jack, www.dohertyporcelain.com, Courtesy of the Leach Pottery, www.leachpottery.com, pp.220b, 236tr, 237tr
Drenk, Jessica, http://jessicadrenk.com, p.14tl
Drysdale, Pippin, www.pippindrysdale.com, pp.244, 261t
Dyer, Sue, p.193tr
Eastman, Ken, www.keneastman.co.uk, pp.6, 74tr
Eden, Michael, www.michael-eden.co.uk, Photographer: Adrian Sasson, pp.16tc, 166b, 169l
El Nigoumi, Siddig, pp.171tl, 191tr
Elms, Fenella, www.fenellaelms.com, pp.4, 59tr, 69t
Evans, Damian, p.127tr
Evans, John, www.jevceramics.co.uk, pp.219tcr, 241bl
Follano, Miche, www.michefollano.com, pp.261br, 287b, 291bl, 288b
Gaunce, Marion, p.195

Special credits

Thank you to those who have helped me along the way on this wonderful journey with clay. Starting with Ms Billings at school and evening classes with Claire Heath. Lifelong friends from a terrific B.A. degree course in Bristol and an M.A. in Cardiff, the exceptional support when moving to London from the influential South Bank Crafts Centre folk and my lifelong mentor and wife Claire West. The cast of critical eyes—Claire, big brother Rob, and mate Pete Silverton. Apologies for all those lost weekends and late nights! Thank you to all those makers whose images are included in this book. Also to all those makers and educators who have provided invaluable information along the way. Thanks especially to Jack Doherty and all at the Leach Pottery for their time and to Marta at C.P.A. (Craft Potters Association). I must finally thank my co-author, Mr Tony Quinn, for all the "full English breakfast" meetings.
—Duncan Hooson

Working on a book of such ambition requires a lot of support and I would like to thank the following people: Chai-Ying Lin for her invaluable, unassuming and instinctive help as a studio assistant on many of the step-by-step demonstrations. Steve Brown for his extensive knowledge of all things surface design and the step-by-step demonstrations he prepared for the surface decoration sections of the book, his insight was invaluable. I would also like to thank Andy Allum for his thorough demonstration of the Jigger/jolleying process and David Morris for his help with the glaze recipe conversions. I would like to thank my colleagues on the B.A. ceramic design course at Central Saint Martins College of Art and Design where much of this tacit knowledge has been explored and learnt. Finally I would like to thank the artist Clare Twomey for being the artist Clare Twomey and my fellow author Duncan for rising to the challenge of writing a ceramics book that went deeper and further than the books that have preceded it.
—Anthony Quinn

Thanks to the following institutions for the use of their workshops: Central Saint Martins College of Art and Design, Morley College, and the University of Hertfordshire.

Thanks to Jacqui Atkin for all her work on the tools and equipment section

Quarto would also like to thank the following manufacturers for kindly supplying images:

Amaco AMACO/brent, American Art Clay Co., Inc., 6060 Guion Road, Indianapolis, IN 46254 USA, (317) 244-6871, www.amaco.com (pp.40br, 41tr, 42b, 43t, 47br)

AXMINSTER
TOOL CENTRE

Axminster courtesy Axminster Power Tool Centre Ltd, www.axminster.co.uk (p.44b)

POTCLAYS
LIMITED

© Potclays Ltd, www.potclays.com (pp.41b, 45tr, 49b, 221t)
© Mudtools (40tr)
© Ohaus (46tl, 46b)
© Nidec Shimpo (47cr)

Tools supplied by Top Pot Supplies, www.toppotsupplies.co.uk, photographer: Rebecca Wright (pp.44tr, 45br, 46tr, 47tr)

All other images are the copyright of Quarto Publishing plc. While every effort has been made to credit contributors, Quarto would like to apologize should there have been any omissions or errors—and would be pleased to make the appropriate correction for future editions of the book.